AMERICAN TRUCK & BUS SPOTTER'S GUIDE 1920-1985

TAD BURNESS

Motorbooks International
Publishers & Wholesalers Inc
Osceola, Wisconsin 54020, USA ®

Library of Congress Cataloging in Publication Data

Burness, Tad.
    American truck & bus spotter's guide, 1920–1985.

    1. Trucks—United States—Identification.   2. Buses—United States—Identification.   I. Title.   II. Title: American truck and bus spotter's guide, 1920–1985.
TL23.B784   1985   629.2'24'0973   85-7209
ISBN 0-87938-198-1 (soft)

Acknowledgements

The following is a list of individuals and organizations who've kindly lent a hand. They helped in tracking down many needed pictures, specifications and tidbits of information to add to what had already been found. Their help was much needed in gathering the pieces of the puzzle, to assemble this more detailed *American Truck & Bus Spotter's Guide 1920–1985.*

Special thanks to Victor W. Brown, who first suggested that I do this expanded new edition. And special thanks to Bob Redden and the International Bus Collectors' Club, for a nice box of rare bus photos which were much needed for this new book. Most of the pictures were unobtainable elsewhere!

By the way, two clubs of great value to the vintage bus and truck enthusiast are the International Bus Collectors' Club (18 Lambert Ave., Lynn, MA 01902) and the American Truck Historical Society (201 Office Park Dr., Birmingham, AL 35223). Each of these fine clubs publishes an excellent magazine full of fascinating facts and photos. If old buses and trucks are of real interest to you, I strongly recommend that you send a self-addressed, stamped envelope to these clubs for information on how you may join and what they offer!

I'm also particularly grateful to Lee Kinzer, Elliott Kahn and R. A. Wawrzyniak for the many helpful truck photos and data that each cheerfully provided—and for the time they spent in rounding up the items.

Without the cooperation of others, detailed reference projects such as this are virtually impossible! I'd also like to thank my wife, Sandy, and daughter, Tammy, for their willing assistance with some of the "busy work" of filing, sorting, alphabetizing and so on. And I'd like to thank by mother for her kind help in locating literature on some of the modern trucks.

Many thanks to Gentry Akers, David Amburgey, Wendall Amburgey, American Motors Corporation, American Trucking Associations, Inc., Jeff Anderson, Larry Auten, Autocar Trucks Division of White Motor Corporation, *Automotive Fleet,* Warren Baier, Brockway Motor Trucks, Edwill J. Brown, Robert Burrowes, Richard M. Buttenheim, Jeff Caplan, Swen H. Carlson, Bob Carney, Champion Home Builders (Commuter Vehicles Division), Chevrolet Truck Division of General Motors Corporation, Valerie Chet, Chrysler Historical Collection, Marian Chiulli, John A. Conde, Contemporary Historical Vehicle Association (CHVA), John C. Cooper, Jr., John C. Cowling, Jon H. Cox, Creative Transportation Systems, Inc., Deane Davies, Bob De Carlo, Dodge Truck Division of Chrysler Corporation, El Dorado Bus Sales, Inc., Euclid, Inc., Jim Evans, Fabco, Mike Fanderys, Jack H. Fleming, Flexi-Truc, Inc., Ford Motor Company, Fred K. Fox, Bruce Gilbert, GMC Truck & Coach Division of General Motors Corporation, *Go West,* Greyhound Corporation, Greyhound Lines West, Jon Griffith, Griswold-Eshleman, Grumman Aerospace Corporation, Grumman Olson, Jack H. Hickey, Larry Holian, International Harvester Company, Zoe James, Alden Jewell, Greg Johnson, Ali Kaplan, Bruce Kennedy, Kenworth Motor Truck Company, Bob Knox, Mark F. Kubancik, Jean-Claude Labrecque, Greg Lennes, Randy Liedermann, David B. Lockard, Alberto M. Lowenstein, Mack Trucks, Inc., D. L. Marchand, Keith Marvin, Don Massy, Stuart A. Matlow, Larry Mauck, Loraine McAvene, Douglas T. McClure, John McDonald, Jim Miller, John Montville, Peter Mosling, National Coach Corporation, David Newell, Lynn Nygard, H. E. "Gene" Olson, Oregon State Highway Department, Oshkosh Truck Corporation, *Owner Operator,* Pacific Grove Middle School Art Department, Paramount Equipment Sales, John M. Peckham, Larry Pollock, Buzz Priestly, Bart Rawson, REO *Echo,* Tim Ressler, Charles Rhoads, Gregory Rickett, Walter F. Robinson, Jr., Karla A. Rosenbusch, Wendell Samson, Roy Scheuneman, Mark Simon, George L. Snyder, Society of Automotive Historians, Bryon Stappler, Studebaker Drivers' Club, Bob Sutherlin, Tom Terhune, WABCO, Wayne Corporation, James E. Wenzel, W. P. Wescott, Nick West, Wheeled Coach, Ken Wilson, Ray Wood, WPC/Chrysler Products Restorers' Club, WPC *News,* Al Zeinemann, Robert Zimmerman.

Introduction

Thank you for your interest in this new book!

It's the latest in a series of Spotter's Guides: the new and expanded *American Truck & Bus Spotter's Guide, 1920–1985*. Nearly seven decades of truck and bus development fill this new identification guide, which I hope will be a handy reference tool for you—and entertaining, as well!

Here, you'll discover thousands of different pictures of trucks and buses, most of them selected from original factory literature and advertisements for greatest authenticity. Many of the pictures have never appeared in any other book and may be available nowhere else. As in the other Spotter's Guide books, the pictures and specifications are arranged chronologically by make, so that you can quickly identify the era, brand and year of most any American truck or bus. In cases when a certain model was continued without change, and serial numbers were available, such numbers are included. There were even a few mid-year changes, as you'll note when you become familiar with this material.

Should you have the previous *American Truck Spotter's Guide, 1920–1970*, compare it with this expanded edition and check the many improvements. Now, for your greater interest, sixteen later years of trucks have been added to bring the coverage right up to the mid-eighties.

Also, buses new and old are now included. For example, you'll see Greyhounds from the early models (with back ends like railroad observation cars) to the recent M.C.I. variations. Then there are those interesting A.C.F./Brill buses used for years by Trailways, and the weird-looking double-deck Pickwick Nite Coaches with, as one bus expert put it, "a face only a mother could love!"

In addition to the large intercity buses, local transit buses are included, even the electric ones such as the Marmon-Herringtons ordered in fleets by large cities. There are even some school buses; if you don't see the exact school bus you rode as a kid you can still imagine it, because most school buses usually had the same front end design as the light and medium trucks of the same year and make.

Arranging this new book was a year-long job: to add so much additional material and not get something the size of a Los Angeles phone book that would command the price of a good used car! Most of the older pictures have been improved. The introduction of the old edition explained that "certain illustrations must rely on reprints from original advertisements, some of which were in poor or faded condition." Happily, most of the old pictures that were fuzzy or faded have been replaced by sharp new copies. And there are many pictures of the older models now seen for the first time.

Notice the many interesting types and sizes of trucks, and the interesting brand names. (I've always liked the Wild Rose Lard Republic truck, and included a much better view of it along with many others for this edition.)

You'll find a new, updated and much-expanded alphabetical list of the many trucks and buses manufactured since 1920, following the pictorial section.

Thanks again, and I hope this is a book you'll find of lasting interest, to browse through many times!

Tad Burness
Pacific Grove, California

Table of Contents

AA
ALSO KNOWN AS
ALL-AMERICAN
(1918-1927)

ALL-AMERICAN TRUCK CO., CHICAGO, ILL. (AUG., '22, CHANGED TO FREMONT MOTORS CORP., FREMONT, O.)

CHASSIS

MODEL **A** (1 TON, 130" WB) WITH 4 CYL. HERSCHELL-SPILLMAN ENGINE, 3-SP. TRANS., 6.5 GEAR RATIO, 25 MPH @ 2500 RPM (1920) (1918 MODEL RAN ON KEROSENE, SOLD FOR $__1295__.)

Acme Motor Truck Co., 314 Mitchell St., Cadillac, Mich.

ACME
(1915 TO 1932)

REG. U.S. PAT. OFF.

"E" 5-TON →

4-CYL. CONTINENTAL ENGINES (CYLINDERS CAST IN PAIRS IN MODEL "C" and "E")

(AUG., 1918)

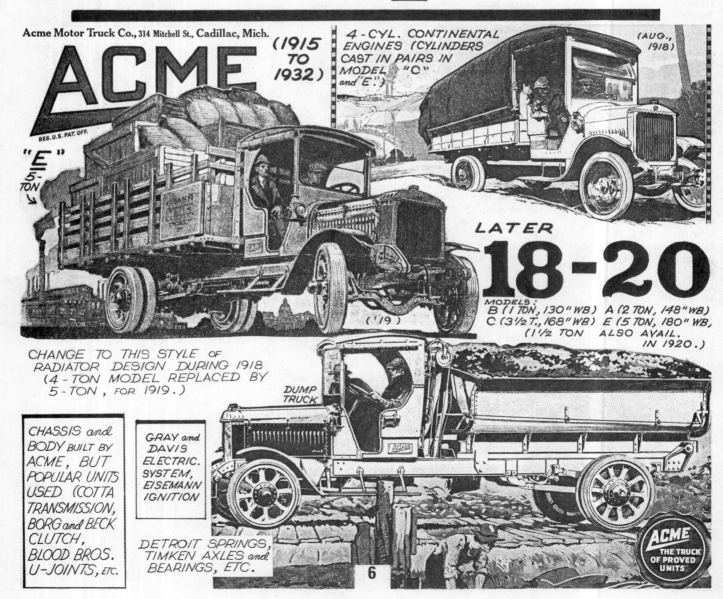

('19)

LATER
18-20

MODELS: B (1 TON, 130" WB) A (2 TON, 148" WB) C (3½ T., 168" WB) E (5 TON, 180" WB, (1½ TON ALSO AVAIL. IN 1920.)

CHANGE TO THIS STYLE OF RADIATOR DESIGN DURING 1918 (4-TON MODEL REPLACED BY 5-TON, FOR 1919.)

DUMP TRUCK

CHASSIS and BODY BUILT BY ACME, BUT POPULAR UNITS USED (COTTA TRANSMISSION, BORG and BECK CLUTCH, BLOOD BROS. U-JOINTS, ETC.

GRAY and DAVIS ELECTRIC. SYSTEM, EISEMANN IGNITION

DETROIT SPRINGS, TIMKEN AXLES and BEARINGS, ETC.

ACME THE TRUCK OF PROVED UNITS

6

ACME

"SEAL OF DEPENDABLE PERFORMANCE"

ACME · THE TRUCK OF PROVED UNITS

SEMI-ENCLOSED CAB

The Pinnacle of Performance

STAKE

20 (CONT'D.)

USED AS ACME RADIATOR EMBLEM

New type dump body as built in Acme factory

21

NEW MODEL "G"

¾ Ton—Worm Drive—$1790 CHASSIS F.O.B. CADILLAC

Speed-TRUCK OPEN CAB

WITH DISC WHEELS 130" W.B. 35 × 5" TIRES

'23 = MODELS ALSO KNOWN BY NUMBERS.

1924 MODELS:
1 TON 20-L
1½T 30
2 T 40, 40L
3 T 60, 60L
4½T 90, 90L
6¼T 125

(25-30 PASS. MODEL "K" BUS AVAIL.)

24 ('24)

25

CLOSED CAB

new 6-CYL. MODELS

INTRO. 3-25:
MODEL "21" 4-CYL.
1-TON "FLYER" 5.0 G.R.
130" W.B. "S-4"
CONT. ENG. (4¼" × 4½" B+S)
50 HP @ 2200 RPM

STAKE (SEMI-ENCLOSED CAB)
MODEL 60 3 TON 152" WB
4 CYL. (4⅛" × 5¼") 4-SP. TRANS.

4 and 6-CYL. MODELS IN '27.
¾ TO 6¼-TON MODELS IN '28.

28

6-CYL. "56"
2½-TON
167¼" W.B.

HEAVY-DUTY CLASS

('29)

29

1-TON TO 7½-TON CHASSIS MODELS

6-CYL. 2-TON MODEL "346" 156" W.B.

DISC WHEELS

7

A.C.F. BRILL

(1926–1953)

AMERICAN CAR and FOUNDRY CO., PHILADELPHIA, PA. (IN DETROIT, MICH. UNTIL 1932) (IN 1925, A.C.F. BOUGHT BOTH J.G. BRILL CO. OF PHILADELPHIA and FAGEOL MOTORS CO. of OHIO.)

1928 TO 1932 : "METROPOLITAN" CITY TRANSIT (UNDERFLOOR-ENGINED) BUS AVAIL., SIMILAR TO "TWIN COACH" BUT LESS SUCCESSFUL.

('35)

37-PASS. DUAL MOTOR ELECTRIC TROLLEY COACH

(OLDER-STYLE TROLLEY COACHES INTRO. 1930.)

1931 and 1932 ACF TRUCKS AVAIL., with HALL-SCOTT ENGS.

PRE-WAR INTER CITY BUS, with ITS BULGING FRONT FENDERS AND FAR-BACK ENTRY DOOR, HAS THE LOOK OF A PUSHER BUS THAT COULD HAVE BEEN PLANNED AS A CONVENT'L.   ('37)

1930s

SILVERSIDES LATER ADDED, TO MODERNIZE PRE-WAR TYPE.

CONVENTIONAL FRONT-ENGINED MODELS DISCONTINUED AFTER 1932.   ('39)

8

A.C.F. BRILL

('41)
LOCAL USE
TRANSIT BUS

POSTWAR IC TYPE has CONCEALED FRONT FENDERS, BUT ODD, BULGING HEADLIGHTS AT SIDES

INTERCITY
IC-37

BUS PRODUCTION SUSPENDED 1942, IN FAVOR OF DEFENSE PROJECTS. RESUMES AFTER WAR.

UNDER-FLOOR 6-CYLINDER HALL-SCOTT ENGINES USED, AS IN PREWAR ERA.

REAR DETAILS

('46-47)   NATIONAL TRAILWAYS BUS (BELOW)

BURLINGTON

IC-41

1940s

new GRILLE, CHANGED FROM VERTICAL TO HORIZONTAL.

('47-48)

Comfort-planned
BUSES

NATIONAL TRAILWAYS BUS SYSTEM

CHICAGO

A LARGE NUMBER OF IC ACF/BRILL BUSES BLT. FOR TRAILWAYS.

9

1948 FARE SCHEDULE

BETWEEN AND	CHICAGO	DALLAS	DENVER	ATLANTA	LOS ANGELES	NEW YORK
CHICAGO		$15.50	$18.45	$10.80	$36.85	$13.60
DALLAS	$15.50		13.70	13.15	26.15	22.20
DENVER	18.45	13.70		22.70	20.15	28.50
ATLANTA	10.80	13.15	22.70		37.15	13.10
LOS ANGELES	36.85	26.15	20.15	37.15		45.25
NEW YORK	13.60	22.20	28.50	13.10	45.25	

C-36 and C-44 ARE LARGE CITY TRANSIT POSTWAR MODELS. (HALL-SCOTT ENGS.)

A.C.F. BRILL

('49)

SMOOTH-SIDED IC TYPES (NARROW GRILLE)

LOWER SIDE VENTS ELIMINATED (1949 AD)

new WIDE GRILLE ON TYPE BELOW

SINCE **47**

1948: SMALL C-27 and C-31 CITY BUSES AVAILABLE, with INTERNATIONAL GAS ENGINES and BEARING ONLY THE "BRILL" NAME.

INTERIOR GLIMPSE OF IC (INTERCITY) TYPE.

SILVERSIDES IC

TRAILWAYS' new UPPER BODY PAINT SCHEME IN LATE 1950.

A.C.F. BRILL INTERCITY TYPES CONTINUE TO PLACE FRONT WHEELS AHEAD OF ENTRY DOOR.

(ABOVE) A FEW ALSO SOLD TO **Greyhound**

TRAILWAYS USED MOSTLY A.C.F. BRILL BUSES TO 1953, THOUGH GMC and OTHER BRANDS SOMETIMES WERE PURCHASED. EAGLE BUSES USED, PRIMARILY, BY TRAILWAYS AFTER 1956.

CITY TRANSIT BUS

10

Aerocoach - *THE COACH OF TOMORROW* - *Today*

BUS

TRADE MARK

GENERAL AMERICAN AEROCOACH
MOTOR COACH DIVISION
General American Transportation Corporation
300 West 151st Street • East Chicago, Indiana

THE AEROCOACH SAFETY FRAME

P-37
INTERCITY TYPE

AS USED BY TRAILWAYS

1940s

INTERNATIONAL ENGINE
(CONTINENTAL ENG. ALSO
AVAIL., 1947)

AS USED BY PACIFIC GREYHOUND
(ABOVE)

('48)

the Safest

coach for every type of service

Aerocoach WITH THE
ALL-WELDED, TUBULAR STEEL FRAMEWORK

Passengers riding in Aerocoach transit, intercity or Astraview sight-seeing busses enjoy protection they cannot get in any other make of coach. Beneath the handsome exterior and comfortable interior of every Aerocoach is a unique framework that keeps everyone safe when unavoidable accidents occur.

Unlike conventional construction, this tubular steel framework does not transmit shock. It merely bends upon impact. Collision damage is confined to a small area around the impact point. No other coaches have this type of framework.

If you are a bus operator*, ask an Aerocoach representative to show you actual case histories of people who have been saved from serious injury because of this exclusive Aerocoach frame.

*Aerocoach is economical, too. Lighter weight cuts fuel costs and tire wear.

CITY TRANSIT BUS INTRO. 1948.

TOOK OVER
GAR WOOD

BUS MFG. BUSINESS, 1939. CON'T. GAR WOOD TYPE, ALSO ADDED ALL-NEW *AEROCOACH*, 1940.

1940-1943 = 250 GAR WOOD TYPES and 300 new AEROCOACHES BLT. (PRODUCTION HALTS 1943 TO APRIL, 1944.) 1944-1952 = 2350 MORE AEROCOACHES BLT., INCL. TRANSIT TYPE.

TRANSIT BUS 36 and 44 passenger coach for city and suburban runs.

ASTRAVIEW 37 passenger sight-seeing bus with Solex-glass roof panels for greater vision without heat or glare.

MASTERCRAFT P-372 37 passenger Intercity Coach

('49) 3 TYPES AVAILABLE, STARTING 1948.

ATTERBURY
MOTOR TRUCKS OF ▼ MAXIMUM SERVICE

('19)

(1½-TON "7-R" *and*
2-TON "7-C"
AVAIL. THROUGH
1919;)
1½-TON CONT'D.
IN 1920.)

TYPICAL GAS STATION
OF 1920

19-20

('19)

4-CYL. CONTINENTAL
ENGINE
1920 MODELS :
"7-CX" 2½ TONS 153½" WB
"7-D"   3½   167½ *
"8-E"   5   167½ *
 (* - CONT'D. FROM 1919)

('20)

new 1½-TON
"20-R" *with*
144" W.B.

(3 OTHER '20
MODELS CONT'D.)

(3½-TON IS "7-DX" IN '22,
BUT "7-D" AGAIN IN '23.)

21-23

5-TON
"8-E" →
4 CYL.
(4¾ x 6)
$5775

167½" WB SOLID TIRES
(TOOLS INCLUDE FIRE EXTINGUISHER)

('21)

"20-R" CONTINUED
also "22-C" 2½ TON 156" WB
"22-D" 3½ 174

"22-D" ('24)

24

1925 MODELS :

24-R	1½ TON	150" WB
22-C	2½	156
22CL-LWB	2½	180
22-D	3½	174
24-E	5	174
24E-LWB	5	204

with SOLID TIRES,
SEMI-ENCL. STEEL CAB
4-CYL. (4½" x 5½", CAST IN PAIRS)
CHASSIS *and* CAB = $4275.

25

('25)

"24-R" 4-CYL.
(PNEUMATIC TIRES) BUDA eng.)
(with

12

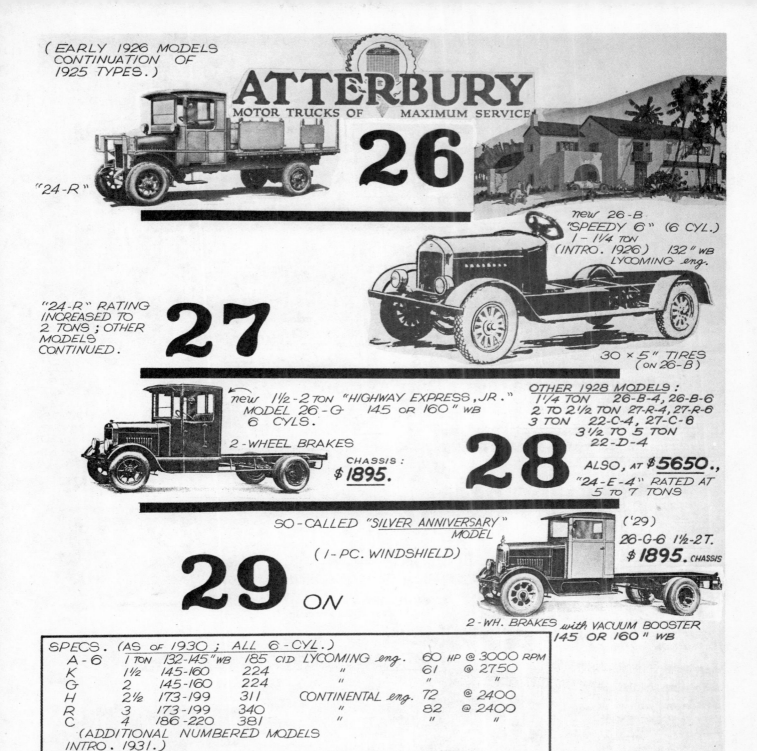

(EARLY 1926 MODELS
CONTINUATION OF
1925 TYPES.)

ATTERBURY
MOTOR TRUCKS OF MAXIMUM SERVICE

"24-R"

26

new 26-B.
"SPEEDY 6" (6 CYL.)
1 - 1¼ TON
(INTRO. 1926) 132" WB
LYCOMING eng.

"24-R" RATING
INCREASED TO
2 TONS; OTHER
MODELS
CONTINUED.

27

30 x 5" TIRES
(ON 26-B)

new 1½-2 TON "HIGHWAY EXPRESS, JR."
MODEL 26-G   145 OR 160" WB
6 CYLS.

2-WHEEL BRAKES

CHASSIS:
$1895.

OTHER 1928 MODELS:
1¼ TON   26-B-4, 26-B-6
2 TO 2½ TON 27-R-4, 27-R-6
3 TON   22-C-4, 27-C-6
3½ TO 5 TON
22-D-4

28

ALSO, AT $5650.,
"24-E-4" RATED AT
5 TO 7 TONS

SO-CALLED "SILVER ANNIVERSARY"
MODEL

(1-PC. WINDSHIELD)

('29)
26-G-6 1½-2 T.
$1895. CHASSIS

29 ON

2-WH. BRAKES with VACUUM BOOSTER
145 OR 160" WB

SPECS. (AS OF 1930; ALL 6-CYL.)

A-6	1 TON	132-145"WB	185 CID	LYCOMING eng.	60 HP @ 3000 RPM
K	1½	145-160	224	"	61 @ 2750
G	2	145-160	224	"	" "
H	2½	173-199	311	CONTINENTAL eng.	72 @ 2400
R	3	173-199	340	"	82 @ 2400
C	4	186-220	381	"	" "

(ADDITIONAL NUMBERED MODELS
INTRO. 1931.)

1933 MODELS INCLUDE "A," "K," "G,"
"R," "C," and also "45" (2-2½ TON;)
"50" (2½-3 TON;) "60" (3 TON;) "65" (3-3½ TON;)
"70" (3½-4 TON;) and "100" (5-6 TON)
(CONT. and LYC. 6-CYL. engines CONT'D.)

Atterbury

Established **1897**

Autocar

SINCE MANY MODELS OVERLAP, EXACT AGE OF UNIT IS BEST DETERMINED BY SERIAL NO.

2-CYL. MODELS AVAIL. 1909 TO 1926.

Chassis (1½-2 Ton)
$2300, 97-inch Wheelbase
$2400, 120-inch Wheelbase ('19)

('20) 120" W.B.

Uneeda Biscuit

EAT Uneeda Biscuit EVERY DAY NATIONAL BISCUIT COMPANY

NATIONAL BISCUIT COMPANY

2 CYL. **21-UF** (97" WB) AVAIL. 1913-26.
21-UG (120" WB) AVAIL. 1919-26.)

AVAIL. WITH WINDSHIELD (AS AT LEFT)

26-Y and 26-B ARE FIRST 4-CYL. MODELS INTRO. 1920.

The 4-cylinder 5 ton Heavy Duty Autocar

16-foot body

Chassis, body and load, 22,000 lbs.

Unladen chassis weight only . 7,400 lbs.

26-B

('22) 156" WB

Chassis, $4100

('22 '23)

4-CYL. **ENGINE**

Overall length only 23 feet

13-26

SLOGAN : "Wherever there's a road"

ELECTRIC "E-5-M" 5-TON MODEL ('25)

27-H (INTRO. '22) SIMILAR TO TRUCK BELOW, BUT W. 114" WB)

27-K 4 CYL. 2-3 TON 138" WB (INTRO. 1922)

MODEL **XXI-F**

1½ TO 2 TON

97" WB

('25)

('23)

$3075.

14

The engine of all Autocar trucks is placed under the seat

NEW FRONT-ENGINE MODELS

Autocar

Autocar SEMI-ENCLOSED

(FULLY ENCLOSED)

(SEMI-ENCLOSED)

ATWATER KENT MFG. CO.

The New 1½ Ton Autocar

27

MODEL "A" PANEL DELIVERY

OWN 4-CYL. ENGINE (4" x 5½" B.+S.)

4-WH. BRAKES 136" OR LONGER W.B.

BELOW: 3½ TON, T MODEL "RANGER" 6-CYL. (187 OR 213" WB) 2-WH. BRAKES 36 x 8" TIRES

('28)

"DISPATCH" 1½ and 2 TON

2-TON **A** CHASSIS 4 CYL. ('28)

28-29

('29)

1½-7 TON MODELS, 4 or 6 CYL., IN 1929.

NEW 5-TON 6 CYL. ('28)

15

3-TON "TRAIL BLAZER" 114" W.B. ('28) 6 CYL.

DIESEL

6-T
220" WB

CALIFORNIA MOTOR EXPRESS LTD.

Autocar

C.O.E.s RE-INTRODUCED 1933

AT RIGHT: **UT** NON-STREAMLINE C.O.E.

WITH STREET FLUSHER BODY

MODEL **S**

DUMP TRUCK

PRODUCERS OF **MACASPHALT** STANDARD BITUMINOUS PAVING MATERIALS

WM. P. McDONALD CONSTRUCTION CO. PAVING CONTRACTORS FLUSHING, N.Y.

6-WHEEL DIESEL TANKER (SHELL)

SHELL

MODEL **C** DIESEL
165" WB

ORB

ORB Road Materials Inc. TEL. 165 SUFFERN, N.Y.

RADIATOR EMBLEM

Autocar

(C. '36)

DIESEL **DH**

136

1930s

('37)

HIGHWAY FREIGHT

NEW YORK · NEW JERSEY · PENNSYLVANIA

('37)

RM, RL FROM $1980.

new 1937 STYLING CONTINUED INTO (INTRO. 5-37)

C.O.E.s

new SHORT-W.B. "UA," "UB" 84", 106", OR 124" WB 6 CYLS., 263 (UA) OR 282 (UB) CID 73 OR 78 HP @ 2300

50 MODELS IN 1937!

FREIGHT HIGHWAY FREIGHT

NEW YORK · NEW JERSEY · PENNSYLVANIA

16

Autocar

C.O.E.s ARE U SERIES
4-W-D and 6-WHEELERS ALSO

('44)

GARFORD TRUCKING CORP.

1940s
(CONVENTIONALS)

ALL 6 CYL.
AUTOCAR,
HERCULES, and
CUMMINS ENGINES
73 TO 150 HP
260 TO 707 CID
1940 CHASSIS PRICE
RANGE:
$1250.
TO $9500.

('45)

AIR REDUCTION
AIRCO
AIR REDUCTION
PHILADELPHIA, PA.

VARITIES WITH EITHER
HORIZONTAL OR VERTICAL
HOOD
LOUVRES

DAVIDSON

('46)

('46)

17

Autocar

HORN
CONCEALED.

OTHERWISE,
STYLING SIMILAR
TO PRE-WAR
C.O.E.

LIKE
'38
"U"
TYPES

with GRILLE VARIATION
('40)

('44) →

TANKER
(LEFT SIDE)

('45)

1940s
(C.O.E.)

(MILITARY)

TANKER (RIGHT SIDE)

18

Autocar

"U70 – U90"
QUICK
REMOVABLE
CAB
(INTERIOR)
('51)

(DISPLAY MINUS STEERING WHEEL)

note:
GASOLINE-POWERED MODELS BEAR "Autocar" NAMEPLATE ON SIDES OF HOOD, AND DIESEL MODELS BEAR "Autocar-Diesel" NAMEPLATES.

DIESEL
ENGINE IN "DC-102TL" ('57)

LIGHTWEIGHT ALUMINUM CAB

('52)

12.00 × 24 TIRES

"C-90-D" with 5-YARD JAEGER MIXER (GASOLINE ENGINE)

RIVETS REPLACED BY NUT-AND-BOLT ASSEMBLY, for EASY SERVICING.

1950s

...Specifically Developed for West Coast On-Highway Operations

Weight Distribution
MODEL DC 102TL

4500 lbs.   10,700 lbs.   6200 lbs.

Autocar 60-61

DC-9564 ('60)

WITH CEMENT MIXER

MODEL "A-10264" ('63)

62 6-CYL. DIESEL 220 H.P. 4-SPEED MAIN, 3-SPEED AUX. TRANSMISSIONS 12,675 pounds

POPULAR IN THE WEST

MODEL "A-75-T" OR MODEL "DCV72-64TL"

6-CYL. DIESEL 220 H.P.   V-8 DIESEL 265 H.P.

WITH FIBER-GLASS HOOD

OTHER MODELS, RESEMBLING EXAMPLE   12,850 pounds

BELOW : "D6V72-64TL" WITH 6-CYL. DIESEL "A-102-T" (6 CYL. DIESEL, 220 HP, 4-SP. MAIN, 3-SP. AUX. TRANS. "A-7564-T" (6-CYL. DIESEL, 220 HP, WT. 12,750 lbs.

(235 HP DIESEL V8s OPT. FOR 6-CYL.)

MUCH ALUMINUM USED IN "A" TYPES

63

10 SPEED TRANSMISSION, UNLESS NOTED OTHERWISE.

20

Autocar

DIVISION OF
THE WHITE MOTOR COMPANY
EXTON, Pennsylvania

64

AU–7064–T
TRACTOR *with*
TANK TRAILER

DC–7654–T
(ABOVE)

TANDEM AXLE MIXER TRUCK

Autocar

65

DC–9964–OHNES

66-67

('67)

('67) *with*
SAND
TANKER

21

QUADRUPLE
HEADLIGHTS
NOT
TYPICALLY
SEEN.

Autocar

68-69

with 218-H.P. DETROIT DIESEL ENGINE and FULLER RT00-913 "ROADRANGER" TRANS.

HALF-CAB MIXER

('70)

('70)

CONVENTIONAL MIXER

TRACTORS ('71)

70-72

CAB ('72)

MODEL A64F (3-AXLE) ('70 TO ('72)

325-HP DIESEL ENG. STD. and 13-SPEED TRANSMISSION* (* FULLER "ROADRANGER")

434 HP V12 DETROIT DIESEL ENG. AVAIL.

Autocar

VARIOUS MODELS

('73½)

better--buy--Autocar

TILT HOOD
MADE OF
FIBERGLASS

73 ON

air conditioning

('74)

radiators

Our specially designed radiator is available in 975-, 1300-, and 1440-square-inch frontal areas. Our engineers will recommend the size most suited for the job your Autocar will be doing. They are all nut-and-bolt construction with superior de-aeration characteristics. To eliminate any possibility of damage from frame twisting and racking motions, they're mounted to the frame at three points. Its all-aluminum construction eliminates the need for a sheet-metal radiator shell.

NEW 1977 MODEL DC-7386-DC HAS TANDEM AXLES BOTH FRONT and REAR. (NOT ILLUSTR.)

A, DC, KK, and HALF-CAB CK SERIES IN 1975 144-295" WB

S and A SERIES (B and F MODELS); C and DC SERIES (INCL. U MODELS) IN 1978

INTERIOR

23

"CONSTRUCKTOR 2" CONVENTIONAL REPLACES WHITE "CONSTRUCKTOR, 1978.

Autocar

('84)

INSTRUMENT PANEL

84 ON

TRADITIONAL RADIATOR EMBLEM

BY-PASS FILTER AND POWER STEERING RESERVOIR

A PRODUCT OF VOLVO WHITE TRUCK CORPORATION

IN THE 1980s

BETHLEHEM

Bethlehem Motors Corporation
Allentown, Pa.

(1917 – 1927)

3/4-TON ('20)

('19)

LOW SIDE

CAB CLOSE-UP
(WEATHER CURTAINS
ATTACHED)

ALL with
4-CYL.
ENGINES

1919 MODELS:

D 1½ TON 136" WB
E 2½   144
F 3½   162

ATWATER-KENT IGN. (TO '20)
GRAY + DAVIS
ELECTRICAL SYSTEM
(TO '27)

Right Side Model D and E Motor

('19)

Left Side Model D and E Motor

20

new MODEL DESIGNATIONS IN '20:
3/4 TON DELIVERY ("DELIVERY BOY")
DG 1½ TON 136" WB
EH 2½   144
FJ 3½   162

HIGH
SIDE

CYLINDERS CAST IN
PAIRS BEFORE 1920;
OWN CAST-EN-BLOC
ENGINE FROM 1920 ON.

21

(new '21 MODELS:)
K 1 TON 125" WB
G 2   135
H 3   143
J 4   162

BOSCH IGNITION
(1921 ON)

1923–1924 : KN 1-TON 125" WB
GN 2   137
HN 3   143
MODEL "L" 2½ TON new IN 1925 (145" WB)
"M" 3½ TON " " " (168" WB)

SOLID TIRES ON 2-TON
and HEAVIER MODELS.

(LATE '20)

HEAVY DUTY

TWO 3½-TON
MODELS
IN '26-'27:
"M" (168" WB)
and
new "CS"
(145" WB)

H
3-TON
('21) 143" WB

CHASSIS-CAB
$ 3095.

(DISCONTINUED 1927)

Bethlehem

25

BROCKWAY MOTOR TRUCKS
Cortland, New York

BROCKWAY

(1912 — 1977)
4 - CYL. CONTINENTAL ENGINES ON *ALL* THRU 1921.

2½ TON
K-5

('21)   152" WB

I - TON
MODEL "E"
(1922 - 1923)
USES 4 - CYL.
BUDA ENGINE.

4 - CYLINDER
WISCONSIN
ENGINES ON
"E" and "S"
(STARTING '24)

6 - CYL. WISCONSIN
ENGINE INTRO. ON
1¼ - TON "E-7" ('26)

5 - TON
"T" (1924)
36 × 5 FRONT (SOLID
40 × 14 REAR   TIRES)
4 CYL., 4¾" × 6" CONT'L. ENG.

1920s

4 - CYL. BUDA ENGINE
RETURNS IN 1927, IN
new 7½ - TON
"BT"

BROCKWAY   ACQUIRES
INDIANA TRUCK CORP.,
OF MARION, INDIANA,
IN   1928.

('28)

26

1929 MODELS	
JUNIOR	1¼ TON
JF, CJBF	1¼, 1½
CJB	1½
E, S	1½, 2
EM	1½
EYW, SY	2 TON
K	3
KW	3
KR, R	3, 4
RT, T	4, 5
T-18	5 TON
BT	5½

BROCKWAY

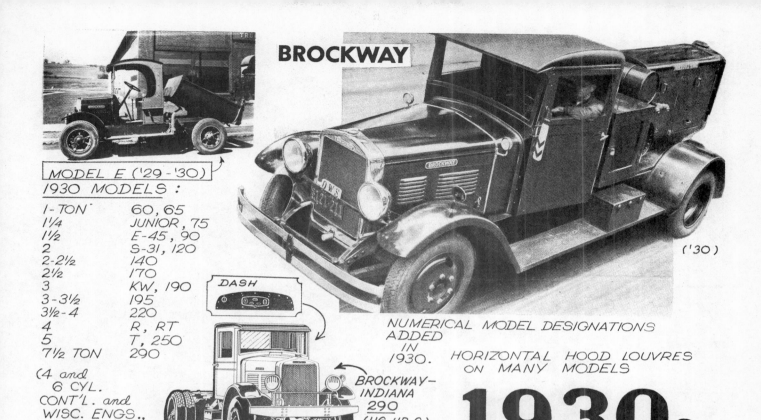

('30)

MODEL E ('29 - '30)

1930 MODELS :

1-TON	60, 65
1¼	JUNIOR, 75
1½	E-45, 90
2	S-31, 120
2-2½	140
2½	170
3	KW, 190
3-3½	195
3½-4	220
4	R, RT
5	T, 250
7½ TON	290

(4 and
6 CYL.
CONT'L. and
WISC. ENGS.,
38 TO 116 HP)

DASH

BROCKWAY-
INDIANA
290
(116 HP 6)
('31)
HEAVY-DUTY

NUMERICAL MODEL DESIGNATIONS
ADDED
IN
1930. HORIZONTAL HOOD LOUVRES
ON MANY MODELS

1930s

WHITE PURCHASES
INDIANA TRUCK ('32)

('37)

FACTORY SCENE (MID-'30s)

THIS BROCKWAY STYLING CONT'D.
THROUGH 1940s and to EARLY '50s,
WITH ADDITION of GRILLE GUARD.
(SEE FOLLOWING PAGE)

27

1939 MODELS :

1½-2 TON	78 ; 83 (1½-2½;) 88 (1½-3)
2-2½	87 92 (1½-4;) 94 (1½-5)
2½-3	90X, 96, 120
3 TON	110, 112, 125X ; 140 (3-3½ TON)
3½-4	128, 130, 141, 145
4	150X4, 150X5 ; 130 PS (4-4½)
4-5	160X, 170X
5-7	165X
5-7½	175X, 195X
6-7½	240X
7½-10	220X
10	260X, 260S

ALL '39s with 6-CYL.
CONT'L. ENGS., EXCEPT=
15-TON V-1200 (V-12 AM. La FRANCE ENG.)

1940
PRICE RANGE
FROM
$ **895.**
(MODEL 78)

TO

$ **6380.**
(MODEL
260-S)

210 TO 501 CID
6 - CYLINDER
CONTINENTAL
ENGINES
(71 - 135 HP)

DURING
THE
1940s,
A
FRONT
GUARD
CONCEALS
GRILLE
OF
MID - '30s
STYLE

BELOW : TANKER WITH SLEEPER CAB ('46)

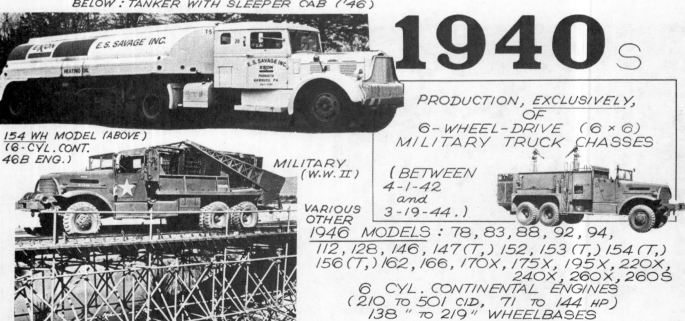

1940s

154 WH MODEL (ABOVE)
(6-CYL. CONT.
46B ENG.)

MILITARY
(W.W. II)

PRODUCTION, EXCLUSIVELY,
OF
6 - WHEEL - DRIVE (6 × 6)
MILITARY TRUCK CHASSES

(BETWEEN
4-1-42
and
3-19-44.)

VARIOUS
OTHER
1946 MODELS : 78, 83, 88, 92, 94,
112, 128, 146, 147 (T,) 152, 153 (T,) 154 (T,)
156 (T,) 162, 166, 170X, 175X, 195X, 220X,
240X, 260X, 260S
6 CYL. CONTINENTAL ENGINES
(210 TO 501 CID, 71 TO 144 HP)
138 " TO 219 " WHEELBASES

BROCKWAY

1951 MODELS :
88WH, 128W, 146W, 148W,
152W, 260XWL, 154W (T,)
154WH (T,) 260 XW (T)
6 CYL.
290 to 572 CID, 100 to 203 HP
138" to 221" WB

PANORAMIC WINDSHIELD

with GRILLE GUARD

DAIRYLEA MILK

1950s

WITH

EATON MORE THAN 2 MILLION EATON AXLES IN TRUCKS TODAY
EATON MANUFACTURING COMPANY, CLEVELAND, OHIO
2-SPEED *Truck* **AXLE**
AVAILABLE
(SINCE 1940s)

1954 MODELS : 260 XL, 260 XWL,
88WH, 128W, 146W, 148W, 151W, 152W,
153W ;   TRUCK TRACTORS : 154W
                                    154WH,
154WHS, 154WHL, 260XW
(SPECS. AS IN '51.)

SINCE EARLY 1950s,
VARIOUS MODELS USE
6- CYLINDER "BROCKWAY - CONTINENTAL"
                    ENGINES

BROCKWAY BECOMES AN
AUTONOMOUS (SELF- GOVERNING)
DIVISION OF MACK TRUCKS, INC.,
AS OF OCTOBER 1, 1956.
(PRODUCTION CEASES 1977.)

1957 MODELS :
128WX, 147WL, 148WD,
153WD, 260LD, 260WLD,
TRUCK- TRACTORS : 147W,
          155W, 254W,
255W, 256W, 258W,
260 WD
  330 to 572 CID
  125 to 230 HP
135" to 221" WB
5- SPEED FULLER TRANS.

('57)

*new "HUSKIE" LINE
INTRODUCED 1958.*

4.77 to 7.80 GEAR RATIOS

INSIGNIA
('57)

(FITS
JUST ABOVE
V- SHAPED
GRILLE)

BROCKWAY

CHROMED "HUSKIE" DOG SYMBOLIC RADIATOR MASCOT (ABOVE) CHANGED TO GOLD IN 1962, TO COMMEMORATE BROCKWAY'S GOLDEN ANNIVERSARY OF MOTOR TRUCK PRODUCTION.

"HUSKIE" LINE and STYLING EXTENDED INTO LIGHTER MODELS, 1961.
new "44 BD" ENGINE has O.H.V., 6 CYL., 478 CID, 200 HP @ 3000 RPM.

NEW C.O.E. MODELS INTRO. 1963.

ORIGINAL HUSKIDRIVE
OTHERS WILL IMITATE BUT NONE CAN DUPLICATE THE TRUE HUSKIDRIVE THAT COMES FROM BROCKWAY

1960s

TWIN GOLDEN HUSKIE DOG RADIATOR MASCOTS ON "HUSKIDRIVE" MODEL.

This is the little switch destined to revolutionize heavy-duty trucking, because it's an integral part of a new diesel power concept currently available only from Brockway.

With Huskidrive, you multiply a constant flow of high torque to start or back any legal load through a five-speed box. With Huskidrive, you merely flip a dash-mounted switch to attain cruising speed and increase engine horsepower while simultaneously improving fuel economy and extending truck life. Engineered and introduced by Brockway, Huskidrive is a great new power train combination that provides all the advantages of a high torque rise engine with a five-speed transmission. It utilizes the highly-acclaimed Cummins NHCT Custom Torque

Diesel to provide constant horse-power through the operating range of 1500 to 2100 r.p.m. Dana 1700 joints and shafts transmit this power from the Fuller five-speed twin countershaft transmission to a single or tandem Eaton Multiplier Rear Axle. You're assured of top performance and economy when you "switch" to Huskidrive.

Huskidrive permits you to cruise in the ideal operating range of 1800 r.p.m., where the engine develops 248 h.p. Huskidrive utilizes all of the advantages offered by this outstanding engine to maintain the highest legal highway speeds, so there's little need for downshifting.

You get maximum starting ability, also. Huskidrive in low multiplies torque at the rear wheels and not forward in the power train where excessive torque can cause transmission, drive shaft or bearing failure. You get flexibility, too. There's no firm pattern—shift through five, and switch to Huskidrive, anytime. This gives greater acceleration plus fuel savings and longer life for the entire power train. You easily reduce over-the-road time and driver fatigue.

new 300-SERIES CONVENTIONALS BEGIN IN MID-1960s.

TANKER

('70)

"HUSKIDRIVE" INTRODUCED 1968.

C.O.E. INTERIOR

C.O.E.

CONVENTIONAL

('69

(REPLACED BY WRAP-AROUND DASH IN MID-1971.)

('70)

SERIES 358LL TANDEM AXLE

BROCKWAY

TANDEM AXLE SERIES 359LL

169" OR 182" WB

1970s

182" STD. WB   ('70)

IMPROVED COOLING SYSTEM

BACK-MOUNTED RAD. SHUTTERS

CAB

MODEL NUMBERS *have* LETTER PREFIXES INDICATING ENGINE TYPES
6 CYL.= C, E, F, N PREFIXES
V8 = K, T, V
V12 = U

DUMP TRUCK ('70)

358 T

ITHACA DELIVE INC
ITHACA, N.Y.
P.S.C. 3398
ICC·MC 55817

('71)

('70)

SERIES 361T SINGLE AXLE TRACTOR

148" STD. WB

(CONT'D. NEXT PAGE)

CAB

359 TL   ('71)

"HUSKITEER 527"
C.O.E.
new ('72)

BROCKWAY

MIXER

WITH AVAIL. CUMMINS OR DETROIT DIESEL ENGINE (185 TO 270 HP) 10.00 × 20 TIRES

WITH OVERHANG. HIGH DUMP BODY

('71)

230 HP DIESEL
6.14 G.R.
11.00 × 22
TIRES
(10.00 × 20
TIRES ON
MOST
OTHER
MODELS.)

160" WB

360 TL   (TANDEM - AXLE MODELS)

360 TYPES *have* FORWARD-SET FRONT AXLE. 361s *with* SET-BACK FRONT AXLE →

1970s
(CONT'D.)

359 TYPE RADIATOR DETAIL

(1976 C.O.E. WITH SINGLE HORIZ. PC. ACROSS RAD., AS ON CONV'T'L., ABOVE.)

SERIES 361TL

400 Series Cabover   ('71)

new

700 SERIES CONV. (1974-77) *has* 1-PC. CURVED WINDSHIELD. SOME LATE – MODEL CONVENTIONALS ALSO AVAIL. WITH 2-PC. WINDSHIELD (TYPE SEEN IN C.O.E. AT RIGHT.)

700 *has* **new** SUPERIOR-BLT. CAB, LIKE MACK R *and* U SERIES CONVENTIONAL.

32

PRODUCTION ENDS 1977

Champion

600 SERIES REAR-ENTRANCE Share-a-Van BUS

HOME BUILDERS CO.
COMMUTER VEHICLES DIVISION
DRYDEN, MICH. TO '81

CHAMPION
COMMERCIAL VEHICLE DIVISION
331 GRAHAM ROAD
IMLAY CITY, MICH. 48444
('82 ON)

700 SERIES ALSO AVAIL., W. "CUSTOM CROWN" (RAISED) ROOF

1980s

coaches from Champion.

SHAREAVAN COMMUTER VEHICLES

↗ INTERIOR

11-TO-26-PASSENGER BUS (17' OR 24')

CHEVROLET CHASSIS (DODGE ALSO AVAIL.)

('82)   ('80-81)

Champion Medium-Duty Bus

('83)

WITH FORD CHASSIS ←

33

RV
MODELS ALSO AVAIL.

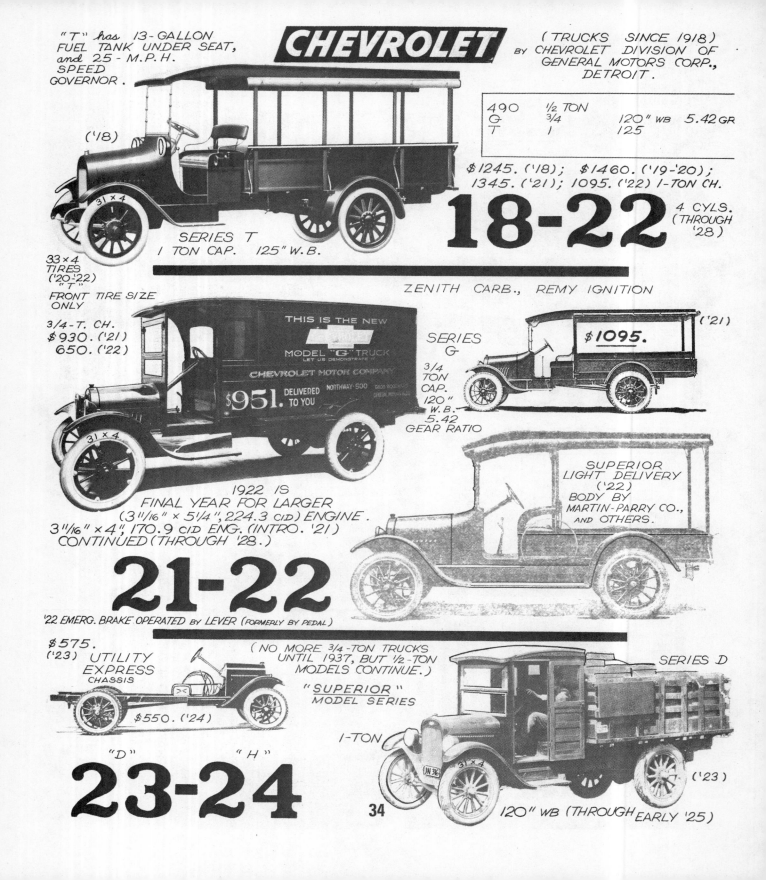

"T" has 13-GALLON FUEL TANK UNDER SEAT, and 25-M.P.H. SPEED GOVERNOR.

CHEVROLET

(TRUCKS SINCE 1918) BY CHEVROLET DIVISION OF GENERAL MOTORS CORP., DETROIT.

('18)

490	½ TON			
G	¾	120" WB	5.42 GR
T	1	125	

$1245. ('18); $1460. ('19-'20); 1345. ('21); 1095. ('22) 1-TON CH.

18-22

4 CYLS. (THROUGH '28)

SERIES T 1 TON CAP. 125" W.B.

31 × 4

33 × 4 TIRES ('20-'22) "T" FRONT TIRE SIZE ONLY

ZENITH CARB., REMY IGNITION

¾-T. CH. $930. ('21) 650. ('22)

THIS IS THE NEW MODEL "G" TRUCK LET US DEMONSTRATE IT CHEVROLET MOTOR COMPANY $951. DELIVERED TO YOU NORTHWAY-500 5600 WOODWARD GENERAL MOTORS BLDG.

31 × 4

SERIES G ¾ TON CAP. 120" W.B. 5.42 GEAR RATIO

$1095. ('21)

1922 IS FINAL YEAR FOR LARGER (3¹¹/₁₆" × 5¼", 224.3 CID) ENGINE. 3¹¹/₁₆" × 4", 170.9 CID ENG. (INTRO. '21) CONTINUED (THROUGH '28.)

SUPERIOR LIGHT DELIVERY ('22) BODY BY MARTIN-PARRY CO., AND OTHERS.

21-22

'22 EMERG. BRAKE OPERATED BY LEVER (FORMERLY BY PEDAL)

$575. ('23) UTILITY EXPRESS CHASSIS $550. ('24)

(NO MORE ¾-TON TRUCKS UNTIL 1937, BUT ½-TON MODELS CONTINUE.) "SUPERIOR" MODEL SERIES

SERIES D

1-TON

31 × 4

JN 316

"D" "H"

23-24

34

120" WB (THROUGH EARLY '25)

('23)

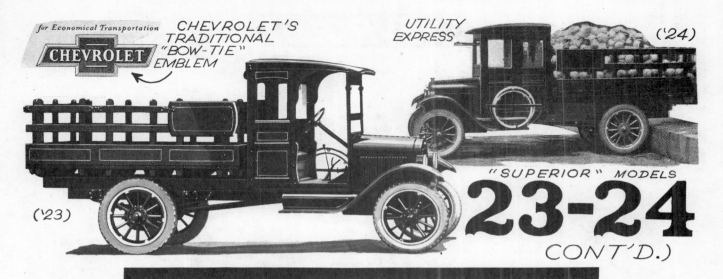

for Economical Transportation

CHEVROLET

CHEVROLET'S TRADITIONAL "BOW-TIE" EMBLEM

UTILITY EXPRESS

('24)

('23)

"SUPERIOR" MODELS

23-24

CONT'D.)

"SUPERIOR" NAME CONTINUES

103" WB ON ½ TON CHASSIS
124" " " 1-TON REPLACES
120" ('26.)

EARLY '25 IS MODEL "M." $550. (UTILITY EXP. CHASSIS)

25-26

STAKE

LATE '25 "R" WITH HERCULES BODY

LATE '26 MODEL "X" has NEW CHEVROLET-BUILT, FULLY ENCLOSED BODY.

('27)

"LM" HAS 1 TON CAP., 124" W.B., 30×5 TIRES ALL AROUND, AS DOES 1926 MODEL "X."

DELUXE 1-TON PANEL $755.

STAKE $680.

OPEN EXPRESS

27

DASH

"CAPITOL" MODEL NAME
(YEAR-MODEL NAMES USED UNTIL 1933.)

new RADIATOR HAS DIP AT CENTER OF UPPER PAN.

CHEVROLET

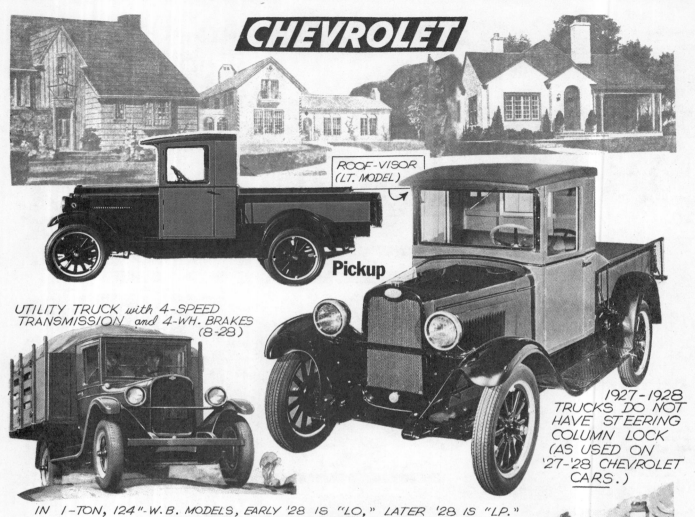

ROOF-VISOR
(LT. MODEL)

Pickup

UTILITY TRUCK *with* 4-SPEED
TRANSMISSION *and* 4-WH. BRAKES
(8-28)

1927-1928
TRUCKS DO NOT
HAVE STEERING
COLUMN LOCK
(AS USED ON
'27-'28 CHEVROLET
CARS.)

IN I-TON, 124"-W.B. MODELS, EARLY '28 IS "LO," LATER '28 IS "LP."

28
"NATIONAL"

new RADIATOR
SHELL DESIGN
ON ½-TON
LT. DUTY
(107" WB)

4-WHEEL BRAKES *on*
LT. DUTY MODELS

JENESEN
FANCY GROCERIES
TELEPHONE MAIN ____

*Illustrating the Light Delivery Chassis
equipped with Panel Body*

29 x 4.40 TIRES (30 x 5 REAR *on* I-TON)

36

CHEVROLET

CANOPY ('29)

SEDAN DELIVERY STYLING MORE LIKE THAT OF A CHEVROLET CAR.

NEW

NEW 6-CYL. ENGINE IN 1929

"INTERNATIONAL" "UNIVERSAL"

29-30

The Utility 1½ Ton Chassis with Chevrolet cab, equipped with power dump body built of reinforced steel to withstand concentrated weight. Popular among coal dealers, contractors, road builders, etc.

STARTING 1930, SOME CANADIAN MODELS BEAR THE "MAPLE LEAF" NAME.

194 CID (THROUGH '32)
'29 : AC (½ TON) 107" WB (THROUGH '30)
    LQ (1½ TON) 131" WB

1930 MODEL HAS new DASH with SMALL CIRCULAR GAUGES (INCLUDING ELECTRIC FUEL GA.) ILLUSTRATED AT RIGHT

ALL MODELS HAVE 4-WH. BRAKES IN 1930.

('30)

1½ Ton

POWER DUMP COMBINATION ('30)

The 1½ TON **chassis**
50 HP and 4-SPEED TRANSMISSION

1930 is FINAL YEAR FOR THIS STYLE OF LIGHT DISC WHEELS.

SPARE TIRE and RIM MOUNTED HORIZONTALLY

STAKE ('30)

'30 : AD (½ TON)
    LR (1½ TON) (LATER BECOMES "LS") 131" WB

1½-TON CANOPY EXPRESS

BELOW, AND RIGHT : DELIVERY MODELS OF 1930

SEDAN DELIVERY

PANEL DELIVERY

CHEVROLET ACQUIRES MARTIN-PARRY BODY CO. IN 1930.

SIMILAR CANADIAN-BUILT "MAPLE LEAF" TRUCKS AVAIL. FROM 1930 THROUGH THE LATE 1940s.

LIGHT DELIVERY

37

CHEVROLET

31

"INDEPENDENCE"

IND. COM. ½ TON 109"wb
Y UTILITY 1½ 131
UL DUAL 1½ 157

(ALSO KNOWN AS AE (½ T.)
LT, MA, MB, MC, MD
(1½ T.) MODELS)

50 HP @
2600 RPM.
CARTER CARB.

4.75 x 19 TIRES
ON ½-TON.
(ALSO EARLY '32)

new
LONGER GROUP
OF MORE
HOOD LOUVRES,
SET in SURROUNDING
PANEL.

SEDAN DELIVERY
(EARLY MODEL with TWO-BLADE
BUMPERS)

LATER MODEL with
SINGLE BLADE BUMPER

DISC WHEELS
STILL AVAILABLE,
BUT WIRE WHEELS
TYPICAL AFTER 1930.

38

Open Cab Pick-up — Pick-up box 66 inches long, 45 inches wide and 13 inches deep. Body sides are so designed that they meet floor at right angles, permitting compact loading and generous capacity. Roadster-type cab. Disc wheels. Price of complete unit $440.

1½-TON
OPEN EXPRESS
(HEAVY PICKUP)
with 157" WB.
30 x 5
TIRES

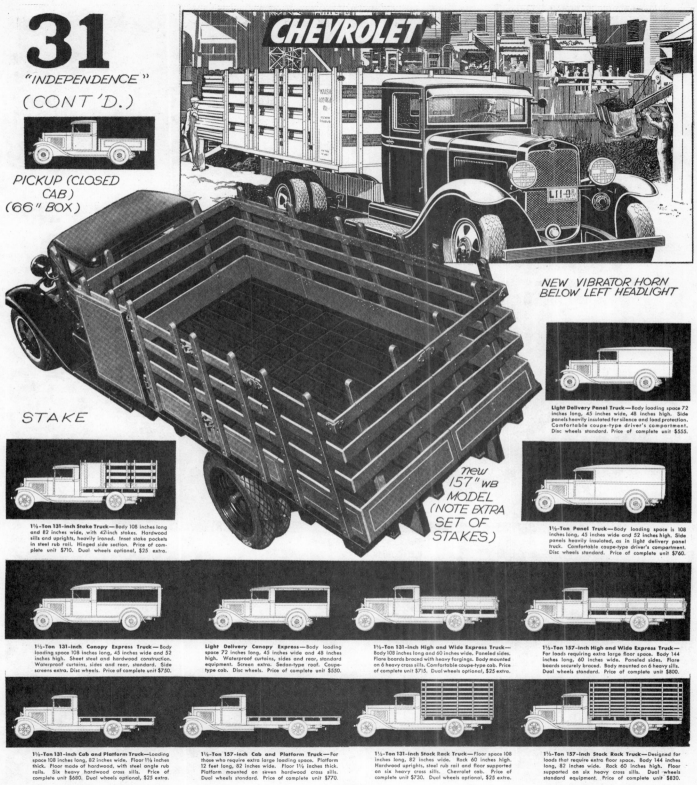

31
"INDEPENDENCE"
(CONT'D.)

PICKUP (CLOSED CAB) (66" BOX)

CHEVROLET

NEW VIBRATOR HORN BELOW LEFT HEADLIGHT

STAKE

new 157" WB MODEL (NOTE EXTRA SET OF STAKES)

Light Delivery Panel Truck—Body loading space 72 inches long, 45 inches wide, 48 inches high. Side panels heavily insulated for silence and load protection. Comfortable coupe-type driver's compartment. Disc wheels standard. Price of complete unit $555.

1½-Ton 131-inch Stake Truck—Body 108 inches long and 82 inches wide, with 42-inch stakes. Hardwood sills and uprights, heavily ironed. Sheet steel and hardwood construction. Inset stake pockets in steel rub rail. Hinged side section. Price of complete unit $710. Dual wheels optional, $25 extra.

1½-Ton Panel Truck—Body loading space is 108 inches long, 45 inches wide and 52 inches high. Side panels heavily insulated, as in light delivery panel truck. Comfortable coupe-type driver's compartment. Disc wheels standard. Price of complete unit $760.

1½-Ton 131-inch Canopy Express Truck—Body loading space 108 inches long, 45 inches wide and 52 inches high. Sheet steel and hardwood construction. Waterproof curtains, sides and rear, standard. Side screens extra. Disc wheels. Price of complete unit $750.

Light Delivery Canopy Express—Body loading space 72 inches long, 45 inches wide and 48 inches high. Waterproof curtains, sides and rear, standard equipment. Screen extra. Sedan-type roof. Coupe-type cab. Disc wheels. Price of complete unit $550.

1½-Ton 131-inch High and Wide Express Truck—Body 108 inches long and 60 inches wide. Paneled sides. Flare boards braced with heavy forgings. Body mounted on 6 heavy cross sills. Comfortable coupe-type cab. Price of complete unit $715. Dual wheels optional, $25 extra.

1½-Ton 157-inch High and Wide Express Truck—For loads requiring extra large floor space. Body 144 inches long, 60 inches wide. Flare boards securely braced. Body mounted on 6 heavy sills. Dual wheels standard. Price of complete unit $800.

1½-Ton 131-inch Cab and Platform Truck—Loading space 108 inches long, 82 inches wide. Floor 1½ inches thick. Floor made of hardwood, with steel angle rub rails. Six heavy hardwood cross sills. Price of complete unit $680. Dual wheels optional, $25 extra.

1½-Ton 157-inch Cab and Platform Truck—For those who require extra large loading space. Platform 12 feet long, 82 inches wide. Floor 1½ inches thick. Platform mounted on seven hardwood cross sills. Dual wheels standard. Price of complete unit $770.

1½-Ton 131-inch Stock Rack Truck—Floor space 108 inches long, 82 inches wide. Rack 60 inches high. Hardwood uprights, steel rub rail and floor supported on six heavy cross sills. Chevrolet cab. Price of complete unit $730. Dual wheels optional, $25 extra.

1½-Ton 157-inch Stock Rack Truck—Designed for loads that require extra floor space. Body 144 inches long, 82 inches wide. Rack 60 inches high. Floor supported on six heavy cross sills. Dual wheels standard equipment. Price of complete unit $830.

new SYNCHRO-MESH TRANS. ON LIGHT DLVRY. MODELS

Half-ton De Luxe Panel, $595
Half-ton Standard Panel, $560
1½-ton Panel, $755
Half-ton Standard Canopy Express, $560
Half-ton Standard Canopy Express with Screen Sides. $579

With High Racks, $855
With Tip-Tops, $820   1½-ton Combination Farm Body

Half-ton Closed Cab Pick-up, $470
Half-ton Closed Cab Pick-up with Canopy Top, $500
Half-ton Special Canopy Express, $580
Half-ton Special Panel, $580
Half-ton Open Cab Pick-up with Canopy Top, $470

BB (½ TON) 109" WB CHEVROLET

MODELS AS OF 3-32

CHASSIS PRICED AS LOW AS $355

32

"CONFEDERATE"

NA, NB, NC, ND (1½ TON) 131" and 157" WB)

1½-ton 131" Open Express, $695
1½-ton 131" Stake Express, $710
1½-ton 157" Stake, $785
1½-ton 157" Van Panel, $1020
1½-ton 131" Platform, $670

RADIATOR STYLE LIKE 1931 CHEV. CARS.

1½-ton 131" High and Wide Express, $705
1½-ton 131" Stake, $700
1½-ton 131" High Rack, $715

(HOOD VENT DOORS

DE LUXE ½ TON PANEL = $595. ON SOME SEDAN DELIVERY MODELS.)

½-T. CHASSIS + CAB $420.

NO TRICKS – Camel just COSTLIER TOBACCOS

1½-T. PANEL $715.

131" STAKE $655.

1½ T. OPEN EXPRESS $650.

DUMP TRUCK $815.

SEDAN DELIVERY $545.

33

"EAGLE" and "MASTER" MODELS.

RADIATOR STYLE LIKE 1932 CHEV. CARS.

CB, OA, OB, OC, OD MODELS 109", 131", 157" WB

OLD-STYLE CABS ON PICKUPS and LG. TRUCKS THROUGH '33.

The Chevrolet Closed Cab Pick-Up........ $440

FINAL YEAR FOR '31-STYLE HOOD LOUVRES

new 206 CID (THROUGH '36)

½-TON PANEL $530.

40

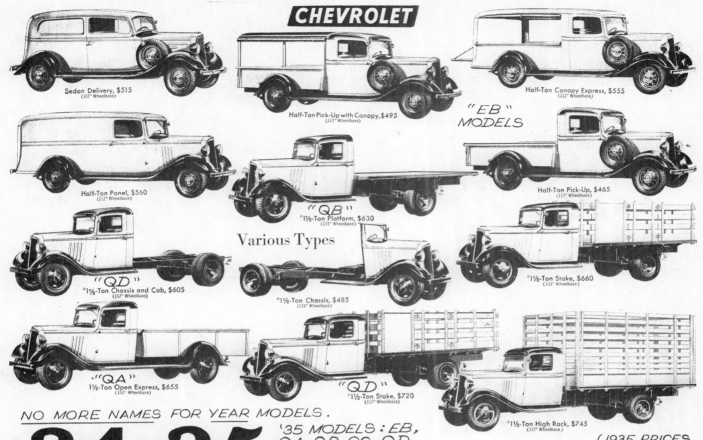

CHEVROLET

Sedan Delivery, $515
(107" Wheelbase)

Half-Ton Pick-Up with Canopy, $495
(112" Wheelbase)

Half-Ton Canopy Express, $555
(112" Wheelbase)

"EB" MODELS

Half-Ton Panel, $560
(112" Wheelbase)

"QB" *1½-Ton Platform, $630
(131" Wheelbase)

Various Types

Half-Ton Pick-Up, $465
(112" Wheelbase)

"QD" *1½-Ton Chassis and Cab, $605
(157" Wheelbase)

*1½-Ton Chassis, $485
(131" Wheelbase)

*1½-Ton Stake, $660
(131" Wheelbase)

"QA" 1½-Ton Open Express, $655
(131" Wheelbase)

"QD" *1½-Ton Stake, $720
(157" Wheelbase)

*1½-Ton High Rack, $745
(157" Wheelbase)

NO MORE NAMES FOR YEAR MODELS.

34-35

'35 MODELS: EB, QA, QB, QC, QD IMPROVED BRAKING ON 1935 MODELS.

(1935 PRICES SHOWN)

(MOST PRICES AS IN 1934.)

'34 MODELS: DB, PA, PB, PC, PD FROM $445. (½-T. CH.+CAB)

			new		
COMMERCIAL	½ TON	112" WB		4.11 GR	(107" WB also)
UTILITY	1½	131		5.43	
"	1½	157		"	

CLOSER VIEW OF CANOPY EXPRESS ('34)

12500
GROC

ROWELL WOODS GROCERY

RO-51

8-PASS. SUBURBAN CARRYALL WAGON (ON TRUCK CHASSIS) INTRO. 1935. (WITH STEEL BODY)

TIRE SIZES
5.50 × 17   (½ TON)
30 × 5 (FRONT)   32 × 6 (REAR)
(6.00 × 20)   (1½ TON)
207 CID "BLUE FLAME" ENG. (70 HP @ 3200 RPM)
CARTER CARB.

SHALLOW OUTER VISOR ON EARLY '36 STYLE CAB

CHEVROLET

new INSTRUMENT PANEL SIMILAR TO THAT IN 1936 CHEV. "MASTER" SERIES CAR (THROUGH '39.)

HYDRAULIC BRAKES ON ALL BUT EARLY 1½-TON "R."

36

new HORIZONTAL HOOD LOUVRES

SCREENSIDE CANOPY TRUCK

GEAR RATIOS
4.11 (½ TON)
5.43 - 6.17 (1½ TON)

VISORLESS LATER '36 CAB STYLE

PANEL DELIVERY === $565.

½ TON : "FB" MODEL (112" WB)
1½ TON MODELS :
RA (131" WB) $590.
RB (131" WB, DUAL REAR WHEELS)
RC (157" WB) $615.
RD (157" WB, DUAL REAR WHEELS)

LATE '36 1½-TON PICKUP has STEEL ARTILLERY WHEELS.

½-TON CHASSIS-CAB $450.

$475.

FB LIGHT-DUTY ½-TON PICKUP

10,110 POUNDS PAYLOAD

AAA CERTIFIED WEIGHT

SAFE DRIVING ROAD TEST CONDUCTED BY CHEVROLET MOTOR CO. DETROIT, MICH.

1½-TON

42

SEDAN DELIVERY HAS GRILLE LIKE 1936 CHEVROLET CAR.

CHEVROLET

PICKUP

37

new 216 CID ENG. 78 HP @ 3200 RPM

WITH WRECKER BODY →

$515.

PERFECTED HYDRAULIC BRAKES — NEW HIGH-COMPRESSION VALVE-IN-HEAD ENGINE — MORE LOAD SPACE — IMPROVED LOAD DISTRIBUTION — NEW STEELSTREAM STYLING — IMPROVED FULL-FLOATING REAR AXLE WITH NEW ONE-PIECE HOUSING (on 1½-Ton Models) — NEW ALL-STEEL CAB — PRESSURE STREAM LUBRICATION

UP GOES POWER

DOWN COME COSTS

PANEL

new GRILLE

GD ¾-TON MODELS RE-INTRODUCED IN MID-SEASON.

FROM $555. (CHASSIS-CAB)

INTER-CITY S-4

½-TON
TYPES = 6.00 × 16
OR 7.50 × 15 TIRES

SEDAN DELIVERY NOW HAS SPARE TIRE UNDER REAR FLOOR, INSTEAD OF IN FENDER WELL AS BEFORE.

½ TON MODEL IS "GC" (112" WB) (4.11-3.82 GRs)
1½ TON MODELS = MASTER SA, MASTER SB,
MASTER SP. SB (131" WB)
MASTER SC, MASTER S.D,
MASTER SP. SD (157" WB)
(5.43-6.17 GRs ON
1½ TON)

GE IS NEW
1- TON MODEL
(122¼" WB, LIKE ¾ TON)
FROM $590.
(CHASSIS CAB)

1½ - TON
(NOTE
CLEARANCE
LIGHTS ON
CAB ROOF.)

INTER-CITY TRUCKING SERVICE INC. GR. WT. 4250

43

IMPROVED DIAPHRAGM-
SPRING CLUTCH,
VOLTAGE -
REGULATOR
GENERATOR

CHEVROLET

1/2 TON PICKUP $560.

C.O.E. (RARE)

CAB ('38)

HC, HD, HE, TA, TB, TC, TD MODELS

38

1938 MICHIGAN RO-10-9 COMMERCIAL

1½-TON STAKE FROM $750.

new TRUCK GRILLE with HEAVIER HORIZONTAL MEMBERS ←

39

JC (1/2 TON ;)
JD (3/4 TON ;)
JE (1 TON ;)
VA, VB, VC, VD (1½ TON;)
VE, VF, VG, VH, VM,
VN (1½ TON C.O.E.)

78 HP @ 3200 RPM
new 113½ " WB and up
1/2-T. PICKUP === $545.
3/4-T. PICKUP === 630.
1/2-T. PANEL === 630.
1½-T. STAKE = FROM 730.

New Chevrolet-Built
CAB-OVER-ENGINE
MODELS

45 MODELS, 8 WHEELBASES IN 1939.

new V-WINDSHIELD ON ALL 1939 MODELS.

$645.

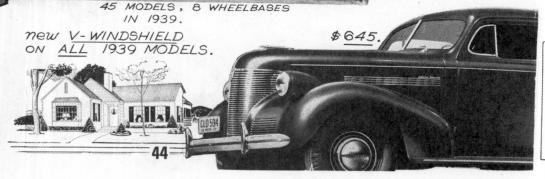

UNLIKE PANEL TRUCK, SEDAN DELIVERY IS STYLED LIKE CHEVROLET CAR. ←

TOP PIECE OF GRILLE IS VERT. WIDENED

new HYPOID REAR AXLE

40

FULL-FLOATING REAR AXLE ON HEAVY-DUTY MODELS *with* VACUUM-POWER BRAKES *and* 2-SPEED REAR AXLE OPTIONS.

CHEVROLET

new
SEALED-BEAM HEADLIGHTS, *and* PARKING LIGHTS ON FENDERS.

new 4.55 GR ON ¾ TON *and* 1-TON

C.O.E.
(LOGGER)
C.O.E STAKES
$845.
(107"WB)
$900.
(131"WB)

MODELS : KC (½ TON;) KD, KE (¾ TON;) KF (1 TON)

KP (½-TON PARCEL DELIV.;)*
WA, WB (1½ TON;)
WD, WE,
WF (1½ TON
C.O.E.)

* = SPRING INTRODUCTION

(1940 CHEVROLET CAR-TYPE INSTRUMENT PANEL REPLACES 1936 TYPE (EXCEPT IN SCHOOLBUS AND FLAT-FACE COWL TYPE.)

BEFORE WORLD WAR II, ALL GM-BUILT TRUCKS OVER 1½-TON CAP'Y. SOLD UNDER GMC NAME.

"WC" IS 1½-TON SCHOOL BUS CHASSIS.

6 CYL., 216 C/D 78 OR 80 HP

PRICED FROM
$541. f.o.b.
(½-TON, 113" WB CAB/CHASSIS)

HEAVY DUTY DUMP TRUCK

MILITARY ('43)

CHEVROLET

60 bigger
models
IN '41

216 or
new
235 C.I.D.,
STARTING
1941.

DUMP
TRUCK
→
('41)

nine longer wheelbases
massive new truck styling

41-47

new
90 or 93
H.P. ('41.

CHEVROLET

EMBLEM MISSING FROM '43-'45
WARTIME MODELS.

1941 MODELS: AK, AJ (115" WB;)
AL (125";) AN, YR (134";) YS (160".)
1942 LETTERS START WITH B or M
(1943 - EARLY 1945 WARTIME, SAME.)
1946 LETTERS START WITH C or O
1947 "   "   "   D or P

TANKER
(C.O.E.)

WARTIME
MODELS
HAVE
LESS CHROME
and
NO
FLOOR MAT.

2-TON
MODELS AVAIL. IN 1946.

46

ENTIRE LINE EXPANDED TO 99 MODELS IN 1946.
1946-47 PRICES FROM $884., f.o.b. (1/2-TON)

90 OR 93 HP IN 1948.

1948
1½-T. STAKE
$1256.
UP

TRACTOR-TRLR.

Chevrolet

New Advance-Design

(TOTALLY RESTYLED)

INTRO. SUMMER, 1947

STAKE CONV.

HOG TRANSPORT WITH RAMP (OTHER APPLICATIONS ALSO, CUSTOM-MADE)

NARROW BRIDGE

48-53

('48)

I.D. TIPS:
EARLY '48 HALF-TON has
GAS FILLER NECK on BOX SIDE,
INSTEAD OF IN CAB SIDE.
1952 has NEW PUSH-BUTTON
DOOR HANDLES.
1953 has NEW 60-LB. OIL PRESSURE GA.
(92, 102, 105 HP INCREASES
IN 1950 ; 92, 107, 108 HP
IN 1953.)

DUAL REAR-
WHEELED
STAKE
C.O.E.

PANEL

('48)

('49)

YEAR DETERMINED
BY FIRST LETTER IN
MODEL DESIGNATION :

E, Q	=	1948
G, S	=	1949
H, T	=	1950
J, U	=	1951
K, V	=	1952

WIDE VARIETY of ALPHABETICAL
SINGLE LETTER 1953 MODEL
DESIGNATIONS.
1953 SERIAL # STARTS with
53-001 001, FOLLOWING
LETTER PREFIX.

HVY. PANEL

Claudier FLORIST

('51)

CHEVROLET

"**ADVANCE-DESIGN**" NAME CONT'D.

THREE 6-CYL. ENGINES: "THRIFTMASTER 235,"
"LOADMASTER 235," OR
"JOBMASTER 261"

54-EARLY 55

FIRST STYLING CHANGE SINCE EARLY '48 MODELS.

CAB INTERIOR OF CAB-OVER-ENGINE

DRIVER'S COMPARTMENT OF PANEL TRUCK

CABS.

New GRILLE and 1 PIECE WINDSHIELD

'54 FROM: $1419.
EARLY '55: 1494.

New Comfortmaster Cab: Offers new comfort, safety and convenience. New one-piece curved windshield provides extra visibility.

New Chassis Ruggedness: Heavier axle shafts in 2-ton models . . . newly designed clutches, and more rigid frames in *all* models.

New Ride Control Seat:* Seat cushion and back move as a unit to eliminate back-rubbing. It "floats" you over rough roads with ease.

New Automatic Transmission:* Proved truck Hydra-Matic transmission is offered on ½-, ¾- and 1-ton models.

New, Bigger Load Space: New pickup bodies have deeper sides. New stake and platform bodies are wider, longer and roomier.

1/2 TON SERIAL # 1154-001001 UP

STAKE

PANEL FROM $1776.

$1956.

New styling in trucks

CAMEO NEW

CHEVROLET

new V8 ENGINES AVAIL.

new 12-VOLT IGNITION

NEW

1½-TON STAKE, $2310.

(2-TON AVAIL. IN 14' OR 16' BED LENGTHS.)

NEW CHEVROLET Task·Force TRUCKS

55

TOTALLY RESTYLED EARLY IN 1955.

"WRAP-AROUND" PANORAMIC WINDSHIELD

LIGHT DUTY SERIAL NO. STARTS AT H-255-001001

(THE EARLIEST 1955 CHEVROLET TRUCKS RESEMBLE THE 1954 MODELS)(6-CYL. TYPES ONLY)

48

New Overdrive or Hydra-Matic Your choice of Synchro-Mesh or, as extra-cost options, new Overdrive (½-ton models) or Hydra-Matic (½-, ¾- and 1-ton).

New Power Brakes, Tubeless Tires Power Brakes are standard equipment on all 2-ton models, optional at extra cost on others. Tubeless tires on all ½-ton models.

SERIAL NO.
STARTS AT
3A 56-
001001

1956
HOOD
EMBLEM
has
LOWER
SIDE
WINGS
THAN
1955.

56

DUAL
REAR
WHEELS

CAB-FORWARD
STAKE

1956 RESEMBLES 1955,
EXCEPT THAT '56 SIDE
NAMEPLATE IS MOVED UP,
ABOVE FENDER CREASE

DUMP TRUCK
(BELOW)

HVY. TRACTOR

DELUXE-STYLE
"CAMEO" →
(WIDE BED w.
FIBERGLASS
OUTER SIDES)
AVAIL. '55-57

SHOWN ON ALCAN
HIGHWAY
(CANADA-ALASKA)

STD. 1/2-TON "3104"
PICKUP = $1626.
(6-CYL.)

LONG-WHEELBASE
MODEL "3204"
(123" ↓
WB)

57 **new**

GRILLE
(LT. DUTY)
SERIAL NO. STARTS AT
3A 57-10000I

NEW TASK·FORCE 57
CHEVROLET TRUCKS

V8 = $113. EXTRA

49

NEW ⟩⟨

"FLEETSIDE" REPLACES "CAMEO."

58 FRONT END RESTYLED. new 4 HEADLTS.

SERIES 100 TANKER WITH "WORKMASTER" V8.

TOTAL PRODUCTION : 278,632

Inside.

('59)
1959 DASH AND INT. SIMILAR TO 1958.

TOTAL PRODUCTION : 326,102

Task·Force 59
Trucks

HEAVY-DUTY COMPACT L.C.F. TRACTOR (V8 ENG.)

SERIAL NO. 3A59 - 100001 UP

59
new HOOD-VENT FRONT EMBLEM

CHEVROLET

L2714

THIS WAY TO THE ELEPHANTS RHINOS HIPPOS

50

Chevrolet New "TILT-CAB" C.O.E.

MOD. C-6402 SCHOOL BUS CHASSIS TAKES 48 TO 54-PASS. BODY.

TANKER

Spartan Models

VARIOUS 6-CYL. and V8 ENGINES AVAIL.

STURDI-BILT TRUCKS

Rotary Valve Power Steering
AVAIL. ON 60, 70 and 80 SER.

| TEMPERATURE GAUGE | GENERATOR TEL-TALE INDICATOR | HIGH BEAM INDICATOR | OIL PRESSURE INDICATOR | GASOLINE GAUGE |
| L.H. DIRECTION SIGNAL INDICATOR | ODOMETER | SPEEDOMETER | | R.H. DIRECTION SIGNAL INDICATOR |

INSTR. PANEL (IN TRUCKS TO 2-TON CAP'Y.)

60

FRONT END RESTYLED

THRIFTMASTER (6-CYL. 235 c.i.d.)

SEDAN DELIVERY (FINAL YR.) $2361.

new "K" SERIES 4-W-D AVAIL. (CHASSIS-CAB, PICKUP, PANEL, CARRYALL)

PROD.: 394,017

51

Chevrolet

70 SERIES

CHEVROLET 70

60 SERIES
(Middleweight)

61

PROD. : 342,659

LIGHT DUTY

LT. DUTY
FRONT END

62 FRONT ENDS RESTYLED, WITH OVAL HOOD PODS ELIMINATED and A RETURN TO ONLY TWO HEADLIGHTS.

PROD.: 396,940

60 SERIES

JOBMASTER

52

FOR BETTER VISIBILITY, DISTANCE (WIDTH) ACROSS FENDERS UP TO 7" NARROWER ON CONVENTIONAL MEDIUM and HEAVY-DUTY MODELS, WHICH HAVE STD. SOLID FRONT AXLE and VARIABLE-RATE SPRINGS. *new* GRILLE ON LT.-DUTY

63

Conventional

C SERIES ON 115, 127, 133 and 157" WB

new HIGH-TORQUE 230 C.I.D. and 292 C.I.D. 6-CYL. ENGS.

1½-TON STAKE 157" WB $2896.

C SERIES I.D. # 3C140(A) 100001 UP

DUMP TRUCK

L SERIES C.O.E. (2-TON) 145"-WB TYPE PRICED AT $3245. (L-5309)

53

the "New Reliables"

SERIES 80 DIESEL TANDEM WITH 6 CUBIC YD. CONCRETE MIXER

(C-50 IS CHASSIS-CAB CONVENTIONAL)

$2629.

CARRYALL (4-W-D. AVAIL.)

$2324.

½-TON PANEL (1-TON also)

Conventional

T SERIES 80 DIESEL TILT-CAB (C.O.E.) TRACTOR, WITH 40' SEMI-TRAILER

SERIES 80 TANDEM 10-CU.-YARD DUMP TRUCK (409 CID V8 ENGINE)

C, 80 SERIES I.D. # 4C140 (A) 100001 UP

WITH 292 CID 6-CYL. ENG.

SERIES 60 TRAILING-AXLE TANDEM WITH 15' PLATFORM BODY.

STD. CAB

SCHOOL BUS

64
new GRILLES

CHEVROLET FLEETSIDE—best for all-around use. Full-width body has double-wall construction.

C-10 (½ TON)
C-20 (¾ TON)
C-30 (1-TON)
4-W-D MODELS ALSO

54

CHOICE OF 18 LIGHT-DUTY, 258 MEDIUM and HEAVY-DUTY MODELS IN 1965! FROM $2023.

HEAVY-DUTY STYLING UNCHANGED

STAKE FROM $2284.

CHEVROLET

THE LONG STRONG LINE FOR '65

PROD.: 619,690

65

4, 6, and V8 GAS ENGINES, (also FOUR DIESELS.)

C SERIES SERIAL # FROM C1445 (-) 100001 UP

VARIOUS OTHER 1965 TYPES ILLUSTRATED BELOW

SEEN FROM FRONT TO REAR:

CHEVY-VAN, STEP-VAN 7, 60 SERIES TRUCK with VAN BODY, 80 SERIES DIESEL TRACTOR

($2324. ½-TON PANEL ACROSS THE STREET.)

$2066. UP

NEW LT.-DUTY 250 CID 6. TO 327 CID V8 IN 1/2-TON.

PROD.: 621,354

SIDE EMBLEM RETURNED TO A LOWER POSITION ON COWL.

66

SERIES 60 MEDIUM-DUTY
I.D. # FROM C-1446 (-) 100001 (C SERIES LT. DUTY)

new SERIES 70000 and 80000 LARGE TRUCKS with new V6 GAS ENGINES TO 478 CID, also V6 and V8 DIESELS TO 637 CID.

UP TO 48,000 LBS. GVW

new CONVENTIONAL MIDDLEWEIGHT TRUCK with new 96" SHORT CAB

HEAVY-DUTY TRUCK

TANDEM DUMP TRUCK (GAS OR DIESEL)

New 4-WAY HAZARD FLASHER SYSTEM, REDUCED-GLARE INSTRUMENT PANEL, IMPROVED DOOR LOCKS.

LT. DUTY

CAMPER

new 250 CID 6 IS STD.; 327 CID V8 OPT.

FLEETSIDE

DASH

MED. DUTY and PICKUP

67

("CST" PLATE ON WINDOW SILL DENOTES A new "CUSTOM SPORT TRUCK" MODEL.)

TOTALLY RESTYLED
I.D. # STARTS AT CE147 (-) 100001.
PICKUPS FR. $2152.

DESIGN IS **NEW**

56

CHEVROLET '68 *Job Tamer* TRUCKS

PICKUPS FROM $2371.

PROD.: 680,931
I.D. # STARTS AT CE148(-)10000/

NEW
SIDE SAFETY LTS. AT EITHER END.

68

note HUBCAP CHOICES (LT. DUTY)

250 CID 6 (155 HP) STD.
292 CID 6 (170 HP) AVAIL.
new 307 CID V8 (200 HP)
327 CID V8 OR 396 CID V8 (310 HP) ALSO

MORE BRIGHTWORK AT FRONT

464 DIFF. MODELS FOR 1968.
TOTAL REDUCED, FOR SIMPLICITY, TO 272 FOR 1969.

PROD.: 684,748

New

ALUMINUM GRILLE WITH CHEVROLET NAME ACROSS CENTER PIECE.

new SEAT BACKS

MED. DUTY

CAMPER SHELL OPTIONAL (ABOVE)

FLEETSIDE CST

new 350 CID V8 AVAIL. (200 OR 250 HP)

69

I.D. # STARTS AT CE149(-)10000/

4 new LP-GAS ENGINES ALSO AVAIL.

PICKUPS FR. $2435.

TO 76,800 LBS. GVW

LT. DUTY FROM 115" WB
$ 2654. UP

250 CID (115 HP) 6
or 307 CID (200 HP) V8
ALSO 292 CID 6,
350 CID V8,
or 400 CID
V8
AVAIL.

new
LONG
CONVENTIONAL CAB
HVY. DUTY DIESEL
TANDEM TRACTOR
90 SERIES
(ABOVE) 2-CYCLE
DETROIT DIESELS and
4-CYCLE CUMMINS DIESELS
TO 855 CID
(218 TO
335
HP)

new
LT. DUTY
GRILLE
WITH 12 SETS
OF SMALL
HORIZONTAL
RIBS ↗

3
OR
4-SP.
MANUAL
TRANS.
OR 2-SP.
POWERGLIDE
OR 3-SP. Turbo
Hydramatic AVAIL.
(LT. DUTY)

I.D. #
CE 140 (-)
100001

70
New
←

Titan 90
HEAVY
DUTY
WITH
SLEEPER
CAB
(ALUMINUM)
(PREVIOUS STYLE
STEEL TILT-CAB
ALSO CONT'D.)

58

TOTAL
1970
PROD.: 492,601

Conventionals
Short

Series 70·80·90

Long

Water and oil-fill access doors speed maintenance checks.

CHEVROLET

1 TON CH.-CAB = $3376.
1½ T. = $4037.
2 T. = 4352.

71
new GRILLE (LT. DUTY)

Titan 90
Aluminum Tilt

1-TON STEPSIDE $3265.

CHASSIS-CAB STAKE

I. D. NO.
CE 141 (−)
100001 UP

Chevy conventionals may be adapted to an almost unlimited range of applications with available power-plants. Gasoline models are powered by a standard 401-cubic-inch V6 or optional 478 V6. Both have established outstanding durability records on the job.

Diesel models offer a wide selection of Detroit Diesel and Cummins engines. 2-cycle Detroit Diesels available are: 6V-53N, 6-71N and 8V-71N. Four-cycle Cummins diesels available are: NH-230, NHC-250, NHCT-270 and NTC-335.

CHEVROLET

9' BOX 133" WB

LT. DUTY = FRONT DISC BRAKES

Sure-stopping long-lasting disc brakes now standard.

Functional, easy-to-read main instrument cluster.

Steel
Tilt

Steel Tilt Cab

59

Chevrolet

4511

SERIES 60 TANDEM TRACTOR

Forward-control rear-engine

School Bus

chassis:

LT. DUTY I.D. #
CE 142 (−) 100001 UP

SERIES 50 CONV.

Step-Van
Step-Van bus conversions are available with bodies to seat up to 30 students.

THESE, and VARIOUS OTHER 1971 MODELS, ARE CONTINUED WITH LITTLE CHANGE.

72

CONVENTIONAL SCHOOL BUS FRONT END SIMILAR TO SER. 50 CONV. TRUCK

SCHOOL BUS

BUS BODIES BY SUPERIOR, CARPENTER, WARD, THOMAS, BLUE BIRD, WAYNE, ETC.

Conventional cab interior

SCHOOL BUS DASH

60

school bus

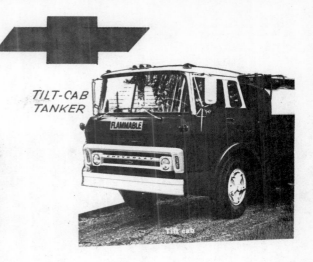

TILT-CAB TANKER

Tilt cab

Refrigerated Transport
TANDEM 90

1973 MODELS ILLUSTR., UNLESS OTHERWISE INDICATED.

new STYLING FOR 1973 LT. and MEDIUM-DUTY MODELS.

Chevrolet's medium-duty models feature all-new styling for '73.

73-74

LT. DUTY '73 I.D. # CC (X or Y) 143 (F) 100001 UP

LT. DUTY '74 I.D. # CC (V) 144 (F) 100001 UP

Detroit Diesel options include the 6-71, 8V-71 and 12V-71. The Cummins NH 230, NHC 250, NTC 290, NTC 335, NTC 350, and V903 are also available.

GCW's up to 76,800 lbs., GVW's up to 50,500 lbs.

('74)

Chevrolet heavies

61

Chevy Suburban seats up to nine facing forward.

SUBURBAN and PICKUP *have* SAME FRONT STYLING.

SCHOOL BUS

SERIES 70 CONVENTIONAL DIESEL TRACTOR ('76)

75-76

LT. DUTY 1975 I.D. # FROM CC (Q) 145 (F) 100001

LT. DUTY 1976 I.D. # FROM CC (V) 146 (F) 100001

Four wheelbases take bus bodies with capacities from 48 to 66.

Series 50, 60, 65 Conventional

DASH (CONV. 50, 60, 65)

Custom Deluxe Interior

Chevy K30 Chassis Cab Big Dooley

WITH WRECKER BODY

← SOME 1979 LT. DUTY MODELS WITH BLACK VERTICAL PCS. IN GRILLE.

MEDIUM-DUTY

Chevrolet

77-79

Series 90 long and short conventional diesels.

SERIES 90

HEAVY-DUTY TRUCKS

new FOR 1977

BISON

New FOR 1978: **BRUIN**

TITAN 90 C.O.E. has new LARGE GRILLE (1979 ON.)

('79)

63

FROM $7787.*

* MIN. PRICE INCR. TO $8265. DURING 1980.)

$6195. – $12,683.
1/2 – 3/4 – 1 – 2 TON PRICE RANGE

3-TON TILT CAB STILL AVAIL. FROM $15,176. BISON, BRUIN, TITAN AVAIL.

17 Main Transmissions. Take your choice of standard 4-speed or available synchromesh automatic and manual transmissions. There's even a Fuller 13-speed transmission available.

15 Wheelbases. Our wheelbases range from 125" to 254," with GVWRs from 13,800 to 50,000 lbs., and GCWRs from 32,000 to 60,000 lbs. And (in most states) our short cabs let you pull longer trailers with bigger payloads.

CHEVY SUBURBAN.

SEATS UP TO 9.

NEW GRILLE (LT. DUTY/ SUBURBAN MODELS)

80

4870 WAYS TO SPEC ONE TOUGH TRUCK Above all, 1980 Chevy Mediums offer you choice. There's such an incredibly wide range of dependable components that you're bound to find the combination you need for your job.
25 Rear Axles. Choose from single, tag and tandem axles with capacities from 11,000 to 38,000 lbs.

NEW KODIAK
FIBERGLASS TILT-HOOD CAB WITH WIDE GRILLE IS A REQUIRED OPTION WITH THE ORDER OF A CATERPILLAR OR CUMMINS ENGINE.

Chevrolet's commitment to Medium-Duty trucks is demonstrated by our broad range of power and components for 1980.

BIG NEWS FOR 1980!

3 DIESEL CHOICES FOR TOUGH CHEVY MEDIUMS.

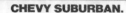

THE CATERPILLAR 3208
The "Cat" has built its reputation on high performance (up to 199 net HP in 49 states, 189 net HP in California). (Available after March 1, 1980.)

THE CUMMINS VT-225
This Cummins diesel features a heavy-duty design and it delivers 212 net horsepower at 3000 RPM. (Delivery later in 1980.) Not available in California.

THE DETROIT DIESEL ALLISON "FUEL PINCHER"
Direct from a leading diesel maker comes a brand-new 8.2 Liter V8 engine that's suited for the '80s. "The Fuel Pincher." (Available after March 1, 1980.)

DIESEL ENGINES ILLUSTRATED

MEDIUM / HVY. 1981 MODELS AS BEFORE *

FRONT OF LT. DUTY MODELS TOTALLY RESTYLED. 2 HEADLIGHTS OR 4.

Chevrolet

DIESEL ENGINES.
6 HP VARIATIONS

DISPLACEMENT AND TYPE	8.2L V8 DIESEL	8.2L V8T DIESEL
BORE & STROKE (IN.)	4.25 x 4.41	4.25 x 4.41
COMPRESSION RATIO	18.3 to 1	16.9 to 1
SAE GROSS HORSEPOWER @ RPM	165 @ 3000	205 @ 3000
SAE NET HORSEPOWER @ RPM	153 @ 3000	193 @ 3000
SAE GROSS TORQUE (LBS.-FT.) @ RPM	350 @ 1200	431 @ 1700
SAE NET TORQUE (LBS.-FT.) @ RPM	332 @ 1200	414 @ 1700
DISPLACEMENT AND TYPE	3208 V8 DIESEL*	3208 V8 DIESEL*
BORE & STROKE (IN.)	4.5 x 5.0	4.5 x 5.0
COMPRESSION RATIO	18.2 to 1	18.2 to 1
SAE GROSS HORSEPOWER @ RPM	160 @ 2800	166 @ 2600
SAE NET HORSEPOWER @ RPM	149 @ 2800	154 @ 2600
SAE GROSS TORQUE (LBS.-FT.) @ RPM	365 @ 1400	398 @ 1300
SAE NET TORQUE (LBS.-FT.) @ RPM	352 @ 1400	383 @ 1300
DISPLACEMENT AND TYPE	3208 V8 DIESEL	3208 V8 DIESEL
BORE & STROKE (IN.)	4.5 x 5.0	4.5 x 5.0
COMPRESSION RATIO	16.4 to 1	16.5 to 1
SAE GROSS HORSEPOWER @ RPM	175 @ 2800	185 @ 2600
SAE NET HORSEPOWER @ RPM	164 @ 2800	175 @ 2600
SAE GROSS TORQUE (LBS.-FT.) @ RPM	(c)405 @ 1400	452 @ 1400
SAE NET TORQUE (LBS.-FT.) @ RPM	(d)390 @ 1400	425 @ 1400
DISPLACEMENT AND TYPE	3208 V8 DIESEL**	3208 V8 DIESEL
BORE & STROKE (IN.)	4.5 x 5.0	4.5 x 5.0
COMPRESSION RATIO	16.4 to 1	16.4 to 1
SAE GROSS HORSEPOWER @ RPM	200 @ 2800	210 @ 2800
SAE NET HORSEPOWER @ RPM	189 @ 2800	199 @ 2800
SAE GROSS TORQUE (LBS.-FT.) @ RPM	490 @ 1400	500 @ 1400
SAE NET TORQUE (LBS.-FT.) @ RPM	473 @ 1400	473 @ 1400

*Not Available in Calif. **For use in Calif. only
(c) Federal ratings. 425 @ 1400 Net in California
(d) Federal rating. 413 @ 1400 Net in California

292 CID 6; 350, 366 or 427 CID V8s (USED IN MED. DUTY)

$6679.-$9197. ('81)

1/2 - 3/4 - 1 TON PRICE RANGE

$7297.-$10,572. ('82)

('81)

81-82

GAS ENGINES. 4 DIFFERENT MODELS (125-210 HP)

KODIAK OPTION ('82)

* HVY. DUTY MODELS DISCONTINUED 1982.

LT. DUTY USES 110 HP 250 CID 6 or 160 HP 305 CID V8.

Chevy Kodiak in Medium Tan

FARM TRUCK

MEDIUMS FROM CHEVY ('82)

There are over 4800 ways to custom-build one for your job.

LT.-DUTY TYPES SIMILAR TO 1981, BUT WITH 1982 I.D. # 1GC (-) C14(-)(-) C (-) 000001 UP

S-10 new FOR 1982
COMPACT PICKUP 119 CID 4 (82 HP) OR 173 CID V6 (110 HP)

4-CYL. ENG. BY ISUZU

108.3" OR 117.9" WB

MEDIUM-DUTY DUMP TR. (WITH DELUXE EQ.) ('82)

454 CID GAS V8 HVY.-DUTY ENG. ALSO AVAIL.

65

CREW / BONUS CAB

Chevrolet

MEDIUM DUTY

C-60, C-70

KODIAK

FURTHER DETAILS ON 1945-1982 PICKUPS and VANS CAN BE SEEN IN THE BOOK, "PICKUP and VAN SPOTTER'S GUIDE."

4-W-D STEPSIDE →

83 new GRILLE ON LT.-DUTY MODELS $7551.- $10,797. CONVENTIONAL 1/2 – 3/4 – 1 TON PRICE RANGE

pickups

CHASSIS-CAB

CAB (MED. DUTY)

6.2 L

CHEVROLET

21M058

66

SPORTVAN.

Chevrolet

S-10 COMPACT MODELS

CHASSIS-CAB

MAXI-CAB

S-10 4X4 BLAZER

PICKUP GRILLE IS SIMILAR (LIKE '83)

84 brand new

C.O.E. TILTMASTER

TURBO-DIESEL STEEL TILT CAB

165 NET HP @ 3000 RPM (155 HP IN CALIF.)

KODIAK

142", 165", 181" OR 197" WB

MEDIUM-DUTY GRILLE

C20 Crew Cab Scottsdale in Doeskin Tan.

C20 Stepside Custom Deluxe with long box i

C30 Chassis-Cab Custom Deluxe in Frost White with stake body provided by an independent supplier.

Electronic speed control and intermittent wiper shown on standard multi-function switch.

PUSH

CRUISE WIPER OFF ON DELAY LO

85

LT. DUTY HAS new GRILLE w. FEWER HORIZ. PCS., new HEADLIGHT PLACEMENT. →

new 4.3 L "VORTEC" 262 CID V6 (155 HP)

ALSO 305, 350 OR 454 CID (GAS) V8s OR 379 CID DIESEL V8 AVAIL.

WHEEL STYLES

Cast aluminum wheels

Styled sport wheels

Rally Wheels

Wheel covers

SCOTTSDALE →

← REAR STEP BUMPER IS OPTIONAL, AS IS SLIDING REAR WINDOW AND THE CARGO LIGHT ABOVE IT.

CHEVROLET

TFW·202

MODEL DESIGNATIONS:
C = 2WD
K = 4WD

10 = ½ T.
20 = ¾ T.
30 = 1 TON

(MED.-DUTY ON NEXT PAGE)

Silverado instrument panel.

VARIATION IN LTS. (SCOTTSDALE) ↘

Shown: C10 Fleetside Silverado Custom Two-Tone in Silver and Midnight Black.

68

Chevrolet

TILTMASTER
WITH 5.7 LITER
TURBOCHARGED DIESEL ENG.
165 HP @ 3000 RPM
(155 HP IN
CALIFORNIA)

C-70 KODIAK
(KODIAK CAB OPTION
REQUIRED WITH THE
CATERPILLAR 3208
DIESEL ENG.)

(ABOVE)
TILTMASTER C.O.E.
DIESEL (137-209" WB)

85
(CONT'D.)
(16 AVAILABLE WHEELBASES, AS
WELL AS A CHOICE OF 4 GAS
AND 15 DIESEL ENGINES.)

MEDIUM-DUTY
CONVENTIONAL
DUMP
TRUCK

INSTRUMENT
PANEL (ABOVE)

C-50
(GAS)
125-167"
WB
C-60
(GAS, DSL.)
125-218"
WB
C-70
(GAS)
(DIESEL OPT.)
125-254"
WB

Grab
handles

CLOSER
DETAILS OF
REAR QUARTER
SECTION (CONV.
MED. CAB)

Corbitt

CORBITT CO., HENDERSON, N.C.
TRUCKS 1913-1958 *

* NO TRUCKS 1953 TO 1956

RICHARD J. CORBITT, FOUNDER

CORBITT BUSES ALSO, STARTING 1915

('21) 3½-TON "A" $4650.

LEELAND HOTEL

('23) 1-TON SPEED TRUCK

MODELS (1927)
(CONTINENTAL ENGS.)

Model	Tonnage	Cyl.
20-21	1 TON	6 CYL.
25	1½	4
40, C	2	"
B	2½	"
3-4 TON		"
70	5	"

Truck

ALL 4-CYL. UNTIL 1926

('24) 2½ TON B $2970. 152" WB

NOTE OVAL QUARTER WINDOWS IN CAB.

NEW 56 2½-TON TANKER

('28) 4 CYL., 152" WB

CONTINENTAL ENGINES
BUDA ENG. IN SOME 5-TON MODELS.

1920s-1930s

('29) 1¼ TON "620"
$1400 6 CYL.
(CHASSIS) 137" WB
HYDRAULIC BRAKES

SCHOOL BUS
(C. '36)

COCA COLA BOTTLER'S TRUCK ('34)

1935-1936 MODELS, USING 1934 BODY DIES BOUGHT FROM AUBURN
AVAIL. TO 1938 w. LYCOMING ENG.

LIGHTWEIGHT SER. SAME FRONT END AS A 1934 AUBURN CAR.

70

Corbitt Trucks

('37)

note OLD-STYLE CAB W. ARCH WINDOWS

HVY. TRACTOR

CORBITT ('34) BUSES

('40 TO '48)

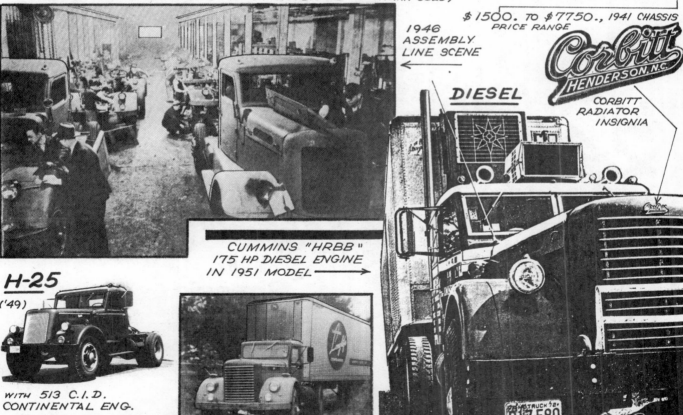

50-SD6 MILITARY PRIME MOVER WITH HERCULES 855 CID 6-CYLINDER ENGINE *(LATER ADAPTED TO CIVILIAN USES)*

1941 MODELS INCLUDE: 13-B; 17-B; 21-B; 26-D; 14BT; 17BT; 18BT; 22BT; 27BT (DIESEL: D-18BT; D-27B6T)

1940s

CONTINENTAL, HERCULES, and CUMMINS ENGINES

$1500. TO $7750., 1941 CHASSIS PRICE RANGE

Corbitt HENDERSON, N.C.

CORBITT RADIATOR INSIGNIA

DIESEL

1946 ASSEMBLY LINE SCENE ←

CUMMINS "HRBB" 175 HP DIESEL ENGINE IN 1951 MODEL →

H-25

('49)

WITH 513 C.I.D. CONTINENTAL ENG.

1950s

('52) WITH *new* 1-PC. WINDSHIELD

71

DENBY

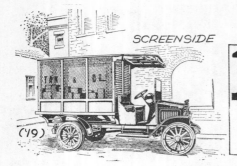

SCREENSIDE

('19)

1915–1931
DENBY MOTOR TRUCK CORP.,
DETROIT

('19)

19

EISEMANN IGNITION
ON ALL (TO '25)

12	1 TON	124" WB	8.2 GR
13	2	144	10.2
15	3	144	10.9
210	5	170	12.55

ALL with 4-CYLINDER
CONTINENTAL
ENGINES (TO '25)

STROMBERG CARB.
(THROUGH '22)

20-21

new 1921 $4600.
4-TON
MODEL
"27"
→

('21)

NOTE
RADIATOR
GUARD

1½-TON "33"
('21) new IN 1921,
REPLACING 1-TON
"12." 4-TON
"27" ALSO new.

1920
MODELS

12	1 TON	124" WB	3-SPEED	3½" × 5" BORE and STROKE
134	2	144	4	3¾ × 5
25	3	150	4	4⅛ × 5¼
210	5	170	4	4½ × 5¼

22

1922 MODELS

31	¾ TON	130" WB	5.85 GR
33	1½	136	6.83
134	2	144	10.20
25	3	150	9.45
27	4	170	10.0
210	5	170	12.55

23

MODEL "33" IS
2-TON IN 1923,
with 136" WB, 7.25 GR,
3-SPEED TRANS.
MODEL "35" IS
new 3-TON, with
4 SP., 8.0 GR, 155" WB.

2-TON
"33"
(144" WB)
CHASSIS
$2375.

('24)

24

31	¾ TON	130" WB
33	2	136
35	3	155
27	4	170
210	5	170

NEW

IN
1925
↓

1-TON
('25 TO '28)

MODEL 41
Chassis

25-28

4-CYL. HERCULES "O"
ENGINE (4" × 5")
USED ON '26 and
LATER "41," "41-A" TYPES,
AS WELL AS AUTO-LITE
IGNITION.

1927-1928 MODELS:

41, 41A	1 - 1½ T.	128" WB	5.8 GR
43	2½	155	9.0
35	3	155	8.15
27	4	170	10.0
210	5	170	12.5

Chassis

29

THIS 2-TON "42"
IS new IN 1929 →
(154" WB)

$2275.

"35" 3-TON MODEL NOT LISTED
IN 1929; OTHER MODELS
CONTINUED.

(DISCONTINUED 1931)

Diamond Reo

EMBLEM

DIAMOND REO TRUCKS
A Division of White Motor Corporation / Lansing, Michigan 48920

(FORMED 1967 THROUGH A MERGING OF _DIAMOND T_ and _REO._)

(MAY 1, 1967 IS OFFICIAL DATE OF CONSOLIDATION.)

68-69

CF-59 COMPACT (BELOW)

FORWARD TILT HOOD SECTIONS (ON C-90-D, C-114, OPTIONAL ON C-101)

(SHORT 90" BBC)

"CF-68 TREND" with (GASOLINE OR DIESEL ENGINES)

← TILT CAB OF PLASTIC-LIKE "Royalex."

C-90-D

"GOLD COMET" 6 CYL. and V-8 GASOLINE ENGINES (130 H.P. TO 235 H.P.)

ALSO, A SELECTION of 27 DIESELS (CUMMINS, DETROIT, CATERPILLAR.)

"CF-83" (with FORWARD-TILT CAB = FIBERGLASS OPTIONAL.)

C-101

(SHORT W.B., GAS OR DIESEL)

LOW-MAINTENANCE ELECTRICAL SYSTEM

CO-78

(with 84" SLEEPER BUNK, 190 TO 335 H.P. DIESEL ENGINES

C-114

(CHOICE OF STEEL OR ALUMINUM COMPONENTS, FRONT AXLE FORWARD OR SET BACK.)

CAB (C-90-D, C-114, DC-101 MODELS)

DIESEL ENGINES TO 335 H.P.

73

Diamond Reo

C-101

('72)

with
STEEL
CAB
(new ENLARGED
CAB in 1970.)

70-72

SUMMER, 1971:
FRANCIS L. CAPPAERT
PURCHASES DIAMOND REO
FROM WHITE.

"C-101" has 134" WB
(236" WB with
TANDEM AXLES.)

CAB (C-101, '72)

CONVENTIONAL "BUTTERFLY"
HOOD

VERTICAL MUFFLER
ON ALL BUT
"8-250" GAS and
"8-230 LPG
MODELS.

C-114

('70)

TILT-UP
(OPTIONAL)
FIBERGLASS
HOOD -AND-
FENDER ASSEMBLY (AVAIL.'71 ON
DC-101: '72 ON C-101.)

"VARI-RATE"
(SLIDING)
REAR
SPRINGS

74

DOUBLE TOP TANK REMOVES TRAPPED AIR FROM RADIATOR.

Diamond Reo

50 - GALLON FUEL TANK STANDARD (40 , 43 , 62 or 65 - GAL. TYPES ALSO AVAIL.)

DC-101

("ROYALE" C.O.E. INTRO. FALL, 1972. 6, V8 or V-12 DETROIT DIESEL ENGS. USED)

gasoline, LPG and diesel

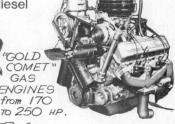

"GOLD COMET" GAS ENGINES from 170 to 250 HP.

"CLEAN - AIRE" LPG ENGINES from 190 or 230 HP.

72 ON

CUMMINS OR DETROIT DIESEL ENGINES

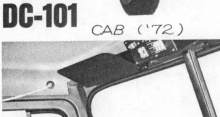

DC-101

CAB ('72.)

"C-92-D" new FOR '72.

CONVENTIONALS RENAMED "APOLLO," WITH 6 CYL. OR V8 CUMMINS, DETROIT OR CATERPILLAR ENG.

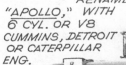

('72)

(SPRING, 1974 new "RAIDER" C-119 CONVENTIONAL has COLUMN OF 7 DIAMONDS ON LARGE GRILLE.)

DIAMOND REO TAKEN OVER NOV. 3, 1975, BY CONSOLIDATED INDUSTRIES, COLUMBUS, OHIO.

POWER HYDRAULIC STEERING optional

(DIAMOND REO MILITARY TRUCKS PRODUCED IN 1968, BUT NOT AGAIN UNTIL SUMMER, 1972.)

PRODUCTION OF 6 AVAIL. MODELS SUSPENDED SEPT., 1975. RESUMES 1977 with ONE MODEL, BY OSTERLUND, INC., HARRISBURG, PA.

DIAMOND REO "GIANT" AVAIL. SINCE 1978.

MODEL C-11664-DB

75

DIAMOND T TRUCKS (1911-1967)

1919 MODELS:

J-5	1 TON
J-4	1½
J-3	2
LB	3½
R	5

(132" TO 170" WBS)

4-CYLINDER CONTINENTAL ENGINES (THROUGH '20)

DIAMOND T MOTOR CAR COMPANY
Chicago, Illinois   Established 1905

EARLY INSIGNIA — DIAMOND

LATER INSIGNIA — T

('19)

19-20

('20)

7.75 GEAR RATIO IN 1919 MODELS TO 2-TON; LB has 10.33, R has 11.66 GR.

1920 MODELS:

T	1½ TON	144" WB	8.25	GR
*FS	1½	144	8.25	
J-4	1½	154	7.75	
J-3	2	154	7.75	
LB	3½	170	8.75	
R	5	170	13.66	
S	5	180	13.66	

21

1½-TON "T" WORM DRIVE 144" WB ('21)

"DIAMOND T" INSCRIPTION ON HOOD

4-SPEED TRANSMISSIONS ON 1921 2-TON and up.)

1921 MODELS:

T	1½ TON	144" WB	8.25	GR
U	2	160	7.75	
K	3½	170	8.75	
EL	5	180	11.66	
S	5	180	11.66	

new 4-CYL. 1921 HINKLEY ENGINES (TO '26, ON SOME MODELS.)

* "FS" MODEL = "FARM SPECIAL" (INTRO. 1919; AVAIL. THROUGH '23.)

22-25

O3	1-1½ TON
FS (T)	1½
U (U-2 IN '24)	2 (2½ IN '23)
K	3½
EL	5
S (INTRO. '23)	5

(new "75" ¾ TON MODEL INTRO. '24, with 4-CYL. HERCULES "OX" ENGINE.)

('26)

26-27

new TR-TR MODELS IN '26.

K-2 (3½ TO 4 TON) 170" OR 180" WB

HERCULES ENGINES ON ALL 1927, 1928 MODELS

28

('28)

U-66   (2½ TON)

HORIZONTAL HOOD LOUVRES AS IN 1927, S-7 IS 7½ TON MODEL (171" WB)

29

new BODY STYLING ON 1929 MODELS:

151, 76 (1 TON;) 3, 290 (1½ T;) T5, T4 (2 T;) U5, U56, 550, 502 (2½ T;) U5S (3T;) K-3, K36 (3½ T;) 800 (4 T;) S3, S (5, 7, 7½ T;) TR-TR : T3T, U4T, K2T, S2T
151 has CONT. 6 ENG., S, S3 have BUDA 4 CYL. HERCULES 6 ENGS. IN ALL OTHERS.

290 CANOPY (1½ TON) ('29)

151 (1-TON)

76

550 (2½ TON)

DIAMOND T TRUCKS

30

MODELS: 200, 151 (1 TON;) 290 (1½ T;) 303 (2 T;) 551, 503, 506 (2½ T;) 602, 606 (3 T;) 700 (3½ T;) 1000 (5 TON;)
TR.-TR.: 303 (2 T;) 503, 551 (2½ T;) 602 (3 TON)

31

HOOD VENT DOORS AS ON '33 (BELOW)
4- CYL., 57 HP BUDA ENG. IN "200."
6- CYL., 61 HP BUDA ENG. IN new "215" (1-TON, 135" WB.) "503" DISCONTINUED.

32

new 8- TON "1603" 6-WHEELER has 6-CYL., 127-HP WAUKESHA ENGINE. 6- CYL. HERC. ENGS. (56 TO 124 HP) CONT'D. IN OTHERS.

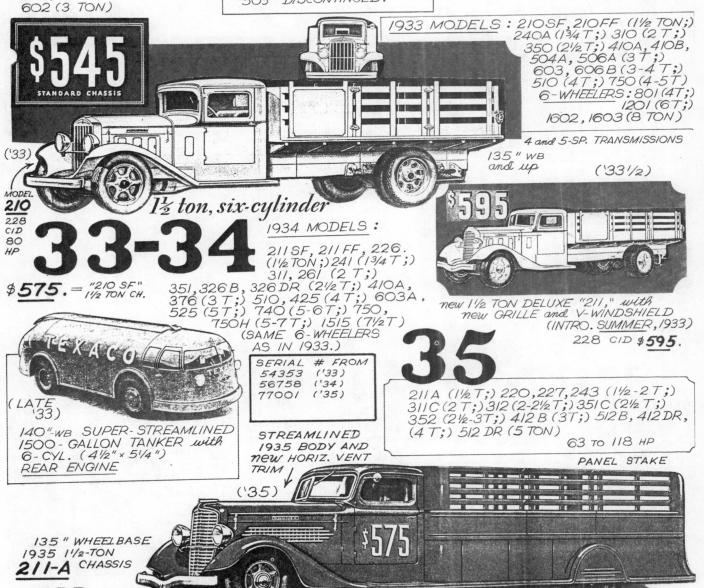

$545 STANDARD CHASSIS

('33)

MODEL **210** 228 CID 80 HP

1½ ton, six-cylinder

1933 MODELS: 210SF, 210FF (1½ TON;) 240A (1¾ T;) 310 (2 T;) 350 (2½ T;) 410A, 410B, 504A, 506A (3 T;) 603, 606 B (3-4 T;) 510 (4 T;) 750 (4-5 T;)
6-WHEELERS: 801 (4 T;) 1201 (6 T;) 1602, 1603 (8 TON)

4 and 5-SP. TRANSMISSIONS

135" WB and up

('33½)

$595

33-34

$575. = "210 SF" 1½ TON CH.

1934 MODELS:
211 SF, 211 FF, 226. (1½ TON;) 241 (1¾ T;) 311, 261 (2 T;) 351, 326 B, 326 DR (2½ T;) 410A, 376 (3 T;) 510, 425 (4 T;) 603A, 525 (5 T;) 740 (5-6 T;) 750, 750H (5-7 T;) 1515 (7½ T) (SAME 6-WHEELERS AS IN 1933.)

SERIAL # FROM
54353 ('33)
56758 ('34)
77001 ('35)

new 1½ TON DELUXE "211," with new GRILLE and V-WINDSHIELD (INTRO. SUMMER, 1933) 228 CID **$595.**

TEXACO

(LATE '33)
140"-WB SUPER-STREAMLINED 1500- GALLON TANKER with 6- CYL. (4½" × 5¼") REAR ENGINE

35

STREAMLINED 1935 BODY AND new HORIZ. VENT TRIM

211A (1½ T;) 220, 227, 243 (1½-2 T;) 311C (2 T;) 312 (2-2½ T;) 351C (2½ T;) 352 (2½-3T;) 412 B (3T;) 512B, 412 DR, (4 T;) 512 DR (5 TON)

63 TO 118 HP

PANEL STAKE

('35)

135" WHEELBASE 1935 1½-TON CHASSIS
211-A
$555.

$575

(LENGTH EXAGGERATED)

DIAMOND T TRUCKS

301 CHASSIS

3CI
1-1½ TON STARTS JUNE, 1937.

¾ TON 80 →

new GRILLE and LOUVRES

$525.*

*= CHASSIS PRICE

PANEL

36-37

80 (¾ TON) IS new FOR 1937, with 205 CID ENG. (61 HP @ 3300 RPM) and 119" WB (4.5-5.1 GR) D-20, D-30 DIESELS also new. 412 B and 228S DISC. 4.5 TO 7.27 GRs
'37 SER. # FROM 302003 (¾ TON); 3010001 (I TON); 209276 (1½ TON)

1936 MODELS :
212 AS (1½-2 TON ;) 212 BS (1½-2½ T;) 221S, 228S (1½-3T;) 244S (2-3T;) 313, 320 (2-4T;) 353, 360 (2½-4T;) 412 B (3-4T;) 512 B, 412 DR (4-5T;) 512 DR (5-6½ TON)
1936 SERIAL #s START AT 204001 (I TON, I½ TON) 300001 (¾ TON)

63 TO 118 HP, 228-404 CID ALL HERC. 6 ENGINES, AS BEFORE.

38

'38 = 304324 (¾ TON); 3010427 (I T.); 213077 (1½ T.)

INTRO. OCT., '37: new C.O.E. MODELS →

80 (¾ TON;) 301, 304 (1-1½ T;) 401 (1½-2T C.O.E.;) 402 (1½-2½ T C.O.E.;) 404, 212 AS (1½-2½ T;) 212 BS, 221S, 405, 406 (1½-3T;) 507 (2-3T C.O.E.;) D-20 (2-3½ TON DIESEL ;) 244S, 509 (2-3½ T;) 607 (2-4T C.O.E. ;) 313, 320, 611, 612 (2-4T;) 609 (2½-4½ T C.O.E.;) 353, 613 (2½-4½T;) 360, 614 (2½-5T;) D-30 (2½-4½ TON DIESEL ;) 512 B, 412 DR (4-5½ T;) 512 DR (5-6½T)

78 TO 118 HP   4.5 TO 7.37 GRs

new GRILLE ('38)

GRILLE JOINED with LOUVRES ON 1938 CONVENTIONALS.

PANEL STAKE ←

('38)

1939 SERIAL #s FROM 2010368 (I TON) 3060183 (1½ TON)
61 TO 118 HP 4.5 TO 8.4 GRs

39

new HEAVIER GRILLE, STRAIGHT BUMPERS

201 (I TON;) 305 (1-1½ T;) 306 (1½ T ;) 401 (1½-2T C.O.E.;) 402 (1½-2½ T C.O.E.;) 404 (1½-2½ T;) 405, 406 (1½-3T;) 507 (2-3T;) 513 (2-3½ TON DIESEL ;) 509 (2-3½ T;) also, MANY OTHER MODELS, from #231 to 804, up to 5-6½ TON "512-DR."

('39)

new DOOR-TO-DOOR DLV. UNITS : 231, 332, 333

78

1940 PRICE RANGE :
$**575**. (MODEL 201)
TO
$**5600**. (MODELS 807 OR 808 DIESELS)

C.F. and C.O.E. TYPES AVAIL.

STARTING 1940, CUMMINS ENGINES AVAIL. IN SOME DIESEL MODELS. (100 or 150 HP)

1940 SERIAL NOS. FROM 2011012 (201-S, D) 306/259 (306-S) 4045002 (404-S LT. MODELS)

('40)

"PaK-Age-Car" DELIVERY UNITS INCLUDED IN LINE (1940-1942) (PURCHASED IN SPRING, 1939 BY DIAMOND T, has 133 CID, 4-CYL. LYCOMING ENGINE with 32 HP @ 2400 RPM.) FROM $1095. ('40)

AS BEFORE, 6-CYL. HERCULES GAS and DIESEL ENGINES IN OTHER MODELS. UP TO 132 HP (1940)

1940 MODEL LINE UP =
201, 306, 404, 404-H, 406, 509, 509-H, 612, 612-H, 614, 614-DR, 614-H, 614-HDR, 805, 806, 513*, 615*, 807*, 808*, 900, 306-SC (C.F.), 404-SC (C.F.), 404-SCH (C.F.)   C.O.E.s: 201-C, 404-C, 509-C, 612-C, 614-C, 805-C, 806-C, 513-C*, 615-C*   (ALSO MODELS 91 and 117 PAK-AGE-CARS)
(* = WITH DIESEL ENGINE)

heavy-duty

EARLY **1940**s

DIAMOND T

('42)
LT.

('42)
HVY.
(note HEADLIGHT and BUMPER DIFFERENCE BETW. LT., HVY.)

ARMORED "HALF TRACK" (ABOVE)

('42)

MILITARY VEHICLES
(W.W. 2 YEARS)

REAR SECTION OF THIS TYPE USUALLY COVERED BY CANVAS IN COLD OR RAINY WEATHER.

('43)

MILITARY 6 × 6 "PRIME MOVER"

1941 LT. CIVILIAN SERIAL NOS. FROM 2011639 (201-L, 201-S or 201-D) FROM 4046817 (404-S)

79

DIAMOND T
LATER
1940s

GAS ENGINES = HERCULES
DIESEL " = CUMMINS
77 to 150 HP

('45) GRILLE and TRIM PAINTED IN BODY COLOR.

FEWER POSTWAR MODELS FOR 1946 : 404HH, 509, 509 SC, 614H, 702, 806H, 900; 910 DIESEL

6 WHEELERS : 900 SD300PA; 910 SW3002PA DIESEL, 910 SD462W DIESEL

('47) CAB-FORWARD TANKER

STANDARD OF CALIFORNIA

ROY E. SMITH

MORE MODELS IN 1947:

201, 306, 306H, 404HH, 404 SC, 404 SCH, 509, 509H, 509 SC, 614H, 703, 809, 901;

910 DIESEL

ALSO, 5 6-WHEELERS

CONTINENTAL ENGINES IN 703, 809, 901 MODELS (START. 1947.)

AIR BRAKES

MODEL 201 ('49)

DIAMOND T TRUCKS

DIESEL "910" TRACTOR-TRAILER ('47)
172" TRACTOR WB CUMMINS "HB-600"
672 CID ENGINE 150 HP @ 1800 RPM
7.08 and other GEAR RATIOS

Diamond T Model 910 handles 68,000 pounds gross weight with Diamond T reliability. Golden Gate Bridge in background.

80

DIAMOND T TRUCKS

NO LT. DUTY
MODELS AFTER 1951.

1950s
and
LATER

1953
MODELS:
323, 422, 522, 622,
660, 720, 722, 920;
DIESELS: 723, 921, 921 BR,
921 FN, 950 RS,
951 S
6-WHEELERS ALSO

(SOME O.H.V. ENGINES)

('53)

OWN, CONTINENTAL, HERCULES,
CUMMINS and BUDA 6-CYL.
ENGINES ('53) (112 to 300 HP)

C.O.E. DESIGN LATER
SOLD TO
INTERNATIONAL.

MODEL
"660"
162 HP (164 HP @ 2700 IN '53.)

('52)

new
TILT-CAB (C.O.E.)
SPRING, 1953.
INTRO.

T-662 ('59)
(AVAIL.
THROUGH
1950s)

OWN, CUMMINS, and
HALL-SCOTT ENGINES (6 CYL.)
IN 1958 (153 to 262 HP)

C.O.E. (1960s)

DIESEL

('67)

DIESEL ('61)

81

DURING
1967, BECOMES

Diamond Reo
DIAMOND
REO

FIRST TYPE

DIVCO

DIVCO, DETROIT, MICH.
(1926 ON)
ORIG. DETROIT INDUSTRIAL VEHICLE CO.

27

'27 COULD BE DRIVEN FROM FRONT SEAT OR FROM EITHER RUNNING-BOARD.

28

MODEL B →

PRE - 1929 TYPES DO NOT HAVE EXTENDED HOOD AT FRONT.

29

(IMPROVED MODEL)

HOOD EXTENDED IN FRONT ; SHORTER BODY

('29 STYLE CONT'D. TO 1933)

33-37

→

REPORTEDLY, NO MAJOR CHANGES DURING MID-1930s.

DIVCO BUYS TWIN COACH TRUCK OPERATIONS, 1936. KNOWN AS <u>DIVCO-TWIN</u> UNTIL 1944.

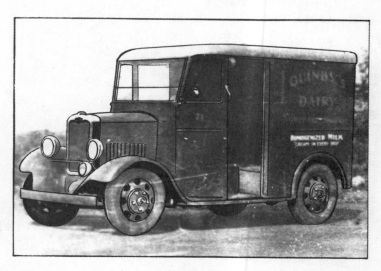

MODEL S (EARLY 1937)

DIVCO

4 - CYLINDER CONTINENTAL ENGINE

(IN "UM," ILLUS. BELOW)

MODELS UM, ULM (ULM has 6 CYL., 218 CID ENG.)

NEW STYLING IN 1937

('41)

THREE OAKS Creamery
MILK CREAM BUTTER

RO828

PLAZA 1472

INTERIOR with ONLY MINOR CHANGES, 1938 TO 1970.

3 DIVCO-TWIN Models for

RETAIL MILK ROUTES
SEMI-WHOLESALE MILK ROUTES
BAKERY ROUTES
ICE CREAM DELIVERY
LAUNDRY • DRY CLEANERS
FLORISTS • PARCEL DELIVERY
DEPARTMENT STORES

U SERIES

37 ON

THE PATENTED *Divco-Twin*

DIVCO-TWIN TRUCK COMPANY • DETROIT

POST-WAR TYPES
MODELS 11, 13 (4 CYL.)
MODEL 15 (6 CYL.)
100 3/4" WB

note SMALLER FR. QTR. WINDOW (LIKE "ULM") →

MODELS 33, 37 (6 CYL.)
115" WB

MODEL 21 (6 CYL.)
DUAL REAR WHEELS
← 127 1/2" WB

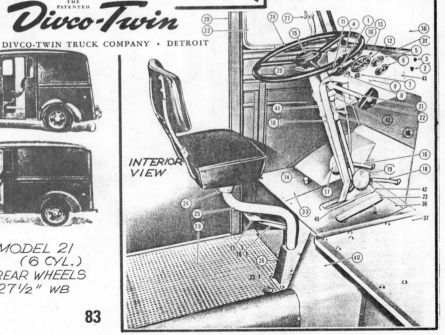

INTERIOR VIEW

DIVCO

DIVCO CORPORATION
22000 Hoover Road
Detroit, Michigan

MODEL 334 ('54) HAS *new* CLEARANCE LIGHTS ON ROOF (OVER WINDSHIELD.)

3½ TO 7 TONS GROSS VEHICLE WT.

NEW

MODEL 52-10' BODY

412 CU. FT. CARGO CAPACITY

MODEL 42-12' BODY

117"

56

130"

470 CU. FT. CARGO CAPACITY

IN 1956, OVER 80% OF ALL DIVCO TRUCKS BUILT SINCE 1927 WERE STILL IN SERVICE!

OLDER STYLE DIVCO ALSO CONTINUES.

58

DIVIDEND SERIES MODEL 12 130" WB (THIS TYPE AVAIL. TO 1966.)

60

new 4-CYL. O.H.V. DIVCO ENGINE

80 H.P. @ 3500 RPM

'60 MODELS (47 TO 102 HP)
WITH 4-CYL. CONTINENTAL ENGINES : 11, 114, 12, 124, 13, 134, 244, 364, 364HD
WITH 6-CYL. HERC. ENGINES : 15, 154, 214, 224, 334, 344, 374
WITH OWN SUPER 6 ENGINE : 42, 52, 41, 51, 71, 72, 57

TOP H.P. UP TO 128 IN 1961

FROM 1957 TO 1967, A PART OF

DW **DIVCO-WAYNE** CORPORATION
EXECUTIVE OFFICES: 680 FIFTH AVENUE, NEW YORK, N.Y. 10019

65

WAYNE SCHOOL BUS ('65)

(FOR RECENT EXAMPLES OF WAYNE BUSES, SEE **WAYNE** SECTION.)

WITH OLD-STYLE FRONT BODY

72

APPROX. 5600 LBS. CURB WT.

1-MAN GARBAGE TRUCK *with* 15 CU. YD. PACKER BODY UP TO 9 TONS GROSS VEHICLE WT.
127½", 139½", OR 151½" W.B.

DIVCO TRUCK CO.
DIVISION OF HUGHES-KEENAN MFG. CO., DELAWARE, 01110

S/T-STAND CONTROLS CONT'D.

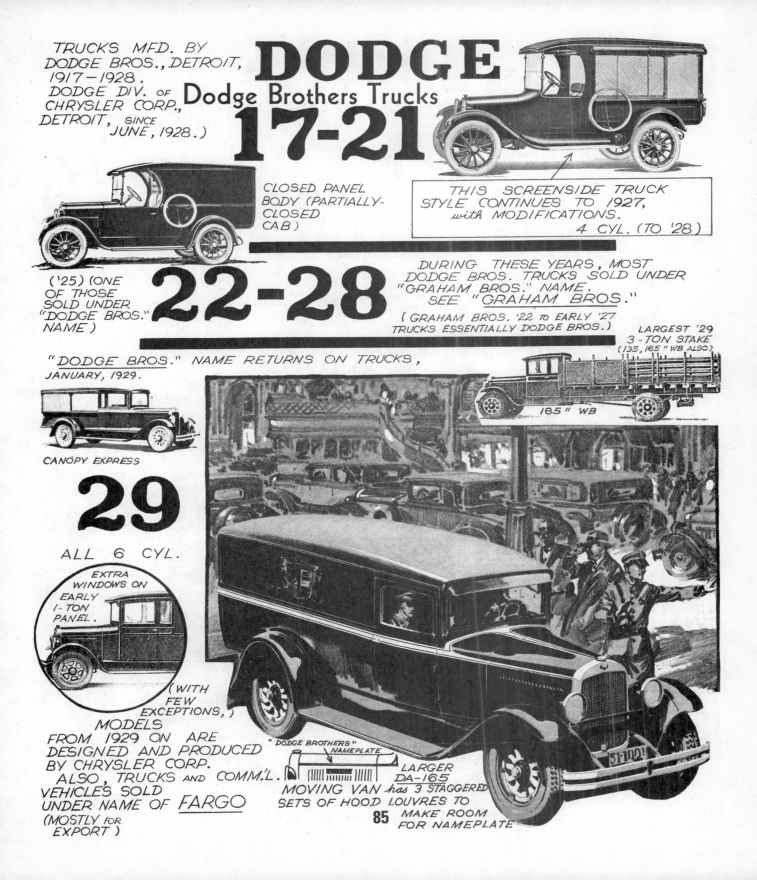

TRUCKS MFD. BY DODGE BROS., DETROIT, 1917-1928. DODGE DIV. OF CHRYSLER CORP., DETROIT, SINCE JUNE, 1928.)

DODGE
Dodge Brothers Trucks
17-21

CLOSED PANEL BODY (PARTIALLY-CLOSED CAB)

THIS SCREENSIDE TRUCK STYLE CONTINUES TO 1927, with MODIFICATIONS.
4 CYL. (TO '28)

('25) (ONE OF THOSE SOLD UNDER "DODGE BROS." NAME)

22-28

DURING THESE YEARS, MOST DODGE BROS. TRUCKS SOLD UNDER "GRAHAM BROS." NAME. SEE "GRAHAM BROS."

(GRAHAM BROS. '22 TO EARLY '27 TRUCKS ESSENTIALLY DODGE BROS.)

LARGEST '29 3-TON STAKE (135,165" WB ALSO)

185" WB

"DODGE BROS." NAME RETURNS ON TRUCKS, JANUARY, 1929.

CANOPY EXPRESS

29

ALL 6 CYL.

EXTRA WINDOWS ON EARLY 1-TON PANEL.

(WITH FEW EXCEPTIONS,) MODELS FROM 1929 ON ARE DESIGNED AND PRODUCED BY CHRYSLER CORP. ALSO, TRUCKS AND COMM'L. VEHICLES SOLD UNDER NAME OF FARGO (MOSTLY FOR EXPORT)

"DODGE BROTHERS" NAMEPLATE

LARGER DA-165 MOVING VAN has 3 STAGGERED SETS OF HOOD LOUVRES TO MAKE ROOM FOR NAMEPLATE

DODGE
Profitable
30
Truck Engines

CANOPY TRUCK

6 CYL., L-HEAD

SOME CANOPY and STAKE TRUCKS (UP TO 3 TON) AVAIL. WITH SAME FRONTAL STYLING AS 1927½-1928 GRAHAM BROS. (AS ABOVE)

(10', 1½, 2 OR 3 TON)

HALE AND SON HAULING

Nº 24

BASIC MODELS:

½ TON	109" WB	4 CYL.	45 HP
1 TON	140	6	
1½ TON	150, ETC.	6	63
2 TON	" "	6	
3 TON	135-185	6	78

¾ and 1-TON AVAIL. SUMMER, 1930, with 4 OR 6 CYL. ENGINE, AFTER 4-CYL. RETURNS. (40 MODELS WITH 12 WHEELBASES)

PANEL TRUCK 8', 1 TON 4 OR 6 CYL.

LATER IN YEAR, 1½ TON PRICES BEGIN AS LOW AS $595.

NOTE THE DIFFERENCES IN THE RADIATOR DESIGNS

86

DODGE

QUARTER WINDOWS CONT'D.
IN SOME HEAVY DUTY MODELS.

3 TON F-60, 61, 62 w.
96 HP 6

2-TON
6-CYL.
F-40
and
F-41 WITH
96 HP @
3000
RPM

31

UNUSUAL "DB" SPIDER
RADIATOR GUARD

STAGGERED LOUVRES ON HVY. DUTY

F-41 165" WB
TRACTOR TRAILER (SEMI)
WITH SLEEPER CAB

(F TYPES CONTINUE)
ALSO, 2 TON **CHASSIS**
73 HP   136" OR 165" WB
5-SPEED   TRANSMISSION

7.00
× 20
DUAL REAR
WHEELS W.
HELPER SPRINGS

32

HEAVY-DUTY MODELS UP TO
7½ TONS GROSS CAPACITY.

DODGE

('33)

COMMERCIAL PANEL

"DODGE BROTHERS" NAME STILL ON SIDE OF HOOD.

EXTERNAL VISOR ELIMINATED

33-35

Walter P. Chrysler

AS OF 8-35, LOWER WINDSHIELD CORNERS CURVED, and NAME ON SIDE OF HOOD IS SHORTENED TO "DODGE."

BROOKSIDE FARMS

COMMERCIAL PANEL   116" WB

NEW GRILLE ON SOME TYPES; OTHERS CONTINUE 1935 GRILLE AS SHOWN BELOW.

70 TO 96 HP, 201 TO 309 CID 6-CYL. ENGINES. (STRAIGHT-8, 385 CID, 115 HP ENG. IN G-80.)

(VERTICAL FRONT EDGE OF DOOR STARTS AUGUST, 1935.)

36

MODELS :
LC (COMMERCIAL)
LE-15 (3/4 TON)
LE-20; LF-28; LH-29 (1 TON)
LE-30; LHD-30; LF-35 (1½-2 TON)
LD-35; LS-35 (1½-3 TON)
LG-40 (1½-4 TON)
LT-35; LH-45 (2-4 TON)
K-50 (2-5½ TON)
K-60 (3-5½ TON)
G-80 (4-8 TON)

96 HP
3-TON →
$1695. (CH.)

88

DODGE TRUCKS

('38)

STAKE

37-38

new GRILLE WITH HORIZONTAL PCS.

"AIRFLOW" TANKER (AVAIL. TO '40)

Swift's Premium · Swift

HAM · BACON · SAUSAGE

SWIFT & COMPANY · PURVEYORS OF FINE FOODS

CHASSIS-CAB

"DODGE" NAME ON BOTH SIDES, ABOVE GRILLE

C.O.E.

39

COMPLETELY RESTYLED

CAB

9 ft. Platform body . . 133" wheelbase
12 ft. Platform body . . 160" wheelbase

2-TON

9 ft. Stake body . . 136" wheelbase
12 ft. Stake body . . 160" wheelbase

ON 17 WHEELBASES

40

"DODGE" NAME MOVED DOWN TO CENTER OF GRILLE

9 ft. Express body 133" wheelbase

CHASSIS with FLAT FACE COWL
3-TON to 1/2-TON

In wheelbase lengths ranging from 220" to 116"

CHASSIS with WINDSHIELD COWL -3-TON to 1/2-TON

In wheelbase lengths ranging from 220" to 105" including C.O.E. models

CHASSIS with CAB -3-TON to 1/2-TON

In wheelbase lengths ranging from 220" to 105" including C.O.E. models

1½-TON C.O.E.

9 ft. Platform body—C.O.E. 105" wheelbase
12 ft. Platform body—C.O.E. 129" wheelbase

Job-Rated MEANS: A Truck That Fits YOUR Job! Here's Why!

	DODGE	TRUCK 2	TRUCK 3
ENGINES	6	1	3
WHEELBASES	17	9	6
GEAR RATIOS	16	6	9
CAPACITIES (Ton Rating)	6	3	4
STD. CHASSIS and BODY MODELS	96	56	42
PRICES Begin At	$465	$450	$474¹⁸

DODGE

C.O.E.

112 BODY and CHASSIS TYPES ON 18 DIFF. WBs. 100-HP (DIESEL AVAIL. IN 3-TON TYPE.)

41

PRICED WITH THE LOWEST

Chassis .. $500 (WITH COWL) Pick-Ups $630

Chassis .. $595 (WITH CAB) Panels .. $730

Stakes .. $740

CENTER of GRILLE RE-DESIGNED, and new HORIZ. CHROME STRIPS (DLX. CONV.)

ICE CREAM DELIVERY TRUCK WITH STREAMLINED REFRIG. BODY

42-45

WHETHER YOU NEED ½ TO 3-TON GAS OR HEAVY-DUTY DIESEL ... YOU CAN **DEPEND ON DODGE**

OVER 75,000 DODGE MILITARY TRUCKS BUILT BY JANUARY, 1942.

REMEMBER THE DODGE POWER WAGONS OF WWII? Dodge has been building four-wheel-drive Power Wagons for military and civilian use. In World War II, Dodge supplied over 20 variations of these hard-working vehicles to our armed forces.

"BLACK-OUT" MODELS HAVE LESS CHROME TRIM.

BOTTLER'S

ICE CREAM

DODGE "Job-Rated"

6 CYL. (217, 236, 250 CID) 95, 115, 120 HP

46-47

'46 MODELS
WC; WF 31;
WF 32; WFM 38; WFA 31;
WFA 32; WH 47; WH 45;
WHA 45; WFMA 38; WD 20; WD 21; WF 33; WH 46;
WHA 46; WHA 47; WH 48; WHA 48; WH 49;
WHA 49;   WHM 45; WHMA 45;
WHM 48;   WHMA 48;
WFM 35;

WFMA 35;
WFM 37;
WFMA 37

EAST SIDE LUMBER CO.

STAKE

"POWER WAGON" (4-W-D)
6 CYL. 230 CID with ENGINE
(94 HP @ 3200 RPM)
('47)

116-220" WBs

Free Press No 15

HEAVY-DUTY CONVENTIONAL (IN 14 MODELS)

INTERIOR

('46)

NEW "AIR CONTROLLED" SEAT CUSHION ADJUSTER

JOHN F. IVORY STORAGE CO. Inc.

91

175 BASIC *Job-Rated* CHASSIS MODELS

C.O.E. (IN 4 MODELS)

important NEW features

TOTALLY **NEW** STYLING!

48-49

B-I-B SERIES

FLUID DRIVE AVAIL.
new STEERING-COLUMN GEARSHIFT *and* SYNCHRO-SHIFT TRANS.

2½ TON

"B-2" SERIES

50

RESEMBLES 1948-49, BUT 3 VERTICAL BUMPER GUARDS ARE ELIMINATED (AS OF LATE '49.)

"Powered by NEW 377 cu-in. Heavy-duty Engine!"

154 H.P.

"NEW Twin Carburetion for High Power, with Economy!"

"NEW 5-speed, Helical Constant-mesh Transmission!"

"Rugged 10⅛" Frame... 7 Big Cross-members!"

"Extra-heavy 18,000-lb. Capacity Rear Axle!"

BIG New 4-TON Heavy-Duty

"Y" SERIES (ABOVE)

ROUTE VANS *have* 102" WB ; OTHER MODELS *have* SAME WB RANGE AS BEFORE.

DODGE

MIXER

PANEL
FR. 1493. ('51)
1627. ('52)
1640. ('53)

DUMP

C.O.E.

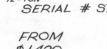

LIGHT PICKUP
WITH REAR
QUARTER WINDOWS

51-53

MEDIUM-DUTY
STAKE TRUCK

"B-3" SERIES *
new GRILLE

½-TON
SERIAL # STARTS AT 82215001 (DETROIT, 1951)
85308001 (SAN LEANDRO, 1951)

FROM   82257601 (DETROIT, 1952)
$1420.   85313701 (SAN LEANDRO, 1952)
             82302001 (DETROIT, 1953)
('52)   85322001 (SAN LEANDRO, 1953)
* 1953 IS "B-4"

93

DODGE

"C-1" SERIES

54 RESTYLED new GRILLE, 1-PC. WINDSHIELD

LT. DUTY FROM $1331.
100 TO 172 HP 6 STD., BUT 241 OR 331 CID V8 AVAIL.

REAT LAKES SHIPPING

SER.# FROM 82338001 (DETROIT)
85328001 (SAN LEANDRO)
('1/2-TON)

4WD

School Bus

STOP LITTLEVILLE SCHOOL DISTRICT

POWER WAGON

DODGE

CENTRAL OIL CO.

C.O.E. OIL TANKER

(MODEL G SIMILAR)

1½ TON MOD. F (ALSO BELOW)

55 -56

C-3 SERIES

new "WRAP AROUND" WINDSHIELD

LT. DUTY FROM
$1501. ('55) *
$1530. ('56)

* SALE PRICE $1368.

CANINE FEED CO.

J.&L. AUTO PARTS

GRILLE CENTER TRIM MODIFIED

(1955 EXAMPLES ILLUSTR.)

1956 MODELS START 10-7-55.

94

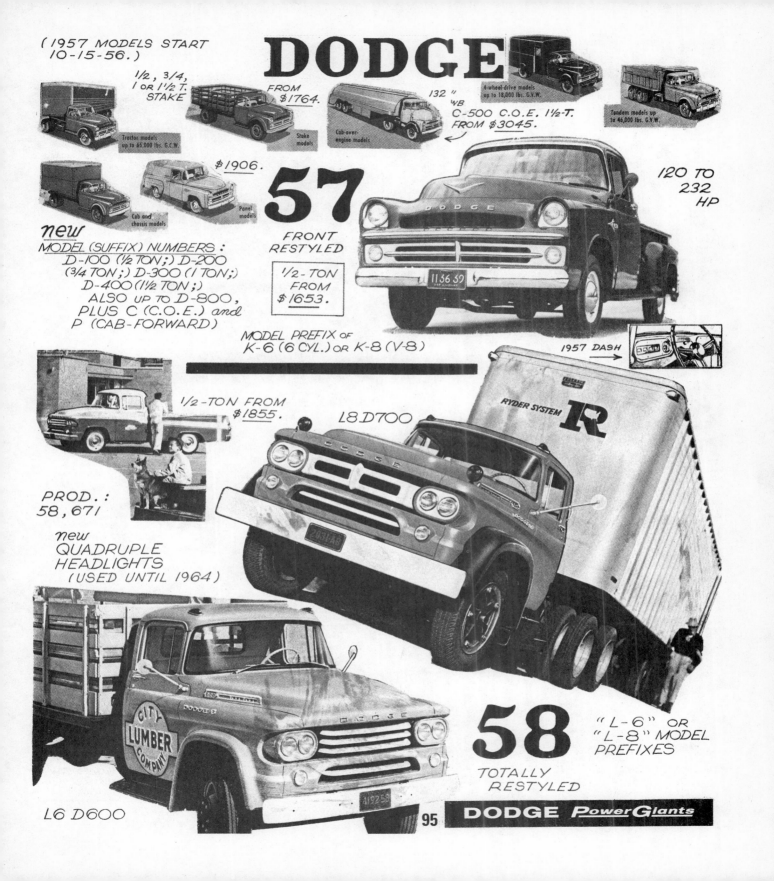

DODGE

(1957 MODELS START 10-15-56.)

1/2, 3/4, 1 OR 1 1/2 T. STAKE

FROM $1764.

Stake models

132" WB

Cab-over-engine models

C-500 C.O.E. 1 1/2-T. FROM $3045.

4-wheel-drive models up to 18,000 lbs. G.V.W.

Tractor models up to 65,000 lbs. G.C.W.

$1906.

Cab and chassis models

Panel models

Tandem models up to 46,000 lbs. G.V.W.

57 FRONT RESTYLED

1/2-TON FROM $1653.

120 TO 232 HP

new
MODEL (SUFFIX) NUMBERS:
D-100 (1/2 TON;) D-200 (3/4 TON;) D-300 (1 TON;) D-400 (1 1/2 TON;) ALSO UP TO D-800, PLUS C (C.O.E.) and P (CAB-FORWARD)

MODEL PREFIX OF K-6 (6 CYL.) OR K-8 (V-8)

1957 DASH

1/2-TON FROM $1855.

L8 D700

RYDER SYSTEM R

PROD.: 58,671

new QUADRUPLE HEADLIGHTS (USED UNTIL 1964)

CITY LUMBER COMPANY

58 TOTALLY RESTYLED

"L-6" OR "L-8" MODEL PREFIXES

L6 D600

95

DODGE *Power Giants*

DODGE

PROD.: 71,680

59
new GRILLE

I.D. # M6DI-
LOIOOI UP (CONV.)
(C.O.E. M-8 1½-TON
132" W.B.
PRICED FROM
$3515.)

BUMPER GUARDS
AVAILABLE

M6 D100

½-TON
LT. DUTY
FROM $1927.

"M-6"
OR "M-8"
MODEL
PREFIXES

POWER GIANT

P6 NC 1000
DIESEL
(134" TO 182" WB)

4 *new* DIESEL
ENGS. or 5 *new*
GAS V8s.
DIESEL CAB-FWD. MODELS
(P6 KC, P6NC SERIES)
USE 464, 672 or 743 CID
6-CYL. CUMMINS DIESEL ENG.
104" TO 254" COMPLETE
WHEELBASE RANGE

108" TO 116" W.B. ON
D100 PICKUPS (BELOW)

60
CHOICE
OF 140
MODELS!

"P-6" AND "P-8"
SERIES

BIG-220

SWEPTLINE

new
GRILLE
ALUMINUM)
STD. FROM
$1958.

PROD.: 70,305

SWEPTLINE
OFFERS
OPTIONAL
"LOAD-
FLITE"
PUSHBUTTON
AUTO.
TRANS.

120
TO 228 HP
(V8 PICKUP TO
200 HP)

6-CYL. P-6 I.D. # STARTS AT
1160-100001

96

DODGE

C-800 ('62)

('63)

5-YARD DUMP

HEAVY-DUTY TRACTOR ('63)

ENGINES:
225 CID 6 (140 HP @ 3900 RPM)
251 CID 6 (125 HP @ 3600 RPM)
318 CID V8 (202 HP @ 3900 RPM)
361 CID V8 (178-194 HP @ 3600 RPM)
(228 HP, 413 CID V8 IN '62 C-1000)

"DART" PICKUP $1958. ('61)

LT. DUTY RESTYLED new 114" WB

61-64

D-100 FR. $1957. ('63-'65)

↑ 114" WB new "PALOMINO" PICKUP ('64)

PRODUCTION (all types)
1961 (64,886)   1962 (96,102)
1963 (110,987)   1964 (135,630)

NEW MODELS START OCT. 1 OF PREVIOUS YEAR (THROUGH '66)

LATE '62

Crew Cab

WHEELBASES:	
A-100 =	90"
D-100 =	114, 128"
D-200 =	128, 146"
D-300 =	133"
D-400 =	157"
D-500 =	"
C-500 (V8, 2 TON C.O.E.) =	145

L-600, L-700 new MED. DUTY TILT-CAB WITH 89" TO 192" WBs

65-66

COMPACT A-100

L-700

1964 THROUGH '70

STARTS 2-66

LT. DUTY D-100 FROM $1957. ('65) --- ---and $2056. ('66)

FRONT RESTYLED WITH new GRILLE and LARGE-RIMMED SINGLE HEADLTS. (LIGHT-DUTY TYPES)

D-100 ('66)

DODGE

DODGE

new GRILLE →

D-100 PRICED FROM $2196. ('67)
$2390. ('68)
$2442. ('69)

Adventurer ↓

DASH (ADV.)

PRODUCTION :
141,685 ('67)
173,769 ('68)
165,133 ('69)

"C-700"

67-69

CN-900 has CHOICE OF 3 OPT. CUMMINS DIESEL ENGS., 13½ TO 26½ TON GVW ('68)

Dodge Builds Tough Trucks

DODGE DIV.

MED. DUTY (ABOVE)

HVY. DUTY (RT.)

('69)

✓ ILLUSTRATED 1969 LT. DUTY HAS *new* SIDE SAFETY LTS. (ROUND) NEAR FR. END, and RESTYLED HOOD.

CHRYSLER CORPORATION

ADVENTURER

DODGE

WITH G78-15 B TIRES

D-100 CUSTOM SWEPTLINE

CUMMINS 6 OR DETR.
DIESEL 6 OR V8 IN
SLEEPER-CAB
HEAVY-DUTY
TILT

(4 MODELS
AVAIL.)
('70)

('71)

(GAS
LOW CAB FWD.
AVAIL. WITH V8s
TO 549 CID)
DIESELS
AVAIL.
ALSO

LNT-
1000
DIESEL
TILT-CAB
(CUMMINS
NH-230
ENGINE)

SIMILAR
LN-1000
TYPE AVAIL.
SINCE MID-'60s

SHORT (OR 2 SIZES SLEEPER CABS)

SCHOOL BUS

70-71

NEW GRILLE (LT. AND MED.)

BELOW:
B-300 127" WB (EXTENDED)
SEATS UP TO 14 CHILDREN.
OPTIONAL AIR COND.,
POWER STEER., POWER FRONT
DISC BRAKES, AUTO. TRANS.
(SMALLER 109" WB 5, 8, OR 12-PASS
BUS ALSO)

('71)

S600 DODGE SCHOOL BUS CHASSIS

1972 SCH. BUS
SAME AS ABOVE

SCHOOL BUS ENGINES

318-3 HEAVY-DUTY PREMIUM V8 (STANDARD)

Lightweight, powerful, high in torque, this Dodge 318-cubic-inch V8 is great for economy. Its premium features include these: hardened and shot-peened forged crankshaft; trimetal main and connecting rod bearings; Stellite-faced exhaust valves with Roto-Caps; stainless steel head gaskets. Standard V8 for all Dodge school bus chassis, this engine uses regular fuel.

361 HEAVY-DUTY PREMIUM V8

Biggest, most powerful Dodge school bus engine. Optional in all models. With a displacement of 361 cubic inches and with such premium features as: induction-hardened crankshaft journals; trimetal main and connecting rod bearings; hydraulic valve lifters; sodium-filled exhaust valves with Roto-Caps; and a chrome-alloy, cast-iron cylinder block. Uses regular fuel.

U.S. SERVICE CENTERS

99

DODGE

CREW CAB PICKUP.

Go camping with Dodge. The only all-new pickup for 1972.

LIGHT-DUTY TOTALLY RESTYLED

DODGE FOUR-WHEEL-DRIVE POWER WAGON.

WHEEL COVER VARIATION

SWEPTLINE D100 (6½' BOX, 115" WB) $2871.

72

DODGE D100 UTILINE PICKUP.

LIGHT-DUTY STAKE.

D-100 STAKE = $3059. D-200 = $3322.

CONVENTIONAL STAKE MEDIUM-DUTY

MEDIUM-DUTY LCF (GASOLINE).

THIS STYLE OF DODGE VAN STARTS '71.

DODGE FORWARD CONTROL VAN.

DODGE TRADESMAN VAN.

DODGE TRADESMAN VISION VAN.

FOR FURTHER INFO. ON PICKUPS, VANS, PLEASE SEE "PICKUP AND VAN SPOTTER'S GUIDE."

DODGE TRADESMAN MAXIVAN...AMERICA'S BIGGEST COMPACT VAN.

Dodge. Depend on it.

100

(CONT'D. NEXT PAGE)

Dodge. Depend on it.

72 (CONT'D.)

TYPICAL SERVICE STATION OF 1972, WITH HIGH CANOPY (TO ACCOM. LARGE TRUCKS, RVs, ETC.)

The easy-to-service Dodge LCF now has four new engines to choose from.

new CN-900 SER.

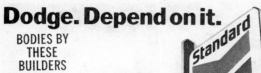

DODGE HEAVY-DUTY CONVENTIONAL.

Heavy Duty Low Cab Diesels from Dodge

DODGE HEAVY-DUTY LCF TANDEM (GASOLINE).

LS-1000

DODGE HEAVY-DUTY TILT CAB (DIESEL).

"PRACTICAL" IS THE WORD for Dodge Truck's new CN 900 series. For starters, eye those swing-out fenders, providing walk-in accessibility to powerful and economical engines. Single axle wheelbases range from 134" to 182". Tandem wheelbase lengths range from 146" to 200", with a BBC of less than 90 degrees for both models. This means easier manueuverability in close quarters. GVW ranges from 28,000 to 52,000 lbs.; top GCW for both single and tandem axle models is 76,800.

HEAVY-DUTY LCF TANDEM (DIESEL).

DODGE HEAVY-DUTY LCF (GASOLINE).

LCF's

CN-900, CNT-900 WITH CUMMINS V-903 OR DETROIT 8V-71 DIESEL ENG. new CUMMINS V-555 OR V8-210 AVAIL. IN C-800, CT-800.

DODGE HEAVY-DUTY LCF (DIESEL).

DODGE

Camper

LT. DUTY

BI-TORQUE GAUGES. Except for the speedometer and the tachometer, every gauge in the Bighorn is an expensive Stewart-Warner waterproof bi-torque gauge.

new Club Cab 73

1972 TYPES

CONTINUE

BIGHORN

all-new heavy-duty truck.

INTRO. SPRING, 1973

(BELOW, AND RIGHT)

MODEL CN-950 (LONG CONV.)

WITH CUMMINS NTC-350 OR CATERPILLAR 1100 DIESEL ENGINE (OR OTHERS AS AVAIL. (INCL. GAS) DURING THE 1973 SHORTAGE OF HEAVY-DUTY TRUCK ENGINES.

(NEW MEDIUM-DUTY "KARY-VAN" CONV. ALSO INTRO. EARLY '73. SEE NEXT PG. FOR ILLUSTRATION.)

102

INTERIOR

(new BIGHORN)

Extra care in engineering makes a difference in Dodge...depend on it.

BIGHORN HOOD MASCOT →

DODGE HITS THE ROAD WITH CAT POWER.

Now you can get Caterpillar power in a Dodge light heavy-duty truck.

Dodge announces a wider choice of fine engines for the Dodge LCF . . . Caterpillar diesels join the Cummins diesel and a full line of Dodge gas engines. Here's power to handle your midrange hauling needs whatever they are . . . pick the power plant that fits the job. And you get some truck to go along with it! The Dodge LCFs are a natural for you people who do a lot of hauling in cities. They're also one of the easiest trucks to service. With a lift of the hood and a swing of the fenders, Dodge gives you fantastic engine compartment accessibility.

Today . . . open it up, and here's what you'll find.

Caterpillar 1145	175 HP
Caterpillar 1150	200 HP
Caterpillar 1160	225 HP
Available on C800s or CT800s.	

Caterpillar, Cat and ⬛ are Trademarks of Caterpillar Tractor Co.

CHRYSLER
MOTORS CORPORATION

CLUB CAB DETAILS →

LT. DUTY I.D. # D13 (A)(E)
4 (S) 000001 UP ('74)
D13 (-)(-) 5 (-) 000001 ('75.
" 6 " ('76.

('74)

new GRILLE (LT. DUTY)

Club Cab.

new

new D-700 MEDIUM "KARY-VAN"

← *LT.*

900

(D-800 STYLED LIKE D-700)

$3368. AND UP FOR CONV. LT. DUTY D100 ('74)

3779. ('75)

3777. ('76)

FINAL TYPE OF LCF MODELS (ABOVE)

TILT HOOD DETAILS

74-76

1975 LT. DUTY HAS *new* DASH, *new* SIDE TRIM ('76-77 D-600 STILL RESEMBLES '74 D-700 ILLSTR.)

(THE PROD. OF HEAVY-DUTY MODELS DISCONTINUED 1975.)

BIGHORN 900

DODGE

LIGHT TRUCK SALES :
385,125 (1977)
396,268 (1978)
FROM $4137. (1977)
4147. (1978)

I.D. # D14 (-)(E) 7 (-) 000001 UP (1977)
D14 (A)(E) 8 (-) 000001 UP (1978)

(D-150 MODELS
ADDED TO ½-TON
LINE, JOINING
D-100 .)

(W MODELS
ARE F-W-D)

OPT. 6 CYL., 243.3 CID
(103 HP @ 3700 RPM)
MITSUBISHI DIESEL AVAIL. '78.

FROM $4587. ('77); $4851. ('78)
(EXCEPTION = $4147. SPECIAL PRICE ON
D-100 OFFERED SPRING, 1978)

77-78

new GRILLE and
LIGHTS. "DODGE"
NAME ON TOP
GRILLE BORDER.

('77)

I.D. #
EXPLANATION :
EXAMPLE : D14 (A)(B) 9 (9) 012345
D = 2WD PICKUP ; 1 = ½-TON CLASS ;
4 = CONV. CAB SWEPTLINE ; A = TO 6000 lbs. GVW;
B = ENGINE TYPE ; 9 = MODEL YEAR ; S = CITY
WHERE ASSEMBLED ; 012345 = UNIT NO.

FROM $5169.
I.D. # D14 (A)(E) 9 (-)
100001 UP
LIGHT TRUCK SALES :
400,945

79

new HORIZONTALLY-
SPLIT GRILLE.
new HEADLIGHTS.

(D-50 MINI 4
MITSUBISHI
PICKUP
ALSO
AVAIL.,
STARTING 1979.)

✗ PROSPECTOR

I.D. # = D14 (-) EA (-) 100001 UP
½-TON D150 FROM $6155.
¾-TON D200 FROM 6976.
1-TON D300 STAKE FROM 7661.
1-TON D300 CAB-CHASSIS FROM 8247.
CLUB CABS $7131. TO $8943.
CREW CABS $8220. TO $9158.

new
GRILLE WITH
BLACKED-OUT
PCS.

80
LT. TRK. SALES =
347,138

*Use EPA mpg number for comparisons. Your
mileage may vary depending on speed, distance
and weather. Est. Hwy. will probably be less.
California estimates lower.

Dodge Trucks

RAM TOUGH

104

(ABOVE = ROYAL S.E. DASH)

CREW CAB

('82)

D-250, D-350 STAKE

AT RIGHT: LEE A. IACOCCA, SUCCESSFUL NEW CHRYSLER CORP. CHAIRMAN

new GRILLE **81** ON

DODGE RAM

D-350 DUMP

"KARY VAN"

C

"RETRIEVER" WRECKER

E

4WD "SNO-COMMANDER"

CONV.
I.D. NO. EXAMPLES
1B7F (-) (-) 4E (-) B (-)
100001 UP ('81)
1B7FD (-) 4 (-) (-) C (-)
100001 UP ('82)

2WD PRICES ('83 EXAMPLES)
½ T. D-150 6½' SWEPTLINE	$	7581.
½ T. D-150 8'	"	7735.
¾ T. D-250 8'	"	8482.
1-TON D-350 8'	"	9493.
" CAB/CHASSIS FROM		9332.
" CREW CAB 6½' SW.		10,647.
" " " 8' SW. D.R.		11,417.

F

D-350 "DYNA TRAC" WITH DUAL REAR WHEELS
131, 149, OR 165" W.B.

4-W-D W-150
POWER RAM

DODGE

POWER RAM

DODGE

225 CID SLANT 6
318 OR 360 CID V8
D-100, D-150,
D-250 OR D-350
(W MODELS ALSO)
D SERIES = 2WD
W " = 4WD

AVAIL. RAM'S HEAD
HOOD MASCOT

DODGE

('81)

(1917 – 1935)

Douglas TRUCKS

"TA" 1½-TON (127" WB)
ONLY MODEL
LISTED FOR 1919.

DOUGLAS
MOTORS CORP.,
OMAHA, NEBR.

SCHEBLER CARB. (THROUGH '27) ZENITH CARB. ('28 ON)

4 CYL. (UNTIL 1933)
(ALSO, 6-CYL.
MODELS AVAIL. BY 1927.)

BUDA ENGINES EXCLUSIVELY*

new MODELS
20 C 1 TON 120" WB
E 2½ 136

21 *new* MODELS AGAIN

G 1½ TON 128" WB
H 2 136
I 3 144 (140 IN '23)
D 1½ (REPL. G, 1923-24)
C 1 (new IN 1923-24)

27 6-CYL. ENGS. IN 2, 3-TON MODELS. (4 CYL. IN 1½ T.)

28 CHOICE OF 4 OR 6-CYL. ENGS. and 3 WHEELBASES IN 1½, 2, 3-TON DOUGLAS SPL. IS *new* 3-TON with 210"° WB. (new BOSCH IGN. REPLACES EISEMANN.)

note UNIQUE SHAPE OF ARCHED CAB WINDOWS.

L-N IGN. IN SOME **29** *new* 5-TON 185" WB MODEL and 5-TON 6-WHEEL. (210" WB)

('20)

* 4-CYL. WEIDLEY ENG. BRIEFLY USED IN 1921 ½-TON "G."

30-33 new MODELS (36 TO 114 HP) A6 (1T, 6 = '31-33;)
BGC4, B4 (1½ T, 4 CYL.;) B6 (1½ T, 6;) CG4, C4 (2T, 4 CYL.;)
C6 (2T, 6 CYL.;) CD4 (2½ T, 4 CYL.;) CD6 (2½ T, 6 CYL.;) D4 (3T, 4 CYL.)
D6, D6 5P. (3T, 6 CYL.;) F4 (5T, 4 CYL.;) F6 (5T, 6 CYL.;) F66 (5T, 6-WH., 6 CYL.)
116" TO 216" WBS (FINAL YEARS PROBABLY UNSOLD STOCK SALES)

DOVER (1929-1930)

MFD. BY THE HUDSON MOTOR CAR CO., DETROIT

(MECHANICALLY SIMILAR TO HUDSON'S LOW-PRICED 1929 ESSEX CAR.)

3/4 TON

New 29

110 ½ WB
6-CYL.
160 CID
L-HEAD ENG.
55 HP @
3600 RPM

SIGN ON SIDE RESEMBLES RADIATOR EMBLEM.

DOVER
THE COMMERCIAL SUPER SIX
Built by HUDSON

(2,130 SOLD)

MANY BOUGHT BY U.S. POST OFFICE FOR MAIL DELIVERY SERVICE.

(1,066 SOLD)

30

1929 SPECIFICATIONS CONTINUE

new LOWER ROOFLINE *and* BODY LAMPS *on* PANEL DELIVERY.
FLYING HORSE RADIATOR EMBLEM MISSING *from* SCREEN-SIDE EXPRESS (AT UPPER LEFT)

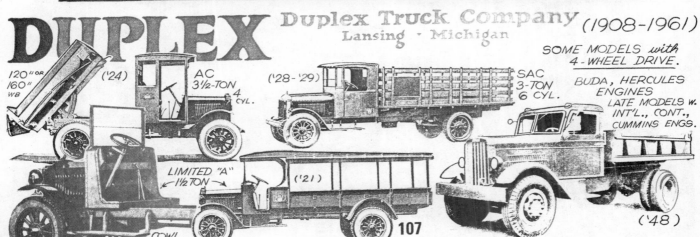

DUPLEX

Duplex Truck Company (1908-1961)
Lansing · Michigan

SOME MODELS *with* 4-WHEEL DRIVE.

BUDA, HERCULES ENGINES
LATE MODELS *w.* INT'L., CONT., CUMMINS ENGS.

120" OR 160" WB

('24) AC 3½-TON 4 CYL.

('28-'29) SAC 3-TON 6 CYL.

LIMITED "A" 1½ TON

('21)

('48)

COWL

107

T/A MODEL
460 C.I.D FORD V8 ENG.
176" WB

ElDorado Falcon

EMC
ElDorado Motor Corporation
Minneapolis, KS 64767

INTERIOR (T/A)

460 CID FORD OR 350 CID CHEV. ENG.

22 Passenger

Base Floor Plans

23 Passenger

"Tee" Type Passenger Windows have emergency egress capability and a 31% tint. Upper portion slides open for ventilation.

MST

HANDICAPPED BUS

capacity range of 12 to 25

31 Passenger **MST**

Paratransit

MST

REAR

NEW $65,000.

1984 EXAMPLES ILLUSTR. V8 8.2 L. DETR. DIESEL ENG. IN MST (165 H.P.)

Falcon MST

108

30" Double Opening Entry Door is driver-controlled and air operated. Stainless steel grab rail, padded stanchions, modesty panel and automatically lighted step well are standard features. Optional clear opening widths, wheelchair access doors and power lifts also available.

FAGEOL and TwinCoach

CORPORATION
KENT, OHIO

(EST. 1927
AFFILIATED WITH
FAGEOL

(1916 – 1954)

FAGEOL MOTORS,
OAKLAND,
CALIF.
(THROUGH '38)

2½,
3½,
5 TON
MODELS

4 CYL.
WAU.
ENGS.
('20)

CONVENTIONAL FAGEOLS OF
1920s and 1930s have UNIQUE,
CHARACTERISTIC "SAWTOOTHED"
RIDGE RUNNING ALONG
TOP CENTER OF HOOD.

SOME WITH
"7 SPEEDS"
PAINTED ON
RADIATOR CORE.

144"
OR 172" WB ('20)

MODEL
130
"FLYER"
1½ TON
('28)

CHASSIS:
$1900.

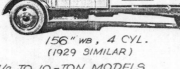

156" WB, 4 CYL.
(1929 SIMILAR)

1½ TO 10-TON MODELS
AVAILABLE.
"GOLDEN
BEAR" TRUCK ('29) BELOW

TANDEM
TRACTOR
(ALUMINUM
CAB)

('29)

TRUCKS
1920s

New

TWIN COACH
TRANSIT BUSES
INTRO. 1927

FAGEOL
SAFETY COACH

('22)

('27)

A TYPICAL
FAGEOL TRUCK OF 1920s.
(1930 VIEW)

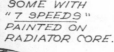

44-PASS. (EARLY 1927)

FLAT-FRONT TYPE
WITH WIDER ENTRY

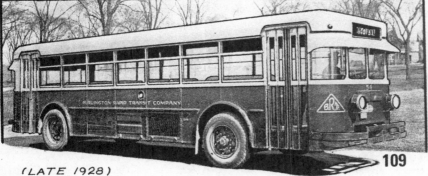

(LATE 1928)

109

FAGEOL and TWIN COACH

RIGHT SIDE VIEW

BUY BREAD AT YOUR DOOR

TWIN COACH

LEFT SIDE

('30) TRUCK
FAGEOL HEAVY DUTY

Frank R. Fageol
President

CITY DELIVERY

THESE QUAINT, BOXY LITTLE DOOR-TO-DOOR ROUTE DELIVERY VANS WERE MFD. FROM 1929 TO 1936, WHEN OPERATION ABSORBED BY DIVCO.

STILL IN USE IN THE 1950s

← THIS LITTLE TYPE ALSO AVAIL. AS AN EARLY MINI-BUS. USED IN VARIOUS CITIES, SUITABLE FOR SHORT OR HILLY ROUTES. AS IN BERKELEY, CALIF.

"AS IS" UNRESTORED 1936 FAGEOL TRUCKS. NOTE 2 DIFFERENT CAB TYPES. ↓ →

1930s

REAR END OF LATER '30s BUS IS STREAMLINED. →

New ('37-38) TWIN COACH
2 VIEWS

SMALL TRANSIT BUS WITH REAR ENGINE

FAGEOL

60-VISITACION

25

1½ TO 10-TON MODELS (1938): 106 BK 135 BK 250 BK MK RA 300 HP, ETC. 6-CYL. WAU. OR CUMMINS ENGINES, 82 TO 150 H.P.

('37) NOTE ↑ 2 DIFFERENT FRONT END STYLES ('38) ↓

FAGEOL

FREIGHTWAYS

110 **C.O.E.** OAKLAND PRODUCTION ENDS JAN. 1, 1939 =STERLING TEMPORARILY ACQUIRES ASSETS.

FAGEOL and TWIN COACH

TRANSIT BUS

THIS 6-PC. WINDSH. STYLE LATER ON FLXIBLE. ↙

INTERCITY TYPE

STK. YARDS-MOSLEY

DOUGLAS

250

250

(note: NO FAGEOL TRUCKS DURING 1940s.)

Propane-power
OPTION on BUSES

Fageol Twin Coach

(POSTWAR, WITH MULTI-PIECE WINDSHIELD)

FAGEOL
TWIN COACH
KENT-OHIO

40-53

(90 TO 250 H.P.)
1952 ENGINES ILLUSTR.

FAGEOL GASOLINE ENGINES

HORIZONTAL

PROPANE ENGINES RESEMBLE THESE 2, BUT LABELED "PROPANE"

VERTICAL

as used by the Flxible Co.

FAGEOL LEYLAND DIESEL ENGINES

HORIZONTAL

VERTICAL

FAGEOL LEYLAND

Twin Coach of 1950. Operating on 125 octane Propane, it saves an average of up to 2 cents per mile on fuel costs alone.

FAGEOL TRUCKS RESUME 1950, BY TWIN COACH CO.
(RE-ORGANIZED)
new SERIES STARTS 1950.

Super Freighter

Designed with Fruehauf Model SS (GT55) Stainless Steel Van

(New) 50

FAGEOL SUPER FREIGHTER
KENT-OHIO

DESIGNED BY

TWIN COACH COMPANY
KENT, OHIO

In Canada: Twin Coach of Canada, Ltd.
Toronto 5, Ontario

FAGEOL GAS/PROPANE ENGINES IN CONVERTED FRUEHAUF TRAILERS ('50)
6 CYL., 162 TO 250 HP

POWER STEER. AVAIL

L. J. FAGEOL

L.J. Fageol

111

FRONT VIEW

CAB

FAGEOL VANS

FAGEOL and TWIN COACH ('51)

SUPER FREIGHTER (ROUNDED END, CORRUGATED SIDES)

210 HP FAGEOL TWIN COACH PROPANE ENGINE UNDER FLOOR

GASOLINE-POWERED ALSO AVAIL.

MODEL **SS** IN STAINLESS STEEL

PONY EXPRESS "1954 MODEL!"

MAIL ROUTE TRUCK (ABOVE) SOLD UNDER TWIN COACH NAME

OTHER VEHICLES ON THIS PAGE ARE FAGEOLS.

MODEL FV-24 ('52)

51-54

COAST GUARD VAN

('52)

AFTER 1951, FAGEOL VANS USE INTERNATIONAL ENGINES and MECHANICAL PARTS.

O'NEIL'S

THE M. O'NEIL COMPANY

48

('53)

('54 SIMILAR)

MODEL FV-24 ('52)

U.P.S. DELIVERY

MOST MECH. COMPONENTS INTERCHANGEABLE with INTERNATIONAL MODELS L-150, 160, 170, 180, 190 and 200.

NOTE THE GRILLE GUARD

LIVESTOCK MODEL ('51)

112

(CONT'D. NEXT PAGE)

FAGEOL VANS

THE FAGEOL
Twin Coach "CONVERTIBLE"

DESIGNED BY L. J. FAGEOL ('51½)

INTERIOR (CIVILIAN)

FAGEOL T·C·C KENT·OHIO

SEATS CAN BE REMOVED, SO FREIGHT CAN BE HAULED

With seats in place, "Convertible" is light, airy, comfortable, deluxe bus.

CIVILIAN TYPE 35' LONG

51-54
(CONT'D.)

BRAND NEW

MILITARY TYPE, RT., HOLDS A JEEP, AND ALSO 24 SEATED PASSENGERS. →

ONE OF 1509 CONVERTIBLE BUSES BLT. FOR U.S. ARMY

Seats telescope into compact pile to permit use as cargo truck carrying 5-ton payload (or seats can be removed completely).

REAR OF MILITARY TYPE

Rear view. Locking hasp protects cargo. Emergency release inside vehicle permits opening of rear doors even if doors are locked by outside hasp. Rear step is retractable.

for Military Service

(IN 1953, (FLXIBLE BUYS TWIN COACH BUS PROD.)

The "Convertible" fills the long existent military need for a high speed vehicle which can be used separately or simultaneously as a personnel-carrying bus, high capacity cargo truck or field ambulance. Each vehicle can be divided into separate sections for combination use of any desired type.

WITH CHRYSLER V8 ENG. ('68)

TWIN COACH NAME RETURNS 1968, ON SMALL BUSES BLT. AT KENT, OHIO, BY HIGHWAY PRODUCTS CO.

The University of California at Santa Cruz is presently running a propane-powered Twin Coach Model TC-29.

68
ON

25 OR 33-PASS. AVAIL. W. CHRYSLER HT-413 LP GAS POWER (ABOVE) ('71)

113 RADIO-DISPATCHED "DIAL-A-RIDE" BUS ('72)

FEDERAL (1910–1959)

FEDERAL MOTOR TRUCK CO.

FEDERAL MOTOR TRUCK COMPANY, Detroit

4-CYL. CONTINENTAL ENGINES
(3¾" × 5," 4⅛" × 5¼," OR
4½" × 5½")
EISEMANN IGN.

20

The Tenth Year FEDERAL TRUCKS

SD (1 TON, 132" WB, 6.2 G.R.); TE (1½ T., 144" WB, 8.5 G.R.); UE (2 T., 156" WB, 9.25 G.R.); WD (3½ T., 156" WB, 10.33 G.R.); XC (5 T., 156" WB, 13.66 G.R.); LIGHT TRACTOR (120" WB, 9.25 G.R.); HVY. TRACT. (114½" WB, 12.0 G.R.)

36" TIRES, EXCEPT 35×5 (FRONT) ON SD; 40×6 REAR DUALS, XC

"WF" 3½ TON CHASSIS $3950.

21

CHASSIS $2500.

(new "WE" and "XE" MODEL DESIGNATIONS REPLACE "WD" and "XC".

SD 1 TON 132" WB

RE-NAMED "X-2" has 4¾" × 6" BORE and STROKE.

22

IMPROVED MODELS (NOTE CHANGES)

				TIRE SIZES, FRONT and REAR
SD	1 TO 1½ TON	132" WB	7.2 GR	35 × 5 , 36 × 6 (PNEUMATIC)
TE	1½ TO 2	144	8.5	36 × 3½, 36 × 5
UE	2 TO 2½	156	9.25	36 × 4 (REAR DUALS)
WE	3½ TO 4	154	10.25	36 × 5 " "
X-2	5 TO 6	163	10.25	36 × 6, 40 × 6 REAR DUALS

MODERN 1923 HOME OF HOLLOW TILE AND STUCCO CONSTRUCTION

"TE" BECOMES "T" MODEL.

"SD" HAS 6.2 GEAR RATIO.

sixteen truck models. 23

new 36 × 7 REAR WHEELS ON "UE." "UE" WB SHORTENED TO 144". "WE" WB LENGTHENED TO 156", " HAS 10.33 GEAR RATIO.

TASTELLS ICE CREAM

ZENITH CARBURETOR (ALL MODELS)

24

new MODEL DESIGNATIONS

new 6-CYL. BUS CHASSIS

Prices of Federal Trucks

1-Ton	R-2	$1675	5-6 Ton	X-2	$4750
1½-Ton	S-23	2150	7-Ton		5000
2½-Ton	U-2	3200	Light Duty Tractor		3200
3½ to 4 Ton	W-2	4200	Heavy Duty Tractor		4235

"U-2" CHASSIS (157" WB)

132" WB "R-3" FAST EXPRESS CHASSIS (132" WB, 33 × 5 TIRES, 3¾" × 5" BORE AND STROKE)

FEDERAL

note FRONT CORNER WINDOWS

"U-2" ('25)

157" WB

25

MODELS			CONT. ENG. #	
R-2	1 TON	132" WB	J-4	5.6 GR
S-23	1½	144	J-4	7.25
U-2	2½	157	K-4	7.45
WL	4	157	L-4	10.3
X-2	5	163	B-5	10.2
LT. DUTY TRACTOR		125	K-4	8.5
HVY. DUTY "		121	L-4	10.3

W.E. WOOD CONSTRUCTION COMPANY

CROWLEY, MILNER CO. DETROIT

'26 STEERING GEAR RATIOS LOWERED

'26 MODELS

R-3	1¼ TON	132" WB
U-3	2½	157
UB-6	3	190
W-3	4	157
X-4	5	163
X-5	5½	163

U-3 (has HEADLIGHTS ON COWL)

new HIGHER RADIATOR with ALUMINUM SHELL

'27 MODELS

"SCOUT"	1 TON	124" WB	(WAUKESHA 4)
U-4	2½	157	
2-B-6	3	190	(CONT. 6)
W-3	4	157	
8	5½	163	
LD	(TT)	121	
HD	(TT)	125	

1926 "UB-6" IS FEDERAL'S FIRST 6-CYL. TRUCK.

26-27

4-CYL. TT (TRACTOR-TRAILER) MODELS STILL AVAIL.

('26)

2½ TON CAPACITY. 6 Different Wheelbases

(EXCEPT FOR FEDERAL-KNIGHTS, new WAUKESHA-ENGINED 4-CYL. '27 "SCOUT" IS FIRST FEDERAL W/o CONT. ENGINE.)

"UB-6" BIG 6 (3¾ × 5) CONTINENTAL "6-B" ENG.

WAUKESHA ENGS. IN new 1927½ 2-TON MODELS.

"FW SCOUT" CHASSIS (124" WB)

2-WHEEL BRAKES

FEDERAL 28

CONTINENTAL and WAUKESHA 4 and 6-CYL. ENGINES

2 TON : T-20, T-2B, T2W, T6B, T6W
2½ TON : U-5   3 TON : 2B6
4 TON : W-4   7½ TON : X-8
TRACTOR TR. : LD, HD

"F-6" IS new 1-TON 124" WB MODEL with 6-CYL. CONTINENTAL ENGINE.

A-6

6-CYL. "A6" 1½-2 TON CHASSIS 151" WB

JOHN MORRELL & CO. *Morrell's Pride* HAMS. BACON

L. BAMBERGER & CO.

29

ON "SCOUT," new, FLATTER FUEL TANK REPLACES CYLINDRICAL TANK

new HYDRAULIC BRAKES (ON "A-6," ETC.)

F-7 PANEL DELIVERY

new 1½-TON "F-7" INTRO. 4-29. 6 CYLS., 65 HP 132", 144" OR 152" WB 4-WH. HYDR. BRAKES

FRONT BUMPER INCLUDED

BIG 6 STAKE

C&S TRUCK NO 3

OTHER MODELS

F-6	1 TON	6-CYL. CONT. "34-L" ENGINE	
SCOUT	1	4	WAUKESHA "X"
T21, T3W	2½	4	WAU. "V"
A6, T7W	2, 2½	6	CONT. "16-C"
U-5	3	4	CONT. "K-4"
3O6	3½	6	CONT. "20-R"
UL-7, W-4, HD	3½, 4	4	CONT. "L-4"
X-8	7½	4	CONT. "B-7"
LD	TT	4	CONT. "K-4"

15-TON CARRYING CAPACITY WITH TRAILER

P.W. ROEHL No 1
P.U.C.O. No 8 REGULAR
FEDERAL BIG SIX
THE LIBERTY HIGHWAY CO. DETROIT TOLEDO CLEVELAND
CAPACITY 15 TONS

BIG 6 15-TON TRACTOR/TRAILER WITH SLEEPER CAB FOR 24-HOUR-A-DAY SERVICE →

116

FEDERAL

30-31

MODELS ('30)
"D" 1-1½ TON 131" WB (4 CYL.)
"E-6" 1- TON 132"
"F-7" 1½-TON 132"
"A6T(W)" 2½ 151"
"T-10-B" 2½-3 TON 165"
"T-10-W" "
"U-6" 3-3½ TON "
"46A" 4-5 TON 192" (4C6A)
"46AB" " (4C6AB = '31)
"X-8" 7½ TON 162" (4 CYL.)
"X-8R" "
TRACTOR-TRUCKS ALSO AVAIL. IN 2½-TON and LARGER ('31)
CONTINENTAL ENGINES : 6-CYL. UNLESS OTHERWISE NOTED.

(FLAT RADIATOR CONTINUES)

ALSO "A6" 151" WB 2-TON ('31)

32-33

'32 6-WHEEL : D2SW, E2SW, D2D, E2D, A6SW (2½ TO 4 TON)

D-2, E-2 (1½ TON,) F-7 (1¾ TON,)
A-6 (2-TON,) A6T, A6TW, T3W,
T8WF (2½-TON,) T-10-B, T-10-W,
(2½ TO 3-TON,) U63 (3½ TON,) C-7,
C-8 (5 TO 6 T.,)
X-8, X-8R
(7½ T.)
4-CYL. (9-32)

DROP-FRAME MILK TRUCK 108" OR 120" WB

new for 1933: DM, D4, E-4, F-8, G-5, T3WFA, A-7, A8, T-10-DR, A-600, U6, X-8DR, etc.

('34) **$645** and up with hydraulic brakes and full-floating axle

V-GRILLE

34

new for 1934 : MODELS 15, 20, 25, 30, 40, 40-DR, etc.

new 6-CYL. HERCULES ENGINES (IN "15," "20," "25.")

MODELS "DM"		MAKE of ENGINE	
15, 15-X	1½ TON	CONTINENTAL "W-10"	50 HP
18-X	2	HERCULES	61 HP
20	2	"	
25	2½	"	
30	2½ TO 3	"	
40, 40-DR	3½ TO 4	WAUK.	
T-10 (VARIATIONS)	"	"	
50	4½ TO 5	CONT. WAU.	
C-7, C-7W	6		
C-8, C-8W	6		
X-8, X8DR	7½ CONT.		
X-8RDR, X8R	7½ WAU.		

new HORIZONTAL HOOD LOUVRE TRIM

DM IS ONLY 4-CYL. MODEL ; OTHERS 6-CYL.

35 (RESTYLED)

$745. (1½ TON CHASSIS)

UP TO 110 HP (IN 517 CID WAUKESHA "6-SRK" ENGINE)

IN 1935 "25TH ANNIVERSARY" MODELS

FEDERAL

CONTINENTAL 4 and 6,
HERCULES 6, and
WAUKESHA 4 and 6-CYL. ENGINES
199 to 517 CID
50 to 110 HP

36

The New
¾-1 TON FEDERAL

MODELS DM, 10, 15, 18, 20,
25, 28, 29, 30, 40, 40DR,
T-10B, T-10W, 50, C7, C7W,
C8, C8W, X-8, X8DR,
X8R, X8RDR

5.14 to 11.14 GEAR RATIOS

CAPACITIES TO 7½ TONS

¾ TON
4-CYL.
CHASSIS
FROM
$645.
(THROUGH
'39)

new MODEL "9" REPLACES "DM," with 4-CYL. "C-400"
CONT. 143 CID ENGINE (33 HP @ 2500 RPM) (for MILK ROUTES)
105" WB, ¾ to 1-TON CAP'Y.,
MODEL 11 ALSO new
GR: 5.14-5.83

37

SLEEPER-CAB TYPE
(AVAIL. '38,
WITH V-WINDSHIELD
ON DE LUXE CAB)

new LOWER
RUNNING-
BOARDS

new GRILLE with
RADIATOR FILLER
UNDER HOOD.
V-WINDSHIELD ON
DE LUXE CAB

(CAB-OVER-ENGINE TYPES:
new 75, 80, 85, 89 MODELS INTRODUCED.)

STANDARD CAB

MODEL 28 NO
LONGER AVAIL.

FINAL YEAR
FOR 7½ TON
"X"
MODELS

104" TO 249"
WBs

50 TO 115 HP
HENRY DREYFUSS
STYLING

38

MODELS 9, 10, 11, 11-H, 15, 15-H, 18, 18-H,
20, 20-H, 25, 25-H, 29, 29-H,
40, 40-DR, 50, 50-H, C-7, C-7W,
C8, C-8W, C-8H (¾ to 7½ TONS)

C.O.E.s: 75, 75-H, 80, 80-H, 85,
85-H, 89, 89-H. (1½ to 5 TONS)
(43 MODEL VARIATIONS)

5.14 to 11.2 GEAR RATIOS

6 CYLS., EXC. 4-CYL. "9" (CONT. ENG.) and 4-CYL. "10"
HERC. ENGINE

PANEL
DELIVERY

SAME MODELS AS 1938

39

2-3½
TON
COE

BUT
6½
TO
7½ T.

"62," "63" ARE new, AS ARE 6-8 TON
"65" * and "68" * CONVENTIONALS.

159"
WB

new
GRILLE ON ¾-TON (ABOVE)

140 TO 517 CID
52 TO 138 HP

* = 24"
WHEELS

PICKUP
(¾-TON)

HEAVY-DUTY

new "62" and
"65" have
501-CID 6CYL.
CONTINENTAL
"22-R" ENG.
138 HP
@
2400
RPM

¾-TON STAKE

PACKAGE DELIVERY
(¾-
TON)

C.O.E.

new "202" to "892"
6-WHEELERS

20" WHEELS,
MOST MODELS

118

40-45 FEDERAL

52 TO 139 HP (1940)

'40 MODELS : 7, 8, 11, 12, 14, 15, 18, 20, 25, 29, 29-H, 40, 50, 50-H, 62, 63, 65, 66
C.O.E.s : 75, 80, 85, 89, 89-H

FINAL WAUKESHA ENGINES IN '41 "63" and "66".

ARMY NAVY E

Federal was cited four times for its excellence in war production—building trucks of all types for the Armed Services.

WARTIME MODEL ('43) WITHOUT FULL-HEIGHT GRILLE

MODELS 11-15, 40, 50, 75 NOT LISTED IN '41. 16, 17, 35, 45, 55, 55-H and C.O.E.s 76, 77, and 90 SERIES new in '41. 7, 29-H, 63-66 NOT LISTED IN '42.

FINAL 4 CYL. IN 1941.

1941 ENGINES:					MODELS USING :
CONTINENTAL	F-4140	4 CYL. 140 CID	52 HP @ 2500 RPM		7
HERCULES	QXB3F	6 205	66 @ 3500		8
"	JXFF	6 232	75 @ 3000		16
"	JXGF	6 245	79 @ 3000		17
"	JXBF	6 263	82 @ 3000		18, 20

OTHER HERCULES 6 ENGINES ALSO, OF 282, 320, 383, 404 CID (85 TO 125 HP.)
ALSO WAUKESHA and CONTINENTAL 6 ENGINES (TO 501 CID, 150 HP.)

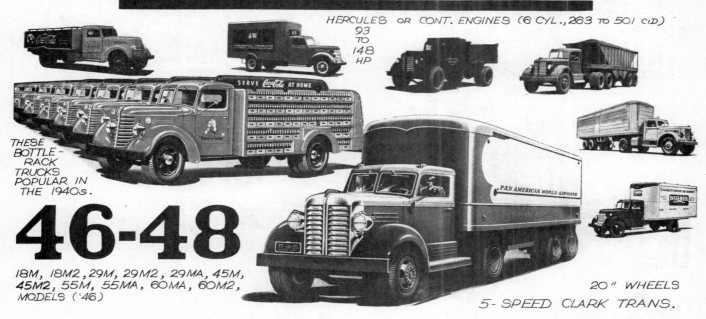

HERCULES OR CONT. ENGINES (6 CYL., 263 TO 501 CID)

93 TO 148 HP

THESE BOTTLE-RACK TRUCKS POPULAR IN THE 1940s.

46-48

18M, 18M2, 29M, 29M2, 29MA, 45M, 45M2, 55M, 55MA, 60MA, 60M2, MODELS ('46)

20" WHEELS

5-SPEED CLARK TRANS.

SEPT., 1947 = 2 SERIES (5 MODELS)
INTRODUCED : "25" SERIES (25M, 25M2, 2½ TO 3½ TON FOR TRUCK-TRAILER COMBINATIONS with HERCULES JXC(F) GAS ENGINE.)
"29ML" SERIES SIMILAR TO EXISTING "29M" SERIES, has HERCULES JXLD(F) GAS ENGINE.

all MODELS with LOCKHEED FRONT BRAKES and TIMKEN (REAR.)

BENDIX Hydrovac on all.

119

FEDERAL 49-50

6 CYL.

15M, 16M, 16M2, 18M, 18M2, 25M, 25M2, 29M, 29MA, 29ML, 29ML2, 29MLA, 35M, 35M2, 45M, 45M2, 55M2, 55MA, 60MA, 60M2, 65M2, 65MA. MODELS ('49)

HERC. ENG BELOW "35M;" CONT. ENGINES IN OTHERS.

5.56 TO 8.53 GEAR RATIOS ('51)

22-24" WHEELS ("45M" and up)

6.50 x 20 TIRES

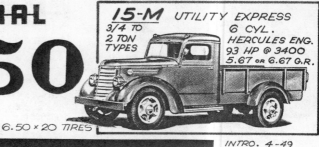

15-M UTILITY EXPRESS
3/4 TO 2 TON TYPES
6 CYL. HERCULES ENG. 93 HP @ 3400
5.67 or 6.67 G.R.

INTRO. 4-49

RESTYLED

new 51

new SWING-UP FENDER SECTIONS

INTRO. LATE SUMMER, 1950

new CURVED WINDSHIELD

9 DIFFERENT 6-CYL. ENGINES, 236 TO 602 CID
90 TO 205 HP   136" TO 250" WB
28 MODELS : 1501-T, 1601-T, 1602-T, 1801-T, 1802-T, 2501-T, 2502-T, 2901-T, 2902-T, 2904-T, 3001-T, 3002-T, 3004-T, 3401-T, 3402-T, 3404-T. 45-M, 45-MA, 45M2, 55-M, 55-MA, 55M2, 60-M, 60-MA, 60M2, 65-M, 65-MA, 65M2

new CONTINENTAL "POWER CHIEF" OVERHEAD-VALVE 6-CYL. 371 CID ENGINE 145 HP @ 3000 RPM

52

Federal Announces New Style Liner Models and Improved Engine Design

1956 MODELS   (133" TO 216" WB)

400 PREFIX : R-1 THROUGH R-8 (427 CID)
500 PREFIX : R-1 THROUGH R-5 (501 CID)
600 PREFIX : R-1 AND R-2   (602 CID)
4-W-D : T-400R-1; T-500R-1; T-600R-1; T600R-4
ALL WITH 6-CYL. CONT. ENGINES (170 HP @ 3000 RPM, 182 HP OR 212 HP @ 2800 RPM) (ALL WITH 5-SPEED TRANS.)

3401, 3402, 3404 MODELS

('52)

WITH new O.H.V. 6-CYL., 371 CID "POWER CHIEF" ENG. (145 HP @ 136 TO 250" WB   3000 RPM)

145" TO 193" WB ('59)

59

MODELS :
200 R1; 200 R2; 300 R1, 300 R2; 400 R1, 400 R2, 500 R1, 500 R2, 600 R1, 600 R2, "D" PREFIX ON ABOVE MODELS INDICATES CUMMINS DIESEL ENG. D700R1, D700R2 and NUMEROUS ADDITIONAL MODELS WHICH END IN R53 OR R54 SUFFIX.
R44 SUFFIX INDICATES 4-WHEEL DRIVE.
R66   "   "   6-WHEELER.

HERCULES, CONTINENTAL, CUMMINS, TD ENGINES 116 TO 232 HP

NAPCO

IN LATER '50s, NAPCO INDUSTRIES OWNED FEDERAL, and MOVED OPERATIONS TO MINNEAPOLIS.

FEDERAL TRUCKS

FEDERAL-KNIGHT (1924 TO 1927)

The only Knight Engined Truck on the market ('24)

24-26

THE FEDERAL MOTOR TRUCK COMPANY

INITIALLY INTRODUCED 1924 AS FEDERAL'S LOWEST-PRICED LINE CHASSIS =

$1095.

1½-TON "S-25-6" and 2-TON "S-27" (BOTH WITH 144" WB) ALSO AVAIL. AFTER '25. KNOWN AS "S-25" and "S-1" IN 1927.

1-TON FEDERAL-KNIGHT with 4-CYL. KNIGHT SLEEVE-VALVE ENGINE

3 5/8" × 4½" BORE and STROKE (TO '27)

Willys-Knight engine

(SPRING, '25) OPEN CAB

OIL TANKER TRUCK (SPRING, '25)

124" WB

SEMI-ENCLOSED CAB

$1095.

BLUE RIBBON MAYONNAISE. C.C. SKAFGAARD DISTRIBUTOR

CLOSED CAB (SUMMER, '25)

(FALL, '25)

1½ TO 2 TON (FALL, '25)

(STILL AVAIL. IN 1927)

FULLY-CLOSED CAB ('26)

1924
Prices of other Federal Models

Fast Express	·	$1675
1½-Ton	·	2150
2½-Ton	·	3200
3½ to 4	·	4200
5-6 Ton	·	4750
7-Ton	·	5000
Light Duty Tractor	·	3200
Heavy Duty Tractor	·	4235

SEE ALSO: FEDERAL

121

FLEETARROW

BY PIERCE

(1928 – 1929)

THE PIERCE-ARROW MOTOR CAR CO.
BUFFALO, N. Y.

1 to 2 Ton

with 6- CYLINDER PIERCE-ARROW L-HEAD ENGINE (70 ⁇ HP)
3½" × 4" BORE and STROKE.
7-MAIN-BEARING CRANKSHAFT.

28½

SOMETIMES REGISTERED AS "EARLY 1929." HORIZONTALLY-SPLIT 2-PC. VENTILATING WINDSHIELD

STAKE WAGON

29

ONE-PIECE WINDSHIELD

Outstanding Features

A Pierce-Arrow 6-cylinder engine . . . More than 70-horsepower . . . 7-bearing crankshaft . . . Unusual gasoline economy . . . Safety 4-wheel mechanical brakes . . . 1500-4000 pounds pay load . . . Short turning radius . . . High carbon steel frame . . . Tubular radius rods . . . 140"–160"–180" wheelbases . . . Dual rear tires.

$2450

for 140-inch wheelbase
$2500 for 160-inch wheelbase
$2550 for 180-inch wheelbase
for chassis only, at Buffalo

Dual Rear Tires Extra

32 × 6 TIRES (DUALS ON REAR, OR 34 × 7, IF DESIRED.

Model C. O.

Highland Coupe Cab

For FLEET ARROW MODEL F A

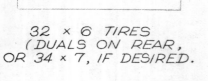

REAR VIEW of DUMP TRUCK

CAST STEEL WHEELS

NOTE SMALL PANE BETWEEN WINDSHIELD AND DOOR →

CHASSIS PRICES	
140" WB	$2450.
160"	$2500.
180"	$2550.

4- WHEEL MECHANICAL BRAKES

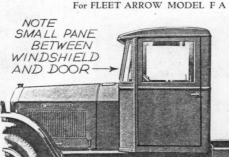

CAB and CHASSIS

BODY
Manufactured by
THE HIGHLAND
BODY MFG. CO.,
Elmwood Place,
Cincinnati, O.

← A Closer Look

SEE ALSO "PIERCE-ARROW"

FLXIBLE

1938, CONVERTED TO PRIVATE COACH

(FIRST TYPES WERE CONVERTED BUICKS, WITH LONG WHEELBASES.)

THE FLXIBLE CO., (1924 ON) LOUDONVILLE, O.

Bowling Green Hopkinsville Bus. Co.

VERMONT TRANSIT

233

(C. '40)

new CLIPPER SERIES (STARTS '37) (BUICK OR CHEVROLET ENGS.)

('48)

('37) NOTE THAT FR. DOOR IS BACK OF FR. AXLE (20-PASS.)
(REAR-ENGINED "CLIPPER 25" STARTS '38

30s-40s

SOME EARLY CLIPPERS have 3-TIERED BUMPERS.

1935 = 16-PASS. "AIRWAY"
1936 = 19-24 PASS. "

MICHAUD BUS LINES INC SALEM MASS
Scenic Special

(SLANTED SIDE WINDOWS SINCE '41)

('48)

VISICOACH   ONE OF THE FINAL "CLIPPER" TYPES, with LONGER WINDOWS.

AIR SCOOP COOLS REAR ENGINE

CHARTERED
673
1251

('55)

TRANSIT LINES
VERMONT TRANSIT
673

50s

new VL100 FLXIBLE ('56) "VISTA-LINER"

(INTRO. 1956)

FLXIBLE CONTINUES TWIN COACH CITY BUS TYPES.

22 BIG SUR
207

FLXIBLE Conversion 1964

H MAIN AND PEARL

GRUMMAN
CONNECTICUT TRANSIT
205
2-757
STATE CONNECTICUT

70s

(ABOVE TYPE STARTS 1961.)
(17-55 PASS. TYPES IN 1972.)

GRUMMAN

NORTH MAIN

BUYS FLXIBLE FR. ROHR INDUSTRIES 1977.

80s

('80)

123

GRUMMAN-FLXIBLE "870" (SINCE '78)

4-cylinder (THROUGH '31)

FORD

Ford Motor Company
Detroit, Michigan
(ESTAB. 1903)

MODEL T

HENRY FORD

20 H.P. (TO '27)

20-24

PLANETARY TRANSMISSION CONTROLLED BY FOOT PEDALS (THROUGH '27)

FORT DEARBORN STEAM LAUNDRY — LAUNDRY

RUNABOUT with PICKUP BODY

$366., f.o.b., with STARTER and DEMOUNTABLE RIMS (JULY, '25)

EXPRESS BODY with CANOPY TOP (OPEN CAB)

$515.

MODEL T AND TT 25-27

EXPRESS BODY with CANOPY TOP and SCREEN SIDES (CLOSED CAB)

$560.

STAKE BODY with CLOSED CAB

$515.

(PRICES f.o.b., FACTORY, AS OF JULY, 1925.)

$505.

Ford

THIS TYPE OF SCRIPT IS STAMPED ONTO UPPER PAN OF MODEL "T" TRUCK and CAR RADIATORS (THROUGH 1927.)
(MODEL "T" and "TT" PROD. CEASES AS OF SPRING, 1927.)

WIRE WHEELS ON LIGHTWEIGHT 1927 "T."

EXPRESS BODY with CLOSED CAB (OPEN CAB ALSO AVAIL.)

124

new MODEL "A"
(COMPLETELY RE-DESIGNED)

FORD

ROADSTER PICKUP

Ford

new OVAL EMBLEM
new CONVENTIONAL-STYLE
SLIDING-GEAR TRANSMISSION

pickup

MODEL **A**
New **28-29**

CAB

New Power

4-CYLINDER
ENGINE IMPROVED
(new 40 HP @
2300 RPM)

1½ TON
STAKE
Truck 125

HEAVY DUTY
WHEELS

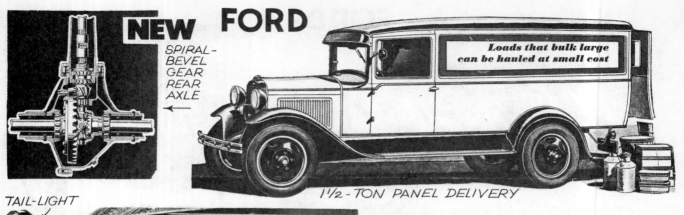

NEW FORD

SPIRAL-BEVEL GEAR REAR AXLE ←

Loads that bulk large can be hauled at small cost

1½-TON PANEL DELIVERY

TAIL-LIGHT ↗

LARGER and HIGHER RADIATOR THAN IN 1929.

REAR CHASSIS DETAIL

30 (RESTYLED) MODEL -32A and AA

SOME 1931½-32 LT. DLVRY., CARS HAVE THIS FRONT END STYLE. ↓

4-SPEED TRANS. IS STD. EQUIP. ON "AA" TRUCKS SINCE AUTUMN OF 1929.

SHIFT PATTERN

(BELOW) 4-SPEED TRANSMISSION

FORD CAR RADIATOR DESIGN (MODEL A)

HVY. FORD TRUCK RADIATOR SHELL DOES NOT HAVE A HEART-SHAPE DIP AT THE CENTER OF UPPER PAN.

1½-TON STAKE (131½" OR 157" WHEELBASE) 200.5 CID 4 CYL. ENG.

126

(CONT'D. NEXT PAGE) ('30)

30-32
(CONT'D.)

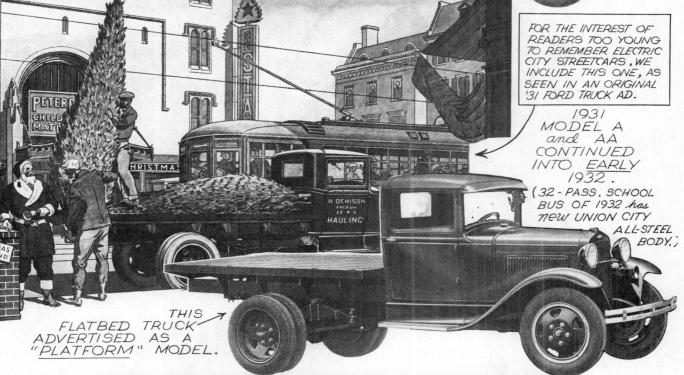

FOR THE INTEREST OF READERS TOO YOUNG TO REMEMBER ELECTRIC CITY STREETCARS, WE INCLUDE THIS ONE, AS SEEN IN AN ORIGINAL '31 FORD TRUCK AD.

1931 MODEL A and AA CONTINUED INTO EARLY 1932. (32-PASS. SCHOOL BUS OF 1932 has new UNION CITY ALL-STEEL BODY.)

THIS FLATBED TRUCK ADVERTISED AS A "PLATFORM" MODEL.

new SMALLER WHEELS

new MODEL **B** (4-CYL.) (ALSO "BB") (new V-8 ALSO AVAIL., LATER IN SEASON.)

NEW

32
(LATER SERIES)

new GRILLE AND BODY TYPIFIES THE "TRUE 1932" FORDS. (ALSO, new OVAL INSTRUMENT PANEL)

(INTRO. SPRING, 1932)

PICKUP CAB

DELIVERY

127

FORD
TRACTOR-TRAILER

BOXY, 1930 CAB STYLING ON **HEAVY-DUTY**

½ TON CHASSIS PRICE FROM $370. ('33) OR $360. ('34)

Checker Express Co MILWAUKEE

('33)

SERIAL # FROM 18-203127 ('33) 18-457478 ('34)

SEDAN DELIVERY STYLED LIKE A FORD CAR.
$565.

('34)
$550.

33-34

OVAL INST. PANEL CONTINUES IN MOST TRUCKS

PANEL

DUMP

CAB

112", 131" OR 157" WHEELBASES (THROUGH '37)

2ND-HAND TRUCK ILLUSTRATED HERE

('34)

NOTE V EMBLEMS ON 1934 V8 MODELS.

4-CYL. ALSO AVAIL. (THROUGH '34)*

½-TON OR 1½-TON MODELS

AC 218

128

* (THROUGH '33, IN CARS.)

VERTICAL BUMPER GUARD and FOG LIGHT NOT ORIGINAL EQUIP.

FORD

TRACTOR-TRAILER

WARREN TRANSFER CO.
CHARLOTTE N.C.

LONG-WHEELBASE
1½ T. PANEL
$760.
ALL
MODELS
RESTYLED

35

MODELS 48
(COMMERCIAL ;)
50 (½ TON ;)
51 (1½ TON)

CUSTOM-BLT. C.O.E.s
AVAIL. 1935 to 1938
(FACTORY-BUILT
C.O.E. STARTS
MAY, 1938.)

(CITY
TRANSIT
BUS CHASSIS
ALSO BLT.,
STARTING '34.
FIRST FLEETS
SOLD TO CITY OF
DETROIT.)

FINAL YEAR FOR
WIRE WHEELS
ON LIGHT FORD TRUCKS.

Checker Express Co.
PARCEL DELIVERY AND TRUCK RENTAL

$565.
½ T. STD. PANEL DELIVERY
V8 ENGINES ONLY (TO '39)

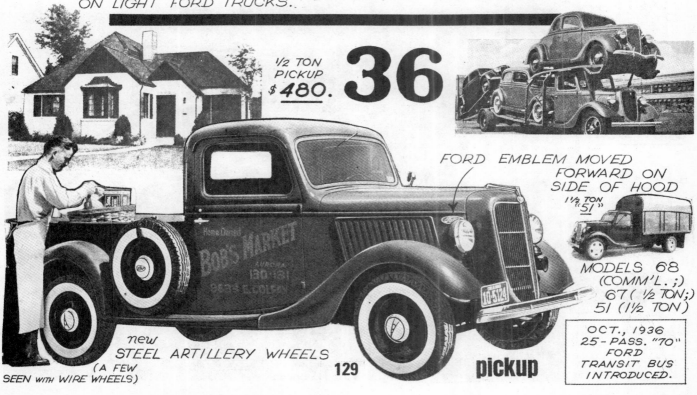

½ TON
PICKUP
$480.

36

FORD EMBLEM MOVED
FORWARD ON
SIDE OF HOOD

1½ TON
"51"

Home Owned
BOB'S MARKET

MODELS 68
(COMM'L. ;)
67 (½ TON;)
51 (1½ TON)

OCT., 1936
25- PASS. "70"
FORD
TRANSIT BUS
INTRODUCED.

new
STEEL ARTILLERY WHEELS
(A FEW
SEEN WITH WIRE WHEELS)

129

pickup

PLATFORM TRUCK

FORD

NEW
STYLING

OPTIONAL GEAR RATIOS AVAILABLE

FORD "70-A" and "70-B" (2' LONGER) CITY TRANSIT BUSES AVAIL. (TO 1939.)

new 37

new CHOICE OF 60 or 85 HORSEPOWER V8 ENGINES, 3 WHEELBASES (PICKUPS FROM $516.)

THIS SEDAN DELIVERY (AND "COMMERCIAL CARS") STYLED LIKE 1937 FORD AUTOMOBILES.

60 HP MODELS:
74 (COMM'L.;)
73 (½ TON;) 75 (1½ TON)

85 HP MODELS:
78 (COMM'L.;)
77 (½ TON;)
79 (1½ TON)

"74" (60 HP) $639.
"78" (85 HP) $649.

new V-WINDSHIELD

new HOOD LOUVRES with V8 EMBLEM

new GRILLE

→ STAKE TRUCK
$526.-683.

WONDER BREAD IT'S SLO-BAKED

WONDER BREAD IT'S SLO-BAKED

TRACTOR with VAN TRAILER

FORD V·8 TRUCKS

130

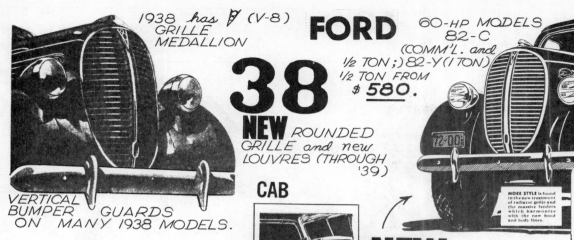

1938 has Ⱳ (V-8) GRILLE MEDALLION

FORD

38

NEW ROUNDED GRILLE and new LOUVRES (THROUGH '39)

60-HP MODELS 82-C (COMM'L. and 1/2 TON;) 82-Y (1 TON) 1/2 TON FROM $580.

MORE STYLE is found in the new treatment of radiator grille and the massive fenders which harmonize with the new hood and body lines.

New This Year! **THE FORD V-8 ONE-TONNER!** A unit that fills the gap between Ford Commercial Cars and the Big Ford Trucks

VERTICAL BUMPER GUARDS ON MANY 1938 MODELS.

CAB

CHASSIS DETAIL

NEW 1-TON MODELS WITH 122" WB $660. UP

85-HP MODELS: 81-C (COMM'L. and 1/2-TON;) 81-Y (1-TON;) 81-T, 817-T (1 1/2 T;) 81-W, 811-W (1 1/2 TON C.O.E.)

FINAL YEAR FOR MECHANICAL BRAKES

(FROM $595., new 3/4-TON MODELS ADDED.) NEW 25'-9", 27-PASS. TRANSIT BUS WITH 95-HP V8 (TRANSVERSE, AT REAR.)

60-HP MODELS: 922-C (1/2 TON) 922-D (3/4 TON) 92-Y (1 TON)

39 NO GRILLE MEDALLION IN 1939

$630. UP

THE "ONE-TONNER"

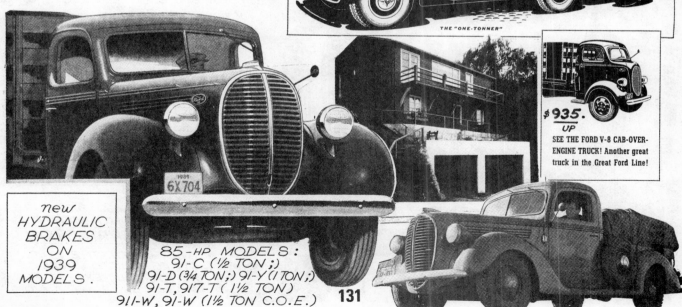

$935. UP SEE THE FORD V-8 CAB-OVER-ENGINE TRUCK! Another great truck in the Great Ford Line!

new HYDRAULIC BRAKES ON 1939 MODELS.

85-HP MODELS: 91-C (1/2 TON;) 91-D (3/4 TON;) 91-Y (1 TON;) 91-T, 917-T (1 1/2 TON) 911-W, 91-W (1 1/2 TON C.O.E.)

131

FORD

SEDAN DELIVERY and COMMERCIAL LINE has FORD AUTOMOBILE STYLING.

$705.

60-HP MODELS :
022-A (COMM'L.;) 02-C (½ TON;)
02-D (¾ TON;) 02-Y (1 TON)

OTHER MODELS : 01-A (COMM'L.;) 01-C (½ T.;)
01-D (¾ TON)
01-Y (1 TON)
01-T, 018-T
(1½ TON)
011-W, 01-W
(1½ TON C.O.E.)

40

NEW LONGITUDINAL FRONT SPRINGS ON TRUCK CHASSIS (NO TORQUE TUBE)

OTHER FORD TRUCK MODELS with OWN GRILLE, HOOD LOUVRES, HEADLIGHTS SEPARATE FROM FENDERS

V/8 EMBLEM PLACED AHEAD OF HOOD LOUVRES.

$775.

158" WB TYPE PLATFORM TRUCK (ABOVE)

CAB VIEW FROM ACTUAL PHOTO →

STAKE CAB

85 and 95-HP V8 ENGINES (FINAL YEAR FOR V8-60) 4 CYL. ALSO AVAIL.

ALSO SEE **MARMON-HERRINGTON**

(NEARLY ALL 42 OF THE 1940 TYPES PRICED UNDER $1000., FOB, EXCEPT FOR 134" WB C.O.E. STAKE @ $1010.

CHASSIS/CAB
122" (¾ T.)
$630.
122" (1 TON
$665.

134" $680.
158" 705.
(ALSO C.O.E.
CHASSIS/CABS AVAIL.)

132

FORD 41

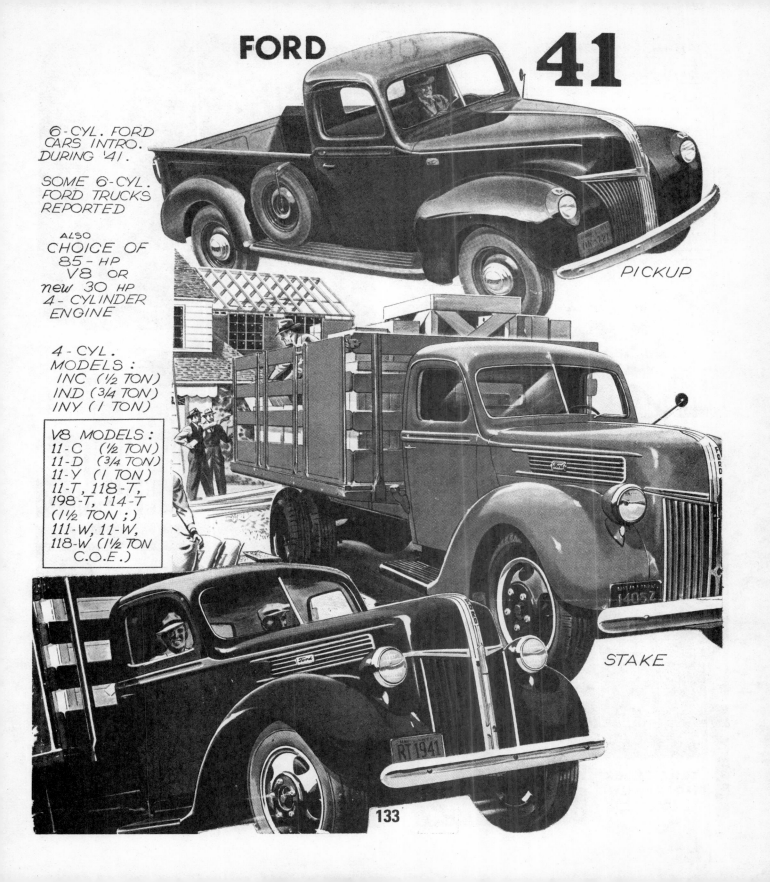

6-CYL. FORD CARS INTRO. DURING '41.

SOME 6-CYL. FORD TRUCKS REPORTED

ALSO CHOICE OF 85-HP V8 OR new 30 HP 4-CYLINDER ENGINE

4-CYL. MODELS:
INC (1/2 TON)
IND (3/4 TON)
INY (1 TON)

V8 MODELS:
11-C (1/2 TON)
11-D (3/4 TON)
11-Y (1 TON)
11-T, 118-T,
198-T, 114-T
(1 1/2 TON ;)
111-W, 11-W,
118-W (1 1/2 TON C.O.E.)

PICKUP

STAKE

133

FORD

FORD 1942-44
CAB-FORWARD MODELS
ILLUSTRATED IN
MARMON-HERRINGTON
SECTION.

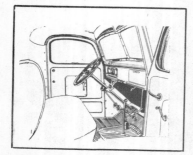

INTERIOR (1944-1947)
V8 OR
new 6-CYL.
90 H.P. and up

42 -47

114, 122, 134, 158 or
194" WHEELBASES
(101, 134 or 158" ON
C.O.E.s)

1942-1945 MODELS:
21-A (SED. DLVRY.)
21-C (½ TON)
21-D (¾ TON) *
21-Y (1 TON)
21-T, 218-T, 214-T
(1½ TON ;)
211-W, 21-W, 218-W
(1½ TON C.O.E.)

1946 MODELS :
69-C, 69-Y,
69-T, 698-T,
691-W, 69-W, 698-W

1947 MODELS :
79-C, 79-Y, 79-T,
798-T, 791-W, 79-W,
798-W

new
STYLING
IN 1942

STAKE
('46)

6 CHASSIS TYPES IN 1945.

SLOGAN : "FORD TRUCKS LAST LONGER."

FLATBED
('45)

TRANSIT BUS   ('46)

PITTSBURGH
1946

THESE
BUSES BLT. BY MARMON-
HERRINGTON AFTER 4-50.
* = ¾-TON TRUCKS
DROPPED AFTER 1944.

TRUE TRUCK ENGINEERING
*Powerful truck engines—Six chassis
types—for 95% of all hauling jobs.*

CLOSE-UP OF INSTRUMENT PANEL

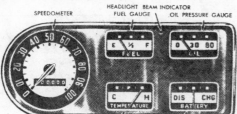

SPEEDOMETER

HEADLIGHT BEAM INDICATOR
FUEL GAUGE   OIL PRESSURE GAUGE

FUEL   O.P.
TEMPERATURE   BATTERY

TEMPERATURE GAUGE   BATTERY GAUGE

FORD

F-4 STAKE

('49)

NEW *1-PIECE*
WINDSHIELD
new GRILLE

Model F-3; 6,800 lbs. G.V.W.
Express or Stake

Model F-4; 10,000 lbs. G.V.W.
with Duals

Model F-5; 14,000 lbs. G.V.W.
Wheelbases; 134, 158 and 176 in.

Model F-5 Cab-Over-Engine
14,000 lbs. G.V.W.

Model F-5 School Bus Chassis
Wheelbases; 158 and 194 in.

Model F-6 Cab-Over-Engine
16,000 lbs. G.V.W.

Model F-6; 15,500 lbs. G.V.W.
Wheelbases; 134, 158 and 176 in.

Model F-7; 19,000 lbs. G.V.W.
35,000 lbs. G.T.W.

Model F-8; 21,500 lbs. G.V.W.
39,000 lbs. G.T.W.

48-50

RESTYLED 1948
3/4-TON MODELS
RETURN '48.

OVER 175 DIFFERENT
MODELS IN 1950.

PARTS NUMBERS INCLUDED

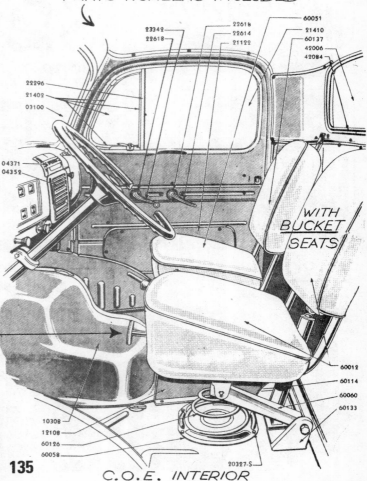

23342
22618   22618   60051
22614   21410
21122   60137
42006
42084

22296
21402
03100

04371
04352

WITH
BUCKET
SEATS

SEAT
ADJUSTMENT
KNOB

60012
60114
60060
60133

10308
12108
60126
60058

20327-S

C.O.E. INTERIOR

WITH
VAN
BODY

('50)

C.O.E.s

CAB-AND-
CHASSIS

135

FORD

New
GRILLE

226 OR 254 CID 6,
239 OR 337 CID V8

F-1 (½-TON)
F-2, F-3 (¾ ")
F-4 (1-TON)
F-5 (1½ ")
F-6, F-7, F-8
and C.O.E.
MODELS
ALSO AVAIL.

51

95 HP @ 3300 (6)
100 HP @ 3800 (V8)
110 HP @ 3400 (BIG 6)
145 HP @ 3600 RPM
(BIG V8)

OVER 180
MODELS
IN
ALL

6 (note
DIFFERENT
HOOD TRIM)

V8

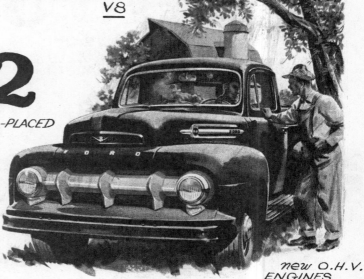

52

new LARGER, LOWER-PLACED
"FORD"
LETTERING
ABOVE GRILLE
and new TRIM
ON FRONT and
SIDES of HOOD.

H.P.
INCREASED
101, 112 HP (6)
106, 145,
155 HP (V8)

FINAL YEAR WITH THIS
INTERIOR

new O.H.V.
ENGINES
AVAILABLE

F-900

HEAVY-
DUTY

RESTYLED

53

(C.O.E.)
C-800

new F-100,
F-250, F-350
and F-500
SERIES

new
INTERIOR,
DASH, and
SYNCHRO-SILENT TRANS.

136

FORD

SERIES F-900
Max. G.V.W. 27,000 lbs.
Max. G.C.W. 55,000 lbs.

CONCRETE MIXER
156- and 175-in. wbs.

LOGGER
156-, 175- and 192-in. wbs.

CONVENTIONALS

NEW F-900 BIG JOB TRACTOR
Max. G.C.W.—55,000 lbs.
Wheelbases: 132 and 114 in.

SAFETY REAR STAKE LOCK

Ford

54

HENRY FORD II

POWER STEERING ON T-800, AVAIL. ON MOST "BIG JOB" HEAVY TRUCKS.

CAB FORWARD
6 New Series
C-500, C-600
C-700, C-750
C-800, C-900

TANKER

1954 CAB

239 or 256 CID POWER KING V8
130 or 138 HP

279 or 317 CID CARGO KING V8
152 or 170 HP

Refrigerator Van

Coal Dump

Furniture Van

Gasoline (Oil, Milk) Tank

Garbage Body

137

('53 CAB SIMILAR)

6-CYL. FROM $1346.

V8 FROM $1462.

HOLLAND MOTOR EXPRESS Inc.

"You Can't Beat the Big Dutch Fleet"

FORD

I.D. #F10D5A 100001 UP

PICKUPS have SHORT-STROKE ENGS. (6 - 118 HP; V8 - 132 HP)

new GRILLE (V8 has V and 8 IN CENTER OF TOP PIECE)

55

IMPROVED FORD-O-MATIC AUTOMATIC TRANS.

MASTER-GUIDE POWER STEER

C-600 (3 V8s AVAIL.)

C-750 UTILITY

C.O.E.s

175 or 186 HP V8s

F-350 WRECKER

CONVENTIONAL

POWER STEERING and AIR BRAKES AVAIL. ON F-800 (TO 200 HP) AVAIL. on SOME OTHER MODELS.

T-800

F-500 1½ TON

F-600 2-TON

6 OR V8

F-750 with TACHOMETER

C-800

C-900

TO 25 TONS G.C.W.

SERIAL # F10-D6A-100001 UP

56

F-700 "BIG JOB" TYPE

CHECK INSIGNIA ON SIDE OF HOOD.

new GRILLE $1346. UP

LT. DUTY 110 OR 118" WB

F-800 12-TON G.V.W.

to 200 HP V8

new 133 HP 6 or 167 HP V8 ("Y-8")

FORD

138

F-900 "BIG JOB" with new HEAVY-DUTY 5-SPEED TRANS.

new SWING-FORWARD CAB FOR ENGINE ACCESS

New TILT-CAB C.O.E. (2 VIEWS)

TRACTOR / TRAILER

60,000 lbs. GCW

LARGE CONVENTIONALS WITH 3 HOLES IN LOWER FRONT SHEET METAL. (LT. DUTY WITH SMALL VERTICAL SLOTS (AS IN ILLUSTRATION BELOW, LEFT)

T-800 TANDEM DUMP 212 HP H.D. V8 WITH new HYDRAULIC CLUTCH and POWER STEERING (65,000 lbs. GCW)

FORD

TOTALLY RESTYLED FOR 1957

57

STANDARD "FLARESIDE" PICKUP

pickup

new PARALLEL GROOVES ALONG HOOD

NEW

F-350 1-TON has SIMILAR FRONT STYLING.

WIDE-BED F-100 STYLESIDE CUSTOM CAB 6½' OR 8' BED LENGTH (NARROW-BED AVAIL. ALSO.)

139

FORD

CONVENTIONAL INSTRUMENT PANEL

TANDEM DUMP

TILT-CAB INSTRUMT. PANEL →

TILT CAB (IN 6 SER.)

PRODUCTION: 242,890
AVAIL.
6½' OR 8' FLARESIDE, BUT SMOOTH STYLESIDE BED STD. EQUIPMENT IN LT. DUTY,

3 new "SUPER DUTY" V8 ENGINES =
401 CID, 226 HP;
477 CID, 260 HP;
534 CID, 277 HP

VARIED IN 6½', 8' and 9' LENGTHS IN 1958.

58 NEW
4 →
HEADLTS., new GRILLE ON CONVENTIONAL

OVER 300 MODELS!

STAKE

PRODUCTION : 331,348

DASH

59
new ALL-HORIZONTAL GRILLE MEMBERS new "FORD" LETTERING ABOVE GRILLE REPLACES BADGE EMBLEM.

CUSTOM CAB
ALSO AVAIL.:
new 4-W-D P.U.

140

FORD

STYLESIDE
(BELOW)

WITH

F-600 STAKE (ABOVE)
6 OR V8

TILT CAB

Certified
Economy

60

new GRILLE. BADGE EMBLEM RETURNS ON CONVENTIONALS.

PROD.: 337,468

CONVENTIONAL INSTRUMENT PANEL AND CONTROLS

DASH

141

102 ALL-NEW H-SERIES TILT CAB MODELS —DIESEL AND GAS

5 Cummins Diesels or 5 Ford "Big V" gas engines in these new highway tractors. Service is coast to coast!

Space-saving sleeper increases cab length by only one inch. Short 28-inch axle setting, GCW's up to 76,800 pounds, permit top legal loads.

984 pounds more payload is big advantage of new, lightweight "pusher type" tandem axles. Over 500 engine-axle-transmission combinations, all told!

107 C-SERIES TILT CAB MODELS

WITH NEW SLEEPER OPTION!

Most popular Tilt Cabs on the American road! Four series—up to 65,000 pounds GCW—with new chassis strength, new weight-saving options for bigger loads.

New compact sleeper adds only 2½ inches to cab length, lets you haul 40-foot trailers in 50-foot states. Wide range of optional tractor equipment available on all models.

Tandem-axle models are also available in the C-Series. As with conventional tandems, aluminum walking beams, wheels and fuel tanks are offered to cut weight, boost payload.

A RETURN TO ONLY 2 HEADLTS.

61

FORD TRUCKS COST LESS

115 NEW HIGH-STRENGTH CONVENTIONAL CAB MODELS

New huskier tractors feature lighter, stronger frames of high-tensile steel . . . heavier gauge metal and stress-isolating mounting for cabs. New 28-in. BA for extra payload!

New tougher tandems offer new strength in chassis, cab sheet metal . . . new shock-swallowing front suspension. Powered by rugged "Big V" engines, Ford tandems range up to 51,000 lbs. GVW, 75,000 GCW.

FORD

SUPER DUTY

142

(CONT'D. NEXT PAGE)

New "Big Six" engine for more power!

FORD

SERIAL # F-10J-100001 UP (F SERIES)

F SERIES

2-TON MEDIUM DUTY

all-new 262 CID "BIG SIX" ENGINE AVAIL. IN 2-TON

NEW TOUGHER HEAVIES
New, stronger hi-tensile frames! Huskier axles! Wider power-train choice! Short, 28-in. front axle setting! New high-durability cabs and sheet metal!

T SERIES

NEW LOW-COST TILTS
New sleeper cabs! New weight-saving options for greater payloads! Money-saving ease of servicing!

Econoline "STATION BUS" 144 CID 6

61
(CONT'D.) **New**

$2130. UP

new GAS-ENGINED "H" TILT-CAB MODELS ALSO AVAIL.

619 new models! It's the biggest change-over in Ford history with more trucks to match more jobs, more savings on any job! New "Big Six" power for two-tonners! New Super Duty Diesel Tilts with the nation's most popular diesel engines! Suspensions that give up to twice the tire life of other types! New Econoline models that pack more load in three feet less truck length! New engines that deliver up to 40% more gas mileage! And all this at prices that give you a flying start to long-term savings! So for super-economy pickups all the way up to super-duty diesels, see your Ford Dealer . . . economy never came in such a choice!

HEAVY DUTY DIESEL C.O.E.

H SERIES →

NEW!

CHOICE OF 5 CUMMINS DIESEL ENGINES OR 5 FORD "BIG V" GAS ENGINES

OVER 500 ENGINE-AXLE-TRANSMISSION COMBINATIONS IN "H" SERIES ALONE!

DIESEL

FORD

NOW! ONLY FROM FORD
100,000-MILE WARRANTY
ON ALL SUPER DUTY ENGINES → 401, 477 OR 534 CID V8s

PROD.: 338,985

143

FORD

SERIAL #
F-10J (A) 205000 UP
(1962 F SER.)

F-250 3/4 TON

62

new GRILLE ON LIGHT
and MEDIUM-DUTY
F SERIES

H SERIES

TON		WB	PRICE
1/2	F 100	114	$1962
3/4	F 250	122	2117
1	F 350	132	2305
1 1/2	F 500	156	2810
2	F 600	156	3225
1 1/2	C 550	111	3913
2	C 600	111	4046

VARIOUS OTHER
SERIES ALSO,
INCLUDING
SCHOOLBUS CHAS.

LOWEST-PRICED MODELS
IN EACH SERIES OF
F and C LISTED
ABOVE.

DIESEL

FORD

FORD

TILT CAB

C-750
SUPER DUTY
TILT CAB
TRACTOR *and*
TRAILER

FORD *Super Duty*

MEDIUM DUTY
F SERIES (*new*
BIG 6
ENGINE AVAIL.)

**FORD TRUCKS
COST LESS**
SAVE NOW...SAVE FROM NOW ON!

144

F-100

FORD

NEW 89" BBC LINE CUTS LENGTH, ADDS MANEUVERABILITY!

SERIAL #
F-10J (A)
325000 UP
STARTS
10-1-62

NEW! Low gear synchronized for easier downshifting!

LARGER F SERIES AVAIL. WITH CUMMINS V6 DIESEL OR FORD "SUPER DUTY" GAS V8.

DIESEL

AVAILABLE
CUMMINS V6 DIESEL ENGINE (588 CID, 200 HP)
CUMMINS V8 DIESEL (785 CID, 265 HP)

63

NEW

N SERIES

64

luxury interior

F-100	114" WB	$2004.
F-250	128"	2163.
F-350	132"	2337.
F-500	156"	2889.
F-600	156"	3247.

SERIAL # F-10J 445000 UP
STARTS 10-1-63

SERIAL #
F-10 (J) (—)
580000 UP
STARTS 10-1-64

THREE ALL-NEW ENGINES! Now standard in Ford pickups: brand-new 240 cubic inch economy Six! Optional: new 300 cubic inch Big Six, powerful new 352 cubic inch V-8!

new GRILLE

65

F SERIES
$1970. UP

WITH

TWIN I BEAM

INDEPENDENT SUSPENSION

145

FORD

F-100
$2125.
AND UP

new
GRILLE ON
F SERIES

66

2 SANGAMO TACHOGRAPHS (OPT.)

W
SERIES
DASH

W SERIES (**new**)
STARTS
SPRING,
1966

STEWART-WR.
GAUGES
STD.

CENTER
CONSOLE

W-1000
TILT CAB

WITH
195 TO 335 HP
DIESEL ENGS.
BY CUMMINS,
DETROIT
DIESEL, OR
CATERPILLAR.

WITH
OR
WITHOUT
SLEEPER
CAB.

146

FORD

F - SERIES CONVENTIONAL CAB:
F-500, 600, 700, 750

F-700

School Bus Chassis
B-500 • 600 • 700 • 750

B-750
(UP TO 66-
PASSENGER
CAP.)

67

F-800

F, T SERIES CONV.: F-800, 850, 950,
1000, T-800, 850, 950, 850-D, 950-D,
STANDARD CAB (F SERIES)

ALSO F-950-D, 1000-D,
F and T-8000

INSTRUMENT PANEL AND CONTROLS

STANDARD CAB

CUSTOM CAB

P. SERIES

DASH of
P SERIES

CUSTOM CAB
(F SERIES)
has "FORD"
STRIP HORIZ.
ACROSS PANEL.

SERIES (LETTER and
1ST 2 DIGITS
OF SERIES
TYPE)

ASSEMBLY
PLANT

MODEL

BODY TYPE

TRANSMSN.

REAR
AXLE

ENGINE

UNIT
NO.

HOW TO READ
A FORD I.D. PLATE

WARRANTY NUMBER

F25 ALA12600

MADE IN U.S.A

Ford

REG US PAT

NOT FOR TITLE OR REGISTRATION PURPOSES

W.B.	COLOR	MODEL	BODY	TRANS	AXLE
131	JM	F250	E81	C	25

MAX.G.V.W. LBS.	CERT. NET H.P.	R.P.M.	D.S.O.
7500	129	4000	72

WARRANTY VOID IF MAX. GROSS VEHICLE WEIGHT IS EXCEEDED
(SEE OPERATORS MANUAL FOR LOAD CAPACITY CHART)

WHEEL-
BASE

MAX. GROSS
WEIGHT
(lbs.)

HORSEPOWER
@ RPMs

DISTRICT
CODE SPEC.
ORDER NO.
(SAN JOSE)

Parcel Delivery Chassis
P-100 • 350 • 400 • 500 • 3500 •
4000 • 5000

(P-350
ILLUSTRATED)

SERIAL #
F-10 (—)
A00001 UP

F-100
$2237. UP

147

(CONT'D. NEXT PAGE)

95 Short-Haul Tractors (N-750's)
N-750

N-SERIES SHORT CONVENTIONAL CAB :
N-500, 600, 700, 750, 850, 950,
1000, N-6000, 7000, 8000,
1000-D, NT-8000 *, 850, 950,
850-D, 950-D

DIESEL OR V8 GAS.

N-850-D

Ryder
Truck Lines modernizes fleet; invests over $5 million in Ford Trucks

67
(CONT'D.)

C-700

C-850

C-SERIES
TILT CAB :
C-550, 600, 700,
750, 800, 850,
950, 1000,
C-6000, 7000,
8000, CT-750,
800, 850, 950,
8000 *

* = AVAILABLE ON
SPECIAL ORDER.

1½ TON
C-550 STAKE $ **4188.**
C-600 STAKE **4570.**
2 TON

W-SERIES INTERIOR

DIESEL W-1000-D CR WT-1000-D   148

W SERIES

FORD

Medium/Heavy F SERIES

BRANCH

SNYDER

GREAT LAKES
EXPRESS
SAGINAW, MICH.

CJ

SNYDER

BRIGGS
TRANSPORTATION CO.
ST. PAUL, MINN.

BLUE RIDGE
TRANSFER CO. INC.
ROANOKE, VA.

HEAVY-DUTY

5686·CR

RANGER
NAME
NEAR
REAR

Ranger

68

F SERIES
INTERIOR
(RANGER)

F-100 "RANGER"

FORD 100

FORD

WITH
CAMPER

GRILLE DETAILS
(RANGER)

WORKS LIKE A TRUCK
RIDES LIKE A CAR

149

V 47 158

NEW!

FORD HEAVY-DUTY TRUCK

W SERIES

The switch is on... to Ford

PRODUCTION: 658,534

FINAL YR. FOR N, F-800 UP, and T-800 UP.

69

new GRILLE (LIGHT F SERIES)

He covers 9% more ground than the rest of the fleet.

Works like a truck. Rides like a car.

F-100

pickup.

"CAT DIESEL POWER" FILLER DOOR EMBLEM (ABOVE) INDICATES CATERPILLAR DIESEL ENG.

CATERPILLAR "1674" DIESEL ENGINE

Medium/Heavies

F-750 (BELOW)

C SERIES

150

FORD

UP TO 335 HP *with* DIESEL.

LN (MEDIUM) SHORT CONVENTIONAL (93.3" BBC)

L SERIES

LOUISVILLE LINE

BLT. AT FORD'S *new* LOUISVILLE, KY. BRANCH FACTORY. (INTRO. 12-69)

NEW

HEAVY-DUTY TRUCKS

DUAL-CIRCUIT AIR BRAKES (*new*)

70

4 DIGITS IN MODEL NUMBER DENOTES A DIESEL ENG. (LS = SHORT W.B., WITH FRONT AXLE SET BACK)

TANDEM-AXLE **LT** DUMP

(CONT'D. NEXT PAGE)

STD. CAB →

AIR CLEANER PORT ON RT. SIDE OF HOOD →

FORD 9000

LINEHAUL PANEL (IN CUSTOM CAB)

(ON ALL BUT "LN." TYPE)

151

FORD

Hertz

Minihome
INTRO. MID-'69

70
(CONT'D.)

C

W

F

(THIS VAN STYLE BEGINS 1968)

5 PICKUP ENGS. TO 390 C/D V8.

(*LTS* STARTS MID-1970, AS '71 MODEL.)

FOR FULL DETAILS on VANS, PLEASE SEE "PICKUP AND VAN SPOTTER'S GUIDE."

ECONOLINE VAN

CREW CAB (F MED. DUTY) →

F-SERIES CREW CAB

F

L

C

W (W-9000 IS new)

HEAVY-DUTY

W SER. HAS new SMALLER "FORD" NAME IN FRONT.

F-100

F-350 CAMPER SPECIAL

new GRILLE WITH FEWER HORIZ. PCS.

71

RANGER XLT INSTRUMENT PANEL

152

FORD

L SERIES

STANDARD CAB
(L SERIES)

Short conventionals with
exclusive tilting front end

Louisville Line Engines
up to 534 cu. in. gasoline
up to 927 cu. in. diesel

(new LT-880 and LNT-880 DUMP TRUCKS
INTRO. EARLY 1972 with 475 CID GAS V8s)

72

new GRILLE (LT. F)
WITH FEWER
VERTICAL PCS.

Over 1,000 big trucks

F-100
LT. DUTY

C SERIES
CUSTOM CAB

Custom Cab Interior

C-800
REFUSE TRUCK

153 (CONT'D. NEXT PAGE)

Ford W-Series tractor

SLEEPER CAB

"DRESS-UP" PAINT PKG. AVAIL. OPTION FROM 5-72.

Choice of 19 popular Diesels

W-Series

EARLY '72 CAB (2 VIEWS)

Spacious super cab—

WOODGRAIN INSTRUMENT PANEL, BEIGE STEERING WHEEL and PADDED ENGINE COVER STANDARD AS OF 5-1-72.

ALUM. CAB OPTION. ON W, WT

72 (CONT'D.)

The newest Ford

W-9000 Series

154

FORD 73-75

ALL F TYPES GET *new* GRILLE, 1973.

CAB (MED. F)

F-700 DUMP

BRIGHT METAL GRILLE

new EXTERIOR SHEET METAL ON F-500-750 *and* F-6000-F-7000 ('73)

F-750

WITH WHITE GRILLE

('74)

RESTYLED <u>W</u> SERIES INTRODUCED SPRING, 1973, WITH GRILLE SIMILAR TO LOUISVILLE (L) MODELS.

MANY *new* MECHANICAL IMPROVEMENTS IN REDESIGNED LIGHT F TYPES

('73)

F-110

155

(CONT'D. NEXT PAGE)

Introducing Ford's SuperCab
...the pickup cab roomy enough for a back seat.

('74½)

FORD PICKUPS
FORD DIVISION Ford

(SUPER CAB INTRO. 6-74)

L SERIES
Louisville Line

73-75
(CONT'D.)

AMERICAN ROAD CAMPER

EXTERIOR

OPT. BATHROOM

INTERIOR

STORAGE

INTRO. SPRING, 1973, AS FORD'S FIRST OFFICIAL, COMPLETE DEALER-AVAILABLE CAMPER-PICKUP COMBINATION (F-350, 140" WHEELBASE)

SCHOOL BUS

FORD

FORD B-SERIES CHASSIS Major school bus body builders install bodies on Ford B-Series chassis.

SUPERIOR COACH DIVISION
Sheller-Globe Corporation
Lima, Ohio; Kosciusko, Mississippi

PERLEY A. THOMAS CAR WORKS, INC.
High Point, North Carolina 27261
Woodstock, Ontario, Canada

WARD SCHOOL BUS MFG., INC.
Conway, Arkansas 72032
Beaver Falls, Pennsylvania

WELLES CORPORATION, LTD.
An Indian Head Company
A Division of Wayne Corporation
Windsor 15, Ontario, Canada

WAYNE CORPORATION
An Indian Head Company
Wayne Transportation Division
Richmond, Indiana 47374

BLUE BIRD BODY COMPANY
Fort Valley, Georgia 31030; Brantford, Ontario, Canada
Blue Bird Midwest, Inc., Mount Pleasant, Iowa 52641

CARPENTER BODY WORKS, INC.
Mitchell, Indiana 47446

GILLIG BROTHERS
Hayward, California 94543

156

C SERIES TILT CAB

_LN_

F
L

F-150.
Runs on any kind of gas.

300 C/D 6 OR 3 DIFF. V8s.

new ↗
GRILLE / HEADLT. DETAILS (LIGHT F SERIES)

76-77

W-SERIES LINEHAULER

New! Long 118" BBC Louisville Line tractor
New
LTL-9000

('76 MODELS ILLUSTR.)

W. 82" BBC
SLEEPER CAB
(52" BBC AVAIL. ALSO)

('78)

New GRILLE
(LIGHT / MED. F SERIES)

CL-9000
C.O.E.

78-79

F, L, LN, LNT, LTL, C, and CL SERIES

157 **NEW heavy-duty truck**

FORD
TRUCKS

HEAVY TRUCKS.

FORD

1981

FLARESIDE

GAS OR DIESEL!

NEW RESTYLED MEDIUM/ HEAVY F-SERIES

WITH ADVANCED 8.2L "FUEL PINCHER" DETROIT DIESEL POWER.

F-600, F-700, F-800

80-81

DDA 8.2L Fuel Pincher Diesel

CUSTOM CAB

SUPERCAB

('81 EXAMPLES ILLUSTRATED)

CAB

FORD F-SERIES. in big trucks.

Built Ford Tough

Ford

Medium and Heavy

C

LN

Tough new
F-700 4x4.

82

F-SERIES.

11,000
LB. MAX.
GVWR

Chassis Cab shown

Chassis-Cab
Models.

Ford

America's Truck.
Built Ford Tough!

NEW OVAL
"FORD" EMBLEM ON
GRILLE (LT. "F" SERIES)

232 CID V-6 STD. IN F-100
(EXCEPT IN CALIFORNIA)

SCHOOL BUS

B-600
B-700

(GAS, LP GAS
OR DIESEL)

DETROIT DIESEL (ABOVE) OR LIMA
370 CID V8 OR
429 CID V8.

**SCHOOL BUS
CHASSIS**

BUS
USES
"FUEL
PINCHER"
8.2 L

159

FORD

STYLESIDE

Ford

C-Series

REFUSE TRUCK

REFRIG. TRUCK

C-SERIES

C-Series
CAB TILTS FOR SERVICING

SCHOOL BUS

School Bus Preparation Package
A School Bus Body Builders Preparation Package is available on the 138-in. wheelbase Econoline Commercial Cutaway model.

AS BEFORE, VARIOUS TYPES OF SCHOOL BUSES, VANS AVAILABLE.

F-SERIES

('83) F-350 137" WB $9352.

F-350 **CHASSIS-CABS** w. 137 OR 161" WB

F-100s FROM $7349.

4WD 4 CYL. FROM $8677. ('83) *RANGER 4WD*

160

83-85 (CONT'D. NEXT PAGE)

Empire
TRUCK STOP

LN

83-85
(CONT'D.)

CL-9000

CL-9000

(1984 EXAMPLES ILLUSTRATED)

FREIGHTLINER (ESTAB. 1939)

(A SUBSIDIARY OF CONSOLIDATED FREIGHTWAYS)

FREIGHTLINER CORP., PORTLAND, OREGON

REGULAR PRODUCTION BEGINS WELL AFTER WORLD WAR II ('47)

C.F.R.*

47

EARLY CONVNT'L. (RARE!)

* CONSOLIDATED FREIGHTWAYS REBUILT; MODIFIED OLDER FAGEOL.

"AS IS" USED EXAMPLE SHOWN

new INSIGNIA-NAMEPLATE IN 1951, AS SALES AND SERVICE TAKEN OVER BY WHITE

WHITE FREIGHTLINER

FREIGHTLINER" IS ONLY NAME ON GRILLE INSIGNIA

50

6-CYL. BUDA OR CUMMINS DIESEL ENGINES, BUT WITHIN A FEW YRS., VARIOUS OTHER ENGINES AVAIL.

53

new GRILLE; NAMEPLATE NOW ON CAB FRONT, ABOVE GRILLE.

TILT-CAB MODEL INTRO. 1958.

6-CYL., 638 CID CATERPILLAR "1674" DIESEL (270 HP @ 2200 RPM) AVAILABLE ('67.)

61

(OPTIONAL QUADRUPLE HEADLIGHTS AVAIL. DURING 1960s.)

66

TRIPLE AXLES AVAIL.

HALF CAB

PRODUCTION DURING 1960s	
1960	931
61	1242
62	1928
63	3053
64	3854
65	4993
66	6704
67	5226
68	7162
69	8674

68

1968 WINDSHIELD WIPERS MOVED TO A LOWER POSITION ON CAB FRONT

70

Freightliner

9 CAB LENGTHS FROM 48" TO 104" BBC

48" 51" 63" 72" 75" 81" 86" 104"

71

White-Freightliner builds more cab body sizes than any other truck manufacturer. Choose from three non-sleeper and six different sleeper cab sizes, including a double bed model and a top mounted sleeper. If your crew numbers more than two men, try our 104 inch, 4-door crew cab for size.

new **VENT SLOTS**

WHITE **FREIGHTLINER**

The Road's Too Long For Anything Less

STD. ENG. IS 6-CYL. CUMMINS 585 CID DIESEL NTC-290 (290 HP @ 2100 RPM)

DASH

72 -73

(SOME '71-STYLE TRACTORS AVAIL. THROUGH '76.)

The hydraulic 90° tilt cab is nothing new to White Freightliner. In fact, we were the first to develop it. And in the years since, we've improved it to the point of perfection. In seconds, the cab is tilted to a full 90°, or stops and locks anywhere in between. Our tilt cab gives you the ultimate in access and ease of service.

new **GRILLE,** *new* **STYLE** OF **NAMEPLATE (SOME MODELS, '72.)**

('72) **RADIATOR FILLER UNDER TILTING NAMEPLATE**

163

Freightliner

CONVENTIONAL

WITH FIBERGLASS TILT-HOOD

WHITE FREIGHTLINER

FINAL USE OF COMBINED

White Freightliner NAME

74-75

NEW CONVENTIONAL

JOINS C.O.E. MODELS

WHITE FREIGHTLINER

164

FREIGHTLINER

"WHITE" PREFIX NAME NO LONGER APPLIED.

STD. C.O.E.

FREIGHTLINER

↗ THIS STYLE OF C.O.E. "POWERLINER" AVAILABLE FALL, 1973.

1978 TYPES: FLC-12042-T; FLC-12064-T; FLC-12064. COEs: FLT-6342-T; FLT-7564-T; FLT-6364. POWERLINER COEs: FLP-6342-T; FLP-7564-T; FLP-6364 (250-600 HP DIESEL ENGINES)

('83)

76 ON

CONVENTIONAL

FREIGHTLINER

CF CONSOLIDATED FREIGHTWAYS

CF

FREIGHTLINER

16-5524

SHOWN WITH INSIGNIA OF PARENT COMPANY ↙

(The **CF** Company)

80 S

('84)

2 OR 4 HDLTS. AVAIL.

FULTON TRUCK (1916—1925)

THE FULTON MOTOR TRUCK COMPANY
OFFICES: 1710 BROADWAY, NEW YORK
FACTORY: FARMINGDALE, L. I.

Canadian Distribution by Grace Motors Ltd., Toronto, Canada.   Export: Fulton Motors Export Co., 1710 Broadway, N.Y.

THERMO-
SYPHON
COOLING
SYSTEM

4-CYLINDER
HERSCHELL-
SPILLMAN
ENGINES
(TO '24)

CARTER CARB.
(TO '24)

FORMER
1919
MODEL
"FX"
RATED AT
1½ TONS,
with 136"WB
SOLID TIRES
34×3 FRONT
34×5 REAR
18 M.P.H. (@
1800 RPM)

MODEL C (1920) INTRO. JUNE, 1919 (ILLUS. ABOVE)

PLAINER
RADIATOR
ON
"A"

new MODELS FOR 1920 SEASON, CONTINUED
THROUGH 1925.

CHARACTERISTIC
ROUNDED
RADIATOR

('21)

"FULL-TON EXPRESS"

('20)

EASY TO
IDENTIFY

MODEL A

1 TON
130" WB (THROUGH '25)
6.8 GEAR RATIO (THROUGH '22)
8.8 GEAR RATIO (1925)

35 × 5 PNEUMATIC
TIRES
35 M.P.H.

MODEL C

2 TON
137" WB
(THROUGH '25)
10.20 G.R. ('21) 10.80 ('22)

SOLID TIRES
34 × 4 (FRONT)
34 × 6 (REAR)
25 M.P.H.
40 HORSEPOWER

20-25

MODEL D TRUCK-TRACTOR
VARIATION OF "C,"
AVAIL. 1920-1922
(1922 MODEL D INCREASED
FROM 2 TO 4½ TON
RATING.)

1925 "A" and "C" MODELS
BOTH HAVE 4-CYL. BUDA "WTU"
ENGINE (3¾" × 5⅛" B. + S.)
and ZENITH CARB.
and SIMMS ELEC. SYSTEM

(SINCE 1912)

FWD Trucks

(4-WHEEL DRIVE)

**FWD CORPORATION
CLINTONVILLE, WIS. 54929**

('17)

('20)

105"-WB TRUCK-TRACTOR
ALSO AVAIL. IN '26, and
"ROAD-BUILDER" 3-TON
DUMP TRUCK, '24-25.

3 TON
MODEL B
124" WB
4-CYLINDER
WISCONSIN ENG.

1920s

MODEL B

TOWN PLEASAN VALLZ
NEW YO

('27)

MODEL B HAS OWN 4-CYL. ENG.
IN 1927. SMALLER 1½-TON "H"
(with 121" WB) INTRODUCED, USING
4-CYL. WISC. ENGINE.

1929 MODELS :

H, HT	2 TON	120"WB	4 CYL.	WISCONSIN ENG.
B, M	3, 3½	124	6	OWN ENG.
U-6	3½	148	6	WAUKESHA "
MF6, X6	5, 5½	170	6	" "

(HORIZONTAL LOUVRES,
LONGER HOODS)

with SNOW PLOW
('28)

CA. 1934

SHORT
CONVENT.

1930s

(C.O.E.)

('38-'42)   C.O.E.

TANKER AND TRAILER

167

('39)

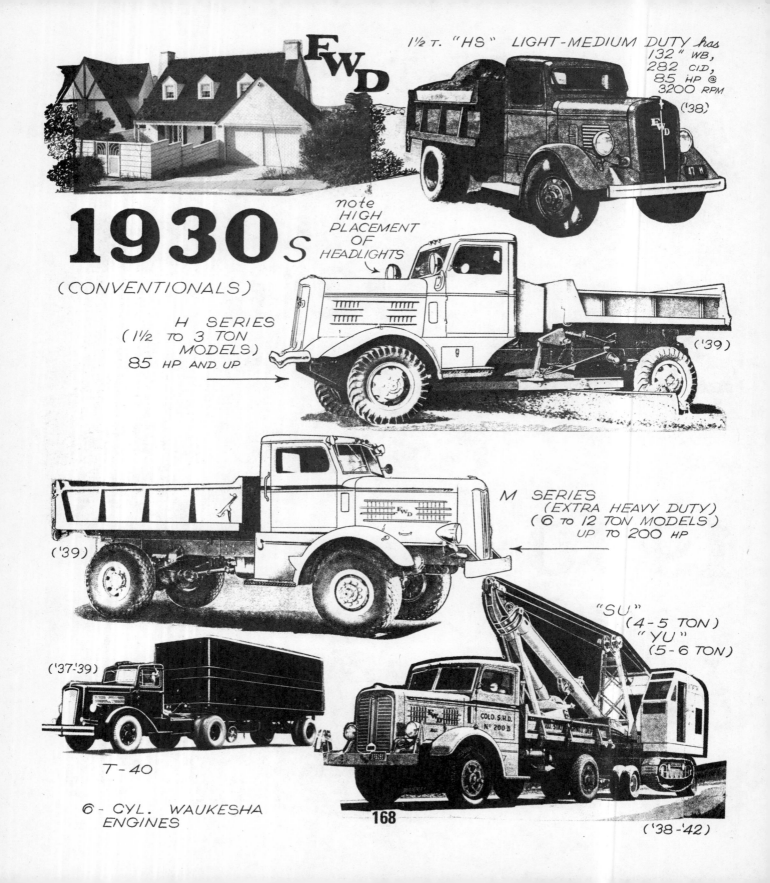

FWD

1½ T. "HS" LIGHT-MEDIUM DUTY has 132" WB, 282 CID, 85 HP @ 3200 RPM ('38)

1930s

(CONVENTIONALS)

note HIGH PLACEMENT OF HEADLIGHTS

H SERIES (1½ TO 3 TON MODELS) 85 HP AND UP

('39)

M SERIES (EXTRA HEAVY DUTY) (6 TO 12 TON MODELS) UP TO 200 HP

('39)

"SU" (4-5 TON) "YU" (5-6 TON)

('37-'39)

T-40

6-CYL. WAUKESHA ENGINES

COLO. S.H.D. No 200-B

('38-'42)

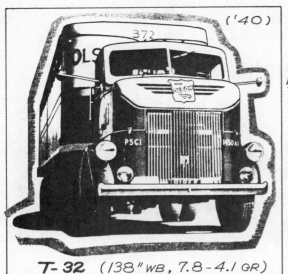

('40)

372

T-32 (138" WB, 7.8-4.1 GR)
$ 3995.
6-CYL.
(91 HP @ 2100 RPM)   381 CID
"MKR" WAUKESHA ENG.

1940s

MILITARY

WORLD WAR II   ('46)

48   MODELS: HA, HR, HG,
SU, M7, M7-D,
M10-D
6-WH.-DR.: M6×6, M6×6D
320-779 CID WAUKESHA GAS OR 844 CID
BUDA DIESEL ENGINES (104-186 HP)
(ALL 6-CYL.)   132-182" WB

EWD   "D" SUFFIX ON MODEL NUMBER
MEANS DIESEL-POWERED.
('46 ON)

1940 WAUKESHA 6-CYL. ENGINES USED:

# BK	282 CID	85 HP @ 3200 RPM	IN MODELS HS, T26
MKR	381	91 @ 2400	IN HH6, T32
MZR	404	96 @ 2400	CUA, CU
SRLR	462	112 @ 2400	SUA, SU
SRKR	517	126 @ 2400	MJ5, MJ6, MJ6×6, T40
RBR	677	152 @ 2400	M7, M6×6, T45

ALSO, HERCULES 6 CYL., 935 CID ENGINE (HXE)
IN MODEL M-10   (198 HP @ 2000 RPM)

CUMMINS DIESEL ENGINES
AVAILABLE IN SOME
POSTWAR MODELS.

36th Year

YU, ZU, M10 GAS-POWERED
MODELS ADDED FOR 1949.
ZU has 188 HP @ 2600 RPM.

FIRE TRUCK

FWD

('52)

1950s

NUMEROUS MODELS ADDED
TO FWD LINE DURING 1950s.

('54)

1954 MODELS : 141, 170, 220, 223-D, 262,
264-D, M262, M264-D,
T273, T285, T286, T284-D, T288-D, 323,
324, 324-D, 327-D, 365, 366, 368-D, A369,
408, 409, 406-D, 409-D, 509, 506-D, 509-D,
ALSO, 6-W-D MODELS *with* 6, L6, or G6
PRECEDING MODEL NO.

HERCULES, WAUKESHA, GMC or CUMMINS
ENGINES (6-CYL., EXC. FOR CERTAIN 4-CYL.
GMC DIESELS. 6-CYL. GMC DIESELS ALSO.)
97 to 240 HP

('55)
TERACRUZER
8 × 8
DRIVE

→

The first FWD 8x8 Teracruzers built for commercial service have been delivered to the Pak-Stanvac Petroleum Project in East Pakistan. The highly specialized Teracruzers and specially built trailers are being used to haul full loads of oil well drilling equipment and supplies in monsoon climate areas inaccessible to conventional vehicles.

The secret of the Teracruzer's maneuverability lies in its unique eight-wheel drive system, its superior articulation, its small turning radius, the very low ground pressure which results from the special characteristics of the design, and the ability to adjust immediately to changing terrain conditions by automatically deflating and inflating each tire separately from the cab.

1957 MODELS : 140 ; U-150;
181 ; 182 ;
202 ; 232 ; 233D ; 284 ;
M284D ; M284 ; 284D ;
285 ; 285D ; M285 ; 305 ;
326 ; 324D ; 327D ; 367 ;
368D ; S326 ; S324D ;
408 ; 409 ; 406D ;
409 D
6-WHEELERS *have* 6,
R6, T, TS, C6 or CS6
PREFIXES

DUETZ,
INT., GMC, CUMMINS OR WAUKESHA ENGINES
USED (240 to 779 CID, 3, 4, 6 or 8 CYLS.,
102 to 240 HP IN 1957.

57

58

3, 4, 6, 8 CYL. MODELS with GMC, INT., CUMMINS DIESEL, WAUKESHA, OR DEUTZ AIR-COOLED DIESEL ENGINES.
213 TO 779 CID
102 TO 240 HP

130" TO 161" WB

PRODUCTION :
1,227 ('58)
1,067 ('59)

TRACTIONEER MODELS FIRST APPEAR IN 1958.

HEAVY-DUTY VEHICLE SPECIALISTS

PROD.: 881 ('60)
989 ('61)
1,029 ('62)
827 ('63)

FWD®

VEHICLES FOR
OIL FIELDS
UTILITIES
* FIRE FIGHTING
CONSTRUCTION
ROAD MAINTENANCE
CRANE CARRIERS
TRANSPORT
READY MIX
LOGGING
MILITARY

(VARIOUS 1958 MODELS ABOVE)

1960s

1,123 ('64)
1,496 ('65)
1,619 ('66)

* STARTING MAY 1, 1962, FWD NO LONGER BUILT NON-MILITARY COMPLETE FIRE TRUCKS, BUT SUPPLIED F.T. CHASSES FOR OTHER MFRS., SUCH AS SEAGRAVE. FWD BOUGHT SEAGRAVE IN 1963 AND CONTINUED TO PRODUCE SEAGRAVE FIRE TRUCKS.

"TRACTIONEER" MIXER TRUCKS

WAUKESHA

('66)

MODEL C6-6461

171

FWD

LATER
1960s
with T.L. SMITH 10-YARD MIXER

MODEL C88-4479
8-WHEEL DRIVE
(ABOVE)

ARROW

FRONT
DETAILS OF
CONVENTIONAL
(TYPE WITH
OPEN GRILLE)

PROD. :
1, 251 ('67)
1, 233 ('68)
1, 403 ('69)
1, 093 ('70)

MIXER TRUCKS OF
VARIOUS
WHEEL ARRANGEMENTS
ARE
ILLUSTRATED.

335 HORSEPOWER CUMMINS DIESEL ENGINE

13-SPEED TRANSMISSION

with 15-YARD MONTONE ALUMINUM DUMP BODY

FWD

11.00 x 24 TIRES

TRACTIONEER

70-71 ON

GENERAL BLOCK & SUPPLY CO.

CONCRETE BLOCK CARRIERS (ILLUSTRATED WITH and WITHOUT TRAILER)

(CONT'D. NEXT PAGE)

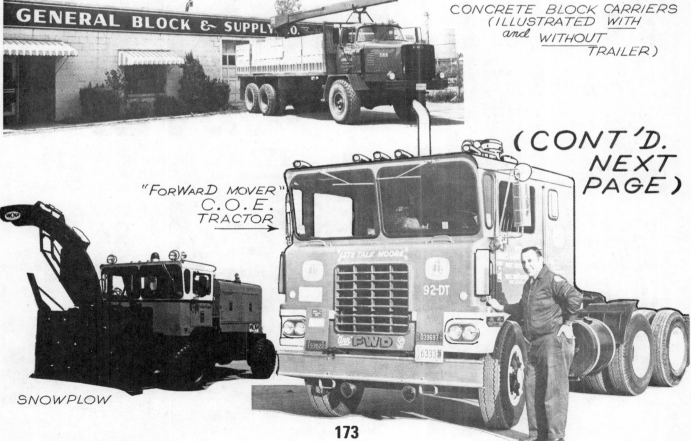

"ForWarD MOVER" C.O.E. TRACTOR →

SNOWPLOW

('70)

150 TO 300 HP GAS, OR 130 TO 300 HP DIESELS (6 OR V-6)

FWD CORPORATION

tractioneer

6X6

(ABOVE)

70-71

ON

(CONT'D.

"FWD" ON DIFFERENTIAL

"FORWARD **mover**"

MODEL B5-2116 6 × 4 LIGHTWEIGHT (FOR MED./HVY. USE)

CF C.O.E. HAS FIBERGLASS/PLASTIC BODY SHELL and FENDERS (METAL DOORS)

DESIGNED FOR MIXER/DUMPER SERVICE (AS ILLUSTR. AT UPPER RT.)

"FWD" ABOVE GRILLE

"FORWARD MOVER" NAMEPLATE IS ON HOOD.

CAB/CHASSIS OF "FORWARD MOVER" MODEL B5-2116 6×4 LTWT.

174

CF ('71)

B, LB ('72)

FWD

B & LB SERIES

C

C SERIES

D

D SERIES

C5-2178

C5-2178

FWD adds conventional and COE tractors

('72)

116" BBC

WITH MERCURY 30" SLEEPER BOX

HEAVY-DUTY

WITH AFTER-COOLED CUMMINS 350 DIESEL ENGINES

SINCE **72**

CA-64 CONVENTIONALS

84" BBC WITH SLEEPER CAB   CO-64   ('72)

CB 4 × 4

('74)

1978 LINE INCLUDES RB and CB CONVENTIONALS OR DF (C.O.E.) W. DIESEL ENGINES OF 195 TO 350 HP MANY CUSTOM-BUILT VARIETIES IN RECENT YEARS.

CF SERIES

DF SERIES

CF   DF

tractioneer ®

4 X 4

RB 4 × 4

truck

TRACTOR

('74)   *tractioneer*

C SERIES   ALL-WHEEL DRIVE ('74)

WITH LOW BED DUMP BODY and HYDRAULICS FOR PLOWING OPERATIONS.

175

GARFORD

1920s

(1909 – 1933)
GARFORD MOTOR
TRUCK CO.,
LIMA, OHIO

CHASSIS
PRICES
LISTED

3½ *Ton* "77-D" 162" WB
$4390.

('21)

2-TON "70-H" 144" WB
$3450.

1¼ TON "25" 135" WB
$2290.

('21)

5-TON "68-D" 162" WB
$5200.

('21)

Garford 5-ton Truck

"51-D" 4-CYL.
25-29 PASS. BUS CHASSIS
187" WB
$4350.

('24)

1-TON "15" 132" WB
CHASSIS ('24)
$1590.

"KB"
17-PASSENGER COACH
6 CYL., 180" WB CHASSIS
('25)

(3³/₈" x 5"
BORE and STR.)
32 x 6"
TIRES

GARFORD BUS ('25)
SINGLE-DOOR STYLE

GARFORD GREYHOUND 17-PASS.
PARLOR CAR BUS   180" WB

('26)

MULTI-DOOR STYLE

1½-2 TON "30" 144" WB
4 CYL.

('28)

MODEL 50
2½ TON
156" WB

RELAY MOTORS
BUYS
GARFORD,
SEPT., 1927.

CHASSIS $2690.

MERGER

GARFORD GREYHOUND
19-PASS.
PARLOR CAR
BUS ('28)

180" WB

('29)

COMMERCE–GARFORD–
SERVICE 2 TON "40-Z"
(RELAY TRUCK SIMILARLY
STYLED)

DEC., 1932
RELAY GROUP
GOES INTO
RECEIVERSHIP.
CONSOLIDATED MOTORS BUYS ASSETS.

176

BUICK 6 ENGS. IN T-20 and T-40
MEDIUM-DUTY MODELS. LT. DELIV.
KNOWN AS PONTIAC
('27) IN '27.
PONTIAC 6
ENG. IN
'28.

('28)

"T20-A"
CHASSIS
132" WB

27-29
TRUCKS
*new RADIATOR SHELL
DESIGN, with
SEPERATE EMBLEM.*

42 MODELS in 1929,
UP TO 15-TON
"BIG BRUTE."

1929
MODELS

DUMP
TRUCK

FINAL 4-CYL.
HEAVY DUTY
MODELS IN 1929.

PANEL
DELIVERY

1½ TON Range $960

2 TON Range $1545

1 TON Range $745

2½ TON Range $1845

¾ TON Range $695

3 TON Range $2080

½ TON Range $625

3½ TON Range $3035

1½ TON Range $1265
Super-power

4 TON Range $3795

six-cylinder

Service Station
OF
1930,
WITH

30

T-60-B
TANKER

395
choices

THIS
"T-60-B"
3½-TON
TANKER has
94 HP ENG.

UNION COAL CO.
COAL

5 TON Range $5885
Six-wheeler

TRACTORS up
to 15 Tons

"T-82-A" 4-TON
DUMP TRUCK
94 HP

178

(CONT'D.
NEXT PAGE)

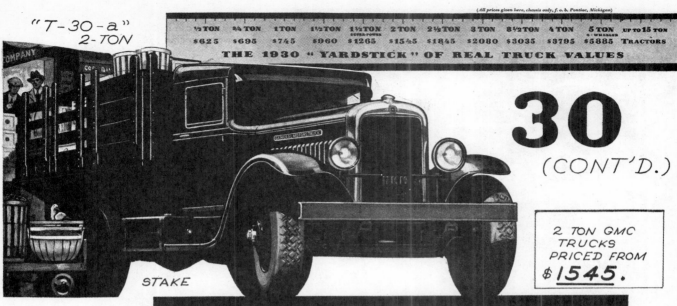

(All prices given here, chassis only, f. o. b. Pontiac, Michigan)

½ TON	¾ TON	1 TON	1½ TON	1½ TON SUPER-POWER	2 TON	2½ TON	3 TON	3½ TON	4 TON	5 TON 6-WHEELER	UP TO 15 TON
$625	$695	$745	$960	$1265	$1545	$1845	$2080	$3035	$3795	$5885	Tractors

THE 1930 "YARDSTICK" OF REAL TRUCK VALUES

30
(CONT'D.)

2 TON GMC
TRUCKS
PRICED FROM
$ **1545.**

STAKE

PANEL DELIVERY

(T 31 and T-45 HAVE 257.5 CID 6 , 76 HP @ 2500 RPM)

The Truck and Coach Division of General Motors

GMC

ALL MODELS *with*
6 CYLINDERS
(THROUGH '54)

31-
32

(9-31:
new
"T-18"
INTRO., W.
SIMILAR SPECS.
TO T-19.)

('31) 1½ - 2 TON "T-19-a"
WITH
200.3 CID 6, 60 HP

MODEL "U"
BUS ('32)

9-32: *new* GMT "400"
ENG. (400.9 CID 6)
112½ HP @ 2800 RPM, FOR
T-61, T-83, 6-WHEEL T-90

AT RT.: "T-26" ('31)
2-3 TON RANGE ↑

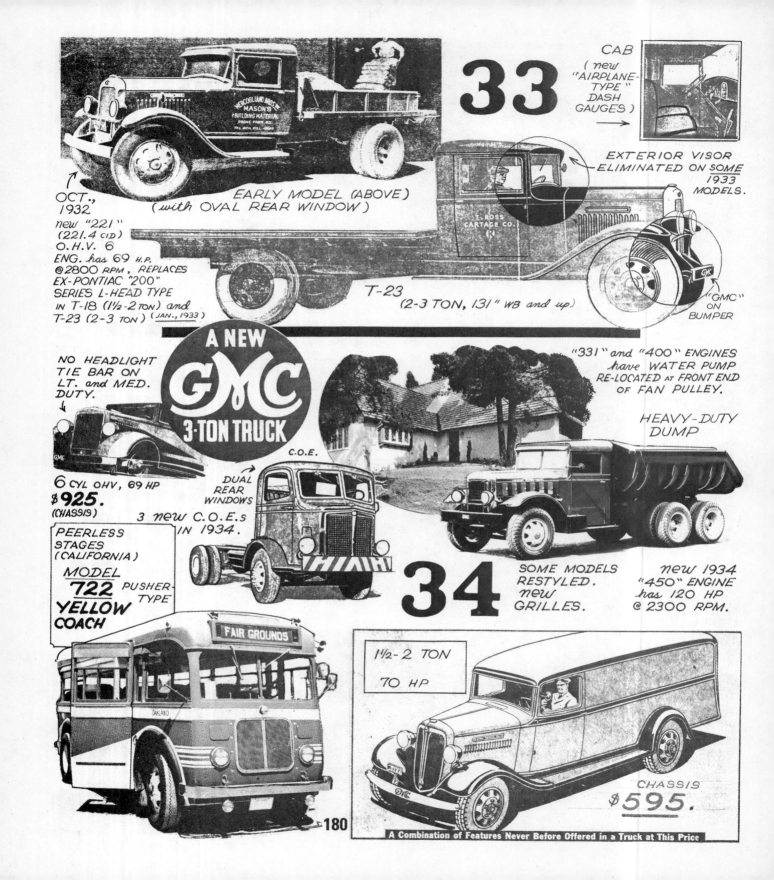

CAB
(new "AIRPLANE-TYPE" DASH GAUGES) →

33

EARLY MODEL (ABOVE)
(with OVAL REAR WINDOW)

OCT., 1932

new "221" (221.4 CID) O.H.V. 6 ENG. has 69 H.P. @ 2800 RPM, REPLACES EX-PONTIAC "200" SERIES L-HEAD TYPE in T-18 (1½-2 TON) and T-23 (2-3 TON) (JAN., 1933)

EXTERIOR VISOR ELIMINATED ON SOME 1933 MODELS.

T-23
(2-3 TON, 131" WB and up)

"GMC" ON BUMPER

A NEW GMC 3-TON TRUCK

NO HEADLIGHT TIE BAR ON LT. and MED. DUTY.

6 CYL OHV, 69 HP
$925.
(CHASSIS)

"331" and "400" ENGINES have WATER PUMP RE-LOCATED AT FRONT END OF FAN PULLEY.

HEAVY-DUTY DUMP

C.O.E.
DUAL REAR WINDOWS

3 new C.O.E.s IN 1934.

34

SOME MODELS RESTYLED. new GRILLES.

new 1934 "450" ENGINE has 120 HP @ 2300 RPM.

PEERLESS STAGES (CALIFORNIA)
MODEL **722** PUSHER-TYPE
YELLOW COACH

FAIR GROUNDS
OAKLAND

1½-2 TON
70 HP

CHASSIS
$595.

180

A Combination of Features Never Before Offered in a Truck at This Price

1½-2 TON **T-16** / **CAB**

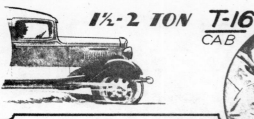

The Truck and Coach Division of General Motors

GMC

NEW for 1935,
HYDRAULIC BRAKES ON ALL LT.
and MEDIUM-DUTY GMC TRUCKS
SLOPING GRILLE
FENDER-MOUNTED HEADLIGHTS

IN ADDITION TO "T-16" and "T-18,"
MODELS ALSO INCLUDE :

T-23	2½ to 3 TON	221 CID	
T-33	3 TO 4½	257	
T-43	3½ TO 5	"	$1795
T-46 (H)	4 TO 6½	331	2625
T-51 (W,H)	4 TO 6½	"	3095
T-61	5 TO 6½	400	4395
T-83	6 TO 8	"	5185
T-84	7 TO 10	450	5760
T-84-SX	7½ TON	"	

C.O.E. MODELS :

T-73 (H)	3 TO 4½ TON	
T-74 (H)	3½ TO 5½	
T-75 (T,H)	5 TO 13	
T-78 (T)	7 AND UP	

(1935 SPECS.)

note VARIATIONS IN GRILLES and HOOD LOUVRES

35

DUMP TRUCK

2 to 3 ton **T-18**
140" W.B. (UP TO 164" AVAIL.)
221 CID 6
CHASSIS FROM **$777.**

"T-16"
EARLY MODEL
with
1934-STYLE
CAB ROOF

213 C.I.D., 6 CYL.
L-HEAD engine
IN
"T-16"
1½-2 TON
131" W.B.
(UP TO 157"
AVAIL.)

GENERAL MOTORS TRUCK

D-7533

ALL BUT "T-16" MODELS have 6-CYL.
OVERHEAD-VALVE ENGINES OF
221, 257, 331, 400 OR
450 C.I.D.

new **T-46** 5 TON
INTRO. JULY, 1934
WITH "331" ENGINE
94 HP @ 2500 RPM
$2135. and up

"DUAL-PERFORMANCE"
2-SPEED REAR AXLES
(5.14 and 7.15 GEAR RATIOS)
AVAILABLE ON LATE '35
1½-2-TON MODELS

"T-16"
LATER MODEL 1½-
2-TON with "BLISTER"
VISOR on CAB, and
SMALL VERTICAL
HOOD LOUVRES and
84 H.P. @ 3500 RPM
FROM **$976.** (TACOMA, WASH.)

CAPACITIES UP TO 22 TONS

181

1931-VINTAGE SERV. STA., COMMONLY SEEN IN 1936.

The Truck and Coach Division of General Motors

GMC

$425. 1/2 TON NEW CHASSIS
T-14
213 CID 6

V WINDSHLD.

EARLY MODEL

PANEL-STAKE 1 1/2-2 T. CHAS. FROM $525.

36

new 1/2-TON PANEL DELIVERY (LATER MODEL DOES NOT HAVE "BLISTER" VISOR ABOVE WINDSHIELD.)

325 GM/YELLOW "719" BUSES BLT. FOR GREYHOUND. (SEE GREYHOUND)

CAPACITIES UP TO 15 TONS

new 239 CID 6 IN T-18, T-18H ALSO 257, 286, 331, 400 and 450 CID ENGS.

NEW GRILLE

"DUAL PERFORMANCE" REAR AXLES NOW AVAIL. IN 1 1/2 TO 6-TON RANGE.

new "DUAL TONE" COLOR DESIGNS

"HELMET-TOP" CAB

C.O.E. PANEL-STAKE

300 "720" and "725" REAR-ENG. DOUBLE DECK BUSES BLT. 1936 TO 1938. (160 FOR NYC, 140 FOR CHICAGO.)

3 MODELS OF 2-WHEEL UTILITY TRAILERS AVAIL. FROM GMC (ALSO IN '38) { OPEN EXPRESS SCREEN-SIDE " { STAKE

new LOW-PRICED 1 1/2-TON C.O.E. TRUCK ($830., f.o.b., for chassis and cab; $635., f.o.b., chassis only.)

37

PICKUPS and PANELS ON 112 OR 126" WB

(INTRO. LATE '36)

The GREYHOUND LINES

INTER-CITY BUS (BLT. FOR GREYHOUND)

GM/YELLOW "743" (1250 BLT., '37-'39) '36 "719" SIMILAR, BUT WITH VERTICAL VENTS BY DESTINATION SIGN.) TRUCK
CAPACITIES UP TO 12 TONS

67302

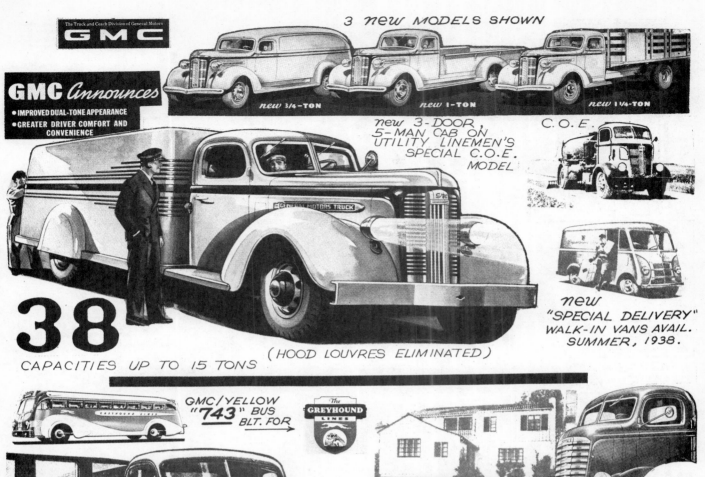

The Truck and Coach Division of General Motors

GMC

3 *new* MODELS SHOWN

new 3/4-TON   *new* 1-TON   *new* 1¼-TON

GMC *Announces*
- IMPROVED DUAL-TONE APPEARANCE
- GREATER DRIVER COMFORT AND CONVENIENCE

new 3-DOOR, 5-MAN CAB ON UTILITY LINEMEN'S SPECIAL C.O.E. MODEL

C.O.E.

new "SPECIAL DELIVERY" WALK-IN VANS AVAIL. SUMMER, 1938.

38
CAPACITIES UP TO 15 TONS

(HOOD LOUVRES ELIMINATED)

GMC/YELLOW "743" BUS BLT. FOR → **The GREYHOUND LINES**

new 10–12–15-TON DUMP MODELS AVAIL. AUGUST, 1939.

C.O.E.

THE TRUCK **GMC** OF VALUE

39
new "228" GMC O.H.V. ENGINES IN ½-TON (80 H.P. @ 3000 RPM)

new GRILLE →

GENERAL MOTORS TRUCK

new C.O.E. MODELS (1½ TO 8 TONS)

New TRUCKS 183 | 7 O.H.V. *New* ENGINES "SUPER-DUTY" | 12 *New* DIESELS 3½ TONS and up | *New* SYNCRO-MESH TRANSMISSION ON MEDIUM AND HEAVY-DUTY MODELS

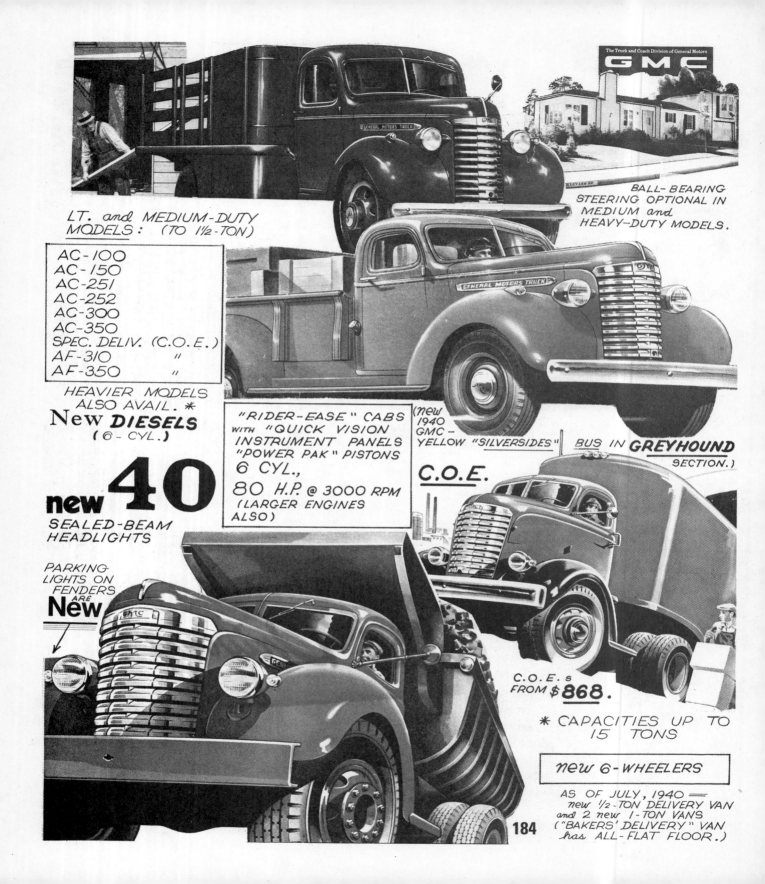

The Truck and Coach Division of General Motors

GMC

BALL-BEARING STEERING OPTIONAL IN MEDIUM and HEAVY-DUTY MODELS.

LT. and MEDIUM-DUTY MODELS: (TO 1½-TON)

AC-100
AC-150
AC-251
AC-252
AC-300
AC-350
SPEC. DELIV. (C.O.E.)
AF-310   "
AF-350   "

HEAVIER MODELS ALSO AVAIL. *

New **DIESELS** (6-CYL.)

new **40** SEALED-BEAM HEADLIGHTS

PARKING LIGHTS ON FENDERS ARE **New**

"RIDER-EASE" CABS WITH "QUICK VISION INSTRUMENT PANELS "POWER PAK" PISTONS 6 CYL., 80 H.P. @ 3000 RPM (LARGER ENGINES ALSO)

(new 1940 GMC - YELLOW "SILVERSIDES" BUS IN **GREYHOUND** SECTION.)

C.O.E.

C.O.E.s FROM $**868**.

* CAPACITIES UP TO 15 TONS

new 6-WHEELERS

AS OF JULY, 1940 ═ new ½-TON DELIVERY VAN and 2 new 1-TON VANS ("BAKERS' DELIVERY" VAN has ALL-FLAT FLOOR.)

184

115" TO 160" WB
new 228 SIX
AVAIL. 6-41
(93 HP)

(TYPE ENDS MID-1947.)

new GRILLES (LT. DUTY'S WIDER)
new PARK. LT. POSITION.*
new "236" (97 HP) ENGINE.
"CRADLE-COIL"
SEATS.

TRACTOR-
TRAILER
W. DUAL
REAR
WH.
('41)

C.O.E.
("CF")
('46)

IN 1947, OLD TYPE NEWSPAPER TRUCK STILL MFD.

TANKER

WITH NEW PARK. LTS.
('42)

* HVY.-DUTY DOESN'T GET PARKING LTS. ATOP HDLTS. UNTIL 1942.

MILITARY TRUCK ('42)

('47)

CC-101   ½ TON
CC-152   ¾ "
CC-262,3 1 "
CC-302, 303,
    304   1½ TON
C.O.E.s :
CF-301, 302, 303
    (353, '41) 1½ TON
1 TON CH. TO CF-252, '42
CC-102 ADDED 1946 :
    (½ TON PANEL, 125" WB)
(OTHER HVY. DUTY
        MODELS ALSO)
EC, EF (CONV., C.O.E.)
IN 1947.

GMC TRUCKS

Two GMCs team up on the tough job of loading and hauling heavy 36 inch pipe for an irrigation project.

185

GMC

INTER - CITY
BUS
GREYHOUND.

New GMC Postwar Cab

('48)

REAR WINDOW VISION
INCREASED 60%

WINDSHIELD VISION
INCREASED 20%

DOOR OPENINGS
FOUR INCHES WIDER

FAMOUS BALL
BEARING STEERING

3-POINT CAB
MOUNTING AND
RUBBER STABILIZERS

EASIER CLUTCH
PEDAL ACTION

SEATING WIDTH
INCREASED 8 INCHES

CIRCULATING FRESH
AIR VENTILATION

73 INDIVIDUALLY
WRAPPED SPRINGS

PD - 4103 ('49-53)

TRAILWAYS

TUBULAR FRAMED
ADJUSTABLE SEATS

GMC's new cabs circulate fresh air by a revolutionary ventilating system. And you can have forced air heating and defrosting, too, if desired.

TOTALLY
RESTYLED
LT. DUTY
1948
MODEL
STARTS
SUMMER,'47.

48-53

DIESEL COACHES—In 1938, less than 200 Diesel-powered motor coaches were in operation. By 1948, the number had multiplied to over 18,000. GMC Diesel coach production has accounted for more than 90 per cent of the industry's total.

New

BOTH 4 and 6 CYL.
DIESEL ENGINES
AVAIL. 1948.

('50)

55 - PASS. CITY BUS ('49)

DIESELS RESTYLED
LIKE OTHER
GMCs IN
1950. HEAVY-DUTY
GASOLINE MODELS
RESTYLED ALSO.
PRE – 1950 TYPE
DIESEL SHOWN
AT RIGHT ——→

GMC Diesel trucks are powered by engines of the same basic design as the Diesel locomotives which pull many of the nation's finest, fastest trains.

This advanced and exclusive GM 2-cycle design cuts Diesel weight without sacrifice of power, thus permitting greater payloads. It also provides outstanding fuel economy, low maintenance costs, exceptional dependability and long life.

GMCs are the only Diesel trucks offering a choice of four- and six-cylinder engines . . . specially engineered Diesel chassis . . . a selection of eight series of models. And, more important, GMC has had unequalled experience in equipping vehicles with these modern, time and money saving Diesel power plants.

GMC TRUCK & COACH DIVISION · GENERAL MOTORS

DIESEL TRUCKS—In 1938, less than 500 Diesel trucks were in service. By 1948, the number had jumped to more than 12,000. In recent months, GMC has produced nearly 30 per cent of the industry's total. Shown is a GMC six-cylinder, 200-horsepower Diesel tractor.

GM
GENERAL MOTORS
COACH

GMC
TRUCKS

186

LOAD CLEARANCE ANTENNA

PANEL TRUCK

SUBURBAN

GMC

HEAVY DUTY

TRACTOR-TRAILER (C.O.E.)

FLEET CARRIER CORP.

('54)

new GRILLE ON 1958 LT. DUTY (ABOVE) NO BUMPER PODS ON LT. DUTY 1959s.

1958

Greyhound

HWY. TRAVELER

54- 59

('54)

TRAILWAYS

SCENICRUISER

Greyhound

G R E Y H O U N D

TRUCK PRODUCTION : 64,216 ('58) 77,473 ('59)

MODEL 374 FLATBED ('59)

CANOPY EXPRESS ('54) 137" WB

('58-59)

DR-860 DIESEL 189 H.P.

187

D-860

GMC

('59)

('59)

59-63

new 72" BBC C.O.E.
TILT-CABS ('60) FROM
19,500 LBS. G.V.W.

BELOW:
"NEW LOOK"
RESTYLED
CITY
TRANSIT
BUS
FOR
1960s

TYPE AVAIL.
1959-1977

NOTE
LOW
WINDSHIELD

DLR-8000 LIGHTWT. ALUMINUM
TILT-CAB (with 6-71 SE GMC
DIESEL ENGINE)

New

('60)

AT
RIGHT,
SHOWN
WITH
LOAD OF
LARGE
NEWS-
PRINT
PAPER
ROLLS →

PROD:
104,310
('60)

74,996
('61)

('63)

CAPACITIES UP TO 60 TONS

188

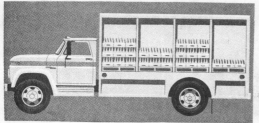

BOTTLER'S TRUCK

UTILITY

TRACTOR / TRLR.

Medium-Ton Trucks

DUMP TRUCK ('64)

64-68

TILT-CAB C.O.E.

('64)

LIGHT-DUTY

('66)

('67)

Buses

('64)

4106
(ADDITIONAL BUS DETAILS IN **GREYHOUND** SECTION.)

New

FOR MED. TON TKS. IN '64.

...only GMC Trucks have V-6 engines

(305 CID V-6)

('65)
4106

('66)

60 PASS. SCHOOL BUS →

1966 GMC Model SV4019

PD 4107

Toro-Flow Diesel Engine

189

GMC

Stake Model

Steel Tilt Model

PD-4107 ('69)

69-72

(1972 EXAMPLES SHOWN)

Conventional

(CONT'D. NEXT PAGE)

195, 217 OR 229 HP ('72)

INTERIOR

Series 7500 Conventional

401 OR 478 CID V6 GAS ENG. OR 318 CID DETROIT DIESEL 6V-53N ENGINE (ILLUSTRATED)

('72)

The Truck People from General Motors

GMC

Series 9500

Conventional Heavy Duty

69-72 (CONT'D.)
(1972 EXAMPLES SHOWN)

WITH OPTIONAL GRILLE GUARD

9500

ASTRO 95 Tilt Cab
C.O.E.

ASTRO 95

Available RPM and MPH Sangamo instruments are located in bezels provided for standard tach and odometer. Both units are placed for rapid reading.

191

GMC

PUSHER TYPE SCHOOL BUS CHASSIS

(GENERALLY SIMILAR TO MOST GMC SCHOOL BUSES OF 1970s.)

WITH FULL AIR BRAKES

WITH 2 AIR RESERVOIRS

73

130 to 200 NET HP

MODEL	RM-7500	RM-7500	RM-7500
WB—WHEELBASE, IN.	172	227	255
**OL—OVERALL LENGTH, IN.	354	409	437

REFER TO LOAD CAPACITY CHART IN DATA BOOK OR OWNERS AND DRIVERS MANUAL FOR MINIMUM EQUIPMENT REQUIRED FOR MAXIMUM GVW.
**ADD 3½" FOR OVERHANG OF TAILPIPE.

WITH ALLISON 4-SPEED MT-640G AUTOMATIC TRANS. AVAIL. (PUSHER CHASSIS)

Cowl Model

NOW 4 WARN. LTS. ABOVE WINDSHIELD

MODEL	SE -6000	SE -6000	SE -6000	SE -6000
				SG -6000
	SM-6000	SM-6000	SM-6000	SM-6000
	SS -6000	SS -6000	SS -6000	
WB—WHEELBASE, IN.	189½	218	235½	254
LA—STD. COWL FACE TO REAR AXLE, IN.	165½	194	211½	230
LE—STD. COWL FACE TO END OF FRAME, IN.	267¾	294¼	322¾	349
*OL—BUMPER TO END OF FRAME, IN.	322¼	349¼	377¼	403½

REFER TO LOAD CAPACITY CHART IN DATA BOOK OR OWNERS AND DRIVERS MANUAL FOR MINIMUM EQUIPMENT REQUIRED FOR MAXIMUM GVW.
* ADD 5" FOR OVERHANG OF TAILPIPE.

Chassis

(HORSEPOWER DECREASED FROM 1972 FIG.)

1973 Engine Specifications

ENGINE TYPE	CUBIC INCH DISPLACEMENT	NET SAE HP @ RPM	NET SAE TORQUE (Lbs. Ft.) @ RPM	BORE & STROKE	COMPRESSION RATIO (TO 1)
GASOLINE					
IN-LINE SIX	292	130 @ 3600	225 @ 2000	3.87 x 4.12	8.0
V-6	305	148 @ 4000	238 @ 1600	4.25 x 3.58	7.8
V-6	379	170 @ 3600	266 @ 1600	4.56 x 3.86	7.5
V-6	432	190 @ 3200	336 @ 2000	4.87 x 3.86	7.5
V-6	478	192 @ 3200	371 @ 1400	5.125 x 3.86	7.0
V-8	350	160 @ 4000	265 @ 2400	4.00 x 3.48	8.0
V-8	366	200 @ 4000	310 @ 2800	3.93 x 3.76	8.0
DIESEL					
V-6 DH 478	478	150 @ 2800	314 @ 2000	5.125 x 3.86	16.5

192

GMC TRUCK & COACH DIVISION
GENERAL MOTORS CORPORATION
Pontiac, Michigan 48053

GMC

('74)
STAKE
Cab & Chassis

3500
← THIS GRILLE USED 1973-1974 ONLY

← 1975 TO 1976 - STYLE GRILLE (LT. DUTY)

('79)

CONVENTIONAL
Series 5000, 6000 and 6500 ('73)

C-3500
('79)

('73)

73-79

INTERIOR ('74)

9500 Conventional

193

('76)

ASTRO 95

GMC DRAGFOILER

C.O.E. ('79)

('80)

BRIGADIER

WITH 2 HEADLIGHTS

GMC introduces the first really new heavy-duty conventional in years.

RADIATOR ORNAMENT

DASH

GEN'L. INTRO. DURING SUMMER OF 1976. note 4 HEAD-LIGHTS.

BUDD ALUMINUM CAB. FIBERGLASS HOOD and FENDERS.

76 ON

1977 SLOGAN: "GET TRUCKIN' - GET A GMC."

1978: "NOTHIN' GOES TRUCKIN' LIKE A GMC."

General 194 **new**

('76½)

LIGHT DUTY

('83)

GMC
80 ON

THREE NEW DIESEL OPTIONS.
GMC now offers the Detroit Diesel Allison "Fuel Pincher" and the Caterpillar 3208. And, you can order the Cummins VT-225 (not available in California) for delivery after June 1, 1980.

('81)

('81)

6000-7000 SERIES MEDIUMS

DETROIT DIESEL ALLISON "FUEL PINCHER" ENGINES DIESEL

('81)

Instrument panel with available radio and air conditioning

MEDIUM-DUTY ADVERTISED IN 1980 WITH BLACK BUMPER

CAT 3208 V8 DIESEL ENGINE

('80)

5000-6000-7000 SERIES (6000 WITH DUMP BODY IS ILLUSTR.) ('83)

TOP KICK

('81)

1979-1983 SLOGAN

195

GMC TRUCKS ARE WHAT WE'RE ALL ABOUT.

GMC A truck you can work with.

DETR. DIESEL. 6V-92TA, OTHERS AVAIL. IN

BRIGADIER SHORT CONVENTIONAL

VANDURA SEATS 16 STUDENTS OR 12 ADULTS

VANDURA SPECIAL SEATS UP TO 20 STUDENTS

84

P-3500 FC CHASSIS SEATS UP TO 30

School Bus

TRANSIT BUS

196 *BUILT ON A* **GMC** COWL MODEL SCHOOL BUS CHASSIS

GMC PICKUPS

FULL-SIZE MODELS

(ABOVE) CAB/CHASSIS WITH VAN, UTILITY, or WRECKER BODY

INSTRUMENT PANEL OF <u>SIERRA CLASSIC</u> WITH BRUSHED PEWTER-TONE CLUSTER FACE ↓

Sierra Classic Instrument panel with brushed, pewter-tone instrument cluster face

LT. DUTY HAS new GRILLE and new HEADLIGHT SETTING. COMPACT S-15 ALSO AVAIL. (MEDIUM DUTY MODELS SIMILAR TO CHEVROLET'S.)

85

FOR ENGINE CHOICES, SEE <u>CHEVROLET</u> 1985 LT. DUTY.

ALUMINUM CABS IN ASTRO and GENERAL HVY.-DUTY.

CUMMINS DIESEL ENGS. AVAIL. IN HEAVY-DUTY TYPES <u>BELOW</u>.

STD. BLACK INSTR. PANEL

C.O.E. <u>ASTRO</u>

STEEL-CAB SHORT CONVENTIONAL **BRIGADIER** ↓

CONV. <u>GENERAL</u> ↓

C-3500 CREW CAB w. DUAL RR. WHEELS

SIERRA CAB/CH. W. DUMP BODY (DUAL REAR WHEELS)

197

GMC

GRAHAM BROTHERS
(1917–1929)

1, 1½ and 2½ - TON "TRUCK-BUILDER" MODELS

CABS and REAR BODIES BUILT BY GRAHAM BROS.

GRAHAM BROTHERS EVANSVILLE, INDIANA

19-20

WITH USED CADILLAC, BUICK, WHITE DODGE BROS. OR FORD ENGINE and CHASSIS

(ILLUSTRATED WITH CADILLAC V8 CHASSIS)

6-VOLT ELECTRICAL SYSTEM (TO 1922)

21

1½-TON "A" SERIES "SPEED TRUCK" 133" W.B. $2495. (CHASSIS)

4-CYL., 3¾" × 5" CONTINENT. ENGINE USED IN 1921.

"SPEED BUS" ALSO AVAIL. ($3455.)

PNEUMATIC TIRES = 35 × 5 (FRONT) 36 × 6 (REAR)

DISC WHEELS

BUILT BY TRUCK DIVISION OF DODGE BROTHERS INC. (STARTING WITH 1922 MODEL)

4 CYL. (DB)

"121" CAB

('24)

GRAHAM BROTHERS DETROIT (EVANSVILLE PLANT RETAINED)

STOCKTON, CALIF. PLANT ADDED 1926.

The Coca-Cola Bottling Co.

('22)

1-TON HAS 140" W.B.

('22)

12-VOLT ELECTRICAL SYSTEM (TO 1927)

ACTUALLY, DODGE BROS. TRUCKS BEARING "GRAHAM BROS." NAME

('25)

1-TON PANEL

1 and 1½ TON MODELS = DODGE BROS. CHASSIS and ENG. on ALL (THROUGH '28)

('25)

17-PASS. SEDAN BUS 140" WB

$3640.

22-26

GRAHAM BROTHERS GB DETROIT

1-TON "G-BOY" CANOPY EXPRESS

('26)

198

SOLD AND SERVICED BY DODGE BROTHERS DEALERS EVERYWHERE

GRAHAM BROTHERS

Carryall Truck
TC

LC School Bus

SCREENSIDE CANOPY EXPR.

SIMILAR IN APPEARANCE TO 1926.

ACME EXPRESS

27

MODELS :
BC (1 TON)
IC, CC (1-1½)
MC, FC, LC
(1½ TON ;)
new ¾, 2-T.

A RETURN TO 6 VOLT ELECTRICAL SYSTEM DURING '27.

2-TON ALL-PURPOSE DUMP TRUCK
OC

BODY SIMILAR TO 1926 GRAHAM BROS. "STREET CAR COACH"

BURLINGTON RAPID TRANSIT COMPANY

BUSES (HIGH, LOW BODY TYPES)

BURLINGTON RAPID TRANSIT COMPANY

WITH RADIATOR SHUTTERS

27½

ON TRUCKS, new 1-PC. WINDSHIELD IMPROVED "124" 4-CYL. ENGINE new RADIATOR (ON HEAVY MODELS, CONT'D. 1928-29)

AUG., 1927 —
2-TON TRK. GETS 6-CYL. ENG., LOCKHEED HYDRAULIC BRAKES, 4-SPEED TRANSMISSION.
SEPT., 1927 — 1½ TON GETS HYDR. BR., 4-SP. TRANS.;
new ½ TON, 108" WB PANEL DELIVERY ALSO INTRO. MID - SEPT.

"AS IS" USED SPECIMEN

199

GRAHAM BROTHERS

ASSEMBLY LINE

28

108" WB and up

MODELS: (EARLY '28)
SD (½ TON;)
DD, DDX (¾ TON;)
BD, ID, IDX (1 TON;)
MD, MDX, LD, LDX (1½ TON;)
OD, ODR, ODX, TD, TDR, TDX,
ED, EDR,
EDX
(2 TON)

CHRYSLER CORP.
PURCHASES
DODGE BROS.,
SPRING, 1928.

2-TON MODELS
have 6-CYL. DODGE
3¼ × 4½
ENGINES.

$4060.

ALL MODELS
6 CYL., AS OF
SUMMER, 1928
SOME AVAIL. WITH
ATTACHED SET OF
HORIZONTAL SHUTTERS
(ON THIS STYLE
OF RADIATOR)

21-PASSENGER BUS
(STREET CAR COACH)
162" WB   6 CYLS.
(1926-1927 SIMILAR,
BUT WITH 158" WB
and 4-CYL. ENG.)

5101-M

PANEL
(new LATE SERIES)

FACTORIES AT
DETROIT; EVANSVILLE, IND.;
STOCKTON, CALIF.

R.W. ADAMS

MODELS BUILT LATE '28
CONSIDERED "1929."

STARTING JAN., 1929,
ALL DODGE BROS.
TRUCKS SOLD
WITH DODGE BROS.
OR
FARGO NAME.

200

1918 PREDECESSOR TO GREYHOUND BUS LINES (MESABI'S FLEET)

GREYHOUND Lines
WORLD'S · GREATEST MOTOR · COACH · SYSTEM

IN ADDITION TO GREYHOUND PAGES, SEE ALSO: GMC, MCI.

EARLY PICKWICK SPLIT-LEVEL COACH

('28)

TO **32**

1931 ROUTES IN USA

('29)

"OBSERVATION PLATFORM" LOOK OF REAR END SHOWS A STRONG RAILROAD INFLUENCE.

PICKWICK NITE COACH

53-PASS. DOUBLE DECK WITH REST ROOM FAC., FOOD AVAIL. ON BUS

PICKWICK'S SPECIAL NITE COACHES INTRO. FALL, '28. GREYHOUND ABSORBED PICKWICK IN 1930.

MOST '27-'30 MODELS BLT. BY WILL MOTORS CORP., MINNEAPOLIS, MINN.

THESE ODD BUSES IN REGULAR SERVICE UNTIL 1933.

SERVICE IN 1931:

SOME PICKWICK NITE COACHES WITH AERODYNAMIC SHROUD OVER RADIATOR, AND ADDITIONAL PORTHOLES ALONG THE SIDE.

These Greyhound Lines Serve the Nation

CENTRAL-GREYHOUND
E. 11 St. & Walnut Ave., Cleveland, Ohio
PENNSYLVANIA-GREYHOUND
Broad St. Station, Philadelphia, Pa.
ATLANTIC-GREYHOUND
601 Virginia St., Charleston, W. Va.
EASTERN-GREYHOUND
Nelson Tower, New York City
CAPITOL-GREYHOUND
405 American Bldg., Cincinnati, Ohio
RICHMOND-GREYHOUND
412 E. Broad St., Richmond, Va.

PACIFIC-GREYHOUND
9 Main St., San Francisco, Calif.
PICKWICK-GREYHOUND
917 McGee St., Kansas City, Mo.
NORTHLAND-GREYHOUND
509 6th Ave., N., Minneapolis, Minn.
SOUTHLAND-GREYHOUND
Pecan & Navarro Sts., San Antonio, Tex.
SOUTHEASTERN-GREYHOUND
101 N. Broadway, Lexington, Ky.
PROVINCIAL-TRANSPORT
1227 Phillips Square, Montreal, Que.

FINAL WILL BUSES DELIV. TO GREYHOUND JANUARY, 1931. THEN GMC'S YELLOW DIV. TAKES NEW BUS ORDERS.

('31)

201

GREYHOUND

INTERIOR

33-34

('33)
6 CYLS.
707 CID
250" WB

GREYHOUND LINES

EASTERN GREYHOUND LINES

NEW YORK · BOSTON · CHICAGO · MINNEAPOLIS · ST. LOUIS · DALLAS · SAN FRANCISCO · JACKSONVILLE · NEW ORLEANS

GMC/YELLOW "Z-250"

DECORATIVE "OBSERVATION PLATFORM" RAILING CONT'D. TO 1934.

Gas ENG.

GREYHOUND'S FINAL OLD-FASHIONED CONVENTIONAL TYPE WITH ENGINE and HOOD IN FRONT

GMC/YELLOW "843"

34-36

NEW "STREAMLINED"

NORTHLAND GREYHOUND LINES

('34)

New

KANSAS CITY

THIS EARLY TYPE has VERTICAL VENT SLOTS ON EITHER SIDE OF DESTINATION SIGN.
('36)

719 REAR VARIATIONS ('36)

743 ('37)

743 INTERIOR

1937

GREYHOUND!

GMC/YELLOW "719" (LATER MODEL IS "743" note HORIZONTAL VENT SLOTS ON LATER TYPE)

36-40

"719" has 3-PC. REAR WINDOW, and "743" has 2-PC. REAR WINDOW.

LIMITED

202

325 = 1936 "719 s" BLT.
1250 = 1937-39 "743 s" BLT.

87 DIESEL BUSES SOLD TO GREYHOUND. 1939.

GREYHOUND

THESE "SILVERSIDES" **SUPER-COACHES** PRODUCED BY GMC 1940-1953 WITH A FEW MINOR CHANGES DURING THOSE YEARS.

PDG-3701 (33') ('40)

EARLY COMPANY PHOTO (ABOVE)

FRONT TOP DETAILS ('44)

New

DIESEL

New Super-Coach!

Enjoy perfected air-conditioning as you travel *"This Amazing America"* by GREYHOUND

('40)

UNTIL 1942, BUILT BY YELLOW COACH DIV. OF GENERAL MOTORS CORP. (SUBSEQUENTLY, GMC TRUCK and COACH)

EARLY MODELS OF 3701 SERIES DO NOT HAVE OPENING SIDE WINDOWS. REPLACED BY 35' MODEL 3751 / 4151.

("YELLOW" NAME ON BUSES MFD. BEFORE 1943; GMC ON POST-'43 BUSES)

40-46

DIESEL BUSES SOLD TO GREYHOUND
1940 - 367
1941 - 288
1942 - 348
1945 - 440
1946-47 - 1518
(NO NEW BUSES FOR GREYHOUND IN 1943-44, BECAUSE OF MILITARY PRIORITIES.)

GMC

('46)

FULL-LENGTH DRIVER'S-SIDE VIEW

203

1946 INTERIOR, W/O VENT and HEATER DUCT PERFORATIONS.

GREYHOUND

45-PASS. SUBURBAN TYPE

('47)

new TYPE FRONT BUMPERS

47 -49 (WINDSHIELD RECESSED)

37-PASS. INTERCITY TYPE

33-PASS. DOES NOT HAVE THIS EXTRA CENTER WINDOW

1—PACKAGE RACK
2—VENT AND HEATER DUCT PERFORATIONS
3—SOLEX WINDOWS (NON-GLARE SAFETY GLASS)
4—HEADREST COVERS

9—HVY. LUGGAGE COMPT. OPENS FROM SIDE

These Greyhound features add up to the smoothest most relaxed ride on American Highways

5—ARMRESTS EACH SIDE
6—LEVER FOR ADJUSTING RECLINING SEAT
(note CHANGE IN STYLE OF SEAT ARMS SINCE 1946 VIEW ON PRECEDING PAGE.)

1949 INTERIOR

FOOT REST

('49)

FABRIC-COVERED FOAM RUBBER

204

GREYHOUND

('49)

49 -51

('50) **GMC**

PDG - 4151 (35')

has

SHORTER SIDE WINDOW JUST BEYOND DRIVER'S SECTION.

(1949 ON, OTHER TYPES OF <u>LARGE INTERCITY</u> BUSES ALSO AVAIL. FROM GMC)

INTERIOR ('51)

DRIVER'S COMPARTMENT ('51)

(51)

205

GREYHOUND

GMC 4104 TYPE (INTRO. DURING '53) WITH AIR SUSP.

54 TO EARLY 60s

NEW

the **Scenicruiser®**

GMC "PD-4501" SCENICRUISER

GH-165-5" WHITE NUMBERS

GH-234R DOG 36"

GH-226R GREYHOUND DECAL

12"

4"

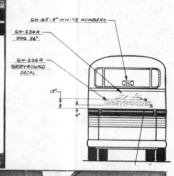

4104 INTERIOR "HIGHWAY TRAVELER"

GREYHOUND

GMC
Model 4106

TOP VIEW

GH-165-5" WHITE NUMBERS

DOG DECAL 36"
GH-234R
(CENTER ABOVE DOOR)

GH-226R
GREYHOUND
(CENTER ON DOOR)

2¼" RED SCOTCHLITE
GH-229

BLUE AMERFLINT
118-M-1155

PAINT FIBERGLASS TAIL LIGHT HOUSING
AS SHOWN ALUMINUM 118-M-790

WHITE AMERFLINT
118-M-1141

WHITE AMERFLINT
118-M-1141

TOP STRIPING 24" #3272 RED SCOTCHLITE
GH-241L & GH-242-R

WHITE AMERFLINT
118-M-1141

BLUE AMERFLINT
118-M-1155

ALUMINUM
AMERFLINT 118-M-790

¾" RIVETS

132 ½

2¼" 14"

GH-222L & GH-223R
GREYHOUND DECAL

GH-82 - WHITE
4" NUMBERS
SCOTCHAL
(4 REQ'D)

GH-140
(INTERIOR FRONT)

ALUM
118-M-790

ALUM
118-M-790

GREYHOUND

GH-235 REG
SYMBOL
7 REQ

GREYHOUND

BLUE 118-M-1155

2¼" RED SCOTCHLITE
#3272 GH-229

GH-113 REV-OWNER
OPER § ICC
(BOTH SIDES)

PAINT WHEELS WHITE
AMERFLINT 118-M-1141

FAIR INTO FENDER

GH-227L & GH-22BR DOG 50"

GH-225F - WHITE SCOTCHLITE
LETTERS WITH BLACK BORDER
(CENTER ON ANODIZED PANEL)

GH-165
5" WHITE NUMBERS

GH-234R
36" DOG DECAL

BOTTOM CURVE STRIPING 24"
#3272 RED SCOTCHLITE
GH-243L & GH-244-R

GMC
Model 4107

GH-226R
GREYHOUND

SEAM

GREYHOUND

ALUMINUM
AMERFLINT
118-M-790

ALL PAINT SCHEMES ON THIS PAGE ARE THE *new* REPAINTS AS OF JULY 1, 1974

TOP VIEW

WHITE AMERFLINT
118-M-1141

BLUE AMERFLINT
118-M-1155

new RAISED WINDOW AT FRONT

BLUE AMERFLINT
118-M-1155

WHITE AMERFLINT
118-M-1141

2¼" RED SCOTCHLITE
#3272 GH-229

ALUMINUM
AMERFLINT
118-M-790

WHITE AMERFLINT
118-M-1141

TOP STRIPING - RED
SCOTCHLITE #3272
GH-237-L & GH-238-R

BOTTOM CURVE STRIPING
#3272 RED SCOTCHLITE
GH-247-L & GH-248-R

99 ½

¾" RIVETS

24" 14"

ALUMINUM
AMERFLINT
118-M-790

GH-82 WHITE
4" NUMBERS
SCOTCHAL
(4 REQ'D)

BLUE AMERFLINT
118-M-1155

GH-140 COACH NUMBERS
(INTERIOR, FRONT)

STARTS 66

4107 IS FINAL GMC BUS SOLD IN QUANTITY TO GREYHOUND. MCI BUSES TO PREDOMINATE.

RIVETS

SEAM

GREYHOUND

SEAM

GH-222L & GH-223R
GREYHOUND DECAL
LETTERS "G" & "D"
LAP OVER SEAM

GH-113 REV-OWNER
OPER § ICC
(BOTH SIDES)

GH-227L & GH-228R
50" DOG - HEAD OF
DOG LAPS SEAM

PAINT WHEELS WHITE
AMERFLINT 118-M-1141

GREYHOUND

GH-235 REG
SYMBOL
7 REQ

GH-225F - WHITE SCOTCHLITE LETTERS
WITH BLACK BORDER GREYHOUND

BLUE AMERFLINT
118-M-1155

2¼" RED SCOTCHLITE
#3272 GH-229

WHITE AMERFLINT
118-M-1141

ALUMINUM
118-M-790

SEE ALSO GMC, MCI PAGES.

ALUMINUM
AMERFLINT
118-M-790

HAWKEYE MOTOR TRUCKS

(1916 – 1933)

HAWKEYE TRUCK COMPANY

R. A. BENNETT, President

634 Sixth Street   Sioux City, Iowa

OR

2702 Floyd Ave.
Sioux City, Iowa

ZENITH CARB. (ALL)
EISEMANN IGN. (TO '26)

BUDA ENGINES USED (ALL 4 CYL., TO '26.)

19

20-25

STAKE ('20)

1919 - 1925 MODELS :

O	(1 TON)	(STARTS 1922)		
K	(1½ T)	148½" WB (ALSO ON M)	7.6 GR	3 SP.
L	(2 T)	(THROUGH 1919)	9.0	
M	(2 T)	(1920 - 1924)	8.0	4 SP.
ML	(2 T)	(THROUGH 1922) (160" WB)		
N	(3½ T)	(INTRO. DURING '20 ; 170-180" WB)	10.0	4 SP.

2-WHEEL MECH. BRAKES
(VAC. BOOSTER AVAIL. IN 1929.)

new MODEL O 1½ T.
SPEED TRUCK CHASSIS

"O" STARTS

22

MAJOR REDESIGNING DURING 1926.

('19)
BUDA ENG. (RT. SIDE)

27 *and* 1928

PRE-'26 RADIATOR

30	1½ TON	160" WB°	4 CYL.
36	"	160°	6
50	2½	OPT.= °	4
56	"	210	6

29 ON

36	1½ TON	160" WB°	6 CYL.
30	"	160°	4
50-75	2½ (new)	210°	6
50-48	"	OPT.= °	4
50-60	" (new)	197	6

31-32

new 100-W *and* 200-W MODELS ADDED

new HERC. 6-CYL. *and* WISC. 4-CYL. ENGINES JOIN 4 *and* 6 CYL. BUDAS.

HAWKEYE-DART ALSO

ENDS 1933

208

SEE ALSO **DOVER**, **TERRAPLANE**.

HUDSON *Six*

(TRUCKS = 1938 – 1947)

MFD. BY HUDSON MOTOR CAR CO., DETROIT

90 PANEL DELIVERY

SERIAL # 90-101 UP (90 SER.) OR 98-101 UP (98 SERIES)

39

HUDSON CARS BUILT FROM 1909 TO 1957. TERRAPLANE TRUCKS REPLACED BY HUDSON TRUCKS AFTER 1938.

$808.

1/2-TON MODEL "90" (86 HP) 112" W.B. (REPLACES 1938 "112" SERIES)

note DIFF. BETWEEN "90" and "98" GRILLE

CAB PICKUP

$651.

3/4-TON "BIG BOY" MODEL "98" 119" W.B. (96 HP)

FRONT CLOSE-UP (**98**)

$695.

new 113" W.B. ON 1/2-TON MODEL "40"

SERIAL # 40-101 UP

40

1940 PRICES

"40" PICKUP	$671.
"40" PANEL	828.
"48" PICKUP	715.
"48" PANEL	884.

new 125" W.B. ON 3/4-TON "BIG BOY" MODEL "48."

new BROAD, LOW GRILLE
new SEALED BEAM HEADLIGHTS

TYPICAL OF MANY "AS IS" UNRESTORED TRUCKS THAT HAVE BEEN FOUND.

HUDSON Six

(*new* SEDAN CARRYALL PRICED AT $1022.)

Van

BODIES 3" LONGER

C.O.E.
MODEL "10"
"ALL-PURPOSE DELIVERY"
116" W.B.
92 HP (98 HP OPTIONAL)
"VACUMOTIVE" DRIVE
PLYWOOD FLOOR (5-PLY)
STARTS 9-40

41
(*new* HEAVY-ARMORED X-TYPE frame)
SER. # FROM C-10101 or C-18101

REAR DETAILS

PICKUP
3/4 TON MODEL **18**
PICKUP and SEDAN CARRYALL *have* 98 HP and 128" WB

1/2 TON MODEL **10**
PICKUP has 116" WB, 92 HP
FROM $782.

42-45
new GRILLE

1942

PICKUPS ONLY (THROUGH '47) 175 CID, 92 HP @ 4000 RPM
SER. # FROM T-20101

1/2-TON "C-20" *has* 116" W.B. $828.

3/4-TON "C-28" *has* 128" W.B. $872.

3/4-TON ONLY AFTER END OF 1945.

HUDSON's TRUCK STYLING SIMILAR TO HUDSON CARS!

REAR DETAILS

46
102 H.P.

MODEL "58"

new GRILLE CONCAVE NEAR CENTER

$1244.

128" WB (THROUGH '47)

---

pickup

47
MODEL "178"

STYLING SIMILAR TO 1946, BUT '47 *has new* HEAVIER CHROME FRAME AROUND MEDALLION ABOVE GRILLE.

$1338.

(SCENE OUTSIDE FACTORY)

(HUDSON CARS TOTALLY REDESIGNED FOR 1948 BUT TRUCK DISCONTINUED.)

210

THE HUG COMPANY
HIGHLAND, ILL.

Hug Model H Contractors' Job
Low center of gravity; two capacities
Complete Line: 1½ and 2 Ton

('24)

HUG (1922-1942)

THE HUG COMPANY HIGHLAND ILLINOIS.

*BUDA ENGINES EXCLUSIVELY
(THROUGH '34)*

22-27

ZENITH CARB. USED

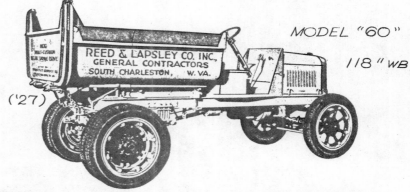

REED & LAPSLEY CO. INC.,
GENERAL CONTRACTORS
SOUTH CHARLESTON, W. VA.

('27)

*MODEL "60"
118" WB*

Sturdy Construction of the Hug Subframe
and Underbody

HUG Camroller Gravity Type Body
"A Roadbuilder's Own Design"

EARLY MODELS :

T   (1½ TON) (1922-1925)
C   "   (1922-1923)
H   (2 TON)   (1923-1924)
HA   "   (1923-1925)
H4   (2½ TON) (1925)
H4K   "   (1926)
HD6 (3½ TON) (1927, 6 CYL.)
*   (FIRST 6-CYL. MODEL)*

*4 CYL. ONLY (TO '27)
(4 CYL. MODELS STILL
AVAIL. THROUGH '32.)*

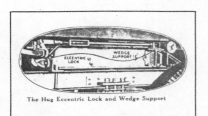

ECCENTRIC LOCK   WEDGE SUPPORT

The Hug Eccentric Lock and Wedge Support

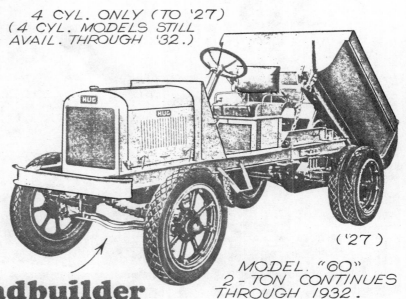

HUG

('27)

*MODEL "60"
2-TON CONTINUES
THROUGH 1932.*

Model "60" Roadbuilder

*with 4-CYL. BUDA "WTU" ENGINE
(3¾" × 4⅝", 37 HP @ 1850 RPM.)* **211**

HUG

28

Hug

MODELS: 20 (1½T;) 60, 25, C60 (2T;)
84, C84 (2½T;) 40, 86 (3T;)
90, C90 (3½ TON)

("20" NOT LISTED AFTER 1928.)

1929 MODELS: 22 (1½T;) 26, 60, 66 (2T;)
81, 84 (2½T;)
40, 86,
486 (3T;)
90 (3½ TON)
(ALL 6 CYL. EXC.
60, 81, 84.)

(APRIL, 1927)

SPEED TRUCK

with new
COUPE CAB BY
THE GENERAL WOODWORK CORPORATION
Cincinnati, Ohio

37 TO 126 HP IN 1931.

← "XPRES 6"
MODELS

Model "42"

6 CYL
298.2
CID

86
HP

3 Ton Commercial Express
143" TO 201" WB

29-32

'32 MODELS: ('32)
22, 23, 60 (2T;)
61, 85, 85D
(2½-3T;)
41, 42,

67, 85-6, 85D6 (3T;) C87,
87M (3½T;) 43 (3½-4T;) C97,
97 (5 TON;) 6-WH.: 97-6 (5T;) 98-6
(7½T;) 99 (10 TON)

Model "43"

6 CYL.
428.4
CID

107
HP

33

MODELS:
23, 63 (2T;)
41S, 42, 42K,
70 (3 TON;)
43, 87K (3½T;)

43L, 87Q (5T;) 99 (10 TON,
6-WHEELER)

34

146" TO
201" WB

3½ Ton Commercial

new
97-L (5 TON) IN 1934.

new MODELS IN 1935 ('35-'36 MODELS)
12 D (1½ TON, ADDED 1936.)
15A, D, T (1¾-2½T;) 19A, D, T (2½-5T;) 23S, A, T
(2½-5T;) 41S (3T;) 42A, T (3-6T;) 43A, T (4-8T;)
70 (3T;) 87K (3½T;) 87Q; 43L (5T;) 97L (7½ TON)
6-WHEELERS: 97 LD (7½T;) 99 (10 TON)
new 4WD MODELS ('36): 43-4; 87K4; 87Q4

35-36

ROADBUILDERS

('36)

Model 87K Hug Roadbuilder with 5-yard Hug scoop type body,
designed for dirt moving and 3-batch hauling.

Model 87Q Hug Roadbuilder equipped with 6-yard Hug scoop type
body and especially designed for dirt and rock moving.

Model 97L Hug Roadbuilder with 8-yard Hug rock type body, for
dirt and quarry operations.

new WAUKESHA 6-CYL. ENGINES IN
MODELS UP TO 19T (1935 ON.)

212

BUDA 6-CYL. ENGINES CONT'D.
IN MODELS 23S and up.

87-Q

5 TON

new DIESELS AVAIL.

HUG 4 CYL., 831 CID CATERPILLAR DIESEL ENGINE (77 HP @ 850 RPM) IN 6-WH. "954 FR" 18-TON.

HUGE 6 CYL., 1246 CID DIESEL CATERPILLAR ENG. (125 HP @ 850) IN 20-TON 4WD "100."

"QUARRY SPECIAL" 10-TON "99"

BUTLER BROS. ST. PAUL, MINN.

99-S

REAR

('37)

98-MB

(WAUKESHA ENG.)

37 MODELS:
12D (1½T;) 16A; 15D, T (1¾-2½T;) 19A, D, T;
23S, A, T (2½-5T;) 41S (3T;) 42A, T (3-6T;)
43A, T (4-8T;) 70K (3T;) 87K (3½T;)
43L, 87Q (5T;)
6-WHEELERS: 97L, LD (7½T;) 99 (10 TON)
4-W-D: 43-4; 87K4; 87Q4 (2 DIESELS: SEE TOP OF PAGE)

"HUG LUGGER" C.O.E. 10-TON MODEL 16 WITH 468 CID CAT. DIESEL ENG.

('38)

('39)

38 MORE DIESELS ADDED '38: (BUDA, CUMMINS, and CATERPILLAR-POWERED DIESELS: D42; D43 (L); (T) HC; D70K; D8, 8; 16; D98, D998 (6 WH.)

COMMERCIAL SERIES 42-T (3-6 TON)

39 MODEL 42-T (SINCE '35.)

1940 CHASSIS PRICES:
$1875. – $8900.

40-42

IN '41, MODELS REDUCED TO 85W ('42;) 87W; 92U; D92U; 98; D98 ('41 6-WH.: 99; D99; 995; D995

51-6, CB7P new for '42

"COMMERCIAL BUILDER DESIGN" CB7P

FINAL HUG STYLE → (SEE ALSO REO.)

REO BODY

('42)

PST DAIRY PRODUCTS CO.

213

(EST. 1946)

LARGER, HEAVY
CONVENTIONAL TYPE
IBEX TRUCKS
AVAILABLE LATER.

RIGHT VIEW   LEFT VIEW

TILTING CAB
('70-'71)

THE EAGER "1" TUG
80" WHEELBASE

EARLY
1970s

('70)

HEAVY
6 × 4
6 - WH.
TRACTOR -
TRAILER

(SHOWN IN
SNOW)

('72)

← CHOICE OF 361 CID FORD V8
GAS ENGINE (168 HP)
OR 4-53 DETROIT DIESEL
(212 CID, 212 HP)

EARLY MODELS ALSO AVAIL. with
504 CID CUMMINS V8 DIESEL
(185 HP) OR 573 CID V8
CATERPILLAR DIESEL
(175 HP)

10.00 × 20"
12 - PLY TIRES
6-SPEED ALLISON AUTO.
TRANS.

41 - GALLON
FUEL TANK

82" WHEELBASE
157½" OVERALL LENGTH
93" HIGH   96" WIDE

FLEXI-TRUC by Ibex...   214

INTERNATIONAL (SINCE 1907)

BOSCH IGN. ON 1-1½ TON; SPLITDORF ON 2-3½ TON. ENSIGN CARB.

INTERNATIONAL HARVESTER COMPANY
CHICAGO, ILL. (SINCE 1907)

15-20

4 CYLINDERS
3½" × 5¼" ON "F" and "K;"
4" × 5" ("G")
4¼" × 5" ("L")

GEAR RATIOS : 7.91 (F)
8.96 (K,G) 10.98 (L)

MODELS ('20)

F	1 TON	128"wb	
K	1½	128	
G	2	138	
L	3½	160	

36" TIRES

STILL AVAILABLE = TRUCKS WITH OLD-STYLE SLOPING HOOD.

note "INTERNATIONAL" NAME ON SIDE OF CHASSIS.

21

MODEL G 2-TON (SOLID OR PNEUMATIC TIRES)

NEW STYLE WITH FLAT RADIATOR

MODELS F, K, G, L CONTINUE

(MODIFIED,) PLUS new ¾-TON MODELS :
"S" (124" WB, LYCOMING 4-CYL., 3½" × 5" ENG.) 6.3 G.R.
"H" (115" WB, OWN 3½" × 5¼" ENG. AS IN F,K) 6.8 G.R.

CONNECTICUT IGNITION on "S"

1922 MODELS :

S	¾-TON	124⅛"WB	6.3 GR
21	1	115	7.0
31	1½	129	8.0
41	2	129	9.0
61	3	138½	9.0
101	5	160	11.0

"RED BABY"

McCORMICK-DEERING
IHC
SALES AND SERVICE
INTERNATIONAL HARVESTER
POWER FARM EQUIPMENT
INTERNATIONAL

1923 WHEELBASES (AS LISTED IN 1-23 "MOTOR TRUCK")

S = 115"		41 = 138"	
21 = 128"		61 = 138"	
31 = 128"		101 = 160"	

22-23

BOTH RADIATOR TYPES AVAILABLE

Betsy Ross BREAD
DORSEY BAKING COMPANY

3 TON "63" ('24 -'26)

1924 MODELS:
WB
S 1 TON 124"
43 2 130
63 3 140
103 5 160

INTERNATIONAL
(ENSIGN CARB. ON LYCOMING-ENG. "S" ONLY; OWN CARB. ON OTHERS.)

ADDITIONAL 1½ TON "33" (128" WB) IN 1925.

DIAGRAM

FRONT END VIEW

4 VIEWS OF new 1924 BALL BEARING 4 CYL., 283 CID O.H.V. ENG. (4¼" × 5")

RIGHT (MAGNETO) SIDE

LEFT (CARB.) SIDE

BUSES ALSO AVAILABLE

new CHAIN-DRIVE MODEL WITH ALL-STEEL CAB ('27)

NATIONAL BISCUIT COMPANY
"Uneeda Bakers"

TRACTOR-TRAILERS new for 1926:
SD-SL (1½ TON) 110" WB
43-TT (TRACT.-TRLR.) 115"
63-TT " " 120"
103-TT " " 134"
OTHERS CONTINUE ZENITH CARB. ON "S" TYPES IN '26.

('26) PANEL

new FOR 1927: ZENITH CARB. ON MORE MODELS
"SPEC. DLV." ¾ TON 116" WB
new 6-CYL. "S-26" 1¼ 130 (LYCOMING ENG.)
("S-24" has 4-CYL. LYCOMING ENGINE.)

Broadway CLEANERS AND DYERS

24-28

'28 "SD-44" (4 CYL.) "SD-46" (6 CYL.)
'28 "54C" and "74C" are TRACTOR-TRUCKS

216

"SPECIAL DELIVERY" ¾-TON
with 4-CYL. WAUKESHA ENG. (INTRO. SPRING, 1927) 116" WB

INTERNATIONAL®

6 - CYL. TYPES
have "6" IN
MODEL NUMBER
(AS IN
"SF-36," etc.)

1929 MODELS : SD (¾-TON;) 6 Sp. (1-TON;) S-24, S-26 (1¼-TON;)
SL-34, SF-34, SF-36, SL-36 (1½-TON;) SD-44, SD-46,
SF-46 (2-TON;) HS-54, HS-54C, 54, 54C (2½-TON;)
74, 74C, HS-74, HS-74C (3½-TON;) 104-C, HS-104-C
(5-TON)

"HS" PREFIX
MEANS HALL-SCOTT
4-CYL. ENGINE.

INTERNATIONAL
SIX-SPEED
SPECIAL

The
2-SPEED
Axle

29
BUS

ZENITH
CARB. ON
ALL MODELS

BRINK'S ARMORED
TRUCK

MIDWEST MERCHANDISE TRANSFER

A DISTINGUISHED SERVICE
30 N. MICHIGAN AVE.
CHICAGO

BRINK'S EXPRESS CO.
OWNED MORE THAN 500
INTERNATIONAL TRUCKS
(AS OF OCT., 1930.)
INT'L. ARMORED TRUCKS
HAVE BULLET-PROOF
WINDSHIELD and 2-
THICKNESS STEEL
IN BODY.

HEAVY-DUTY MODELS

30

MORE 1930 MODELS
AND DETAILS ON
NEXT PAGE.

217

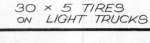

new 3/4 -TON "SPECIAL DELIVERY" PANEL TRUCK (8-30)

STEEL-
SPOKED
WHEELS

130" WB

30 × 5 TIRES
ON LIGHT TRUCKS

SPEC. DLV. and AW-1 have
4 CYL., 173 CID
WAUKESHA "XA" ENGINE
with 30 HP @ 2700 RPM,
AS DOES 1-TON
6-Sp. SPEC.

30
(CONT'D.)

SIMILAR
MODEL SERIES
TO 1929, IN EARLY '30,
with
WAUKESHA 4, LYCOMING 4 and 6,
and HALL-SCOTT 4-CYL. ENGINES.

3/4-TON "AW-1," 1½-TON "AL-3" and
"A-5" TRACTOR-TRUCK MODELS
INTRODUCED SUMMER, 1930.

MOVING
VAN

1920s STYLING CONT'D.
on HEAVY-DUTY of
EARLY '30

OWN INTERNATIONAL 279 CID 6-CYL. ENGINE IN
new "A-5" '30½
3-TON ➤

156-210" WB
65 HP @ 2800 RPM
34 × 7 TIRES
5-SPEED TRANSMISSION

A-5

W-3

new 3½-TON "W-3"
has 160-235" WB,
HALL-SCOTT "152"
4-CYL., 390 CID
ENGINE (60 HP
@ 1800 RPM)
(SAME ENGINE IN
3½-TON "HS-74"
and "HS-74-C."

"W-3"

AMERICAN INSTITUTE LAUNDRY PS 51-7

VAN

A-4

2-TON "A-4" has 145" WB, 32 × 6 TIRES, and OWN "FBB" 6-CYL., 3⅝" × 4½" ENGINE with 65 HP @ 2800 RPM.

1½-TON "6-SPEED SPECIAL" IMPROVED FROM '30 TYPE.

OPEN-SIDED CANOPY EXPRESS (POPULARLY KNOWN AS "PEDDLER'S WAGON")

S.S. PIERCE CO.

BALTIMORE & OHIO R.R.

3-TON **A-5**

"W-3" RATING UPPED TO 5 TONS IN 1931.

32 INTERNATIONAL

INTRO. 7-31: 4-SPEED "A-2" MODEL *with* RECTANGULAR WINDSHIELD

LOWER EDGE of WINDSHIELD ARCHED (A-3 MODEL)

A-2

1½-TON "A-2" (also "B-2") has 136" WB, 4-CYL. WAUKESHA "XAH" 3⅝" × 4½" ENG. (39 HP @ 2400 RPM) 5.50×20(F) 6.00×20(R) TIRES

new 1½-TON **A-3** (12-31) (ABOVE) has 6-CYL., 3¼" × 4½" LYCOMING L-HEAD "SAH" ENGINE (54 HP @ 2700 RPM.) 136" or 160" WB 5.50/6. × 20" TIRES

A-6
3-TON STAKE (BELOW)

3-TON "A-5" and "A-6" have OWN 6-CYL., 3⅝" × 4½" "FBB" ENGINE (67 HP @ 2600 RPM.)

34 × 7 TIRES

1932 MODELS:

A-1	¾ TON	136"WB	4 CYL. (ENG. LIKE A-2, B-2)			
A-2, B-2	1½	136	4			
A-3, A-3½, AL-3	1½	136 UP	6			
A-4	2	145	6	67 HP @ 2600 RPM	
W-1	2½	148	4	59 @ 1800	
A-5, A-6	3	156	6			
W-2	3½	148	4	59 @ 1800	
W-3	5	160	4	69 @ 1800	

ALSO, *new*

Models A-7 and A-8

(INTRO. 2-32)

DELCO-REMY IGN.

6-CYL. 5-TON

"A-7" has OWN "FDB" 4½" × 5½" ENGINE (117 HP @ 2200 RPM.) "A-8" has OWN "FEB" 5" × 5½" ENGINE (136 HP @ 2100 RPM.)

160" WB (STROMBERG CARB. on A-8)

SHIP The UNIVERSAL Way

MUTUAL TRUCK COMPANY 9

WITH EARLY TYPE OF **SLEEPER CAB**

220

INTERNATIONAL

32 (CONT'D.)

INTERNATIONAL TRUCKS

TELEPHONE LINEMAN'S TRUCK

A-3 (1½-TON)

INTERESTING EXAMPLES OF SPECIALIZED BODY TYPES

"EAT ICE CREAM"

ICE CREAM MAKERS OF AMERICA

ICE CREAM FREEZER TRUCK

Illustration shows 3-ton Model A-5, 190-in. wheelbase chassis with mechanically refrigerated body.

A-5 (3-TON)

WILLYS - BUILT new ½-TON "D-1" 6 CYL., 70 HP OWN "D" ENGINE (3⁵⁄₁₆" x 4⅛")

NO VISOR ON SMALL TRUCK.

33

OTHER MODELS : M-2 (1-TON;) A-2, B-2, A-3, A-3½, AL-3 (1½-TON;) B-4, A-4 (2-TON;) A-5, A-6 (3-TON ;) W-2 (3½-TON;) W-3 (5-TON;) A-7 (5-7½-TON;) A-8 (7½-TON)

new ½-TON SERIES PRODUCED BY WILLYS AT TOLEDO, OHIO!

113" WB

113" TO 225" WHEELBASES

221

6 CYL.
78½ HP ('34)

INTERNATIONAL

UNSKIRTED FENDERS ON HVY. MODELS

2-TON AND 3-TON TRUCKS ('34)

WIRE WHEELS ON 1934 PICKUP 5.25 x 18 TIRES

H.J. HEINZ CO.
RICE FLAKES
BAKED BEANS
BOTTLED VINEGARS
PURE FOOD 57 HEINZ VARIETIES PRODUCTS
H.J. HEINZ CO. 57 VARIETIES
489

TRUCKS TO 7½ TONS IN 1934.

4 and 6 CYL., 42 TO 140 HP IN 1935.

11½-TON "C-55-F" ('36)

C-1

new STYLING on MOST (LT.) '34 MODELS.

'33 MODEL DESIGNATIONS CONT'D. IN 1934, and 1½-TON, 6-CYL. "B-3" ADDED. 4.18 TO 8.5 G.R. ('34)

'35 MODELS : C-1 (½-TON ;) M-2 (1-TON ;) A-2, B-3, C-20, C-30 (1½-TON ;) C-35 (1½-2-TON ;) B-4, A-4 (2-TON ;) C-40 (2-3-TON ;) A-5, A-6 (3-TON ;) C-50 (3-4-TON ;) W-2 (3½-TON ;) C-55 (3½-4½-TON ;) C-60 (4-5-TON ;) A-7 (5-7½-TON ;) A-8 (7½-T.)

113" WB PANEL ('34)

New ½-ton
RESTYLED **C** SERIES)
34-36
(EARLY 1937 ALSO)

'36 MODELS : C-1, C-5 (½-TON ;) M-3 (1-TON ;) C-20, C-30, CS-30 (1½-TON ;) C-35, CS-35 (1½-2-TON ;) C-40 (2-3 TON ;) C-50 (3-4-TON ;) C-55 (3½-4½-TON ;) C-60 (4-5-TON ;) A-7 (5-7½-TON ;) A-8 (7½-TON ;) (all with OWN 6-CYL. ENGINES EXCEPT 4 CYL. WAUKESHAS IN C-5. M-3 and C-20.)

222

'36 "C1" has OWN "HD" 213 cid 6 (79 HP @ 3400)

D SERIES
37-40

INTERNATIONAL

INTERNATIONAL STATION WAGONS

('40)

new "D" SERIES (INTRO. MARCH, 1937)
(COMPLETELY RESTYLED)

½-TON "D-2" PICKUP
113" OR 125" W.B.
(¾ TO 1-TON "D-15" has
130" W.B. and HORIZONTAL
RIBS ON BOX SIDES.)

INTERNATIONAL

The ALL-STEEL CAB
is a feature in every new
International. The one-piece
top, the sides, the back and
cowl panels, are welded into
the complete cab frame.
Rubber mountings wher-
ever cushioning is needed.
This is the roomy, well-
appointed de luxe cab.

TRACTOR-TRAILER
MOVING VAN

PANEL-
STAKE

1½-TON "D-30"

'38 MODELS:
C-1, C-5, D-2,
D-5, C-15, D-15, C-20, C-30,
CS-30, D-30, DS-30,
C-35, CS-35, D-35,
DS-35, C-40,
CS-40, D-40,
C-50, D-50,
C-55, D-60,
C-60, DR-60,
DR-70, A-8 (also
e.u.s. 1½-TON D-300
and DS-300.)
(PLUS SEVERAL
6-WHEEL MODELS.)
FINAL "C" MODELS
IN 1938.

DUMP TRUCK

D-15
('39)

ALL 1939-1940
MODELS have
"D" PREFIX
(EXCEPT
A-8.)
D-5 ONLY 4-CYL.
MODEL (132 CID WAU.,
33 HP @ 2800 RPM.)
(OWN 6-CYL. ENGINES
IN OTHERS.)

NOTE HORIZONTAL
RIBBING ON "D-15"
223 PICKUP BOX

33 TO 140 HP IN 1940.

* Heavy Duty means all trucks rated at 2-ton and over.

('40)

SOME HEAVY-DUTY MODELS HAVE CENTER PROTRUSION IN LARGE, PAINTED BUMPER (AS ABOVE.)

HIGHEST-PRICED INT'L. 6-WHEELER IS AR-626-F @ $12,500. ('40)

37-40 (CONT'D.)

('39)

6 WHEELER TRACTOR-TRAILER

FUEL OIL

ROGERS OIL CO.

('39)

STREAMLINED TANKER

WINDSHIELD OPENS →

International Truck sizes range from Light Delivery units up to powerful Six-Wheelers. Diesel-powered models in 12,000 to 42,000-lb. carrying capacities.

Jack's COOKIES

JACK'S COOKIE CO. TAMPA ORLANDO MIAMI

Nº 28

('38)

224

TRACTOR-TRAILER (WITH VAN TRAILER)

INTERNATIONAL

new 1½-TON "C-300" C.O.E. AVAILABLE on MKT. 9-36, with 99" or 117" wb.

ILLUSTRATED AT UPPER RIGHT

RAILWAY EXPRESS VAN
D-400
('38)

RAILWAY EXPRESS for speedy service

RAILWAY EXPRESS AGENCY

RAILWAY EXPRESS

"C-300" 1½ TON (INTRO. 8-36) C.O.E.s

LONG-GRILLE TYPE

CAB-OVER-ENGINE
VARIATIONS

"D-300" ('40)
13,200-lb. G.V.W.
$715. and up (CHAS.)

HOME FURNISHINGS

232 CID 6 CYL.
81 HP @ 3200 RPM

HEAVY-DUTY C.O.E. "D-500" and "DR-700" have 18,800 and 26,900 lb. G.V.W.

37-40
(CONT'D.)

INSIGNIA
INTERNATIONAL

new TYPE of "D-400" ('40) GRILLE
(NOTE = GRILLE DOES NOT EXTEND AS FAR DOWNWARD AS ON OTHERS ILLUSTRATED.)

16,200-lb. G.V.W.

New Model D-400

225

K-1-M OR K-3-M THRU '46

METRO VAN

102" WB 6.00 x 16 TIRES

"Green Diamond" 6-CYL. 82 HP ENG. IN '42 VAN (4.18 G.R. IN 1/2-TON) 4.875-6.5 G.R. IN 3/4-1-TON VAN

INTERNATIONAL HARVESTER COMPANY

THIS EMBLEM APPEARS ABOVE GRILLE

INTERNATIONAL

New **K** SERIES

RESTYLED

HVY. DUMP

WITH TANDEM AXLES

PANEL ('41)

4-CYL., 33 HP "D-5" CONT'D. INTO 1941. AT START OF '41, 51 MODELS and 166 WHEELBASES!

41-46

TRUCK-TRACTOR (3 TO 4 TON)

DIESEL MODELS AVAILABLE

('41)

"K" MODELS IN 1942: 82 TO 140 HP
K-1 THROUGH K-8, K-10, KR-11;
C.O.E.s IN K-5, K-7, K-8, KR-11 LINE.
160"-WB A-8 STILL AVAIL. (BUT NOT IN 1946.)

6-CYL. ENG. (SOME O.H.V. TYPES AVAIL.) 13 TYPES IN 1948, 214 TO 1090 CID

HEAVY DUTY

CAB ('41)

D-500 C.O.E.

"RED DIAMOND" **ENGINE**
USED IN K-8, KS-8, KR-11, KS-11 →

'46: K-1-M, K-3-M new 82 TO 148 HP IN '46.

('45)

21 BASIC MODELS IN 1947

PICKUP

HEAVY-DUTY

GAS OR DIESEL (WEST COAST '46 MODELS SIMILAR. note THE BOXY CAB STYLE.)

KB-8-F
KB-8-F — for mixing and transporting concrete.

THIS EMBLEM INTERNATIONAL IDENTIFIES GREAT TRUCKS.

BOTTLER'S TRUCK KB-6

"KB-8"

WESTERN

K-8 (GAS) ('47)

6-WHEELERS ('47) INCLUDE: KB-6F-4R; KB-8F-4R; KB-11F-4R; W-4064-H (SAME ENGINE AS W-3042-H)

"KBR-12" TRUCK-TRACTOR

"KBR-11"

LOG TRUCK-TRACTOR "W-6564-OH"

new "KB" SERIES

47-49

new "KB" PREFIX IN 1947. LARGEST MODEL IS "W-3042-H," with 749 CID Con. S-6749 ENGINE and 254 HP @ 2600 RPM.

new GRILLE, OTHER CHANGES 82 TO 322 H.P. ENGS. 13 DIFFERENT ENGINES IN 1948, FROM 214 TO 1090 C.I.D. Cummins DIESEL ENG. AVAIL., '48 ON

STATION WAGON

INTERNATIONAL KB5

KB-1 IS 1/2 TON PICKUP $1030. (113" WB) 1188. (125" WB) ('47-48 PRICES) KB-2 = 3/4 TON KB-3 = 1 TON

('48)

INTERNATIONAL-METRO COACH—auxiliary bus for limited passenger transport.

1 1/2 TON KB-5 (ILLUSTR.)

EMBLEM SET IN TOP OF GRILLE.

INTERNATIONAL

METRO COACH PASSENGER BUS-VAN (RARE) (above)

227

INTERNATIONAL

½-TON PICKUP PRICES FROM $1378. ('50) $1438. ('51-52)

½-TON PANEL PRICES FROM $1360. ('50) $1478. ('51-52)

PANEL

New L Series.
50-52

TOTALLY RESTYLED, WITH new 1-PC. WINDSHIELD, 2-PC. REAR CAB WINDOW, new GRILLE (new 115" MINIMUM WB)

Now-International Roadliners offer 3 types of power

GASOLINE, DIESEL and LPG! ('52)

GASOLINE · DIESEL · LPG

HVY. DUTY

L-185, 195 ROADLINER HEAVY DUTY HAS 157" W.B.

DETAILS OF CAB VENT SYSTEM

BOTTLER'S TRUCK

new 220 CID, 101-HP O.H.V. 6-CYL. ENGINE IN LIGHT TRUCKS (STARTING 1950.)

IN 1951, ONE MILLION USED INTERNATIONAL TRUCKS WERE STILL IN SERVICE (MORE THAN ½ OF INTERNATIONAL'S TOTAL OUTPUT SINCE 1907!

130" TO 172" WB ON 1½-TON L-150 MODELS FR. $1919 ('50)

CAB.

INTERNATIONAL HARVESTER

new "IH" CORPORATE TRADEMARK ADDED TO GRILLE.

MILK TRUCK ('54)

AVENUE DAIRY

53-55

RESTYLED "R" SERIES

RAISED SIDE SECTIONS ARE OPTIONAL.

R-110 ½-TON PICKUP $1607. ('55)

WHEELBASES FROM 115" TO 195"
½-TON R-100 LIGHT DUTY JOINS
½ TON R-110 "HVY."; 1955,
PRICED AT $1539.

"LCFD-405" HEAVY
"HIGHBINDER" HIGH CAB
SHORT-BBC STARTS 1954.

HYDRA-MATIC OPTION, 1955

DASH

MILITARY HAULER

"S-100" LT. DUTY FROM $1662.
"S-110" FROM $1735.

new "S" SERIES

56

(and EARLY 1957)

V-8 1956

C.O.E.

LT. DUTY and FRONT DETAILS

new GRILLE, HEADLIGHTS MOVED UP

Heavy-Duty V-8

229

COMPACT CITY DLVRY.

48" SIGHTLINERS

C.O.E.

REFRIGERATOR TRUCK

6-PASS. TRAVEL CREW CAB WITH UTILITY BODY

trucks

note EXTRA WINDOWS BELOW DASH LEVEL.

SCHOOL BUS (CHASSIS MFR.)

DUMP

STAKE

Multi-Million-Mile diesels.

('58)

Golden Anniversary MODELS

Stake or platform-body models.

Powerful, dependable six-wheelers.

PANEL DLVRY. and TRAVELALL WAGON HAVE 2 DOORS ON PASSENGER'S SIDE, and JUST 1 DOOR ON DRIVER'S SIDE.

(57½)

57½-58

"A-100" LT. DUTY TOTALLY RESTYLED.

Conventional tractors for biggest jobs.

Extra-rugged off-highway models.

A-100 $2364.

WITH 240 CID O.H.V. 6-CYL. ENGINE   114" WB (PICKUP STYLING SIMILAR TO TRAVELALL ABOVE.)

190 CONV. TRACTOR WITH TANKER

PRODUCTION: 81,213 ('58)

60110

230

ABOVE:
SIGHTLINER ACO
(THIS TYPE AVAIL. 1959 TO 1965.)
V8

HEAVY-DUTY V8 TRACTOR TRLR. (RT.)

TANDEM-AXLE

MEDIUM-DUTY STAKE (CONVENTIONAL OR ALL-WHEEL DRIVE AVAIL.)

IH

A pickup with a back seat! New Travelette® takes 6 passengers, plus full-size pickup loads.

TRAVELETTE P.U. (6' BED)

OIL FIELD HVY. DUTY

6-CYL. ENGS. WITH 220, 240, 264, 282 OR 308 CID

EVANS

TRAVELALL

C.O.E. TRACTOR-TRAILER

SPECIAL TRIM OPT.

B-110 ½ TON
(8½' BED, 126" WB)

$2094.

V8 ENGINE OPTIONS
266 CID (154.8 HP)
304 CID (193.1 HP)
345 CID (197.6 HP)

BLACK BACKGROUND AROUND FRONT EMBLEM (SEE ARROW)

new 59 B SERIES
new GRILLE and new QUADRUPLE HEADLTS.

B-100 ½-TON PICKUP (7' BED) 114" WB) $2045. **231**

PRODUCTION 143,231

B-100 (7' BED)
PICKUPS
FR.
$2151.

6 CYL.:
220 CID, 112 HP
240 " 141 "
264 " 153 "

new OPT.
154.8 HP
V8 AVAIL.

DUMP
TRUCK

PRODUCTION:
119,696

TANKER

PLEASE NOTE:
OTHER VARIETIES
OF INTERNATIONAL
METRO, METRO-MITE
and METRO MULTI-
STOP VANS ARE SEEN
IN "PICKUP AND VAN
SPOTTER'S
GUIDE."

C.O.E.

METRO-MITE
4 CYL.

W/O REAR BUMPER

60

RESEMBLES
1959,
BUT
WITH
new SILVER
BACKGROUND
AROUND
FRONT
EMBLEM

WITH REAR
BUMPER

TRAVELALL
FR. $2845.

232

MILK DELIVERY TRUCK
RETAINS 1956 PICKUP
STYLING!

('61)

'61 MODELS START 11-1-60, have SUFFIX "—1" FOLLOWING SERIAL NUMBER. '62 STARTS 11-1-61, WITH SUFFIX "—2" FOLLOWING SERIAL NO.

new LOADSTAR CONV. ('62)

C.O.E. ('62)

EVACUATION ROUTE

C.O.E. ('62)

('61)

C-100 PICKUPS PRICED FROM $2187. ('61) 2190. ('62)

61-62

new "C" RESTYLED MODELS

LT. DUTY WITH WIDE CONCAVE ANODIZED ALUMINUM GRILLE (ALSO ANOD. ALUM. HEADLT. TRIM

39 DIFF. PICKUP MODELS, INCL. new C-130 ALL-WHEEL DRIVE

233

PROD.: 142,816 ('61) 147,283 ('62)

'62 SCOUT (INTRO. '61) 2-W-D FROM $1751. (4-W-D OPT.)

IH®

SPECIAL PRESSURIZED GASES TANKER

HOPPER TRUCK

C.O.E. WITH LONG-DISTANCE MOVING-VAN BODY

MIXER

New type inter-city freighter

HEAVY-DUTY DUMP

SLEEPER-CAB ('64) INTERIOR (LONG-CAB C.O.E.)

63 -64

RESTYLED, *new* MODEL NUMBERS. '63 STARTS 11-1-62, WITH SUFFIX "—3" FOLLOWING SERIAL NO.

LT. DUTY IN C-900, C-1000, C-1100 *and* C-1200 SER.

PRODUCTION: 168,296 ('63) 166,892 ('64)

('64)

MODEL 1100 4 x 4

234

↑ ('64) 54" SHORT CAB C.O.E.

6 OR V8

$2705 ('64)

4-DOOR TRAVELALL

900 107" WB 4-CYL. 93 HP

compact 6-ft. body...

Pick your own power—93 to 193 hp—from our 4, 6 and V-8 engines. They're tough, responsive, economical. Naturally, they're built for trucks only.

1/2 TON = C-900, C-1000, C-1100
3/4 TON = C-1200
1 TON = C-1300
1 1/2 TON = C-1500
2 TON = C-1600

2 TYPES SHOWN

C SERIES
65
NEW
GRILLE WITH VERTICAL PCS.

CONVENTIONAL

C.O.E.

SPARE TIRE and WHEEL STORED UPRIGHT.

You don't have to share cab space with a gas tank. You keep all that room for people. We tuck the tank under the cab of INTERNATIONAL pickups. Which makes our pickups safer, too.

LT. and MEDIUM CONVENTIONALS:

1/2 TON PU 7' 119"wb	$2097.
" TRAVELALL "	2705.
" PANEL 7' "	2427.
" TRAVELALL (C-1100)	2731.
" PU 8 1/2' 131"wb	2155.
" TRAV. PU 6' 140"	2769.
3/4 T. PANEL 7' 119"	2550.
" TRAVELALL "	2854.
" PU 8 1/2' 131"	2278.
" TRAV. PU 6' 140"	2893.
1 TON PU 8 1/2' 131"	2362.
" STAKE 9' DUALS 134"	2593.
1 1/2 T " 12' 156"wb	3167.
2 TON STAKE with 12' BED 151"wb	3678.

ALSO C-900 1/2 T. COMPACT PICKUP (4 CYL., 107"wb) = $1952.

235

C.O.E.

½ TON 1000-A PICKUP (7' BED)		$2138.
"A" " 1100-A " (8' ")		2200.
SERIES " 1100-A TRAVELETTE (6' ")		2810.
1200-A (¾-TON MODELS)		2319. UP
1300-A (1-TON ")		2359. UP

METRO VANS
AVAIL. IN
4-CYL. M-800
OR
M-1100
SERIES
and
IN
6-CYL.
M-1200
OR
M-1500
SERIES

(V8
OPT.)

(1966 MODELS START
WITH 11-1-65 REGISTRATIONS)

66 A SERIES

(FINAL YR. FOR 4-CYL. 900-A PICKUP, $1980.)

new ON LIGHT TRUCKS,
CENTER STRIP RUNS ACROSS
FULL WIDTH
OF GRILLE.

Pickup   6 OR V8

PROD.
170,385

PRODUCTION:
167,940 ('67)   145,549 ('68)

1967 I.D. # 1000-B UP

LT. DUTY FROM
$2126. ('67)
2440. ('68)

TRAVELALL
$2841. ('67)

$3146.
('68)

V-8 diesel

CO-LOADSTAR
TILT-CAB
('68)

B SERIES

67-68

C SERIES

236

LT. DUTY
FROM $2623. ('69)
$2795. ('70)

new GRILLE
(LIGHT DUTY)

NOTE THE ODD SIDE WINDOWS

INTERNATIONAL HARVESTER

('69) *with* 16-SPEED SPICER TRANSMISSION

RUAN
4384

"400"

new **D** SERIES

69-70

TRAVELALL
IH

TRANSTAR
(CONVENTIONAL)
SIDE *and* FRONT VIEWS

PRODUCTION:
160,255 ('69)
155,353 ('70)

('70)

('70) CONV. CAB

"8V-71" DETROIT DIESEL ENG. IN TRANSTAR

INTERNATIONAL

C-O Transtar

237

IH "DVT-573-B" DIESEL V-8 ENGINE *with* 230 HP. (260 OR 285 HP AVAIL.) CUMMINS ENGINE AVAILABLE

(LT. DUTY)
new TAIL-LIGHTS

MODELS 1010
and up

STD. PICKUPS
FROM
$2920.

camper pickup

We haven't had a model year since 1907.

Not because we couldn't have done it along with everyone else.

But because we didn't believe in it. Whenever we found a way to change something for the better, we did it right away.

As the early leader of one of our biggest automotive manufacturers once stated, "...the primary function of an annual model introduction is to create a certain dissatisfaction with previous models."

Now, change for the sake of change might win you customers in the Fall. But it's hard to keep their confidence when you tell them they've made a $3,000 mistake ten months later.

So we've never had a model year. Until now.

Because of the need to include certain scheduled safety features, we had no reasonable alternative but to begin having model years.

So we have a 1971 INTERNATIONAL Pickup.

And because so many people look for certain changes in the forthcoming year's models, we've added a few.

A new grill. New hubcaps. A different tailgate treatment. New rocker panel trim. And several new colors.

71

LT. DUTY
RESTYLED

"INTERNATIONAL"
NAMEPLATE ON
DRIVER'S SIDE OF
MESH GRILLE.

LT. DUTY
ENGINES :
V-304
193.1 HP @ 4400 RPM
173 NET HP @ 3900

V-345
196.7 HP @ 4000
182.3 NET HP @ 3800

V-392
253 HP @ 4200
235.9 NET HP
@ 3600 RPM

FLEETSTAR
INTERIOR

The attractive, well equipped cab features easy-reading, individually illuminated and fully-calibrated instruments with air core magnetic voltmeter, fuel, water, temperature, oil and pressure gauges for the greatest accuracy and long-life reliability.

FLEETSTAR® D

(CONT'D.
NEXT PAGE)

choice of IH quality-built gas or diesel engines. Up to 285 horsepower.

For maximum cargo-hauling capacity, you have a short 90 or 92-inch BBC. So you can pull 45-foot trailers in 55-foot states. GVW'S from 25,500 to 54,000; GCW'S from 50,000 to 65,000.

WITH MIXER BODY

new T-415 5-SPEED MANUAL and new 451 and T-454 AUTO. TRANS. AVAIL. MID-1971.

FLEETSTAR A **71**
(CONT'D.)

Loadstar

4200	MAKE	MODEL	DESIGN	GROSS BHP @ RPM.
Std.	Detroit	8V-71NE V8	W/N—55 Inj.—Naturally Aspirated	260 hp @ 1950
Opt.	Detroit	8V-71N V8	W/N—60 Inj.—Naturally Aspirated	290 hp @ 2100
Opt.	Detroit	8V-71N V8	W/N—65 Inj.—Naturally Aspirated	318 hp @ 2100
Opt.	Cummins	V-903 V8	Naturally Aspirated	320 hp @ 2600
4300				
Std.	Cummins	NH-230	Naturally Aspirated	230 hp @ 2100
Opt.	Detroit	6-71N	W/N—65 Inj.—Naturally Aspirated	238 hp @ 2100
Opt.	Cummins	NHCT-CT	Turbo-charged Custom Torque	240 hp @ 2100
Opt.	Cummins	NHC-250	Naturally Aspirated	250 hp @ 2100
Opt.	Cummins	N-927	Naturally Aspirated	270 hp @ 2100
Opt.	Cummins	NHCT-270	Turbo-charged	270 hp @ 2100
Opt.	Cummins	NTC-335	Turbo-charged	335 hp @ 2100
Opt.	Cummins	NTC-350	Turbo-charged	350 hp @ 2100
Opt.	Cummins	NTA-370	Turbo-charged (Aftercooled)	370 hp @ 2100
Opt.	Detroit	12V-71NE V12	W/N—55 Inj.—Naturally Aspirated	390 hp @ 1950
Opt.	Detroit	12V-71N V12	W/N—60 Inj.—Naturally Aspirated	434 hp @ 2100

TRANSTAR SPECS. *(C.O.Es ON NEXT PAGE)*

(HOOD TILTS FORWARD)

FLEETSTAR D

(INTRO. MID-SEASON)

Transstar 4200 and 4300 heavy

(7½)

Fleetstar D offers five big-bore diesels. Choose Cummins or Detroit Diesel 6's from 218 HP to 270 HP.

239

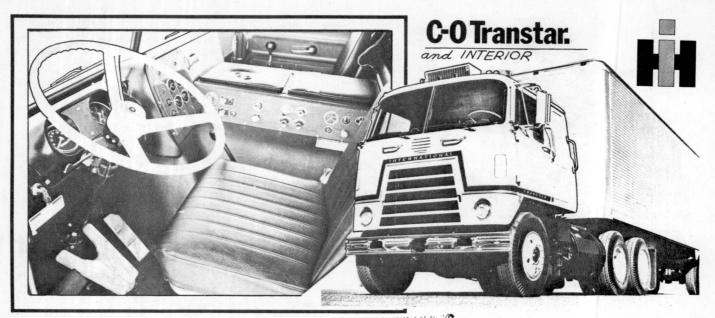

C-O Transtar.
and INTERIOR

IH

V-304	Gas	193 HP
V-345	Gas	197 HP
V-392	Gas	253 HP
VS-401	Gas	206 HP
VS-478	Gas	234 HP
VS-549	Gas	257 HP
DV-462B	Diesel	160 HP
DV-550B	Diesel	180 HP
6V-53N	Diesel	195 HP
DV-550B	Diesel	200 HP

CHASSIS DETAILS, (SHOWING PLACEMENT OF ENGINE) (CARGOSTAR C.O.E.) →

71
(CONT'D.)
C.O.E.

10 MODELS OF CARGOSTAR:

Model CO-1610A
GVW Rating: 19,500 to 24,000 lbs.
Engine Type: Gasoline—Standard: V-304; Largest: V-345.

Model CO-1710A
GVW Rating: 22,000 to 27,500 lbs.
Engine Type: Gasoline—Standard: V-304; Largest: V-392.

Model CO-1750A
GVW Rating: 22,000 to 27,500 lbs.
Engine Type: Diesel—Std.: DV-462B.

Model CO-1810A
GVW Rating: 24,000 to 35,000 lbs.
Engine Type: Gasoline—Standard: V-345; Largest: V-392.

Model CO-1850A
GVW Rating: 24,000 to 35,000 lbs.
Engine Type: Diesel—Std.: DV-550B (180HP); Largest: DV-550B (200HP).

Model COF-1810A
GVW Rating: 37,000 to 46,000 lbs.
Engine Type: Gasoline—Standard: V-345; Largest: V-392.

Model CO-1910A
GVW Rating: 27,500 to 35,000 lbs.
Engine Type: Gasoline—Standard: VS-401; Largest: VS-549.

Model CO-1950A
GVW Rating: 27,500 to 35,000 lbs.
Engine Type: Diesel—Std.: DV-550B (180HP); Largest: DV-550B (200HP).

Model COF-1910A
GVW Rating: 39,000 to 46,000 lbs.
Engine Type: Gasoline—Standard: VS-401; Largest: VS-549.

Model COF-1950A
GVW Rating: 39,000 to 46,000 lbs.
Engine Type: Diesel—Std.: DV-550B (180HP); Largest: DV-550B (200HP).

INTERNATIONAL

Cargostar.

Heavyweights of our Light-Duty Line

Power steering and brakes are especially helpful with all-wheel drive when hauling heavy loads.

Models 1310 and 1510

MODEL 1310, shown above with dump bed which is ideal for contractors, landscapers, cemeteries, municipalities, and many other uses. Wheelbases are 131 inches for 8-foot regular or Bonus-Load pickup bodies, 134 inches for 9-foot regular pickup, dump, stake or platform bodies, 156 inches for 12-foot stake, dump, platform or van bodies. GVW ranges up to 10,000 pounds.

LT. DUTY HAS new GRILLE

Direct-reading gauges are standard on all International vehicles. No idiot lights.

72

CONVENTIONAL TRANSTAR

LT. DUTY OR LOADSTAR OFFERS OPTIONAL 345 CID OR 392 CID V8s

A new optional fiberglass hood and fender assembly tilts forward so a serviceman can walk right up to the engine.

241 **Loadstar**

(CONT'D. NEXT PAGE)

This year you can equip your new FLEETSTAR A truck with any of four dependable diesels. Including 180 and 200 HP International V-8's. Or 225 HP Cummins® or Cat® engines. Or, you could choose one of the time-proven IH gasoline engines. Here your choice includes seven models. Ranging from our 193 HP Six to our big 285 HP V-8.

AVAIL. WITH FIBERGLASS ← TILT HOOD

'72 2050 OR F-2050 FLEETSTAR NOW OFFERS 225 H.P. V8

Cat 1160 Diesel Engine

AS ALTERNATE CHOICE.

Fleetstar A

90 OR 92" BBC CAB

72
(CONT'D.)

Lightweight Western Mixer Chassis from International

8500 M
new
('72 1/2)

WITH 107" BBC, 1160 CAT. DIESEL ENG.

VIEW OF IHC FACTORY ASSEMBLY LINE IN BACKGROUND

INTERNATIONAL

242

(C.O.E. ON NEXT PG.)

CARGOSTAR INTERIOR

72
(CONT'D.)

C-O TRANSTAR 4070A

new BUMPERS

CARGOSTAR

INTERNATIONAL

243

WITH JIFFLOX DOLLY PULLS SINGLES AND DOUBLES

105,569 LIGHT TRUCK SALES

INTERIOR

TRAVELALL
FROM
$3729.

73

FLEETSTAR'S IHC INSIGNIA MOVED FROM FRONT OF HOOD, BACK TO COWL.

Transtar 4200/4300.

FLEETSTAR 2070-A

new BUMPER

(CONT'D. NEXT PAGE)

244

SCHOOL BUSES
(VARIOUS IHC CHASSIS TYPES)

73
(CONT'D.)

Paystar 5000

new F-5010 MIXER INTR. 73½, WITH GAS VS-549 ENG. (227 HP) (1ST GASOLINE POWERED MODEL IN THE PAYSTAR 5000 LINE.)

245

I.D. # 4 (H) I (A)
ODHB UP

Model 500
Chassis & Cab

1/2-TON MODELS DO NOT HAVE THESE ROOF CLEARANCE LIGHTS.

73,656 LIGHT TRUCK SALES, 1974

Model 200
Four-Door Travelette $4093. ('74)

1974

74 new GRILLE (LT. DUTY and CARGOSTAR)

1/2 TON 100 SERIES FROM $3258.
3/4   200   3526.
1 1/2   500 CH./CAB   4230.
2   1600 CH./CAB   4773.

CARGOSTAR

TANKER (ABOVE)
REFUSE TRUCK (RIGHT)

150 HP V-345 ENGINE STD. IN MODEL CO-1610B, CO-1710B, CO-1810B, COF-1810B

180 HP DV-550B ENG. STD. IN CO-1850B, CO-1950B, COF-1950B

186 HP VS-401 ENG. STD. IN CO-1910B, COF-1910B (OTHER ENGS. AVAIL., INCLUDING CATERPILLAR.

INTERNATIONAL

ALD 825

246

IH

1975 LT. DUTY SIMILAR TO 1974, BUT ½-TON NOW IS "150" SERIES (FROM $3952.)

75-77

NEW ('75)

TRANSTAR **II** (STARTS MID-1974)

new SQUARED HEADLT. BEZELS

TRANSTAR 4100 "CONCO"

(CON = CONVENTIONAL
CO = CAB-OVER) COMBINATION

37,630 LIGHT TK. SALES IN 1975

PICKUPS, VANS, TRAVELALLS, LT. DUTY TYPES NOT LISTED AFTER 1975, BUT "SCOUT" MODELS CONT'D.

LOADSTAR, FLEETSTAR A, PAYSTAR, 9, TRANSTAR, C.O.E. CARGOSTAR and CO-TRANSTAR II TYPES AVAIL.

78 GAS OR DIESEL ENGS. (150-430 HP) (DIESEL ENGS. ONLY, IN UNDERLINED MODELS.)

NEW "S" SERIES

CO-TRANSTAR

247

truck is an "S", answer is yes.

NEW

IH **INTERNATIONAL TRUCKS**
The common sense solution.

(CONT'D. NEXT PAGE)

We're not giving in.
We're going on.
(1982-83 SLOGAN)

('81)

MIXER ('84)

DUMP

FINANCIAL DIFFICULTIES INTERRUPTED PRODUCTION FOR A TIME *(1981-1982)*

('80)

80-84

FINAL GAS TYPES, 1984

(CONT'D.)
medium diesel trucks

XL C.O.E.

('84)

6.9 LITER DIESEL

ALSO AVAILABLE :

our 9.0 liter and our DT-466 engines.

The economy 9.0 liter.
Unsurpassed fuel efficiency. The 9.0 liter at 165 and 180 h.p. offers fuel efficiency that can double that of comparable gas engines. It can even save you money if you use it for as little as 8,000 miles a year. And because it's built to meet International's rugged durability standards, the 9.0 liter is even available with an industry exclusive 36 month/75,000 mile warranty.

The premium DT-466.
Number one's #1. It's the engine designed especially to operate efficiently and economically for years and years. At 180 and 210 h.p., the proven DT-466 is the only American built in-line six cylinder diesel with wet-type cylinder sleeves. This allows for in chassis rebuilding which saves time. Saves money. And adds to resale value.

IN 1982, IVECO BLT. new "I" SERIES FOR IHC (AN IVECO TRUCK WITH "INTERNATIONAL" NAME.)

The commitment is forever.

('84)

249

WITH FACTORY-INSTALLED
AERODYNAMICS PACKAGE (WIND SHROUD,
ETC.) AVAILABLE (BELOW)
↓

85

all-new
LONGNOSED
CONV. 9370
REPLACES THE
TRANSTAR
4200 and
4300 SER.

"EAGLE" CAB
(9370
CONVENTIONAL)

NEW: PREMIUM 9370

CONVENTIONAL (STARTS 8-84)

note TAPERED
REAR FRAME RAILS
ON 9370 CONV.

9370 INTERIOR DETAILS

TOGGLE SWITCHES
REPLACE ROCKER
SWITCHES

UNIQUE
MODULAR
GAUGES
CAN BE
PULLED
OR
TWISTED
OUT OF
THE
HINGED
DASH
PANEL.

9670
C.O.E.

DIESEL ENGINES
ONLY,
AFTER 12-1-84.

9370

new
CONVENTIONAL
AVAIL. IN
9370,
F-9370
and
EAGLE
TANDEM
VARIETIES.

A FEW VERY EARLY ('40-'41) JEEPS BUILT BY AMERICAN BANTAM.

JEEP

(SINCE 1941)
WILLYS-OVERLAND, INC.,
TOLEDO, OHIO
4-CYL. L-HEAD ENG.
134.2 CID   6.48 COMPR.
60 H.P. @ 3600 RPM

4-wheel drive

MILITARY JEEP KNOWN AS "G.P.W. ¼ TON 4 × 4 TRUCK."

DASH ('42)

HORN
WIPER
MIRROR
LIGHTS
CHOKE
BEAMS
IGN.
HAND THROTTLE
PANEL LIGHTS
GAS GA.
OIL GA.
SPEEDO.
TEMP. GA.
AMPS.
STARTER
HAND BRAKE
INFO. PLATES

FORD-BUILT MILITARY JEEP ('42)
80" WB

WILLYS BUILT MOST W.W. 2 JEEPS, BUT FORD ALSO PRODUCED EXACT COPIES, TO HELP MEET THE EMERGENCY DEMAND.

1940s
NEW

Jeep Pickup
2-W-D

(MILITARY MODELS ONLY, UNTIL 1946)
6-CYL. ALSO AVAIL., STARTING 1948.

BAR B RANCH

STATION WAGON (ALL-INTRO. 1946.   STEEL)

('47)

118" WB

FRONT	
TRANSMISSION	TRANSFER CASE

TRANSMISSION
Ⓡ   ②
Ⓝ
①   ③

TRANSFER CASE
OUT   LOW
IN   Ⓝ
      HIGH
FRONT AXLE DRIVE   AUX. RANGE

DISENGAGE FRONT AXLE DRIVE WHEN OPERATING ON DRY HARD SURFACED ROADS

← 4-W-D SHIFT PATTERN ('42)

LATER MODELS ILLUSTRATED IN "PICKUP AND VAN SPOTTER'S GUIDE."

251

4-wheel drive

KELLY-SPRINGFIELD MOTOR TRUCKS
Springfield, Ohio.

(1912-1928)
FORMERLY KNOWN AS _KELLY_

EISEMANN IGN. (THROUGH '28)

RAYFIELD CARB. (ON 3½ TON and up, THROUGH '20.) ZENITH CARB. ON ALL OTHERS.

↗ NOTE UNUSUAL SLOPING HOOD, SEEN ON MOST MODELS

WORM, CHAIN, and GEAR DRIVE TYPES

19-23

WOOD OR DISC WHEELS

('20)

RADIATOR IS _BEHIND_ ENGINE

CLOSER FRONT END VIEW

VARIATION IN HOOD VENTS AND LOUVRES

MODELS:

Model	Ton	WB	
K-31	1½ TON	144" WB	(BOTH
K-32	1½	144	THROUGH 1920)
K-34	1½	144	(1921-22; K-340 IN '23)
K-35	2½	144	(THROUGH 1920)
K-36	2½	144	(THROUGH 1921)
K-38	2½	150	(1922-1923)
K-40	3½	150	(THROUGH 1923)
K-41	3½	156	(1921 THROUGH 1927)
K-42	3½	156	(1921; 1923)
K-45	4	150	(THROUGH 1920)
K-50	5	158	(THROUGH 1923)
K-60	6	158	(THROUGH 1922)
K-61	5 to 7	158	(1923 to 1927)

24

33	1½ TON	
K-39	2½	
K-41	3½-5	
K-61	5-7	

K-41 (3½ TO 5 TON) 156" WB

DISC WHEELS

CONTINENTAL ENGINES IN K-70, K-75, K-76, K-75G TT MODELS (1925 THROUGH 1928.)

25-28

2½ TON. K-75 ('25-'26) →

1925:
K-70	1½ TONS
K-75	2½ *
K-76	2½ *
K-41	3½
K-61	7

INTRO. 7-24

* = HAS _new_ FRONT RADIATOR

"K-100" 7-TON and VARIOUS TT MODELS ADDED IN 1926.

"KS" MODELS (HERCULES ENGINES IN SOME) ADDED 1927-1928.)

KNOWN AS "GERSIX" TRUCK,
1917 TO 1923.
FOUNDED AS GERLINGER,
1915.

KENWORTH

(SINCE 1923)

EARLY TRADEMARK

MFD. BY KENWORTH TRUCK CO., SEATTLE, WASH.

KENWORTH
NAMED FOR 2 MAJOR
STOCKHOLDERS :
H. W. KENT and
E. K. WORTHINGTON.

SOLID
36"
TIRES,
EXCEPT ON
REAR WH. OF
MODEL "L"

23

DAIRY TRUCK

EARLY 1923 GERSIX
SPECIFICATIONS :
BUDA engines
WORM DRIVE
STROMBERG CARB. ON
4-CYL.; RAYFIELD ON 6-CYL.

7.75 GEAR RATIO
8.66
10.25

'23 MODEL "M" = 1½-TON 142" w.b. 4-CYL. (4"×5½")
"K" = 2½ 150" 6 (3¾"×5½")
"L" = 3½ 170" 4 (4½"×6")

BOSCH IGNITION ON 4-CYL.,
WESTINGHOUSE S-H IGNITION
ON 6-CYL.

4-CYL. BUDA ENGINES CONTINUE ON
ALL 1924
MODELS.

24
-25

MOVING VAN
('24)

2-TON
"M"
and
3-TON "KS"
AVAILABLE
IN 1925.
new
WINDSHIELD and SIDE CURTAINS

('25)

new KENWORTH MODELS FOR 1924
"N" = 1½-TON 142" W.B.
"KS" = 2½ 160" (new 4¼"×5½"B+S)
"L" = 3½ 170"
2-WHEEL MECHANICAL BRAKES
STROMBERG. CARB. and BOSCH IGN. ON ALL.

253

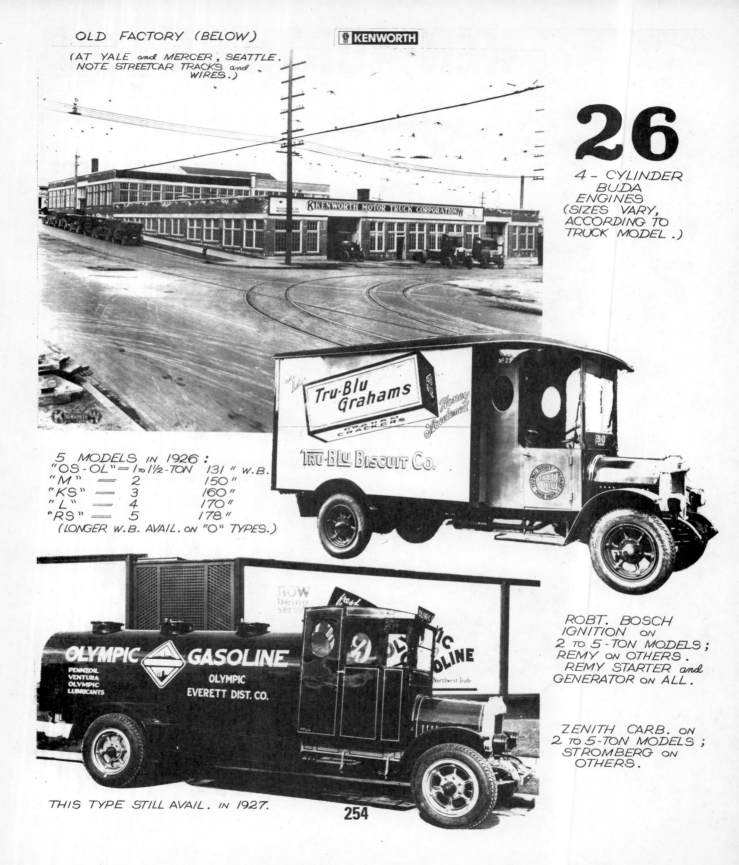

OLD FACTORY (BELOW)

(AT YALE and MERCER, SEATTLE.
NOTE STREETCAR TRACKS and
WIRES.)

KENWORTH

26

4 - CYLINDER
BUDA
ENGINES
(SIZES VARY,
ACCORDING TO
TRUCK MODEL.)

5 MODELS in 1926 :
"OS-OL" = 1 to 1½-TON 131" W.B.
"M" = 2   150"
"KS" = 3   160"
"L" = 4   170"
"RS" = 5   178"
(LONGER W.B. AVAIL. on "O" TYPES.)

ROBT. BOSCH
IGNITION on
2 to 5-TON MODELS;
REMY on OTHERS.
REMY STARTER and
GENERATOR on ALL.

ZENITH CARB. on
2 to 5-TON MODELS;
STROMBERG on
OTHERS.

THIS TYPE STILL AVAIL. in 1927.

KENWORTH

27

new SLANTING
SINGLE GROUP of
HOOD LOUVRES
(ON TRUCKS
ILLUSTRATED
AT LEFT.)

new CABS

new HIGHER-PLACED
HEADLAMPS

('28)

VS-
107

MODELS AVAIL. 12-27 :
"A" =1-TON	131" W.B.	4 CYL.	6.0 GEAR RAT
"A6" =1½	140"	6	7.8
"G" =2	150"	4	7.75
"J" =3	160"	4	7.75
"N" =4	170"	4	8.75
"S" =5	178"	4	8.75

1929 MODELS :

45	1½ TON	152"WB	BUDA WTU ENGINE	4 CYLINDERS
55	2	163	BUDA HS-6	6
D	2½	158	BUDA KBU-I	4
J	3	172	BUDA EBU	4
G	3	172	BUDA DW-6	6
N	4	170	BUDA YBU	4
S	5	178	BUDA BTU	4
10-TON	10	181	WAUKESHA GU	4

28

RADIATOR and
HOOD DETAILS

(OPTIONAL WHEELBASES
AVAIL. ON ALL MODELS.)

29

A TYPICAL
"VISIBLE
SUPPLY"
GAS STATION
PUMP OF THE
LATE 1920s

255

"SPLIT LEVEL" KENWORTH
MOTOR BUS

1930 MODELS :
"70" 1 TON 140-152" WB 6-CYL. CONT. *eng.* (214.7 CID, 61 H.P. @ 3000)
"100" 1½ 164-182" 6-CYL. BUDA 241.6 CID, 57 H.P. @2500 (75 H.P. IN '31)
"125" 2 157½-183" 6 HERC. 298 CID, 67 H.P. @2400
"145" 2½ 158½-184" 6 HERC. 339 CID, 74 H.P. @2400
"184" 3 164-206" 6 HERC. 360.8 CID, 76 H.P. @2600
"185" 3 183¼-211" 6 HERC. 428.4 CID, 94 H.P. @2200
"N" 4 170" 4 BUDA (REPL. BY "240" IN '31.)
10-TON 181" 4 WAUKESHA
"345" 10-T., 6-W. 245" WB 6-CYL. HALL-SCOTT 706.8 CID, 150 H.P. @2000
"165" 3-TON 158-171" WB (ENGINE LIKE "184")
"205" 3½ 172-223" 572.5 CID BUDA 6 CYL., 114 H.P. @ 1900
"240" 4 170-221" 453 CID HERC. 6 CYL., 99 H.P. @ 2200
(103 H.P. IN '31)

30

FURNITURE VAN

31

new FOR 1931 :
"85" 1¼-TON 140" WB 6-CYL. CONTINENTAL
"18-E" *engine* (3⅜" × 4") 61 H.P. @ 3000
"220" 3½-TON 194" WB 6-CYL. HALL-SCOTT
"160" *engine* (4¼" × 5½") 105 H.P. @ 2000
(OTHER MODELS CONTINUED FROM '30.)
(10-TON MODELS NOT LISTED IN 2-28-31
"AUTOMOTIVE INDUSTRIES.")

32

KENWORTH

32
(CONT'D.)

KENWORTH'S EARLIEST FIRE TRUCK (1932) ⟶

RECENTLY IN STAND-BY VOLUNTEER SERVICE, SUMNER, WASH. F.D.

MILK TRUCK ('33)

33

1933 MODELS : 86, 88, 101-B, 89, 127, 90, 146-B, 166-B, 166-A, 186, 241, 241-A, B, C ; 6-WH., 10-TON : 186-SDT, 241-SDT, 346-A, B, C, 386-C

ALL 6-CYL., with BUDA, HERCULES, OR HALL-SCOTT ENGINES. 141-240" WB
1½ TO 10-TON CAPACITIES

6-CYL. GAS ENGINES, AS BEFORE. (2 TO 7-TON) (7 TO 10-TON 6-WHEELERS.)

34

('34)

C.O.E. ('37)

35

"D-146" MODELS are KENWORTH'S FIRST 1935 DIESEL-POWERED.

('37) CONVENTIONAL

ALL with 6-CYL. ENGINES (HERCULES ENGINES, UNLESS OTHERWISE NOTED.)

('37)

36

ADDITIONAL DIESEL MODELS

1937 MODELS :

37

				CID	H.P.	@ RPM
"88"	2-TON	146" WB		282	83	2500
"89"	2½	146		282	83	2500
"127"	2½ - 3	154		360	90	2400
"90"	3	146		282	83	2500
"128"	3 - 4	165		360	100	2400
"146-B"	3 - 4	158	BUDA eng.	393	103	2600
"186"	4 - 5	155		453	98	2200
"241"	5 - 7	169		529	110 H.P. @ 2200	
"241-A" "		169	HALL-SCOTT eng.	468	112 H.P. @ 2200	
"241-C" "		174	CUMMINS DIESEL eng.	707	125 H.P. @ 1800	

257

KENWORTH

38

1938 MODELS:
"88" (146-200" W.B., HERC. 282 CID 6, 5.8-6.8 G.R.)
"89" (SAME W.B. and 83 HP ENG., 6.16-7.4 G.R.)
"127" (154-202" W.B., HERC. 360 CID 6, 6.16-7.4 G.R.,
   90 HP @ 2400 RPM)
"90" (146-200" W.B., HERC. 282 CID 6, 6.8-7.8 G.R.,
   83 HP @ 2500 RPM)
"128" (165-206" W.B., HERC. 360 CID 6, 6.8-
   7.8 G.R., 100 HP @ 2400 RPM)
"146-B" (158-206" W.B., BUDA
   393 CID 6, 6.8-7.8 G.R.,
   103 HP @ 2600 RPM)
"525" "526" (168-204" W.B.,
   BUDA 525 CID 6, 135 HP @ 2200)
"241-A" (169-228" W.B., HALL-
   SCOTT 468 CID 6, 6.02-8.5 G.R.,
   112 HP @ 2200 RPM)

CUMMINS-ENGINED DIESELS:
   (NO. OF CYLINDERS IN PARENTHESIS)
"505" (4 ;) "506" (4 ;)
"507" (4 ;) "511" (6 ;)
"519" (6 ;) "521" (6.)

6-WHEELERS:
   (D = CUMMINS DIESEL)
"89-SBT;" "127-SBT;"
"146-SBT;" "346-C;" "386-C,"
"508" (D;) "509" (D;)
"510" (D;) "512" (D;) "513;"
"514" (D;) "520" (D;)
"522" (D;) "523" (D;)
"524" (D;) "527;" "528."

KENWORTH
BUSES
('38)

6-CYL. GAS ENGINES;
4 and 6-CYL. DIESELS

39

83 TO 150 HP RANGE
282 TO 672 CID RANGE. IN '39 KW LINE,
NO HALL-SCOTT ENGINES LISTED.

EARLY
1940s

$2739.-$9410.
IN 1940

1940 =
new UPRIGHT
RADIATOR
SHELL,
CONT'D.
SINCE THEN.

DURING W.W. 2, KENWORTH BUILT
MILITARY VEHICLES, THE M-1 and M-1A1
WRECKERS and BOMBER NOSE ASSEMBLIES.
COMM'L. PROD. FACILITIES MOVED TO YAKIMA, WA.

1944 = KENWORTH
BECOMES A WHOLLY-OWNED SUBSIDIARY OF PACIFIC CAR
and FOUNDRY CO.
(LATER **PACCAR**.)

1946 = KENWORTH MOVES
TO NEW FACTORY IN
SEATTLE.

(CIRCA '47)

('46-'47)

KENWORTH

1946 - ACQUIRED FACTORY SHOWN IN BACKGROUND

KENWORTH MOTOR TRUCK

47

6-CYLINDER DIESEL OR GAS ENGINES

"521" DIESEL (6¾ TON CAP'Y.)
161-215" W.B.
CUMMINS "HB-6"
ENGINE 672 CID
200 HP @ 2100 RPM
6.42 - 7.84 G.R.

"522" DIESEL (15 TON)
187-245" W.B.
SAME ENG. AS ABOVE,
BUT 150 HP @ 1800 RPM

"587" GAS (9¾ TON)
150-215" W.B.
BU-LO-525 ENGINE 525 CID
135 HP @ 2200 RPM

WESTINGHOUSE AIR BRAKES

ALSO 6-WHEEL
MODELS "523,"
"524," "528,"
"532," "548,"
"552." CUMMINS
"HB-6" DIESEL
ENGINE IN
ALL BUT
"528"
(WITH 135-HP
"BU-LO-525"
ENGINE)
and
"532"
(WITH "6MZR"
WAUKESHA ENG.
404 CID, 112 HP
@ 2500 RPM)

6-WHEELERS
have 186-255"
**WHEELBASE,
DEPENDING ON
MODEL.**

10.00 × 20 TIRES
(UP TO 11.00 × 22 AVAIL.)

259

KENWORTH

SHORT CONVENT'L. TANKER

INFLAMMABLE

"521" DIESEL CONT'D., BUT RATED AT 150 HP @ 1800 RPM.

6 – WHEELERS INCLUDE :
"522" (4-WH. IN '47)
"523"
"524"
"528"
"548"
"552"
"825"
"829"

48

ALL with 150 - HP "HB-6" CUMMINS DIESEL ENGINES EXCEPT "528" and "829"

new "585" has ENGINE SIMILAR TO FORMER "587," BUT WITH 150 HP @ 2200 RPM.

DON E. KEITH
CORCORAN

"BRUCK"

COMBINATION
BUS -AND-
FREIGHT TRUCK

49

Gas &
Diesel Trucks

CONVENTIONAL
HEAVY-DUTY

"521" DIESEL
6-CYL., 621 CID
CUMMINS ENGINE
(150 HP @ 1800 RPM)
161"-215" W.B.
6.42 TO 7.84 GEAR RATIO

"585" GAS-POWERED
6-CYL., 525 CID
BUDA ENGINE
(150 HP @ 2200 RPM)
150"-215" W.B.
6.14 GEAR RATIO

C.O.E.

49
(CONT'D.)

*INDUSTRIAL
HAULER
TRACTOR*

WITH *ONE-MAN CAB*

6 CYL. KENWORTH

50-52

1951 SPECS.:
"521" (D) 165-255" W.B.
672 CID
150 HP @ 1800 RPM
"585" (SAME WBS AS 521)
554 CID
188 HP @ 2600 RPM
6-WHEELERS:
"522," "523," "524,"
"548," "552," "584,"
"825," "829," "888."

ALL DIESELS
EXC. "585" and
"829."

('50)

1953 MODELS:
521
584 (ENDS '53)
585 (188 HP WAUK. GAS)*
801 (200 HP CUM. DIESEL)
6-WHEELERS: (STD.
522   ENG. IS
523-4R   150 HP,
524-4R   672 CID
548-4R   CUMMINS
552-4R   DIESEL.)
825-4R
829-4R (WAU. GAS)*

ON CONVENTIONAL,
"KENWORTH" NAME
MOVED FURTHER
FORWARD ON HOOD
IN 1953.

('53)

...There's more
WORTH in KENWORTH

848-4R,
849-4R,
850-4R ARE
new IN '54
* HAS 200 HP LE ROI
ENGINE IN '54.

53-54

(153¼" WB and up)

('54)

new MODELS:
801; 802; 802-A

"521" NOT LISTED

55

OTHER
REGULAR MODELS
CONTINUED

263

with SPECIAL ½-CAB TRACTOR

KENWORTH

4 HDLTS.
OPTIONAL
('58)

56-58

('56)

('60)

('61)

('61)

59-62

new QUADRUPLE
HEADLIGHTS

MOTOR TRUCK COMPANY
PACIFIC CAR AND FOUNDRY COMPANY

('61)

MODEL
"S"
(SHORT
HOOD)

264

63

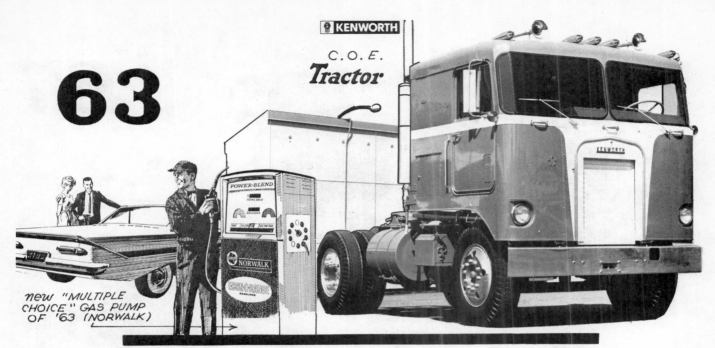

new "MULTIPLE CHOICE" GAS PUMP OF '63 (NORWALK)

POWER-BLEND

NORWALK
ECONO-RANGE
GASOLINE

heavy

64

TANDEM-AXLE TANKER AND TRAILER

BOB'S GARAGE
445 So. MAIN ST. ORANGE, CALIF.
DIAL 543-7042

65

6-WHEELER
WITH WRECKER
BODY (RARE)

265

KENWORTH

66-67

('66)

CONVENTIONAL

C.O.E.

C.O.E. GETS " KW " RADIATOR BADGE, 1969.

68-71

MODEL "K" C.O.E.

BASIC 1970 MODELS :
(DIESEL = 6, V-8 OR V-12)

"CS2" (S2s
"W" with
"WS2" NARROW,
LOWER HOODS FOR
SMALL ENGINES.)
"WS-12" (WIDE-FRONT
HOODS and
LARGER RADIATORS
FOR 300 + HP
ENGINES.)
"K" (C.O.E.)
OTHER
VARIATIONS
UNDER THE
ABOVE MODEL
HEADINGS.

('70-71)

"WS-12" TYPE

TILT-CAB

CONVENTIONAL
'72s have AMBER LIGHT ABOVE
EACH PAIR OF HEADLIGHTS.

INSTRUMENT
PANEL
(CONVENTIONAL)

266

SYMBOL ON CONV. SINCE 1940s, ON C.O.E. SINCE 1969.

KENWORTH CONVENTIONALS

Construction Truck   C-500 (STARTS SUMMER, '72)

SINCE 1972

W-900 IS STD. TYPE CONVENTIONAL.

"BRUTE" (STARTS SUMMER, '72) (note GRILLE GUARD)

('83)

Fifty years old and still setting the pace.

The FIRST factory-installed diesel engine in a motor truck.

The FIRST extruded aluminum frame.

The FIRST aluminum disc-type wheels.

The FIRST gas turbine powered truck in scheduled freight service.

The FIRST threaded spring pins and bushings in a motor truck.

The FIRST dual drive torsion spring bogey.

The FIRST grille/condenser air conditioning system.

The FIRST tilt hood in an American motor truck.

The FIRST piano-hinged bulkhead type door.

The FIRST tilt-out instrument panels.

('73)

KENWORTH "FAMOUS FIRSTS" innovations (AS OF 1973)

new 1976½ VIT-200 has AERODYNAMIC ROOFLINE WITH 2ND (UPPER) SLEEPER CAB WINDSHIELD (AVAIL. AS C.O.E. OR CONVENTIONAL)

SQUARE HEADLIGHTS ON SOME MODELS OF THE 1980s

267 (C.O.E.s ON NEXT PAGE)

KENWORTH

LOW - CAB MIDDLEWEIGHT "P D" ('72)

UP TO 250 HP ('74)

C.O.E. MODELS

('74)

LOW - CAB MIDDLEWEIGHT Kenworth Hustler

SINCE 1972 (CONT'D.)

K100E (new)

↓

('85)

SUPERSEDES FORMER K-100

new ACCESS DOOR FOR W.W.

↑ REAR (WITH TRIPLE BACK WINDOWS) (SINGLE BACK WINDOW TYPES ALSO.)

K-100 TYPE

↗ AERO-DYNAMIC SHROUD OVER CAB HELPS TO CONSERVE FUEL IN 1980s. K-100 and K-100 "AERODYNE" C.O.E.s AVAIL. 1978, WITH 228 TO 450 HP DIESEL ENGS.

KEYSTONE TRUCKS

(1919–1924)

Keystone Motor Truck Corporation
OAKS, MONTGOMERY CO.   PENNSYLVANIA

4 CYLS.

BERLING MAGNETO IGN.

ZENITH CARBURETOR

35 × 5, 36 × 6 TIRES
(1920 MODEL "40"

1920 TO 1922 SERIAL NUMBERS RUN FROM #2000 TO 2300.

20

MODEL 40 (2-TON)

(MODEL 20 1-TON DISCT'D. 1920)

WITH "OWN" 4³/₄ × 5¹/₈" ENGINE (17 M.P.H. @ 1350 RPM WITH PIERCE GOVERNOR) 26 HP

144" WB (THROUGH '24)
8.90 GEAR RATIO (THROUGH '21)
CHASSIS PRICE **$2200.**

new BUDA ENGINE (3³/₄" × 5¹/₈", 30 H.P. (THROUGH '24)

21

MODEL **40** →

new CHASSIS PRICE = **$2550.** (PNEU. TIRES) ($200 LESS with SOLIDS)

POWER-DRIVEN TIRE PUMP AND WHISTLE INCLUDED

1921 CHASSIS (AVAIL. FALL, 1920)

PNEUMATIC TIRES (new SIZES IN 1921)
34 × 5 FRONT; 38 × 7 REAR (THROUGH '24)
(SOLID-TIRED '21 MODEL AVAIL.
with 34 × 4 = FRONT; 36 × 6 = REAR)

8.80 GEAR RATIO ('22)

22-24

2-TON CHASSIS PRICE REDUCED TO $2175 IN 1922, AND TO $1975 IN 1923.

1923 SERIAL NUMBERS RUN FROM #3000 TO 3300.

ACTUAL PRODUCTION MAY HAVE ENDED 1923, AFTER PENN MOTORS CORP. (HEADED BY KEYSTONE FOUNDER H. W. SOFIELD) BOUGHT KEYSTONE

KISSEL

(1908–1931)

KISSEL MOTOR CAR CO., HARTFORD, WIS.

(CARS, TRUCKS, BUSES AND TAXIS)

2¹/₂-TON FREIGHTER
4 CYL. (4¹/₄" × 5¹/₂")
4 SP. TRANS.
168" WB
('21)

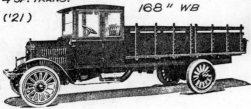

34.75 HP @ 1200 RPM

18-PASS. (4 CYL.)
BUS FRONT END SIMILAR TO CAR.

2¹/₂-TON FREIGHTER
4 CYL.
168" WB

('24)

2-WHEEL BRAKES ('24)

(1925 and 1926 SIMILAR TO ABOVE)

MFD. AUTOMOBILES ALSO, 1924 TO 1929

Kleiber

(1914–1937)
HEADQUARTERS AT SAN FRANCISCO, CALIF.

4-CYL. CONTINENTAL ENGINES

STROMBERG CARBURETOR

KLEIBER MOTOR CO.

11th and Folsom Sts.
SAN FRANCISCO

1800 E. 12th St.
OAKLAND

11th and San Pedro Sts.
LOS ANGELES

LONGER WBs ON ALL BUT "AA" (AS OF 1920) BOSCH IGN.

"B" ('21)

18-23

CHASSIS PRICES (1921) ==
AA (1 TON, 130" WB, $2600.); A (1½ T., 143" WB, $3100.); BB (2 T., 153" WB, $3600.);
B (2½ T., 160" WB, $4200.); C (3½ T., 163" WB, $4900.); D (5 T., 180" WB, $5600) GETS 4 CYL. BUDA ENG. IN '21.

BOYCE MOTO METER

PATENTED MAY-13-13 MAR-17-14

PATENTED JULY-15-18 AUG-13-18

DANGER · STEAM

SUMMER — AVERAGE

A COOL MOTOR CAUSES GASOLINE WASTE USE RADIATOR COVER

A SUDDEN RISE INDICATES TROUBLE STOP AND INVESTIGATE

COOL — MOTOR

THE MOTOMETER CO. INC.
LONG ISLAND CITY, N.Y. U.S.A.

(CONT'L. ENGINES)

24-25

"D" ('24)
$5300.
(CHASSIS PRICE)

5-TON DUMP TRUCK

SOLID RUBBER TIRES

('25 SIMILAR)

2-TON DISCONTINUED UNTIL 1928. MOST WHEELBASES LENGTHENED IN 1925.

↑ THESE BOYCE MOTOMETER GAUGES WERE MOUNTED ON RADIATORS OF MANY VEHICLES OF 1920s WHICH DID NOT HAVE WATER TEMPERATURE GAUGE ON INSTRMT. PANEL. (1925 TYPE ILLUSTR.)

1 TON	130" WB	CONTINENTAL J-4 ENGINE
1	140°	new 6-CYL. CONT. 8R ('27)
1½	147	CONT. K-4
2½, 3	163	CONT. L-4°
3½	170	CONT. B-5
5	185	CONT. B-5

(new 6-CYL. '27 1-TON has DELCO IGNITION; BOSCH. CONT'D. ON OTHERS)

° = OTHER CHOICES AVAIL.

26-27

"A" ('26)   1½-2 TON

('27) NOW RETIRED, THIS TRUCK WAS ONE OF 3 KLEIBERS KNOWN TO BE IN ACTIVE SERV. IN CALIF. AS THE 1970s BEGAN.

Kleiber

28

1½-2 TON SPEED TRUCK

CHASSIS $2450.

147" WB MECHANICAL BRAKES, EXPANDING ON REAR AXLE

3/4 TON	136"	WB	6	CYL.	5.36 GR
1½	158		6		6.42
2	147		4		7.75
2	170		6		6.42
2½ SPEED	190		6		7.75
2½	163		4		7.75
3	163		4		
3 SPEC.	163		6	new BUDA "BUS" ENG.	
3½	170		4		8.75
5	185		4		10.3

29-30

('29) KLEIBER'S FINAL CARS

CONT'L. 6 OR ST. 8 ENGINES WITH

MODELS ('29):

3/4 TON	121" WB	6 CYL.	CONT.	46 HP ('30)	
1, 1½	140	6	CONT.	50 HP ('30)	
2	147°	4	CONT. K4		
2° (SPEED)	170°	6	CONT. 8R	55½ HP ('30)	
2½, 3 (SPEED)	190°	6	CONT. 6B°		
3°	163°	4	CONT. L4		
3 (SPECIAL)	163	6	BUDA "BUS"		
4 (new)	202°	6	BUDA "BUS"	° = OTHER CHOICES AVAIL.	
3½, 5	185°	4	CONT. B5		

6 CYL. ENGINES ONLY IN 1930 (46 HP and up)

170" WB CHASSIS $2450.

('29) 2-TON SPEED

31

new NUMERICAL MODELS:

51 (1 TON;) 52 (1½ TON;) 54 (2 TON;) 64, 56 (2½ TON;) 65, 58 (3 TON;) 657 (4 TON;) 66 (5 TON)

CONTINENTAL AND BUDA ENGINES (6 CYL.) (58 TO 126 HP)

(6-WHEELERS: SAME MODELS AS IN 1932 (SEE BELOW)

32-33

80	1½ TON	140" WB	CONT. 18E	ENGINE	61 HP @ 3000 RPM
100	2	158	BUDA H-260		75 HP @ 3000
120	2½	170	BUDA		86 HP @ 3000
140	3	180	CONT.		74 HP @ 2400
210	3½	190	CONT. 20-R		89 HP @ 2400
225	4	202	CONT. 21-R		102 HP @ 2400 (ENDS '32)
260	5	206	BUDA GF6		126 HP @ 1850

'32 6-WHEELERS: 22DD 5T; 28DD, 34DD, 34DDT (REPLACED '33 BY 280, 340, 340T)

Kleiber

new DIESELS IN 1934

34-37

6-WHEELERS ('35-37):

81	5 TON	HERC. "JXB"	5.14 GR
121	7	CONT. "18R"	6.17
141	9	CONT. "21R"	6.84

MODELS		140" TO 210". WBs	6 CYL.
		new	
80	1½-2 TON	HERCULES "JXB" (263 CID, 68 HP @ 2800) 5.14	
100	2-3½	SAME, BUT RATED 70 HP @ 3000 5.81 GR	
120	2½-4½	CONT. "E601" (318 CID, 80 HP @ 2700) 6.17	
140	3-5½	CONT. "18R" (339 CID, 90 HP @ 2700) 6.84	
210	4-6	CONT. "21R" (427 CID, 118 HP @ 2500) 7.25 GR	
KD-4	4	CUMMINS 4 CYL. (448 CID, 83 HP @ 1800) 5.5 GR	
KD-6	6	CUMMINS 6 CYL. (672 CID, 125 HP @ 1800) 5.5 GR	

THE LANSDEN COMPANY, INC.
229 West 42nd Street   New York City
WORKS AT DANBURY, CONN.

LANSDEN
ELECTRIC
TRUCKS

CHAIN OR
CHAINLESS
DRIVE

(1904-1928)

MODELS : ('21-'22)

G	½ TON	96" WB
M	1	108
M	2	121
M	3½	133
M	5	146

EXIDE
BATTERIES
USED
(44 CELLS)

(1915-1933)

 ('23)

ALSO KNOWN AS **LARRABEE-DEYO**

BINGHAMTON
SPEED
LARRABEE
SIX
NEW YORK

LARRABEE-DEYO MOTOR TRUCK CO.,
BINGHAMTON, N.Y.

1920s

'22
MODELS :

X-2	1 TON
J-4	1½
K-4	2½
L-4	3½
W	5

4-CYL. and
6-CYL.
CONTINENTAL
ENGINES

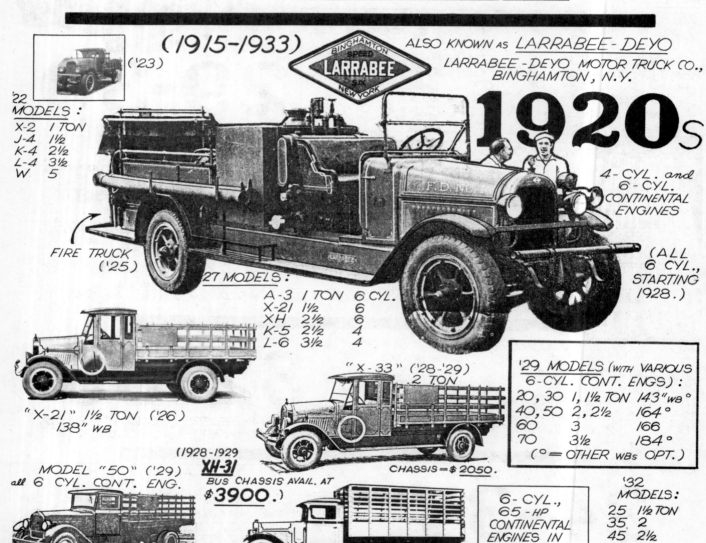

FIRE TRUCK
('25)

(ALL
6 CYL.,
STARTING
1928.)

27 MODELS :

A-3	1 TON	6 CYL.
X-21	1½	6
XH	2½	6
K-5	2½	4
L-6	3½	4

"X-21" 1½ TON ('26)
138" WB

"X-33" ('28-'29)
2 TON

'29 MODELS (WITH VARIOUS
6-CYL. CONT. ENGS) :

20, 30	1, 1½ TON	143"WB°
40, 50	2, 2½	164°
60	3	166
70	3½	184°

(° = OTHER WBs OPT.)

MODEL "50" ('29)
all 6 CYL. CONT. ENG.

(1928-1929)
XH-31
BUS CHASSIS AVAIL. AT
$3900.)

CHASSIS = $2050.

6-CYL.,
65-HP
CONTINENTAL
ENGINES IN
1930 1-TON
"20" and
2-TON "30-TB."

'32
MODELS :

25	1½ TON
35,	2
45	2½
55	3
65	3½
75	4
85	4½

272   ('30)

LECTRA HAUL

**UNIT RIG & EQUIPMENT CO.
TULSA, OKLAHOMA**

(SINCE 1963)

(MFD. OIL FIELD EQUIP. and VARIOUS OFF-ROAD VEHICLES SINCE 1935.)

MODELS M-85 and M-100

700 HP @ 2100 RPM IN CUMMINS "VT-12-700" OR DETROIT "16V-71NT" DIESEL ENGS.

400-GALLON FUEL TANK

21.00 x 49 OR 24.00 x 49 TIRES

29'4" (29'6")

16'8" (16'10") EMPTY

16'3" (16'5") LOADED

15'11" (16'1") EMPTY

15'6" (15'8") LOADED

8'3" (8'3")   15'0" (15'0")

32'4" (32'4")

(M-100 DIMENSIONS IN PARENTHESES)

STARTS **66**

CAB INTERIOR

FRONT WHEEL DETAIL

20' HIGH, 43' LONG, WITH *new* ACCESS STAIRWAY TO CAB, and GUARD RAILING

('70)

STARTS **69**

M-200
200-250 TON CAPACITY

NEW!

ELECTRO-MOTIVE V-TYPE DIESEL ENG. (8 CYL.) 9 1/16" x 10" BORE and ST. 1650 HP @ 900 RPM

36.00 x 51 50-PLY TUBELESS TIRES

(1912–1935) MACCAR

MACCAR TRUCK CO., SCRANTON, PA.

(ORIGINALLY MAC-CARR CO., ALLENTOWN, PA., 1912-1913)
FOUNDED BY JACK MACK — ONE OF MACK BROS. WHO
BEGAN MACK TRUCK CO.— AND ROLAND CARR.)

('21)
4 CYL.
4½" x 6"
BORE + STR.

3½ - TON CHASSIS
174 OR 186" WB
36 x 5 SOLID TIRES
4-SPEED TRANS.

1924 MODELS :	
EX	1¼ TON
L1	1½ T
HAT	2 T
H1	3 T
M2	4 T
G1	5 T

(2-TON BECOMES MODEL VI IN 1925.)

Chassis

('24)

G1 5-TON
DUMP TRUCK
162" WB
2-WHEEL BR
7-SPEED
TRANSMISSION

$5350.

('25) (4 CYL.)
5" x 6"
BORE and STR.

new 6-CYLINDER
ENGINES (BUDA
and WISCONSIN)
AVAIL. IN 1926.

H1 3 TON
162" WB
4 CYL. (4¼" x 6" BORE and STR.)

('26)
(6 CYL.)

H3
3 TON SPEC. TRUCK (TANKER)
186" WB

1920s

46 2-TON MOVING VAN 180" WB 4-SP. TRANS.

('28)

1929 MODELS :			
36	1½ TON	$1950.	
46	2 T	3100.	
64	3 T, 4 CYL.	3800.	
66	" 6 CYL.	4100.	
84	4T, 4 CYL.	4100.	
86	" 6 CYL.	4400.	
G	5 TO 6 TON	5100.	

new TANDEMS and 6-WHEELERS AVAIL. 1929.

46 2-TON TANKER 150" WB

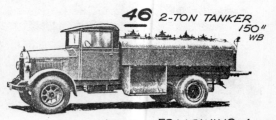

2-WHEEL BRAKES

('29) FOLLOWING A 1929 MERGER, MACCAR A

PRODUCT OF MACCAR-SELDEN-HAHN CORP., ALLENTOWN, PA.

86-A
5 TO 8 TON
CAB AND CHASSIS

note HORIZONTAL HOOD LOUVRES

('30)

30-35

LITTLE CHANGE IN DESIGN AFTER 1930.

$1330 to $5950
CHASSIS PRICE RANGE IN 1933.

1933 MODELS and ENGINES

100	1½-2TON	BUDA	H-260
40A	2½-4T.	"	H-298
180	3-5 T.	"	K-393
60A	4-6 T.	"	BA-6
66A	"	HERCULES	YXC3
220H	"	WAUKESHA	6SRK
220W	"	"	"
86-A	5-8 T.	"	"

274

Maccar

MACK TRUCKS, INC.

(COMPANY TITLE SINCE 1921.)

Mack

(SINCE 1909) ALSO KNOWN, FORMERLY, AS MACK BROS. MOTOR CAR CO., OR INTERNATIONAL MOTOR CO.

PRINCIPAL 1920s MODELS:

AB	1914 – 1936	1½ – 6 TON	4 CYL.
AC	1916 1938	3½ – 15	4
AK	1927 1936	3½ – 5	4
AL	1926 1929		
AP	1926 1938	7½	6	150 HP @ 2000 RPM

UNLIKE SOME OTHER BRANDS, MACK DOES NOT FEATURE YEARLY CHANGES. THERE ARE NUMEROUS MACK MODELS, OVERLAPPING ONE ANOTHER, AND OFTEN CONTINUING FOR SEVERAL YEARS.

1920 SLOGAN: "PERFORMANCE COUNTS"

AC ('19)

19-25

LATE 1922 = "AC" RADIATOR PROJECTS AT COWL SIDES; SCREENING REMOVED

"AB" GETS LARGER FIN-AND-TUBE RADIATOR, 1923.

"AB" COAL TRUCK ILLUSTRATED BELOW

ABOVE IS AC "BULLDOG" MODEL, WHICH MANY THINK OF AS THE MOST "TYPICAL" MACK TRUCK. AC MODEL PRODUCED FROM 1916 TO 1938, WITH A TOTAL OF 40,299 ACs PRODUCED. AC ADOPTS 4-SPEED TRANSMISSION, LATE '22.

BARR & COLLINS.

('25) 2½ TON AB CAB-CHASSIS

146½" WB

AB

FACTORY BRANCH

MACK TRUCKS

5½ - 7 TON AC CAB-CHASSIS ('28)

$5500.

BJ ('27) HORIZONTAL HOOD LOUVRES THROUGH 1929.

MACK'S FIRST HIGH-SPEED 6-CYL. MODEL.

(WITH WINDSHIELD ATTACHED) ('26)

AC "BULLDOG" TYPES

LATER 1920s

AB WITH DUAL REDUCTION DR. $3850.

($450. LESS WITH CHAIN DRIVE)

2½ - 3 TON 4 CYL.

146½ OR 164½" WB ('28)

4 CYL. = 60 HP @ 2200 RPM
6 CYL. = 75 HP @ 2600 RPM
(1931 SPECS.)

('26)

NOTE THE CHAIN DRIVE ON "AC" MODELS ILLUSTRATED ABOVE.

AL
MOVING VAN (MACK BUS ALSO USED THIS CHASSIS)

HERSHFIELD MOTOR TRANSPORTATION CO. STORAGE WAREHOUSE.

SOUTH NORWALK, CONN. 34

HERSHFIELD

1½ - TON MODEL "BB" (INTRO. LATE 1928) IS FIRST WITH HYPOID GEAR REAR AXLE.

276

BUSES

('25)

25-PASS.
CITY-TYPE BUS (AB)
4-CYL. 196" WB
CHASSIS $4250.
WITH BODY $7000.

622 "AL" TRUCKS, BUSES
BLT., 1926-1929.

($11,500. COMPLETE)
29-PASS. PARLOR CAR BUS
6-CYL., 233" WB 34×7 TIRES

AL

('29)
new
4-WH.
BRAKES

AB 29-PASS.
CITY BUS
$8000.
WITH BODY

LEFT
SIDE

BC
(6-
CYL.
126-
HP
BK
ALSO
BLT.
IN
EARLY
'30s,
AS
WELL AS
4-CYL.
AB.)

RIGHT SIDE

3,813 "AB" BUSES
BLT., 1925-1934.

Mack

('25)
(ALSO AVAIL. 1925 W.
230½" WB CHASSIS,
8-DOOR SEDAN
BODY (24-PASS.)
$8850.
COMPLETE, W. BODY)

29-PASS. CITY BUS
4-CYL., 225" WB
34×7 TIRES $4750. (CHASSIS)
BODY $3250.
EXTRA

AB 29-PASS. CITY BUS
225" WB CHASSIS=$4750

$8000.
WITH
BODY

('26)

1928 and 1929
GAS-ELECTRIC TYPES
ALSO AVAIL.,
$6388-8436.
CHASSIS PRICE

('28)

('28)

6-CYL., **AL**
25-PASS. PARLOR CAR
BUS (233" WB)
(2-WHEEL BRAKES
UNTIL END
OF 1928)

AB

25-31

CENTER-AISLE
INTERIOR
VIEWS (BC MODEL)

('30)

"BC" 6-CYL.,
29-PASS.
INTERSTATE BUS

(STREETCAR-TYPE
BODIES AVAIL.
1931-1933)

411 "BC" BUSES
BLT., 1929-1937.

BC 6 CYL. 100 HP @ 2300 RPM

('30-31)

AK 6 CYL. OR 4 (4 CYL. AVAIL. W. CHAIN OR SHAFT DRIVE)

('30-31)

Mack

AB

('30-31)

EARLY **1930**s

BG 6 CYL. 75 HP @ 2600 RPM

NEW bus

(ABOVE) **BT** 40-PASS. CITY TRANSIT BUS ('31) (87 BLT., 1931-1934) (CL IS SHORTER, 30-PASS. VERSION)

AC

PORTLAND LINES, Inc.

('32)

MACK-INTERNATIONAL MOTOR TRUCK CORPN.

Mack TRUCKS

AIR REDUCTION SALES CO

3½ TON

('33)

Models

BB 1928-32 1½ TON, 4 CYL.
BC 1929-33 3-4 T., 6 CYL.
BF 1931-39 (1179 BLT.)
BG 1929-37 1½ T., 6 CYL.
BJ 1927-33 4 T., 4 or 6 CYL.
BL 1929-36 (502 BLT.)
BM 1932-41 (3030 BLT.)
BQ 1932-37
BX 1932-40 (3032 BLT.)
BG BUS 1931-37 (87 BLT.)
BK BUS 1929-34 (544 BLT.)
CG BUS 1933-37 (76 BLT.)
CL BUS 1932-37 (441 BLT.)
CQ BUS 1934-41 (886 BLT.)
CR BUS 1934-43 (275 BLT.)

"BOULDER DAM" MACK

278

('33-34)

Mack

BL VAN ('30-31)

← BC CAB-AND CHASSIS (IN FOREGROUND)

APRIL, 1930 MACK FACTORY PHOTO (AT LEFT)

BJ TANKER →

BJ RACK ↗ ('30-31) 6 CYL. 126 HP @ 2200 RPM

EARLY **1930**s (CONT'D.)

FRANCIS H·LEGGETT & CO

Premier MAYONNAISE

Premier MAYONNAISE

NRA

Premier PURE FOOD PRODUCTS

Francis H·Leggett & Co Hudson River 27th & 28th Sts NEW YORK

196

BJ ('32) LATER TYPE

THESE FINAL '32-33 BJs have HIGHER RADIATOR, LOWER CAB THAN BEFORE.

BX → ('34) WITH COVERED VAN BODY

LATER
1930s

Mack

MODELS:

CB	1941–1950									
CH	1934 1941	126"–180" WB	415	C.I.D.	108 HP @ 2800	6.54	9.82	G.R.	3½–5½ T	
CJ	1933 1941	126 180	468		118 2400	6.54	8.92		4½–7	
DE	1939 1942									
EB	1936 1941									
EC	1936 1941									
ED	1938 1944	120½–136" WB	210	C.I.D.	67 HP @ 3000 RPM					
EE	1938 1950	133 175	253		75 2800	5.14	5.66	G.R.		
EF	1938 1951	133 192	271		78 2800	4.85	6.80			
EG	1938 1950	133 193	290		85 2800	4.86	6.80			
EH	1936 1950	158 194	310		90 3000	4.44	7.40			
EJ	1937 1938	158 194	288		84 2800	4.86	6.80			
EM	1937 1943	158 194	310		90 3000	5.43	6.33			
EQ	1937 1950	158 194	354		100 2800	6.31	8.64			
ER	1936 1941	146 194	310		90 3000	7.7	13.1			
ES	1938 1940	144 210	354		100 2800	9.3	13.0			
ETX	1950 ONLY									
EXBX	1940 ONLY									
FC	1936 1947									
FG	1938 1942									
FH	1937 1941	160 172	468	C.I.D.	118 HP @ 2400 RPM 7.48					
FJ	1938 1943				to 12.4 G.R.					
FK	1938 1941									

1938–1939 SPECS. LISTED
(CH, CJ = 1936 SPECS.)

HP 1936 ONLY
19 THROUGH 125 (1937–1955)

New _EFU_
C.O.E.
('38½)
6 CYL.
78 HP @ 2800 RPM

_EH_ TRACTOR and VAN TRLR.

NEW

DIXIE-OHIO EXPRESS

½ TO 2½ TON
MACK JR. ('36)
$535.–1035.
209 CID 6
72 HP

BLT. FOR MACK BY REO.

new FOR 1936. DISCONTIN. '38
(1937 MACK JR. has V-WINDSHIELD)

PRE WAR PRICE FROM $675.

MACK'S VERY SCARCE
LIGHT DUTY TRUCK
_ED_ 1½–2 TON PICKUP
(1938–1944)
WITH MACK/CONTINENTAL EN-11 ENGINE
210 C.I.D. 6   67 HP @ 3000 RPM

EARLY MODEL "ED"
WITH DUAL SETS OF
HOOD LOUVRES →
(REPLACES "MACK JR.")

LATER MODEL SHOWN
IN EARLY 1940s SECTION.

280

120½" WB
(136½" OPT.)

2,686
"ED"s BLT.,
1938 TO 1944

CH

('38)

LATER
1930s - 40
(CONT'D.)

EHUT
CAB - FORWARD ⟶

INTRODUCED
SPRING, 1938
WITH OTHER *new*
CAB-FORWARD MODELS : EEU, EFU, EGU,
FHU, EMU *and* EQU. HYDRAULIC
BRAKES, *with* MECHANICAL BRAKES *on*
2 LARGEST
MODELS.

WILLISON
OTTUMWA IA

"FN"
STYLED
LIKE TRKS.
OF 1920s!
ONLY VISIBLE
MODERN
FEATURES : WHEELS, BULLDOG MASCOT,
CURVED DOOR HANDLES, OVAL EMBLEM.

MACK'S TRADITIONAL
"BULLDOG" TRADEMARK
(USED AS HOOD
ORNAMENT SINCE
MID - 1930s.)

CHAIN-DRIVE
"FN" CAB-AND-CHASSIS
ONLY
150 BLT., 1940-1941.

6- CYL. C.O.E.
(EC ('79 HP @ 2300 RPM)
(EB (92 HP @ 2300 RPM)
(RESEMBLE '33-4 CJ, CH)

EC, *EB* = TRAFFIC TYPE " C.O.E.
(INTRO. 1936)

1 TO 30 TONS IN 1940.

(SCALE MODEL OF "LF" ILLUSTR.)

Model LF (12,453 LF TRUCKS BUILT, 1940 TO 1953)

MODELS:

FN	1940	1941 (REPLACED BY FT)
FP	1940	1942
FT	1941	1950
FW	1941	1949
HT	1941	1943
LF	1940	1953 →
LH	1940	1953
LJ	1940	1956
LM	1940	1956
LP	1941	1942
LR	1943	1964
LT	1947	1956
LV	1948	1961
LW	1947	(1 ONLY)
MR *	1940	1942
NB, ND	1940 ONLY	
NH	1940	1941
NJU	1941 ONLY	
NM	1940	1945
NN, NQ	1942 ONLY	
NO	1940	1945
NR	1940	1945
NW	1941 ONLY	
SD, SE, SF, SG	(1941-1942)	
SH	1941 ONLY	
T-8 — T-54	(1945-1951)	
CB	1941	1950
LMU	(NEW NAME FOR CH, 1941)	
LJU	(NEW NAME FOR CJ, 1941)	

* = MR IS A C.O.E. DELIVERY TRUCK.

Mack TRUCKS 1 TO 45 TONS

(ABOVE) LF (T) TRACTOR IS **New**

MACK BUILT A WIDE VARIETY OF MILITARY VEHICLES FOR THE WAR EFFORT SUCH AS:

BUSES; FIRE TRUCKS; MARINE ENGINES; VARIOUS TRUCKS (1-45 T.); TANKS (30-T.);

AIRCRAFT SEARCHLIGHT TRUCK; 3/4 TRACK; PRIME MOVER FOR "LONG TOM" GUN; NAVY HELIUM-HAULER TRUCK; PONTOON BRIDGE CARRIER; HEAVY-DUTY WRECKER; MILITARY CONSTRUCTION TRUCK; AIRFIELD CRASH TRUCK; NAVY FUEL TRUCK; FIELD DYNAMOMETER TRUCK; NAVY BUS; MILITARY FIRE TRUCK; 10-TON 6 × 4 PERSONNEL CARRIERS

1940s

3-AXLE TRACTOR ('47)

('49)

CIVILIAN F.T. USUALLY has CHROMED RADIATOR SHELL.

('49)

282

ILLUSTRATED WITH

BARTLETT SKYLIFT... 16'6"
BARTLETT MAKES 21 LIFTING MODELS FOR TOP AND IN-FRAME INSTALLATIONS
In 50,000# and 100,000# Capacities

More Fleets Use BARTLETT HYDRAU. LIFT 5th Wheels Than Any Other

THIS TYPE SKYLIFT WAS ADVERTISED 1971-72 BUT COULD BE USED WITH OLDER TRUCKS, AS SHOWN HERE.

Mack

MOVING VAN TRLR. ('51)

WITH HYDRAULIC SKYLIFT (REAR VIEW)

('51)

KOREAN WAR MILITARY VEHICLES

A20U (1951-1952) IS A REVIVAL OF FORMER EFU C.O.E.

('51-'53)

G744

EARLY 1950s

A SERIES REPLACES E, IN 1950.

SMITHTOWN 1815
SMITHTOWN CONCRETE MATERIALS CORP.

('50)

WITH MIXER BODY
1950 SLOGAN = "MODERNIZE WITH MACK"

MODELS:

Model		
A20	1950	1954
A30	1950	1953
A31		1953 ONLY
A40	1950	1953
A50	1950	1953
A51	1950	1953
A52	1951	1953
A54	1952	1953
A55	1952	1953
B20	1953	1960
B30	1953	1965
B31	1953	1960
B41	1953	1954
B42	1953	1965
B43	1954	1965
B50	1953	1955
B60	1953	1963
B61	1953	1966=(ILLUSTRATED ON NEXT PAGE)
B62	1954	1958
B63	1954	1958
B70	1953	1966
B71	1953	1958
B421	1954	1965
H60	1953	1954
H61	1952	1957=(ILLUSTRATED ON NEXT PAGE)
H62	1954	1958
H63	1954	1958
W71	1953	1958

TRANSIT BUS ('51)

W71-ST C.O.E. DIESEL 6-WHEELER INTRO. SPRING, 1953. (DESIGNED "FOR WEST COAST OPERATIONS."

('52)

DUMP TRUCK

283

with the economy of Mack diesel power! Hydraulically controlled . . .

('50)

EARLY 1950s (CONT'D.)

Bus

More room—greater comfort. Note arrow showing staggered seating arrangement —how shoulders overlap, providing at least 4 inches more effective aisle space for the standing passenger yet giving additional space, more comfort for those sitting.

Other important features: Thermostatically-controlled fresh air heating and ventilating system distributes fresh air throughout the bus—even temperature—no drafts. Hydraulic torque converter drive achieves smooth starting and acceleration . . . sensitive edge hydraulic automatic door controls assure greatest safety . . . fluorescent nonglare lighting for passenger appeal . . . wider entrance and exit doors for faster, safer loading and unloading of passengers.

BUS INTERIOR

B 61 T

WITH SLEEPER CAB →
ENGINE CHOICES ('52) INCLUDE 158 HP GAS (IN A-54 S, T, ETC.) AND 165 HP DIESEL (IN A-55 T, ETC.)

Mack ...outlasts them all!

H 61 T

C. O. E. TRACTOR ('52)

BECAUSE OF THEIR HIGH-SET CABS, THE H-60 TYPES (AS H 61 T, AT RIGHT,) WERE NICKNAMED "CHERRY PICKERS."

MACK MODELS OFTEN OVERLAP.

284

H 61 T 1001 - 1052 C 6907.

D SERIES C.O.E. ('55)

CAB RAISES FOR EASY SERVICING →

('55)

Mack

SCHOOL BUS

TRACTOR / TRLR.

new IMPROVED **B SERIES**

STARTS SUMMER, 1953 (RESTYLED) WITH new ENGINES and SUSPENSION

TRANSIT BUS ('55)

54 -55

MODELS STARTING IN 1955 :

B-33	(TO 1965)
B-44	58
B-64	58
B-65	58
B-613	66
B-653	58
B-655	('55 ONLY)
B-73, B-75	66
B-733, B-753	66
B-81	66
D-20	57
D-30	58
D-42	58
D-44	57
H-64	59
H-65	58
H-628	('55 ONLY)

(IN A TYPICAL TRUCK STOP OF 1955)

MENU

285

Mack TRUCKS

BUS #2101 (1956½ MODEL, BELOW,) has 672 C.I.D. DIESEL ENG., WITH 170 HP @ 2100 RPM and AIR SUSPENSION

(1957 EXAMPLES ILLUSTRATED)

('57)

W/O REAR SIDE DOOR ('57)

2 TYPES of TRANSIT BUS

REAR SIDE DOOR

56-57

VARIOUS MODELS OF LATER 1950s ARE LISTED AT LOWER LEFT, WITH DATES.

('56½)

L 1957 MACK

2101 SURE IT'S A M A C K Z HAIGHT

B46	1958	1965
B66	1958	1965
B67	1957	1965
B72	1956	1965
B77	1958	1964
B80	1956	1965
B83	1956	1966
B85	1956	1964
B86	1957	1959
B87	1956	1964
LY	1958	1962

ALSO INTRO.
DURING LATER
1950s :
  B426, B473,
B633, B673,
B813, B833, B853,
B873, B8136,
G73, G75, G733,
G753, G773,
H67, H69,
H613, H633,
H653, H673,
H693
N42, N44, N60,
N61, N613

286

('58)

('58)

Mack TRUCKS

VARIOUS H-60 C.O.E. TYPES RESTYLED 1954, CONTINUED TO 1962. (EXAMPLE AT TOP LEFT)

1955 to 1958 PRESIDENT OF MACK TRUCKS, INC. (PETER O. PETERSON) HOLDING MODEL OF MACK "AC" "BULLDOG" TRUCK

F.D. 12

58-59

2 VIEWS

1958 INTERCITY "DEMONSTRATOR" BUS (ONE OF A KIND)

new 1959½ G SERIES C.O.E. has ALL-ALUMINUM CAB WITH FLAT FRONT. GRILLE and HEADLTS. LIKE TYPE AT UPPER LEFT OF THIS PG. 205 to 262 H.P. DIESEL ENGINE CHOICES

('58) ↑ C.O.E., newer-style

(CONT'D. NEXT PAGE)

287

Mack B61 Thermodyne Diesel

B-61 THERMODYNE DIESEL

HEADING HEAVY-DUTY
TRACTOR-TRAILER
(164 TONS GROSS)
('57-'58)

Mack

A.LASKA
FREIGHT LINES INC.

INTER-
CITY
BUS

58-59
(CONT'D.)

PROD. :
14,308 ('58)
17,027 ('59)
14,438 ('60)
9,012 ('61)
13,988 ('62)
16,012 ('63)
14,173 ('64)
20,269
('65)

('60)

60-65

('62)

MODELS INTRO.
BETWEEN 1960 and 1965:
R607 to 640, R715, R719,
R737, R609R, R615R, U401 to U615, B13, B23, B37 (1 ONLY,)
B45, B47, B53, B57, B68, B79,
B331, B332, B334, B422, B424, B428, B462,
B576, B615, B755, B815, B4226, B4626 (1 ONLY,)
C607, C609, C611, C615, FC13, FC23, G72, G77,
H68, H81, H813, N68, N422, N442,
18, 20, 25, 30, 32, 40, 45, 50, 60, 65, 70,
DM607, DM815, F607, F609, F611, F615,
F715, F719, F723, F731, F737, F741, F743, F745,
F749, F759, F763, F765, F600R, F700R, MB401,
MB403, MB410, MB605, MB609, R401, R403, R410, **288**
R403R, R763

('64)

UNITIZED FIBERGLASS

CA 361

UNITIZED FIBERGLASS

U SERIES

NEW DESIGN MACK COMMANDCAB

OFFSET CAB

Mack TRUCKS

U SERIES & DM 400 · 600 SERIES CAB

PROD.: 19,579

66

MODELS:

R608F, R611F, DM403, DM410, DM477, DM609, 6076, DM611, DM615, DM640, DM807 to 811, DM819, DM831-845 DM863, F685, MB402, MB607, R402, R709, R711, R731, R611R, U640 ('66 ONLY)

CAB OVER ENGINE NON-SLEEPER CA 38

F MODEL STANDARD NON-SLEEPER CAB

INTRO. 1967: PK5RP, R685F, CF608, CF719, 100, DM401, 6096, 6116, 6118, DM685, 6856, DM823, DM865, DM885, MB477, R477, R685, R723, R773, R685R

67

('66)

C.O.E. MODELS

The Mack FL Western

('67)

Maxidyne®

ENDT- 675 6-CYL. DIESEL ENG. INTRO. 9-67

MACK WESTERN

MACK TRUCKS, INC. ALLENTOWN, PA.

"THE TRUCK CAPITAL OF THE WORLD"

note HORIZONTAL RADIATOR SLOTS

DM-600 HEAVY DUMP

('67)

PROD.: 16,634 ('67)

289

new "RL" (at WESTERN FACTORY)

MACK WESTERN HAYWARD, CAL.

"THE TRUCK CAPITAL OF THE WEST"

PROD. : 19,166

68

Mack

INTRO. 1968 :
FC 607B , CF 611,
CF 685, DM 487,
F 707, F 709, F 711,
F 739, F 773, F 785,
MB 487, MB 611, R 487,
R 607R

INTRO. 1969 :
35
F 795
MB 685
R 489
R 739
R 785

PROD : 23,583

69

Maxidyne

ENDT864 :

- Twin-turbocharged Mack V-8 for highest horsepower requirements.
- 300 hp at 2300 rpm.
- Torque output peaks at 1600 rpm—788 lb.-ft.
- Excellent performance, even when hauling top legal loads at top legal speeds.

← MB →

FL SERIES

LATER '69
(with RADIATOR GUARD)

↖ R SERIES

FL →

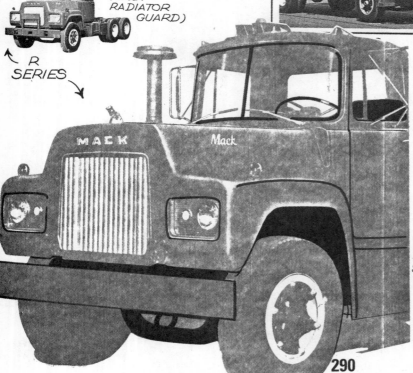

note STYLING SIMILARITY BETWEEN THE "R" and "U" SERIES.

290

U SERIES

BULLDOG HOOD MASCOT

Mack

70

CLOSE-UP VIEW OF FRONT END (R SERIES)

TOP DETAILS OF 6-CYL. DIESEL "MAXIDYNE" ENGINE

MACK

INTRO. 1970 :

FCR-685B, DM491, DM895,
F761, F819 (1 ONLY,)
R761, R795,
R711R (1970 ONLY,)
R715R (1970 ONLY,) R785R (1970 ONLY,)
R795R, U661 (1970-1971,)
U795, RD795

PRODUCTION : 22,057

"R" SERIES

140 TO 380 HP
5 TO 18-SPEED TRANSMISSION

"ALL-AMERICAN"

SOME 1970 MODELS PAINTED IN RED, WHITE AND BLUE PATRIOTIC COLORS, FOR ADVERTISING PURPOSES.

MACK SOLD MORE DIESEL TRUCKS IN 1970 THAN ANY OTHER MFR.

FL700L
FS700L Series

Western

FL700L & FS700L Series

TRUCKS

(SOME OF THESE MODELS AVAIL. DURING FINAL MONTHS OF 1970.)

LIGHTWEIGHT Mack Western "RL" SERIES CONVENTIONAL

Mack western mixer boasts 238 hp engine

RL-600 CHASSIS

71

C.O.E. F SERIES GETS IMPROVED CAB, AUG., 1971. (F SERIES ILLUSTRATED, TOP LEFT, TOP RIGHT.)

325-hp Maxidyne V-8 diesel
ENGINE

new U-700 SERIES

WIDE RANGE OF DIESEL ENGINE OPTIONS 140 HP TO 434 HP

New from MACK

HEAVY CONSTR. DUMP

AVAILABLE 375 H.P. DIESEL V8

The new 375 hp V-8 diesel with companion Maxitorque® 10-speed splitter transmission. An engine-transmission combination for top-performance operations—enough power to easily handle highest gross weight in twin or triple combinations on thruway and interstate runs.

This V-8 Thermodyne diesel produces more horsepower per cubic inch than any engine ever produced by Mack—and provides the power needed for highest gross loads at the highest sustained speeds.

To go with the new 375 hp diesel, Mack engineering has developed the new Maxitorque 10-speed splitter transmission. With selector mounted at the top of the single-stick shift lever, the air-shifted splitter reduces clutching by 40% for substantially prolonged clutch life.

AS AT RIGHT, SOME 1972 C.O.E.s WITH SOLID RADIATOR FILLER DOOR, and 4 FEWER HORIZONTAL BUMPER SLOTS THAN ON TYPE ILLUSTR. BELOW.

72

16000-MILE (OR 300 SHORT-HAUL ENG. HOUR)
EXTENDED SERVICE INTERVAL

Now offered by Mack Trucks
• Increased oil pan capacity
• Improved oil and water flow
6-CYL. DIESEL ENG.

MACK WESTERN F8795LST C.O.E. SLEEP. TRACTOR **Auto Hauler**

(325 HP TURBO V8 DIESEL)

EXTEND. SRV. INTERVAL PKG.
2 SPIN-ON OIL FILTERS.
new " " COOLANT CONDITIONER,
PRIMARY + SECONDARY FUEL FILTERS.
SPLINE-DRIVEN POWER STEER. PUMP.
new AIR COND. COMPRESSOR
3-BELT FAN/ALTERNATOR DRIVE
ETC.

THIS TYPE W. MACK NAME ON GRILLE.

(CONT'D. NEXT PG.)

293

the INTERSTATER

COCKPIT-STYLE WRAP-AROUND CONSOLE features the most important advance in instrument configuration in years — the RCCC and SAE-recommended control and instrument grouping, which makes driver change a safer and surer operation. And the new console with rich wood-grain finish is made of steel to provide greater safety, strength and protection.

Mack

INTERSTATER
(90° TILT CAB)
72 (CONT'D.)

86" BBC SLEEPER (50" BBC NON-SLEEPER ALSO AVAIL.) WITH 180-325 HP DIESEL ENGS.

New 36"-wide sleeper

There's more to the new Mack *INTERSTATER*...

294

Mack INTERSTATER . . . ideal for high-mileage, long-haul operations.

('74 - '75 ↗
FL SIMILAR)

INTERSTATER

WESTERN INTER- STATER (LTWT. C.O.E.)

Mack Western INTERSTATER Series . . . lightweight for maximum payloads

MB SERIES (LOCAL DLVRY.)

R SERIES CONVENTIONAL ↘

73 -75

On August 22, 1972,
the 50,000th Maxidyne-Powered Mack Rolled Off the Assembly Line

The 50,000th engine has the same horse-power and performance as the first—the revolutionary Maxidyne that was introduced six years ago

Mack in-line six and V-8 diesels

LIGHTWEIGHT (HVY. DUTY) DM SERIES MIXER

Mack R Series . . . most popular over-the-road conventional tractor.

Mack R Model's new RCCC-SAE console with high-visibility, standard instrumentation arrangement. Note attractive, non-glare beige color scheme.

★ DRIVER ★ **R** IMPROVED

CF PUMPER FIRE TRUCK

U SERIES (SHORT 90" BBC)

WITH OFFSET CABS

DM SERIES

1973 EXAMPLES ILLUSTRATED

V8 = 285 HP
6 = 237 HP

HEAVY-DUTY CONVENT'L. R SERIES (RT.)

('76)

CRUISE-LINER C.O.E.

← MACK'S FIRST all-new C.O.E. SINCE 1962.

MACK
The Greatest Name In Trucks

EARLIEST (1975½) CRUISE-LINERS had CIRCLE MEDALLION AT CENTER OF GRILLE.

CONVENTIONAL R, RD, RL, RM, RS, U, DM, DMM, HMN, MB (LOW TILT (AB) and F, WL and WS

76-79

C.O.E. TYPES IN 1978, 175 TO 450 HP DIESELS.

('77)

CRUISE-LINER'S DIESEL ENG.

Mack Maxidyne

WITH "MAXI-TORQUE" POWER TRAIN

MACK

SUPER-LINER CONV.

LIVESTOCK CARRIER

('78)

MACK

175 HP (OR 210 HP TRACTOR) IN **MID-LINER** C.O.E.

STARTS 1981

MANY OLDER SERIES ALSO CONT'D.

MC ('80) (MR SIMILAR)

ULTRA-LINER

STARTS 1983

ALSO AVAIL. WITH 2 ROUND HEADLTS.

SINCE **1980**

Bulldog →
HOOD MASCOT CONTINUES

SHOWN WITH SLEEPER CAB →

CONVENTIONAL **SUPER-LINER** ('80)

Super-Liner

('84)

MACK 950

note: AFTER 1982, FRONT BUMPER OF SUPER-LINER has JUST ONE RECTANGULAR SLOT.

297

MARMON-HERRINGTON
INDIANAPOLIS, INDIANA

MARMON CARS BUILT BY MARMON MOTOR CAR CO., UNTIL 1933 (EST. 1902)

NAME OF TRUCKS SHORTENED SIMPLY TO **MARMON** IN 1963 AND SINCE, EXCEPT FOR A SHORT TIME IN 1973 WHEN "MARMON-HERRINGTON NAME RE-APPEARED.

← BUILT MARCH, 1931 WITH 6-CYL. HERCULES ENGINES.

ABOVE: TRUCK PRODUCTION BEGINS 1931, WITH THIS FLEET OF 33 AIRPLANE REFUELING TRUCKS FOR ARMY AIR CORPS.

← ON THESE EARLY MODELS, NOTE THE DOOR-TYPE HOOD SIDE VENTS and ARCHED SIDE WINDOWS.

TH-320-6 SHOWN WITH MARMON V-16 CAR, FOR SIZE COMPARISON

('32)

1930s

L. TO R.: A.W. HERRINGTON, PRES.; WALTER C. MARMON, CHAIRMAN; D. GLOSSBRENNER; B. DINGLEY

40-Ton, 1200-inch Wheelbase Truck-and-Trailer Combination

('32) new STRAIGHT-TOP WINDOWS, VERT. LOUVRES

Truck-Tractor
(5 TO 7 TON)

190-Horsepower, Six-Cylinder Motor Drives All Six Wheels Through a Twelve-Speed Gearset

885 CID ENGINE ('32)

12 MODELS, 2-15 TONS 1932 STYLE STILL BLT. IN 1942!

Marmon-Herrington

6-W-D, 12-SPEED TRANS. WESTINGHOUSE AIR BRAKES ('32-33)

LATER '30s HEAVY-DUTY LINE KNOWN AS "C" SERIES (6 CYL., 78 TO 180 HP)

STARTING 1935, MARMON-HERRINGTON SUPPLEMENTS ITS HEAVY-DUTY LINE BY CONVERTING FORD TRUCKS AND CARS TO SPECIAL ALL-WHEEL DRIVE LIGHT AND MEDIUM-DUTY UNITS. '39 MARMON-FORD ILLUS.

298

MARMON-HERRINGTON

HEAVY MARMON TRUCKS OF EARLY 1940s
SIMILAR IN APPEARANCE TO 1932 MODELS

('41)

('42)

('42)

MARMON—
FORD TRUCK
4-W-D
CONVERSIONS
('40-STYLE)

EARLY
1940s

1940 PRICE RANGE :
$**1557.** (LD-4)(FORD V8)
TO
$**16,105.** (DDS-D-1000)
(WITH 6-CYL., 707cID
HERCULES DIESEL ENGINE
176 HP @ 1800 RPM)

MILITARY VEHICLES

War Service

4-W-D ARMY WINCH TRUCK ('40)

('42)

ARMED
CAR

ARMY
TANK

('45)

"LOCUST"
AIRBORNE
TANK

MARMON-HERRINGTON

TELEPHONE LINE TRUCK (CONVERSION OF FORD) 4-W-D ('44)

('48)

('46)

SINCE 1948, SAN FRANCISCO PURCHASED 174 M-H TROLLEY (ELECTRIC) BUSES.

TANKS, ARMORED CARS, ETC., DURING WW2

SOME EARLIER MODELS SEEN WITH 2-PC. WINDSHIELD 4-W-D OR 6-W-D

NOTE EXTRA DRIVE AXLE IN FRONT

Rancho Framas 74-F-13 NASHVILLE, IND.

('45) **Front-Wheel-Drive**

New "DELIVR-ALL" TRUCK (FRONT WHEEL DRIVE) (AVAILABLE 1945 TO 1952.)

All-Wheel-Drive ('50)

new **RANGER** V-8 FORD 4-W-D CONVERSION

LAUNDRY

('50)

1940s new
AND LATER

M-H TROLLEY BUS FLEETS IN INDIANAPOLIS, CHICAGO, COLUMBUS, CLEVELAND, DAYTON, CINCINNATI, YOUNGSTOWN, MILWAUKEE, K.C., SHREVEPORT, NEW ORLEANS, S.F., DENVER, LITTLE ROCK, PHILADELPHIA, DAYTON-OAKWOOD (AS OF 1950)

STARTS 4-50

MARMON-HERRINGTON 631

('50) 27 or 31-PASS. TRANSIT BUS (GAS) (REPLACES FORD BUS)

TROLLEY BUS AVAIL. 1946 TO 1955, AGAIN IN 1959.

200

BLT. 1950 TO 1955

300   **Marmon-Herrington**

MARMON-HERRINGTON

(TILT-CAB) "HDT" SLEEPER C.O.E.

4-W-D FORD CONVERSIONS AND SCHOOL BUS CHASSES DURING '50s and '60s.)

(INDIANAPOLIS PRODUCTION UNTIL 1963) COMPANY ACQUIRED BY SPACE CORPORATION IN 1964.

ALL-ALUMINUM CABS

special-use truck

('70)

IN ADDITION TO BUILDING OWN UNITS MARMON-HERRINGTON ALSO CONVERTS FORD, CHEVROLET, GMC, DODGE and INTERNATIONAL CHASSIS UNITS TO ALL-WHEEL DRIVE.

"CHDT" CONVENTIONAL (CHOICE OF VARIOUS 6, V-6, V-8, V-12 DIESEL ENGINES): CATERPILLAR, CUMMINS, DETROIT)

1970s ON

('72)

391 CID FORD INDUSTRIAL V8 ENGINE. (4-W-D) ALSO AVAIL. IN 4×2, 6×4, 4×4 and 6×6 DRIVE.

FACTORY IN LEBANON, INDIANA HEADQUARTERS AT GARLAND, TEXAS (and DALLAS) 1964 ON

C.O.E. ('76½)

('76½)

Marmon Designs Sleeper Box

('76½)

CONVENTIONAL

new 86" ALUMINUM SLEEPER CAB (LATE '73) SIMILAR TO 76½

NEW HEADQUARTERS AT MARMON MOTOR CO., DALLAS, TEXAS.

CUMMINS NTC-350 ENG.

1981 = MONSANTO "SPRAY-GUARD" RAIN-FLAPS STD. ON PREMIUM TRACTORS.

301

MOTOR COACH INDUSTRIES, INC.

The Mark of Responsibility

Pembina, North Dakota

ORIGINATED 1937 IN
CANADA ; PEMBINA, N.D.
FACTORY OPENED 1963.

MC-1
(1959 – 1961)

MC-2
(196 – 1963)

MCI

64-65

Model MC-5 Challenger®

('64 – 65)

MCI BUS

—ALUMINUM AMERFLINT
118-M-790

GH-140 COACH NUMBERS
(INTERIOR, FRONT)
(RER)

GH-82 WHITE
4" NUMBERS
SCOTCHCAL

GH-235 REG.
SYMBOL
3 REG.

GH-225-F
"GREYHOUND"

Greyhound

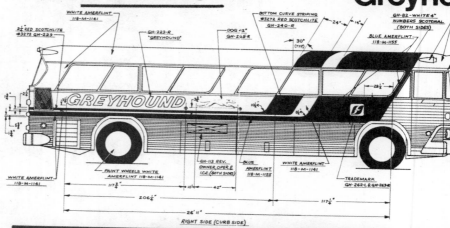

GH-209
5" WHITE NUMBERS

GH-234-R
DOG-REAR

GH-226-R
"GREYHOUND"

WHITE AMERFLINT
118-M-1141

3¾" RED SCOTCHLITE
#3272 GH-229

GH-223-R
"GREYHOUND"

DOG #2
GH-245-R

BOTTOM CURVE STRIPING
#3272 RED SCOTCHLITE
GH-240-R

24"   14"

30"
(TYP)

GH-82-WHITE 4"
NUMBERS SCOTCHCAL
(BOTH SIDES)

BLUE AMERFLINT
118-M-1155

MOULDING REMAINS
UNPAINTED

⅛" ABOVE
RED
STRIPE

WHITE AMERFLINT
118-M-1141

BLUE AMERFLINT
118-M-1155

2½" RED SCOTCHLITE
#3272 GH-229

WHITE AMERFLINT
118-M-1141

PAINT WHEELS WHITE
AMERFLINT 118-M-1141

GH-113 REV.
OWNER OPER.&
I.C.C. (BOTH SIDES)

BLUE
AMERFLINT
118-M-1155

WHITE AMERFLINT
118-M-1141

TRADEMARK
GH-262-L & GH-263-R

117⅜"   10"   42"   117¼"

206½"

26' 11"

RIGHT SIDE (CURB SIDE)

THIS
PAINT
SCHEME
EFFECTIVE
JULY 1,
1974.

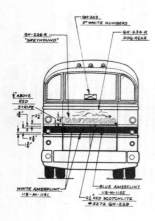

('66 -'67)

65-70

MC-5 VARIATIONS

CONT'D. DURING

THE

70s.

MC-5A

● 1965 and 1966 Model MC-5A "Challengers®", equipped with air conditioning. Lavatory. Air-suspension ride. Reclining seats.

MCI
ADVERTISING
SLOGAN
('78)

MCI
so far ahead
it's all
alone!

261" WB
35' LONG
DIESEL V8
252 HP
('72)

MC-5B

(1971)
1972

MCI MC-5C

A   B

4.00   5.00

FLOOR LINE

29.00 CLEAR
OPENING

54.12
CLEAR
OPENING

A   B

MC-5C

302

('78)

35'

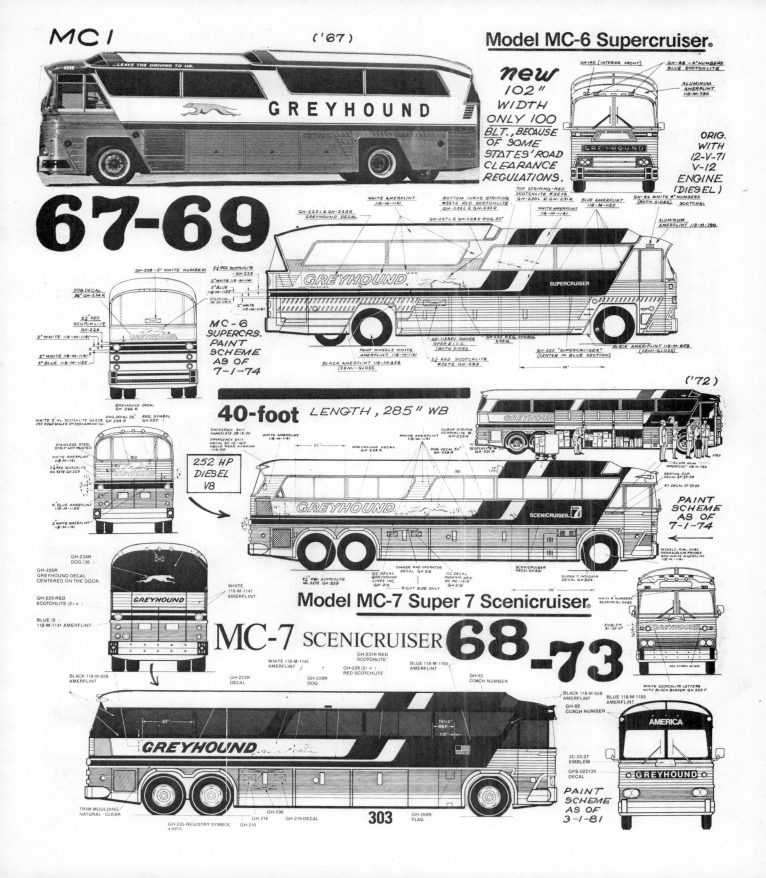

MC 1 ('67)

4589

...LEAVE THE DRIVING TO US.

GREYHOUND

67-69

Model MC-6 Supercruiser®

new 102" WIDTH ONLY 100 BLT., BECAUSE OF SOME STATES' ROAD CLEARANCE REGULATIONS.

GH-140 (INTERIOR FRONT)

GH-88 - 4" NUMBERS BLUE SCOTCHLITE

ALUMINUM AMERFLINT 118-M-790

GREYHOUND

ORIG. WITH 12-V-71 V-12 ENGINE (DIESEL)

TOP STRIPING-RED SCOTCHLITE #3272

GH-230L & GH-231R

BOTTOM CURVE STRIPING #3272 RED SCOTCHLITE GH-232L & GH-233R

BLUE AMERFLINT 118-M-1155

ALUMINUM AMERFLINT 118-M-790

WHITE AMERFLINT. 118-M-1141

GH-222L & GH-223R GREYHOUND DECAL

GH-227L & GH-228R DOG 50"

WHITE AMERFLINT 118-M-1141

GH-82 WHITE 4" NUMBERS (BOTH SIDES) SCOTCHAL

GREYHOUND

SUPERCRUISER

GH-209 - 5" WHITE NUMBERS

DOG DECAL 36" GH-234 R

2½" RED SCOTCHLITE GH-229

2" WHITE 118-M-1141

2" WHITE 118-M-1141

5" BLUE 118-M-1155

2½" RED SCOTCHLITE GH-229

2" WHITE 118-M-1141

5" BLUE 118-M-1155

DOG DECAL 36" GH-234 R

GREYHOUND

MC-6 SUPERCRS. PAINT SCHEME A9 OF 7-1-74

GH-113 REV. OWNER OPER & I.C.C.

GH-235 REG. SYMBOL 6 REQ.

PAINT WHEELS WHITE AMERFLINT 118-M-1141

BLACK AMERFLINT 118-M-858 (SEMI-GLOSS)

2½" RED SCOTCHLITE #3272 GH-229

GH-255 "SUPERCRUISER" (CENTER IN BLUE SECTION)

BLACK AMER-FLINT 118-M-858 (SEMI-GLOSS)

('72)

40-foot LENGTH, 285" WB

GREYHOUND

EMERGENCY EXIT NAMEPLATE 38-15-20

EMERGENCY EXIT DECAL 3C-15-165 ABOVE REAR WINDOW INSIDE

252 HP DIESEL V8

WHITE AMERFLINT 118-M-1141

GREYHOUND DECAL GH-223 R

WHITE AMERFLINT 118-M-1141

DOG DECAL 50" GH-228 R

CURVE STRIPIN SCOTCHLITE # GH-233 R

WHITE 5" No. SCOTCHLITE GH-209 USE EDGE SEALER 3M-3950 AROUND No.

DOG DECAL 36" GH-234 R

REG. SYMBOL GH-235

GREYHOUND DECAL GH-226 R

SCOTCHLITE # 32 GH-231 R

STAINLESS STEEL STRIP NOT PAINTED

WHITE AMERFLINT 118-M-1141

2½" RED SCOTCHLITE No.3272 GH-229

GREYHOUND

6" BLUE AMERFLINT 118-M-1155

2" WHITE AMERFLINT 118-M-1141

ALUMINUM AMERFLINT 118-M-790

SEATING CAP DECAL 3F-37-54

47 DECAL 3F-37-69

GREYHOUND

SCENICRUISER

SUPER 7

PAINT SCHEME AS OF 7-1-74

WHEELS, RIM, HUBS PERMANATE PRIMER AND WHITE AMERFLINT 118-M-1141

GH-234R DOG '36

GH-226R GREYHOUND DECAL CENTERED ON THE DOOR

GH-229 RED SCOTCHLITE (21-4)

BLUE (9) 118-M-1141 AMERFLINT

WHITE 118-M-1141 AMERFLINT

2½" RED SCOTCHLITE No.3272 GH-229

ICC DECAL GREYHOUND LINES INC. GH-210

OWNER AND OPERATOR DECAL GH 216

RIGHT SIDE ONLY

ICC DECAL PHOENIX, ARIZ. 3C-MC-1515 GH-219

SCENICRUISER DECAL GH 221

SUPER 7 INSIGNIA DECAL GH 224

WHITE 4" NUMBERS SCOTCHAL GH 82

GREYHOUND

EMBLEM 3C-33-27

REG. SYMBOL GH-235

Model MC-7 Super 7 Scenicruiser®

MC-7 SCENICRUISER 68-73

WHITE 118-M-1141 AMERFLINT

GH-223R DECAL

GH-228R DOG

GH-231R RED SCOTCHLITE

GH-229 (21-4) RED SCOTCHLITE

BLUE 118-M-1155 AMERFLINT

GH-82 COACH NUMBER

BLACK 118-M-858 AMERFLINT

BLACK 118-M-858 AMERFLINT

GH-82 COACH NUMBER

BLUE 118-M-1155 AMERFLINT

WHITE SCOTCHLITE LETTERS WITH BLACK BORDER GH 225 F

AMERICA

GREYHOUND

57"

15½" REF.

½"

12

GREYHOUND

3C-33-27 EMBLEM

GPS-022139 DECAL

GREYHOUND

PAINT SCHEME AS OF 3-1-81

TRIM-MOULDING NATURAL - CLEAR

GH-235 REGISTRY SYMBOL 4 REQ

GH-210

GH-216

GH-296

GH-219 DECAL

303

GH-268R FLAG

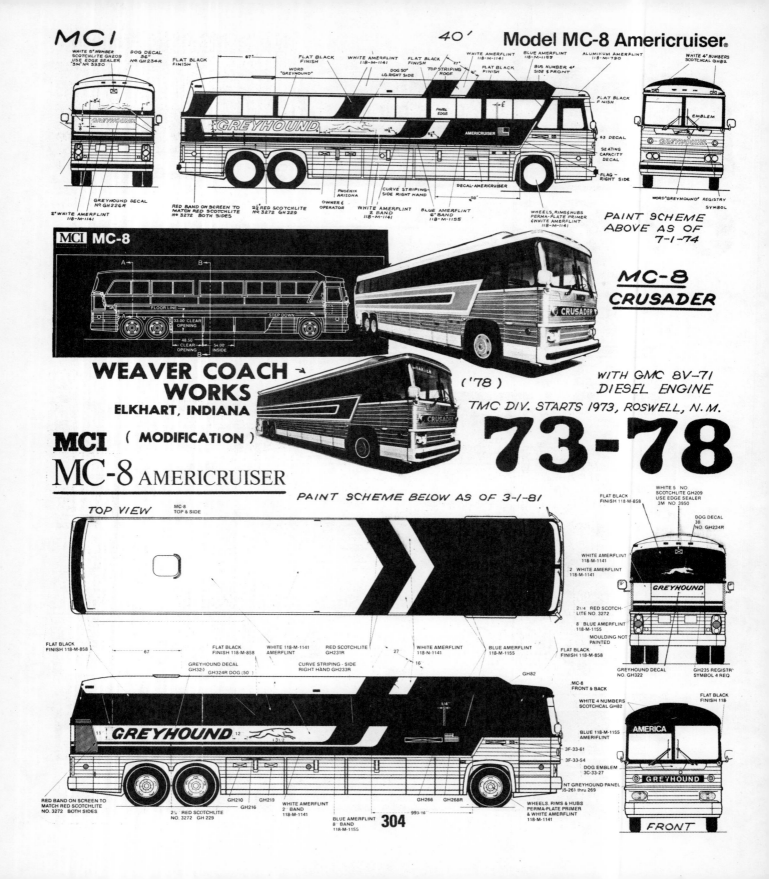

MCI

40' **Model MC-8 Americruiser®**

WHITE 5" NUMBER SCOTCHLITE GH209 USE EDGE SEALER '3M' No 3950

DOG DECAL 36" No GH234R

FLAT BLACK FINISH

67"

FLAT BLACK FINISH

WORD "GREYHOUND"

WHITE AMERFLINT 118-M-1141

DOG 50" LG. RIGHT SIDE

FLAT BLACK FINISH

TOP STRIPING ROOF

WHITE AMERFLINT 118-M-1141

FLAT BLACK FINISH

BLUE AMERFLINT 118-M-1155

BUS NUMBER 4" SIDE & FRONT

ALUMINUM AMERFLINT 118-M-790

WHITE 4" NUMBERS SCOTCHCAL GH82

PANEL EDGE

FLAT BLACK FINISH

EMBLEM

AMERICRUISER

GREYHOUND

GREYHOUND

GREYHOUND

#3 DECAL

SEATING CAPACITY DECAL

FLAG - RIGHT SIDE

GREYHOUND DECAL No GH226R

2" WHITE AMERFLINT 118-M-1141

RED BAND ON SCREEN TO MATCH RED SCOTCHLITE No 3272 BOTH SIDES

2¼" RED SCOTCHLITE No 3272 GH 229

PHOENIX ARIZONA

OWNER & OPERATOR

CURVE STRIPING SIDE RIGHT HAND

WHITE AMERFLINT 2" BAND 118-M-1141

BLUE AMERFLINT 6" BAND 118-M-1155

DECAL-AMERICRUISER

98"

WHEELS, RIMS & HUBS PERMA-PLATE PRIMER {WHITE AMERFLINT 118-M-1141}

WORD "GREYHOUND" REGISTRY SYMBOL

PAINT SCHEME ABOVE AS OF 7-1-74

MCI MC-8

A B

FLOOR LINE

33.00 CLEAR OPENING

STEP DOWN

48.50 CLEAR OPENING

54.00 INSIDE

B

MC-8 CRUSADER

CRUSADER

CRUSADER

('78)

CHARTER

WEAVER COACH WORKS
ELKHART, INDIANA

MCI (MODIFICATION)
MC-8 AMERICRUISER

WITH GMC 8V-71 DIESEL ENGINE

TMC DIV. STARTS 1973, ROSWELL, N.M.

73-78

PAINT SCHEME BELOW AS OF 3-1-81

TOP VIEW

MC-8 TOP & SIDE

FLAT BLACK FINISH 118-M-858

WHITE 5 NO SCOTCHLITE GH209 USE EDGE SEALER 3M NO 3950

DOG DECAL 36 NO. GH234R

WHITE AMERFLINT 118-M-1141

2 WHITE AMERFLINT 118-M-1141

GREYHOUND

2¼ RED SCOTCHLITE NO. 3272

8 BLUE AMERFLINT 118-M-1155

MOULDING NOT PAINTED

FLAT BLACK FINISH 118-M-858

67

FLAT BLACK FINISH 118-M-858

WHITE 118-M-1141 AMERFLINT

RED SCOTCHLITE GH231R

27

WHITE AMERFLINT 118-N-1141

BLUE AMERFLINT 118-M-1155

FLAT BLACK FINISH 118-M-858

GREYHOUND DECAL GH322

GH235 REGISTRY SYMBOL 4 REQ

GREYHOUND DECAL GH320

GH324R DOG (50)

CURVE STRIPING - SIDE RIGHT HAND GH233R

16

GH82

MC-8 FRONT & BACK

WHITE 4 NUMBERS SCOTCHCAL GH82

11

GREYHOUND

12 13½

BLUE 118-M-1155 AMERIFLINT

AMERICA

GREYHOUND

3F-33-61

3F-33-54

DOG EMBLEM 3C-33-27

RED BAND ON SCREEN TO MATCH RED SCOTCHLITE NO. 3272 BOTH SIDES

GH210

GH216

GH219

2¼ RED SCOTCHLITE NO. 3272 GH 229

WHITE AMERFLINT 2" BAND 118-M-1141

BLUE AMERFLINT 8" BAND 118-M-1155

304

GH266

GH268R

993/16"

WHEELS. RIMS & HUBS PERMA-PLATE PRIMER & WHITE AMERFLINT 118-M-1141

NT GREYHOUND PANEL 15-261 thru 269

FLAT BLACK FINISH 118

FRONT

MOLINE (1920–1923)

PROD. BEGINS 10-1-20

MOLINE PLOW CO., E. MOLINE, ILLINOIS

OWN 4-CYL. ENGINE (3½ × 5" BORE and STR.
SPLITDORF IGN.   PNEUMATIC TIRES 34 × 5 FRONT
130" WB   8.00 GEAR RATIO   36 × 6 REAR
25 MPH @ 1800 RPM w. PHARO GOVERNOR
TILLOTSON CARB.

MODEL 10 1½ TON

MORELAND (1911–1941)

MORELAND MOTOR TRUCK CO.

MAIN OFFICE AND FACTORY—BURBANK, CALIFORNIA

Branches: Los Angeles, San Diego, Fresno, Sacramento, San Francisco

'19 = 17 SERIES
'20 = 19 "

4 CYLINDERS (THROUGH '26)

BUDA ENG. IN '20 "19-N" (1 T.) CONTINENTAL ENG. IN OTHERS

21

20-C (2½ TON)
OTHER '21 MODELS:
20-N 1 TON
20-B 1½
20-G 3½
20-J 5

23 24-25

new HERCULES ENG. IN 1½-TON "BX"

AX (3-TON)

('24)   ('25)

AX 1924 and 1925 MODELS NEARLY IDENTICAL. "MORELAND" NAME ON FRAME.

('21)   ('21)

CONTINENTAL ENGS ONLY (1921-22)

TX (10 TON) ('26)

CONT. ENGS. ONLY (1927-1928)

TX-6 (10-TON)

26

OTHER '26 MODELS:
RR, RC (1 T;) BX (1½ T;)
EC (2 T;) EXX (2½ T;)
AC Bus (3 T;) AXX (3½ T;)
RX (5 TON)

$3500. (CHASSIS PRICE)

('28)

28 (ALL 6-CYL. MODELS)

1928-1929 "RC-6" 20-PASS. BUS CHASSIS AVAILABLE AT $2175.

7 TO 8 TON "HDS-6" 6-WHEELER CHASSIS

AUTO-LITE IGN. ON ALL ('29)

29

HERC. 6 ENGS. IN '29 E6, EX6, H6, HDS (3½, 4, 5, 6 TON)

30-32

"ACE" (1¼ TON) and "ROAD RUNNER" (RR-7, 2-2½ TON) ARE LIGHTEST MODELS.

$5800.   172, 196, OR 220" WB
SALES AGREEMENT with FEDERAL

33

ALL ENGINES ARE HERCULES DURING '33.

35

WAUKESHA ENG. USED (1ST TIME SINCE '19) IN TD-34 10 TON 6-WHEELER ('35.)

DIESEL MODELS AVAIL. STARTING 1935 (HERC. ENGS.)

CUSTOM-BUILT TRUCK EQUIPMENT
HERCULES and CUMMINS DIESEL ENGINES AVAIL. IN '37-'38.

MOLINE / MORELAND

MURTY BROS.

(EST. 1949)

DESIGNED FOR CARRYING PIPE, LUMBER, OTHER LONG LOADS THAT WOULD NORMALLY REQUIRE A TRACTOR AND SEMI-TRAILER.

HVY.-DUTY FLAT-TOP CARGO TRUCK (TYPE OF 1952-56)

('53) MURTY BROS., PORTLAND, OREGON

10-TON with SINGLE-AXLE DRIVE has 25' DECK and 179" TURNING WB. 15-TON DUAL AXLE DRIVE MODEL has 30' DECK and 204" WB.

NASH

(1917-1929; 1947-1949) NASH MOTORS CO., KENOSHA, WIS.

19-29

4 CYLINDERS. BUDA ENGINE IN "QUAD" → NASH ENGINES IN OTHERS.

CAB-FORWARD "QUAD" 4-W-D DUMP ↓

('19)

TEXACO PETROLEUM PRODUCTS THE TEXAS COMPANY

('20)

2018	1 TON	(1½ TON IN '22)
3018	2	(2½ IN '22)
4017	2½	(QUAD) (UNTIL '25)
5018	2½	

(BODIES SUPPLIED SEPARATELY)

MOTOR NASH TRUCKS

EMBLEM

(2-TON CHASSIS $2550., 144" WB (1-TON CHASSIS $1895. IN 1921.)

TEXACO GAS STATION (BELOW)

('21)

701 N. Sangamon St. MANUFACTURERS OF SPORTING GOODS AND GUT STRINGS

NASH

('21)

TRUCK PRODUCTION SUSPENDED 1929 TO 1947

1921 2-TON HAS SOLID RUBBER TIRES.

Thos. E. Wilson & Co.

6 CYLS.

47-49

WRECKER BODY ATTACHED (CAB/CHASSIS MODEL)

('49)

NASH CARS ALSO BUILT, 1917-1957 **Nash**

307

"OLD HICKORY"

KENTUCKY WAGON MFG. CO., Incorporated

LOUISVILLE, KY.

(1915-1923)

4- CYLINDER CONTINENTAL
ENGINE
(3¾" × 5" BORE and STROKE

ORIGINAL
WAGON-BUILDING
BUSINESS
BEGAN 1878.

THERMO-
SYPHON
COOLING

EISEMANN
IGN.

FRONT VIEW (EARLY 1920 MODEL
WITH 1919 LICENSE PLATE.)

PIERCE
GOVERNOR

18 M.P.H.
@ 1200
RPM

20-23

new 1- TON MODEL "W" FOR 1920
(REPLACES ¾-TON 1919 MODEL "M.")
"W" has new 135" WB
SOLID TIRES (OTHERS AVAIL.)
36 × 3½ = FRONT
36 × 4 = REAR

WORM
DRIVE

7.75
GEAR
RATIO

3- SPEED
TRANS.

KENTUCKY
WAGON MFG.
CO. ALSO
BUILT
A LINE OF
**URBAN
ELECTRIC**

COMMERCIAL
VEHICLES,
1911 TO 1918.

('20)
WOOD WHEELS STANDARD, BUT
THIS ADVERTISING ILLUSTRATION DEPICTS
TRUCK IN MOTION, MAKING IT APPEAR TO HAVE
DISC WHEELS.

OLDS MOTOR WORKS, LANSING, MICH.

(A DIVISION OF GENERAL MOTORS CORP.)

Oldsmobile
ECONOMY Truck

(1904–1924)

('19–'20) CANOPY EXPRESS

$1250.
CHASSIS PRICE

'21 has FEWER CANOPY SUPPORTS
('24 MODEL STILL SIMILAR)

19-24 T SERIES

4 CYL. 128" WB   40 HORSEPOWER 1 TON CAPACITY

ONEIDA MOTOR TRUCK CO.   GREEN BAY, WIS., U.S.A.
ONEIDA

ONEIDA
(pronounced O-ny-da)
MOTOR TRUCKS
"Uncommon Carriers"

(1917–1931)

Oneida Motor Truck Company
1202-1300 S. Broadway   Green Bay, Wis.

1 to 5 Tons

(OCT., 1919)

('21–'24)

USES OWN and HINKLEY 4-CYL. ENGINES. LATER MODELS USE WISCONSIN and HERCULES ENGS.

D-9 3½ TON CHASSIS

170" WB

B-9 1¾-TON CHASSIS

NATIONAL VARNISH COMPANY
LONG ISLAND CITY
MANUFACTURERS HIGHEST GRADE VARNISHES and ENAMELS

(JULY, 1920)

ONEIDA Electric Motor Truck

('20)

CANOPY

27599

TEICHNER C. SCHNEIDER

(OCT., 1919)

309

America's Most Complete Line of Motor Trucks

Gasoline and Electric Trucks

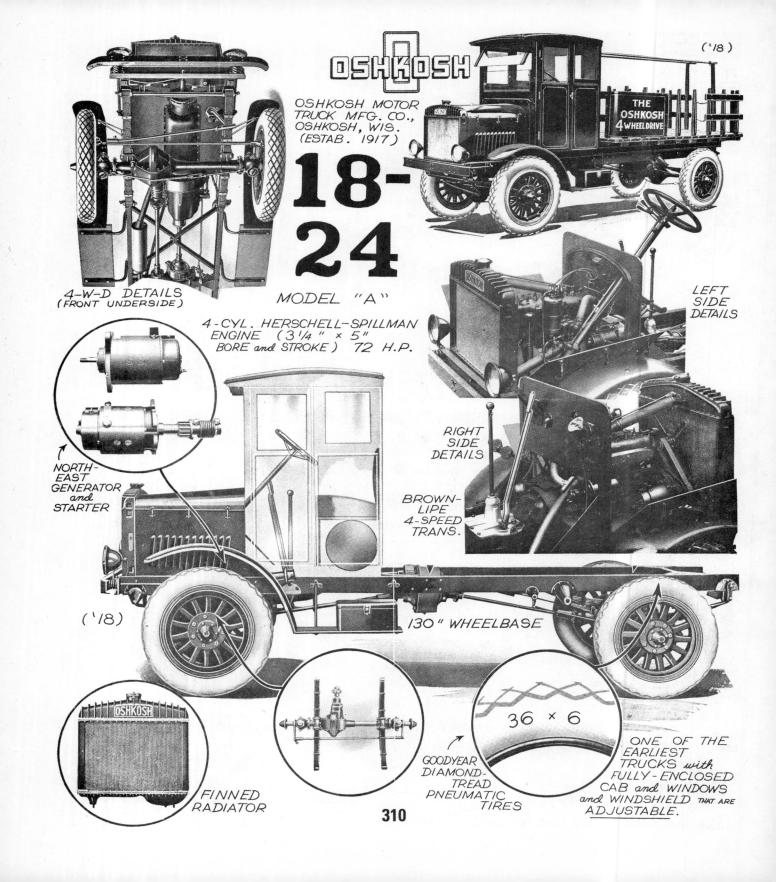

OSHKOSH

('18)

OSHKOSH MOTOR
TRUCK MFG. CO.,
OSHKOSH, WIS.
(ESTAB. 1917)

18-24

THE OSHKOSH 4 WHEELDRIVE

4-W-D DETAILS
(FRONT UNDERSIDE)

MODEL "A"

4-CYL. HERSCHELL-SPILLMAN
ENGINE (3¼" × 5"
BORE and STROKE) 72 H.P.

LEFT
SIDE
DETAILS

NORTH-
EAST
GENERATOR
and
STARTER

RIGHT
SIDE
DETAILS

BROWN-
LIPE
4-SPEED
TRANS.

('18)

130" WHEELBASE

FINNED
RADIATOR

GOODYEAR
DIAMOND-
TREAD
PNEUMATIC
TIRES

36 × 6

ONE OF THE
EARLIEST
TRUCKS with
FULLY-ENCLOSED
CAB and WINDOWS
and WINDSHIELD THAT ARE
ADJUSTABLE.

310

OSHKOSH

25 ON

4-CYL. HERCULES ENGINES IN 2½-TON "B" TYPES.

2-TON "AW" and "AAW" (130", 165" W.B., WISC. ENG.)
2½-TON "BO" and "BBO" (146", 165" W.B.
4-TON "F" (146" W.B., WAUKESHA ENG.)
('25)

(1928 "R" EXPRESS 1½-TON AVAIL. with
4-CYL. HERCULES or 6-CYL. WISC. ENGINES.)
(4 CYL. IN '27.)

4-WHEEL DRIVE,
4-WHEEL STEER
FIRST OF
RUBBER-TIRED
EARTHMOVERS
TO GO INTO
PRODUCTION.

MODEL
"TR"
(INTRO.
1933)

32-35

'32 MODELS			
"L"	2½ TONS	70	H.P.
"H"	3 "	73	"
"HC"	3½ "	90	"
"HXC"	4 "	106	"
"FHX"	5 "	112	"

(H.P. DETERMINED @ 2000 RPM.)
6-CYL. HERCULES ENGINES
IN ALL MODELS.

953A

146" W.B.
STANDARD ('32)

(1½-2-TON "JSW," "JSB"
MODELS AVAIL. 1933.)

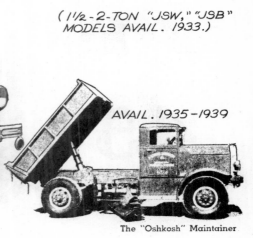

No 3

AVAIL. 1935-1939

The "Oshkosh" Maintainer

OSHKOSH

35-36

6-CYL. HERCULES ENGINES
(283 TO 855 C.I.D.)

CAPACITIES UP TO
10 TONS

DIESEL ENGINES AVAILABLE IN HEAVY TRUCKS.

'35 MODELS

"JB "	1½-2 TONS
"JC "	2 "
"WLD," "WLX"	3-3½ "
"B3S," "B3D"	3½-4 "
"C3S," "C3D"	4-5 "
"FC "	5 "
"FB "	5-6 "
"FD "	6-7½ "
"BG3"	7½-10 "
"GD"	10 TONS

68-180 H.P.

146" STD. W.B. ON ALL BUT 165" W.B. "BG3" AND "GD" BUT LONGER WHEELBASES (165"-201") AVAIL. ON VARIOUS MODELS.

36 ON

("J" SERIES INTRO. DURING 1935)

('37)

7.00 x 20" TIRES

2-TON MODEL 19 "JCB" IN 1936, has 153" W.B. and HERCULES 282 C.I.D. ENGINE (73 H.P. @ 2800 RPM)

10-TON "GD" with SNOWPLOW

1940 RANGE: FROM $2885. "JCB" TO $10,400. "GD" VARIOUS 6-CYL. HERC. ENGINES, 85 TO 199 HP

WARTIME MODEL "W-700"

TRUCKS ILLUSTRATED WERE SHIPPED TO PANAMA

45
and POST-WAR

PRE-WAR STYLING CONT'D. ON SOME TRUCKS.

OSHKOSH

48

THIS POSTWAR-STYLE GRILLE (W/O CHROME) ALSO FOUND ON 1945 CABLESS 4WD TRACTOR →

49

(W SERIES)
MODEL W-312 TO MODEL W-1602 BDH

HERCULES, CUMMINS, BUDA, HALL-SCOTT ENGINES USED

(ALL 6-CYL., 404 TO 893 CID 139 TO 295 HP)

GAS AND DIESEL MODELS

4-W-D AND 6-WHEELERS

50

OSHKOSH-HOWE FIRE TRUCK

OSHKOSH

51-60

SNOW-PLOW ATTACHMENTS (TYPICAL EXAMPLES)

FRONT VIEW
WINGS EXTENDED

('51)

SERIES W   4-W-D
AIR FORCE SNOWPLOW
('53-'59)

24'-2"
TOTAL
WIDTH
(INCLUDING
PLOW BLADES)

MANY
OSHKOSH
UNITS BUILT
FOR FIRE-
FIGHTING
SERVICES.

PEPSI

55

AVAIL. 1955-1966
(INTERNATIONAL CAB)

OSHKOSH

57-62

MIXER TRUCK

AMERICAN

UTILITY

NEW

MANY OSHKOSH TRUCKS CUSTOM-BUILT for SPECIAL PURPOSES.
THIS MODEL SOLD TO COAST GUARD.

61

UNIQUE new FORWARD-SLANT WIND-SHIELDS DESIGNED TO PREVENT GLARE and BUILD-UP OF SNOW on GLASS.

62 SERIES R

CATERPILLAR DIESEL ENG WITH

SERIES C (6×6) (ABOVE)

63

65

NOTE THE GRILLE GUARD.

315

66

OSHKOSH

SERIES C (*new* BROADER NOSE)
CONCRETE BLOCK CARRIER
(STYLE SIMILAR UNTIL 1974)

69

70

NEW

"E" SERIES
(BEGINS
1970)

HAULER TRACTOR

150 TO 270 HP

G SERIES
ARE
6 × 6
TILT-CABS
(C.O.E.)

316

OSHKOSH

MIXER

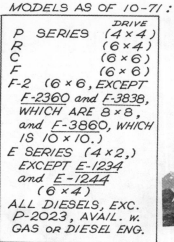

VARIOUS TYPES
OF UTILITY
BODIES AVAIL.
BY SPECIAL
ORDER.

1970s

('75)

210-350 HP
SIMILAR TYPE
P SERIES
SNOW BLOWER
CONTINUES IN
1980s, BUT
WITH UPPER
SECTION OF
HOOD PAINTED
FLAT BLACK
(TO REDUCE
SUN GLARE IN
DRIVER'S CAB.)

317

P SERIES
SNOW BLOWER
(_H SERIES_ SIMILAR)

FOR THE MARINES

MK 48 LOGISTICAL VEHICLE SYSTEM)(LVS) TRUCK

HEMTT* ('84)

* (HEAVY EXPANDED MOBILITY TACTICAL TRUCK)

OSHKOSH HOLDS FIREFIGHTING FOAM and WATER (note THE 2 HOSE-GUNS ON UNIT.)

L, M SERIES FIRE TRUCKS AVAIL.

1980s

J SERIES HEAVY TRANSPT. (ABOVE)

('83)

REAR (T SERIES)

NEW S SERIES CONCRETE CARRIER AND MIXER CHASSIS MIXER (S SERIES) INTRO. 1983.

V SERIES FORWARD CONTROL BUS CHASSIS AVAIL. (210 H.P.)

(ABOVE) T SERIES AIRPORT CRASH / FIRE / RESCUE (T SERIES DASH, BELOW)

BELOW: HEAVY TRANSPT., CONSTRUCTION, OR UTILITY TYPE

F SERIES

318

REAR

PACKARD

PACKARD MOTOR CAR COMPANY, Detroit

TRUCKS
(1903–1923)
(ALSO BUILT AUTOMOBILES, 1899 to 1958.)

OWN 4-CYLINDER ENGINES
4-SP. TRANSMISSIONS
WORM DRIVE

20

VARIOUS MODELS

1½E (EB)	1½ TON	144" WB
2E (EC)	2	144
3E (ED)	3	156
4E (EE)	4	156
5E (EF)	5	156
6E (EG)	6	156

21

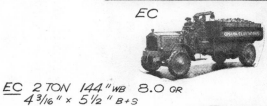

EX (144" WB)   EF (156" WB)

EC (2 TON)   EX (3 TON)   ED (4 TON)   EY (5 TON)
EF (6 TON)

new STEEL WHEELS
ON ALL BUT "EC"

EC

TIRE SIZES, FRONT *and* REAR
(D = DUAL REAR)

EC = 36 × 6, 40 × 8

ED = 36 × 5 D

EF = 36 × 6, 40 × 6 D

<u>EC</u> 2 TON 144" WB 8.0 GR
4³⁄₁₆" × 5½" B+S

<u>ED</u> 3 TON 156" WB 9.0 GR
4½" × 5½" B+S

<u>EF</u> 5 TON 156" WB 10.66 GR
5" × 5½" B+S

22

ED

EC	2-3 TON	144" WB	7.25 GR	15 MPH	@ 1000 RPM
EX	2½	144	8.6	27	@ 1800
ED	3-4	156	9.0	12	@ 1000
EF	5-7	156	10.66	11	@ 1000

PNEUMATIC TIRES ON "EX"

23

VARIATIONS *in* RADIATOR GUARD DESIGN

VAN

(LATER MODEL)

PAIGE MOTOR TRUCKS

The Most Serviceable Truck in America

(1918 - 1924 ;
1930 - 1931)

PAIGE - DETROIT
MOTOR CAR CO.,
DETROIT, MICH.

STARTING 1921,
4 - CYLINDER
HINKLEY ENGINES
(IN 3 SIZES)
REPLACE 4-CYL.
CONT. ENGINES
(IN 2 SIZES.

20-23

MODELS :

5-18	2½ TON	150 " WB	(1920)
52-19	1½	140	(STARTS '21)
54-20	2½	150	(STARTS '21)
51-18	3½	160	

(SOME REPORTS INDICATE THAT
UNSOLD TRUCKS AVAIL. TO 1927.)

PAIGE NAME USED ON TAXIS
AND COMMERCIAL CARS,
1930 - 1931.

PAIGE CARS ALSO BUILT
1908 TO 1927
(REPLACED BY GRAHAM-PAIGE)

NOTE WINDSHIELD VARIATIONS

320

(1917–1926)

★★★ PATRIOT ★★★

4-CYL. ENGINES USED IN ALL MODELS (THROUGH '27)

"LINCOLN" and "WASHINGTON" MODELS HAVE THIS STYLE OF RIBBED (FINNED) RADIATOR.

"REVERE" RADIATOR (NO RIBBING)

BUS BODIES ALSO MFD.
15-PASS.= $**600**.
OR
19-PASS.= $**700**.
FOR USE ON PATRIOT CHASSIS, OR ADAPTED TO OTHER MAKES OF TRUCK CHASSES.

BUDA ENGINES USED 1917–1918. CONTINENTAL ENGS. ON 1919 1½-TON "LINCOLN" and 2½-TON "WASHINGTON." THESE 2 MODELS SWITCHED TO HINKLEY ENGS. (1920,) BUT THE NEW ¾-TON "REVERE" USED A CONTINENTAL. BUDA "WTU" ENGS. IN '26 1½-TON "30" and IN '26–'27 1¼-TON "17-R." HINKLEY IN new '26 2-TON "35," 2½-TON "50," and 3-TON "55-55X." "17-R," 1½-2½ TON, 3 TON MODELS IN '27.

HEBB MOTORS COMPANY, *Manufacturers*
1341 P Street, Lincoln, Nebraska

Revere Model
1500 to 2500 lbs.
128/129" WB

Lincoln Model
3000 to 5000 lbs.
140" WB

Washington Model
5000 to 7500 lbs.
156" WB

HEBB ALSO BUILT TRUCK BODIES (INCL. THOSE FOR PATRIOT.)

20

HEBB MOTORS CO. FAILED LATER IN 1920, BUT IN 1921 HEBB CO. ASSETS ABSORBED BY WOODS BROS. PATRIOT TRUCK PRODUCTION RESUMED. (NAME CHANGED TO WOODS BROS., DURING 1927.)
new MODEL DESIGNATIONS IN 1924: 7R (1 TON;) 9L (2 TON;) 8W (3 TON)

(1928)

(SOME SOURCES LIST 1921 AS DATE OF ORIGIN.)

PENTON

PENTON MOTOR CO., CLEVELAND, O.

THE PENTON CANTILEVER TRUCK

4 CYL.

FRONT-WHEEL-DRIVE

28

AN EARLY "WALK-IN" TYPE OF DELIVERY VAN

321

(HEADQUARTERS LATER IN NEWARK, CALIF.)

EARLY 1939 MODEL WITH GRILLE

(SINCE 1939)

39-49

12-SPEED TRANSMISSIONS

1946 SPECS.: 6-CYL. CUMMINS "HB-600" DIESEL ENGINE with 150 HP @ 1800 RPM 672 CID (THROUGH '53)

6-WHEELER MODELS:
344 DT
345 DT
354 DT
355 DT
ALSO
270 DD (4-W-D)
(1947 and 1948 ONLY)

165" WB and up

EARLY MODELS HAVE CIRCULAR HOLES IN BUMPER.

('48)

new MODELS START 1949: 280(DD); 6-WH.: 350, 360, 370, 380, 390

RADIATOR GUARDS STILL AVAILABLE

1951 = new RED OVAL RADIATOR EMBLEM

('50)

50-55

(1949 TYPES CONTINUE)

"ALL-ALUMINUM" CONSTRUCTION AVAIL.

('52)

ALUMINUM CAB STD. ON C.O.E. MODEL, INTRO. 1950.

LIVESTOCK CARRIER   ('52)

MODELS 281 and 351 ADDED FOR 1955.

C.O.E.

SOME EARLY C.O.E.s have RADIATOR STYLE LIKE '55, (ILLUSTR. LOWER RT.)

STARTING 1954, IMPROVED CUMMINS DIESEL "NHB-600" ENGINE with new 743 CID, new 200 HP @ 2100 RPM.

('55)

Peterbilt CLOSER VIEW OF CONVENTIONAL

('56)

VARIOUS OPTIONAL WBs AVAILABLE

CHOICE OF MODELS REDUCED FOR 1956:

MODEL			GEAR RATIO
280	175" WB	5.91 – 6.51	
280 C.O.E.	114	" "	
281	165	" "	
6-WHEELERS:			
350	193	6.16 – 6.80	
360	198	" "	
381	194	10.16	
350 C.O.E.	135	6.16 – 6.80	
351	190	6.16 – 7.35	
360 C.O.E.	135	6.16 – 6.80	

INSTR. PANEL HINGED, IN DELUXE CAB (RT.)

CAB

NEW STYLE

SPECIFICATIONS CONT'D. THROUGH 1959, BUT 280 C.O.E. MODEL NO. CHANGED TO 281 FOR 1958.

56-59

C.O.E. ('60)

new 1960 GEAR RATIOS, FROM 4.41 TO 11.56

('61)

60-66

IMPROVED CUMMINS "NH-220-B" 6-CYL. DIESEL ENG. FOR 1960. SAME 743 CID AS SINCE 1954, BUT NOW WITH new 220 HP @ 2100 RPM. 15.5 COMPRESSION. (OTHER ENGINES OPT. IN 1961.)

new MODELS FOR 1960: 282 (C.O.E.;) 351; 352 (C.O.E.;) 371.

new MODEL 381-HD ADDED FOR '61, AVAIL. w. OPTIONAL 6-WHEEL DRIVE (AS ALSO OPT. ON 381 IN '61.) '61 GEAR RATIOS START AT 4.11 (351, 352.)

('65)

AVAIL. with 2 OR 4 HEADLIGHTS. RADIATOR VARIATIONS ALSO ILLUSTRATED.

('65)

('66)

323

new WIDE-
RADIATOR
TYPE

Peterbilt

('67)

('68)

C.O.E. "352"

280 HP CUMMINS,
OR OTHERS AVAIL.

('69)

('70)

"359"

('71)

LEFT and RIGHT
VIEW of "359"
CONVENTIONAL
with SLEEPER
CAB

('71)

DASH
(CONV.)

67-71

SPRING, 1970 = new "PACEMAKER"
C.O.E. MODELS INTRODUCED

comfort and convenience

Instruments and controls
are arranged for comfort and
convenience.

('71)

"282"   ('71)

CAB (C.O.E.)

325 or 375-HP, 6 CYL. CATERPILLAR
DIESEL ENGINES AVAIL. (893 CID)
(CHOICE OF OTHER
ENGINES ALSO)

"352"
with
SLEEPER CAB

324

('71)

Peterbilt

COMPACT CB C.O.E.
STARTS LATE '70
COMPACT CB

('82)

('72)

MODEL 348

282, 352 TYPE ('72)

INTRO. 1971

slope-nosed Peterbilt mixer

(MODEL 341 DUMP TRUCK ALSO AVAIL.)

ALSO:
281, 351,
288, 289, 358,
359, 381, 383 CONVENTION.
and CB-200, CB-300
C.O.E. TYPES AVAIL. 10-71.

ALL DIESELS

C.O.E.
(WITH DELUXE EQUIP.)

SINCE

1971

54" TO 110" BBC CAB LENGTHS AVAIL.

('84)

('84)

MODELS of 1980s have SQUARED-OFF HEADLIGHT FRAMES.

CONV. MODELS 289, 359 ('73)

('74)

Model 200/300

210 TO 262-HP DIESEL ENGINES BY DETROIT, CATERPILLAR OR CUMMINS.

(218-HP DETROIT DIESEL # 6172 IS STD.)

DASH. (CONV.)

CONVENTIONAL
new 20" WINDSHIELD WITH NARROW CENTER POST, OTHER IMPROVEMENTS FOR 1973.

MOST MODELS OF '70s CONT'D. INTO 1980s.

PIERCE-ARROW

THE PIERCE-ARROW MOTOR CAR COMPANY, BUFFALO, NEW YORK

TRUCKS 1910-1934*

4-CYL. TRUCKS (TO '28) (4-CYL. AVAIL. THROUGH 1931.)

WORM DRIVE

('19)

1919 ON

* = BUS AVAIL. LATER

OWN ENGINES (TO 1932)

X-2 (2 TON) 150"
R-9 (5 TON) 168" WB

X-4 2 TON ('21)

3½ TON "W2" (162" WB) ADDED 1921, CONT'D. THROUGH '23.

VERY LITTLE STYLING CHANGE DURING THE 1920s.

W-2 (new) 3½ T. ('21)

R-9

5-TON 168" WB ('21)

('23)

1924-1931 4-CYL. TYPES:
XA (2 T, 150" WB
XB (3 T, 150"
WC (4 T, 162"
RD (5 T, 162"
RF (7½ T, 168"

1924 BUS CHASSIS PRICES:
$4600. 196" WB
$4750. 220" WB

new 70 to 130 HP 1932 MODELS (ALL 6-CYL.):
PT (2 TON, 160" WB)
PW (3 TON, 150" WB)
PX (4 TON, 160" WB)
PY (5 TON, " ")
PZ (7 TON, 168" WB)

1924 BUSES TYPE Z 6 CYL. NEW

('24)

5 TON RD TYPES

1933-34 MODELS (6-CYL. HERCULES ENGINES):
13S385 (2-2½ T); 15T298 (3-3½ T); 17T361 (3-4 T);
18W361 (3½-4½ T); 19R479 (3½-4½ T); 21W361 *
(4½-5½ T); 22R479 * (4½-5½ T); 22X479 *
(4½-5½ T); 24X479 (5-6 T); T27T361T *;
28M611 (6-7 T);
28Y479 *; 28K611
(6-7 T);
34K611
(7½-10 TONS)

('33)

"RD" ('29)

THE MATCHLESS PIERCE-ARROW TRUCKS—$1950 to $7550

'26) PIERCE, GREAT-ARROW, PIERCE-ARROW AUTOMOBILES BUILT 1901-1938. SEE ALSO FLEET-ARROW TRUCKS.

FIRST 6-CYL. "FA" (2-TON) INTRO. LATE '28 FOR '29-31 SEASONS.

4-TON "WC" ('28)

New

8-DOOR, 15-PASS. COMMERCIAL COACH
204" WB
STRAIGHT 8
385 CID
140 HP @ 3400 RPM
('37)

326

PLYMOUTH

Trucks and Commercial

(1935 – 1942)
PLYMOUTH DIV. OF CHRYSLER CORP.

NOTE SIDE-MOUNT SPARE

MODEL "PV" SEDAN DELIVERY $635.

35

STYLED LIKE PLYMOUTH CARS.

SUPPLEMENTING THE REGULAR LINE OF DODGE TRUCKS

6-CYL. PLYMOUTH CAR ENGINE

1936 IS ONLY MODEL with SHARP LOWER WINDSH. CORNERS

36

new GRILLE

MODEL "PV" SEDAN DELIVERY $605.

MODELS NOT AS LOW OR WIDE AS EXAGGERATED AD (BELOW) WOULD SUGGEST.

37

"PT-50" MODELS

AD

ACTUAL PHOTO

PLYMOUTH PICK-UP TRUCK: ½-ton...116" wheelbase...powerful six-cylinder "L-head" truck engine...six-foot steel express body...six-inch X-braced frame with five heavy cross members.

PICKUP IS new FOR 1937.

PLYMOUTH COMMERCIAL SEDAN: 116" wheelbase...powerful six-cylinder "L-head" truck engine...ALL-STEEL body of distinctive modern design...with pay-load space 78" x 54" x 45⅜"—105 cubic feet.

327

NOW HIGHER and LONGER THAN PLYMOUTH CAR.

PLYMOUTH

$495.

PICKUP

37 (CONT'D.)

1937 PICKUPS ON ASSEMBLY LINE

CAB ('38)

38

"PT-57" MODELS

PICKUP, COMMERCIAL SEDAN, OR COMMERCIAL CAR CHASSIS WITH CAB.

NOTE THAT *new* GRILLE DOES NOT EXTEND AS FAR DOWNWARD AS IN '37.

4-SP. TRANS. OPTIONAL

$585.

PICKUP REAR VIEW

new DOUBLE REAR DOORS

575.

LUNTE PLUMBING

39

"PT-81" MODELS

ALSO: PICKUP CPE. ('39) AMBULANCE ('39 and '40)

715.

BEAUTIFUL NEW DISTINCTIVE STYLING

COMMERCIAL CAR →

328

LENGTH EXAGGERATED (IN ORIG. ADVERTISING)

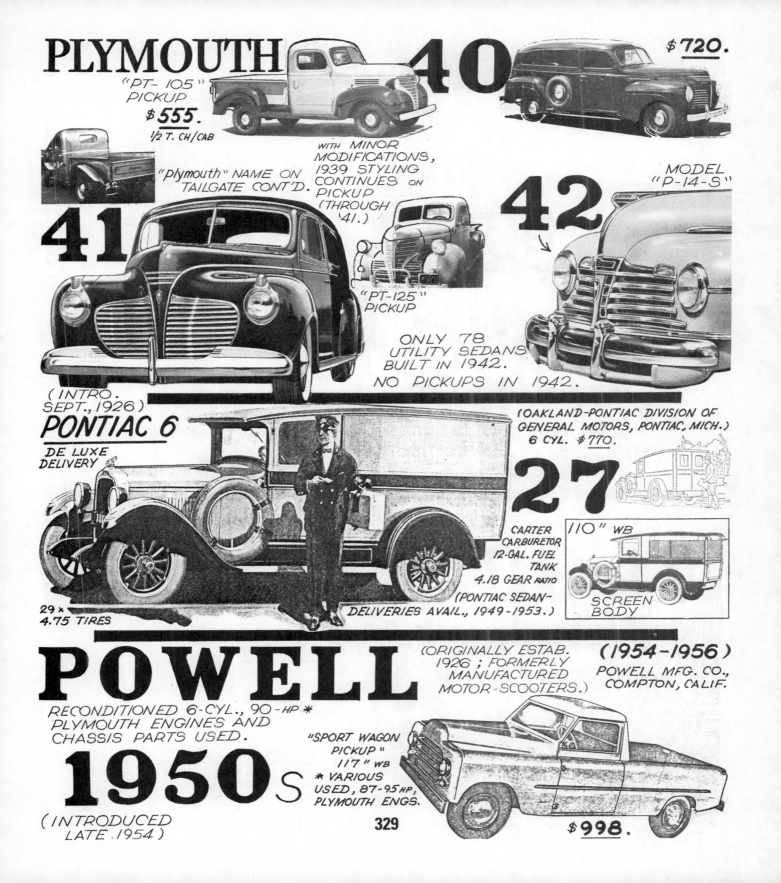

PLYMOUTH

40

"PT-105" PICKUP
$555.
1/2 T. CH/CAB

$720.

"plymouth" NAME ON TAILGATE CONT'D.

WITH MINOR MODIFICATIONS, 1939 STYLING CONTINUES ON PICKUP (THROUGH '41.)

41

42

MODEL "P-14-S"

"PT-125" PICKUP

ONLY 78 UTILITY SEDANS BUILT IN 1942.
NO PICKUPS IN 1942.

(INTRO. SEPT., 1926)

PONTIAC 6

DE LUXE DELIVERY

(OAKLAND-PONTIAC DIVISION OF GENERAL MOTORS, PONTIAC, MICH.)
6 CYL. $770.

27

CARTER CARBURETOR
12-GAL. FUEL TANK
4.18 GEAR ratio
(PONTIAC SEDAN-DELIVERIES AVAIL., 1949-1953.)

110" WB

SCREEN BODY

29 x 4.75 TIRES

POWELL

(ORIGINALLY ESTAB. 1926; FORMERLY MANUFACTURED MOTOR-SCOOTERS.)

(1954-1956)
POWELL MFG. CO., COMPTON, CALIF.

RECONDITIONED 6-CYL., 90-HP *
PLYMOUTH ENGINES AND CHASSIS PARTS USED.

1950s

(INTRODUCED LATE 1954)

"SPORT WAGON PICKUP"
117" WB
* VARIOUS USED, 87-95HP, PLYMOUTH ENGS.

329

$998.

 **Bus**

(SINCE 1947)

(ORIG. MFD. FURNITURE. 1ST WOODEN BUS BODIES ALSO MFD. 1924. COMPLETE BUSES, 1947.)

(MADE IN CANADA, BUT MANY SOLD IN THE U.S.A. IN RECENT YEARS.)

CHAMPION MTS-47 ('79)

(40')

$ 65,000. UP

(35', 1979)

SPECIAL 19-PASS. ROUND-WINDOWED BUS BLT. FOR USE BY MURRAY HILL AT 1976 MONTREAL OLYMPIC GAMES.

1970s

LE MIRAGE MTH-40 (40')

(MTH-35 35' AVAIL.)

DETROIT DIESEL 8V71N ON 40' ('80)
6V92 TURBOCHARGED ON 35' (280 HP)

3.70 G.R.

1980s

RIGHT SIDE

LE MIRAGE

(40')

LEFT SIDE

(PRESTIGE SIGHTSEEING BUS has HIGH-TOPPED SIDE WINDOWS LIKE "LE MIRAGE," BUT OLDER-STYLE FRONT END LIKE 1976 BUS AT TOP RIGHT OF PAGE, AND RAISED SECTION OF ROOF WITH FRONT VIEW WINDOW.)

Just say "Pray-vo . . . the way to go"

LE MIRAGE (W. FULL-LENGTH ROW HIGH WINDOWS.)

330

PREVOST

RELAY MOTORS CORP., LIMA, OHIO 6 CYLS.

BUDA ENGINES USED, BUT CONT. 21-R ENG. IN 5-TON "100-AC" ('30 THROUGH '33.)
HERCULES ENG. IN 1933 "230" (5 T.) and "240" (7T.)

Relay (1927–1934)

(CONSOLIDATED with COMMERCE, GARFORD, and SERVICE TRUCKS.)

note THE UNIQUE RELAY REAR WHEEL DRIVE MECHANISM.

('28) CONTR. HYDR. BRAKES

↑ 30-A (1½-2 TON) 150" WB

DUMP TRUCK

28

also 50-A (2½ TON) 156" WB

('28) MECH. BRAKES

← 70-A (3½ TON) 175" WB note HORIZONTAL LOUVRES

$**4950.** (CHASSIS)

'29 MODELS : 30-A (1½T;) 40-A (2T;) 50-C (2½T;) 60-C (3T;) 70-C (3½T;) 80-C (4 TON) ALSO 20-B (1T;) S11-B (1½TON)

'30 MODELS : 15-AA (¾ T;) 15-AB (1T;) S-11 (1-2T;) 40 (1½-2½T;) 50 (2-2½T;) 60-DA (2½T;) 60-DB (3T;) 60-DC (3½T;) 80 (3-4T;) 100-AC (5 TON) (6 WHEELERS BELOW)

RADIATOR ('30)

RELAY

STAKE

29

DUAL ENGINES (new) 1931 "300-A" with TWIN LYCOMING STR.-8 ENGINES ! 275 HP.

(CONT. ENG. ALSO IN '31-'32 15AA, '33 15-A.)

30

V-FRONT ON "300-A"

50 SW (5T, 6W;) 60 SW (7T, 6W;) 40 TT; 60 TT (TRUCK TRACT.)

31

Westinghouse AIR BRAKES

SHELL GASOLINE SHELL

TANKER ('30) new OVAL EMBLEM, 1930

DEC., 1932 = CO. INTO RECEIVERSHIP, (FOLLOWING PETITION OF HERCULES MOTOR CORP., A CREDITOR.)

331

RELAY

X-66 GEAR RATIO (4.7-'21)

NO CENTER SIDE CANOPY SIDE SUPPORT ON '15 to '19 MODELS.

REO SPEED WAGON *TRADE MARK REG. U.S. PAT. OFF.*

(1904-1967)

REO MOTOR CAR CO. LANSING, MICH.

MODEL "F" 3/4-TON

GRAIN BOX - 50 BU. $1625

Express

20-21

4 CYLS. (4 1/8" × 4 1/2") 128" W.B. 34 × 4 1/2 TIRES

IDEAL DAIRY TRUCK $1575

TRUCK - FARMERS' DOUBLE DECK VAN $1600

CANOPY DETAILS

TAXI CHASSIS INTRO. 12-21

Canopy Express $1435

JOHNSON CARB.

CYLINDRICAL FUEL TANK IN CAB

22

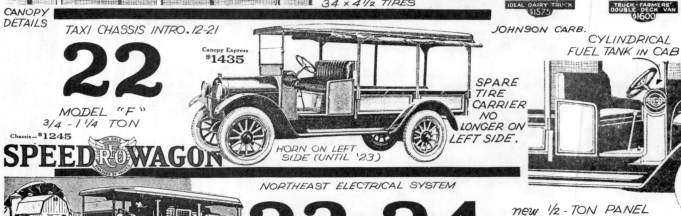

MODEL "F" 3/4 - 1 1/4 TON

Chassis — $1245

SPEED REO WAGON *THE GOLD STANDARD OF VALUES*

SPARE TIRE CARRIER NO LONGER ON LEFT SIDE.

HORN ON LEFT SIDE (UNTIL '23)

NORTHEAST ELECTRICAL SYSTEM

23-24

new 1/2-TON PANEL (WITH 113" WB TAXI CHASSIS) INTRO. 8-23.

RESTYLED

GRAVITY FUEL FEED CONTINUES (TO '27)

12 STANDARD BODY TYPES

('25)

INTRO. AS MODEL "G"

50 HP @ 2000

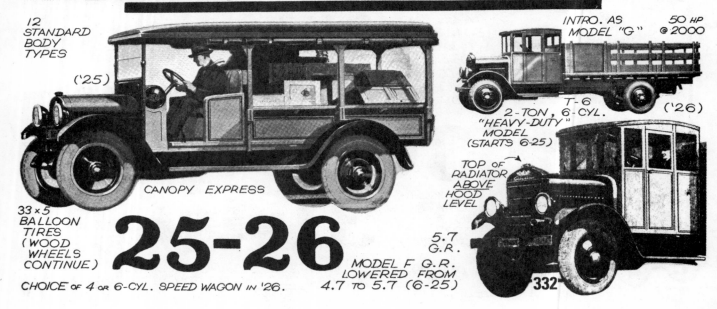

CANOPY EXPRESS

T-6 2-TON, 6-CYL. "HEAVY-DUTY" MODEL (STARTS 6-25)

('26)

TOP OF RADIATOR ABOVE HOOD LEVEL

33 × 5 BALLOON TIRES (WOOD WHEELS CONTINUE)

25-26

5.7 G.R.

MODEL F G.R. LOWERED FROM 4.7 TO 5.7 (6-25)

CHOICE OF 4 OR 6-CYL. SPEED WAGON IN '26.

332

16-PASS. SEDAN BUS **W**

REO

CHAIR COACH BUS **W**

176" WB 6 CYL. ('25)
$5100.

BUSES **25-26**

('26)

21-PASSENGER $6250.

21-PASS. PAY-ENTER BUS **W**
176" WB
$4850.

PAY-ENTER BUS **W** $5025.
(SOME DIFF. IN BODY SIDES AND WHEELS, FROM '25.)

TOTALLY-IMPROVED SPEED WAGON (STARTS APRIL, 1926.)

1¼-TON CANOPY EXPRESS

TRUCK 26½

new CLOSED CAB LONGER HOOD and COWL

new LOWER BODY

new FRONT FENDERS

GAS TANK NOW UNDER SEAT

new LONGER 130" WHEELBASE

Tilt-Ray HEADLIGHTS

MODEL "F"
4 CYL.
(4⅛" × 4½")
6 CYL.
(3³/₁₆" × 5")
("T-6")
4.7 G.R.

JOHNSON or OTHER CARB.; N.E. ELECTR. SYS.

HEAVY DUTY
2-TON 156" W.B.
32 × 6 TIRES
6-CYL. "T-6"
ENGINE (3³/₁₆" × 5")
5.7 GEAR RATIO
SCHEBLER CARB.

27

CHASSIS LUBRICATION BY MEYERS MAGAZINE OILERS on ALL 27½ MIDYEAR MODELS BUT "JUNIOR" (BELOW)

130" WB

1¼ TON
MODEL "F"

new 4-WHEEL BRAKES

STD. SPEED WAGON avail. WITH 133" OR 143" W.B.

new IMPROVED MID-YEAR MODELS

new 6-CYL. 2-TON "MASTER" ALSO JOINS STD. SPEED WAGON (STARTS 7-27.)

27½
new

6-CYL. "JUNIOR" MODEL STYLED LIKE REO'S NEW LOW-PRICED "WOLVERINE" CAR (with HORIZONTAL HOOD LOUVRES, etc.)
114" W.B. 3¼" × 4" BORE + STROKE
SEMI-AUTOMATIC SPARK CONTROL

"JUNIOR" RATED AT ½T. CAPACITY.
333 (NOTE new COWL LAMPS.)

SOME HVY. REOs HAVE THE new

STARTING 9-27, new 6-CYL. IMPROVED 3-TON "HEAVY DUTY" with 159" W.B., DUAL INTERNAL BRAKES

GOLD CROWN ENG.

28 REO

MECH. BRAKES ON ALL BUT "JUNIOR."

SEVERAL BODY VARIETIES ILLUSTRATED

½-TON "JUNIOR" with HYDRAULIC BRAKES $1085.
(LOOKS THE SAME IN 1929,) AS MODEL "BA")

6-CYL. CONTINENTAL ENGINE ("16-E") IN ½ and 1-TON ("JR.," "DA," "DC" MODELS)

HYDRAULIC BRAKES ON ADDITIONAL MODELS

3-TON HEAVY-DUTY "GA" 163" W.B. 32 × 6 TIRES

"TONNER" MODEL "DA" 123" W.B. 30 × 5 TIRES

29

STANDARD SPEED WAGON "FA" → 137" WB 32 × 6 TIRES HYDR. BRKS.

6-CYL. "GOLD CROWN" ENGINE has CHROME NICKEL BLOCK (AVAIL. IN 1½ TON and up.)

14 W.B. LENGTHS, 115" TO 179", IN ½, 1, 1½, 2 and 3-TON MODELS.

SHIP SAFELY BY MAYFLOWER TRUCK

65 Mayflower Transit Co

NATIONAL HOUSEHOLD MOVERS

MOVING VAN (LATE '29)

REO

14 WHEELBASE LENGTHS, UP TO 210"

6 CYL., 268.3 CID ENGINE with 67 HP @ 2800 RPM ON 1½-TON, 2-TON, 3-TON MODELS

CONSUMERS LAUNDRY

6-CYL. CONTINENTAL "16-E" IN "JR.15;" REO ENGINES IN OTHERS

30

new "SPEEDWAGON" LETTERING ATTACHED TO RADIATOR CORE.

"JR.15" ½ TON 115" W.B. 6 CYL. 214.7 CID 60 HP @ 2800 4.45 G.R. 6.00 × 18 TIRES
"DF TONNER" 1 TON 135" W.B. 6 CYL. 268.3 CID 80 HP @ 3200 5.2 G.R.
"FA-137," "FE," "FF" 1½ TON 137, 152, 156" W.B. 5.2 G.R.
"FC," "FD," "FH*" 2 TON 152, 168, 142" W.B. 5.7 G.R. 32 × 6.00 TIRES
"GA," "GC," "GD*," "GCS" 3 TON 163, 179, 144, 210" W.B. 6.14, 6.14, 6.85, 6.14 G.R. 32 × 6.00
HIGH-PRESSURE OR BALLOON TIRES
*-AVAIL. AS TRACTOR-TRUCK

METROPOLITAN DELIVERY

28-45 Passenger School Bus

CAPACITIES TO 7½ TONS (with TRAILERS)

31

MODELS AS IN 1930. FINAL YEAR FOR "JUNIOR 15" ½-TON.

HYDRAULIC BRAKES AND new GRILLE ON LATER 1½-TON MODELS, STARTING 5-31.

EARLY '31 MODEL

MID-YEAR MODEL

335

REO

1½-TON "1A," "1C," "1B," "1D,"
"DFX TONNER;" 2-TON "FAX," "FEX,"
"FFX;" 2½-TON "FCX," "FDX," "FHX;"
3-TON "GA," "GC,"
"GD," "GCS"

REO 1 1/2 TON SPEEDWAGON WITH 4 CYL. ENGINE—CHASSIS F.O.B. LANSING **$625**

6-CYL., 230 CID "GOLD CROWN" ENGINE

EARLY '32 new 4-TON MODELS have 101 HP 6;

32

68 HP @ 2800 RPM, 3⅛" × 5" BORE and STROKE

REO's FIRST STRAIGHT-8 TRUCK ENGINE INTRO. 8-32, IN 4-TON "4H, J, K" TYPES (358 CID, 110 HP @ 2800 RPM) THESE HAVE HIGH, FLAT RADIATORS, LIKE EARLIER "HEAVY DUTY" SERIES.

$595. '34 (CHASSIS)

136"-205" W.B. and 1½ to 4-TON CAP'Y. IN 1933, with 20" WHEELS ON ALL.

33-34

FLAT RADIATORS ON SOME REOS

('34)

A 751

new ¾-TON "BN"(A) IN '34, with 130" W.B., 6.50 × 18 TIRES, 3⅛" × 5" 6 CYL., 4.9 G.R.
1½-2½ T.

new ½-TON "S4P" has 117" W.B., 6.25 × 16 TIRES, 230 CID, 6 CYL., 80 HP @ 3200 RPM 4.3 G.R.

POST HAULING CO DETROIT FLINT LANSING

1 to 1½-TON "1A4, 1C4" 139-166" W.B., 6.00 × 20 TIRES, 209 CID, 6 CYL., 70 HP @ 2800 RPM 5.28 G.R.

(20" WHEELS ON OTHER MODELS)

35

NO 4-CYL. MODELS IN 1935 or 1936.

1-200

*new "SILVER CROWN" 6-CYL. ENGINE IN

NEW 1½ TON SPEEDWAGON

336

C.O.E.

REO

IMPROVED GOLD CROWN and SILVER CROWN ENGINES

36

FINAL YEAR THAT REO ALSO BUILT AUTOMOBILES.

$445* AND UP

In repeated tests, a 1936 Reo 2-3 Ton Truck, equipped with the Reo Gold Crown Engine, pulled an 80-ton load without laboring, in snow! A tough job that only a rough truck can perform!

FINAL YEAR FOR 358 CID STRAIGHT-8 REO ENGINE IN 4 TO 6-TON "4H, J, K, M" MODELS; REPLACED BY STREAMLINED '37-STYLE 3 TO 6-TON MODELS INTRO. 6-36 (156-190" W.B., 428 CID, 6-CYL. BUDA ENGINE, 104 HP @ 2600 RPM

new "Silver Crown" 4 OR 6-CYL. ENGINES

114" W.B. and up   ('37)

★ EXTRA ★★

America's Toughest Truck!   ('37)

new STYLING new V-WINDSHIELD

new C.O.E. MODELS IN 4 WHEELBASES from 105" TO 166," with 228 CID OR 268 CID "GOLD CROWN" 6.

37-39

"6-50," "6-75," "1A4Y" and "1A4(H)" MODELS CONT'D. 1937 THROUGH 1939.

FINAL 4-CYL. REOS ("4-50" and "4-75") IN 1939.

STORAGE AND MOVING

75-011

337 SIDE-LOADING C.O.E. (ADV. 10-37) "ART DECO" STYLING!   ('38)

$656. TO $3350. IN 1940

REO

THIS STYLE CAB ALSO WAS USED BRIEFLY BY HUG TRUCKS.

COWL-HINGED HOOD

SCHOOL BUS

('47)

1941 MODELS (all 6 CYL.):

19, 19R	228 CID	83 HP @ 3200	BM
20	245	89	@ 3100
21, 21R	"	"	"
22, 22R	288	88	@ 2800
23, 23R	310 CID	93	@ 2700
OSL-41, NWL-41	"	"	"

1946 SPECS.:

19	145-165" WB	245 CID 89 HP @ 3100 RPM
20	130-165	288 CID 94 @ 3000
21	130-145	427 CID 127 @ 2600 (CONTINENTAL ENG.)

(C-19 TO C-25 CONT'D. ALSO)

NEW MODELS FOR 1940 (**19-A**, ETC.)

1940s

ASSEMBLY LINE AT LANSING, 1948 (BELOW)

Final inspection for brand new Reo trucks as they roll off the assembly line. From the Reo Model 19 to the giant Model 31, there's a Reo truck to fit the job you want done. See your nearest Reo dealer, now!

37-PASS.

NEW "FLYING CLOUD" TRANSIT BUS 186" WB INTRO. FALL, 1947. 427 CID 6.

1949 ENGINES == <u>245 CID</u> : IN D-19A, 119LS SCHOOLBUS, 119 and 119 L SCHOOLBUSES
<u>288 CID</u> : IN D21A, 121LS, 121 SCHOOLBUSES
<u>310 CID</u> : IN D21RA, D22A, D22RB, D216 *, D226 *, 122 and 122 L SCHOOLBUSES
<u>371 CID</u> : IN D23 SA (ALSO OPT. IN SCHOOLBUS)
<u>427 CID</u> : IN D23A, D23RB, D236 * "
<u>513 CID</u> : IN 30A, D306 *
<u>602 CID</u> : IN 31A, D316 *   * = TANDEM AXLES

1948 REO HEAVY DUTY
MODELS 30—31
TRACTOR CAPACITY UP TO 76,000 LBS. G.V.W.

"EAGER BEAVER" ARMY TRUCK (CAN BE DRIVEN THROUGH WATER.)

STARTS 1949

new F-50 WITH

REO

new "SUPER GOLD COMET" 1953 6 (160 HP)

new IMPROVED "GOLD COMET" 6 ENGINE (INTRO. '49)

292 C.I.D.

('51)

SCHOOL BUS

('51)

('51)

GOLD COMET

new V8 ALSO AVAIL. (1955) 195 OR 220 HP

('51)

1950s

REO MOTORS, INC.

SUBSIDIARY OF **BOHN** ALUMINUM AND BRASS CORPORATION, FROM 12-31-54 UNTIL BECOMING A DIVISION OF **WHITE MOTORS** IN 1957.

('55)

GOLD COMET REO 220

REO WORLD'S TOUGHEST TRUCK

UTILITY S537 SIGNAL TRUCKING SERVICE

REO

W 75 782

1950 E-19, E-21, E-22, E-23, ETC. WITH "R-E-O" VERTICAL ON new GRILLE. new GRILLE AGAIN, IN 1955, AS ABOVE

SUPER V-63 C.O.E. ('56)

REO "ROYALE" POWER MOWERS ALSO

('51)

1960s

new ready-mix truck

(with a flywheel power take-off)

C (GAS;) D (GAS;) E (DIESEL) and DC (GAS, C.O.E.) SERIES IN '61 (145 TO 207 HP) OWN 6 OR V8, ALSO CUMMINS 6-CYL. DIESEL

C.O.E.

BEKINS

REO 6 X

('60)

('62)

34

MAY 1, 1967: WHITE MOTORS COMBINES ITS SUBSIDIARY DIAMOND T and REO DIVISIONS, CREATING A NEW BRAND OF TRUCK= **DIAMOND REO.**

339

REPUBLIC (1913–1929)

Seven Models ¾-ton to 5-ton at Low Prices

REPUBLIC MOTOR TRUCK CO., ALMA, MICH.

2-2½ TON

WILD ROSE LARD + Purily Guaranteed Inspected by Government — FRYE & COMPANY Packers. — INSIST ON GETTING IT.

FRYE AND COMPANY.

REPUBLIC TRUCKS

ABOVE TRUCKS ARE 1919 EXAMPLES OF "YELLOW CHASSIS" SERIES

ABOVE SCENE : SEATTLE, WASH.

('18)

UP TO $4250. (5-TON)

with TORBENSEN "POWRLOK" INTERNAL GEAR DRIVE

SPECIAL ¾ TON

complete with bow top and stake or express body $1095

4-CYLINDER ENGINES (IN ALL MODELS, THROUGH '26)

OWN, CONTINENTAL, BUDA ENGINES (THROUGH '19)

CONT. ENGINES ONLY ('20-'21)

REPUBLIC Yellow Chassis TRUCKS

('20)

18-20

1919 MODELS : (EISEMANN, BOSCH, OR REMY IGN.)

DISPATCH	¾ TON	110" WB	OWN ENG.
9 SPECIAL	¾	128	OWN
10	1	124	CONT.
11-X	1½	144	CONT.
12-X, 12-A	2	144	BUDA
T, TX	3½	165	BUDA
V	5 TON		

Two Improved Republic Models are now ready for delivery

MARCH, 1919 :

Model 19, Republic INVINCIBLE — 2-2½ Tons
Model 20, Republic DREADNAUGHT — 3½ Tons

1920 MODELS :

10	1 TON	124" WB
11	1½	144
19	2½	144
20	3½	165

EISEMANN IGNITION

Ship by Truck

(JUNE, 1920) *with* CLOSED CAB

REPUBLIC
21-23

"20" 3½ TON
165" WB CHASSIS
('21)

75	¾ TON	124" WB	LYCOMING	('22-27)
10	1	124	CONT.	('22 ONLY)
10E	1	124	CONT.	
11X	1½	144	CONT.	
19	2½	144	CONT.	
19W	2½	154	WAUKESHA	('22-'25)
20	3½	165	CONT.	

HEADLIGHTS
IN FRONT

BOSCH IGN.
(AUTO-LITE
ON "75.")

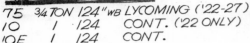

"RAPID TRANSIT"
¾ - TON ('22)

(AVAIL.
SUMMER,
1921.
EARLY TYPE
ILLUSTRATED)

19
3-TON
STAKE

TON RATINGS INCREASED

24
DELIVERY
CAR
4 CYL. (3¾ × 5")
33 × 5 TIRES
124" WB
2-WHEEL BRAKES

75	(1¼-TON)
11X	(2-TON)
19	(3-TON)
26	(4½-TON)

"RAPID TRANSIT"

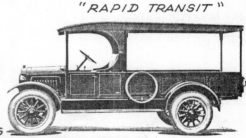

19
(3-TON)
154" WB

GAS FILLER BETWEEN
SEATS (ILLUS. BELOW)

New Five-Ton 35

25

75	1¼ TON
10F	1½
11X	2
19	3
19W	3
20	4
35	5

New
De Luxe Cab
IN IMPROVED 3-TON
(MAY, 1925)

156" 165,"
OR 185"
WHEELBASE

FEATURES
ILLUS. AT LEFT

TOOL
CHEST
UNDER
SEAT
← **341**

REPUBLIC

O = OTHER CHOICES AVAIL.

"85" (1½ TON)

new 25-6 3-TON (BELOW)

NICKEL TRIM

new 85 RB DUMP TRUCK 110" WB

REAR DETAILS

26

MODELS :

75	1¼ TON	124" WB°
85	1½	146°
15,15W	2	153
25W,25	3	165°
30,30W	4½	170°
35	5	170°

NOTE TRANSVERSE REAR SPRING IN ILLUSTRATION AT UPPER RIGHT.

LINN TRACTOR now a division of Republic Motor Truck Co., Inc.

(AS OF FALL, 1927)

It is significant to note that the acquisition of Linn by Republic makes the Republic line of motorized transportation more complete than ever for serving the haulage requirements of industrial America.

TYPICAL REPUBLIC RADIATOR SHAPE

LINN
REPUBLIC
TRACTORS-TRUCKS

"½ TRACK"
6 CYL., 100 HP, OR
4 CYL., 75 HP

Note the Linn exclusive patented flexible traction-unit.

MODELS ('27):

75,76,76-6	1¼-1½ TON
15,15W	2
50	2
60	2½
25,25W	3
30,30W,35	4½,5

27-28

"76-6" (1½ TON)

"60" (2½ TON)

| 85 | 2 TON | 146" WB° |
| S25W | 3½ | 165° |

(BOTH ADDED FOR 1928)

150½" WB° ('28)

163" WB°

LYCOMING, CONT., OR WAUKESHA ENGINES (AS SINCE '22)

29

"65" (3-TON)

179" WB°

"S-25W" (3½ TON) 165" WB°

MODELS :

1¼-1½ TON : 75,75-6,76,76-S ;   2-TON : 15,15W,50,88,88-6 ;
2½-TON : 58,58-6,60,85 ;   3-TON : 25,25W,65 ;
3½-TON : S-25W ;   4½ TON : 30,30-W ;
5-TON : 35

342

CHASSIS
(SAME PRICE FOR "65", "S-25W")
$3695.

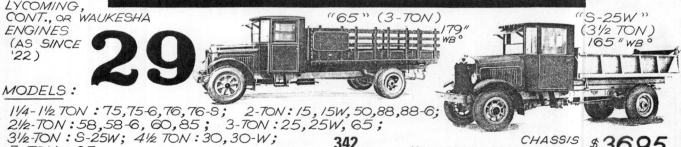

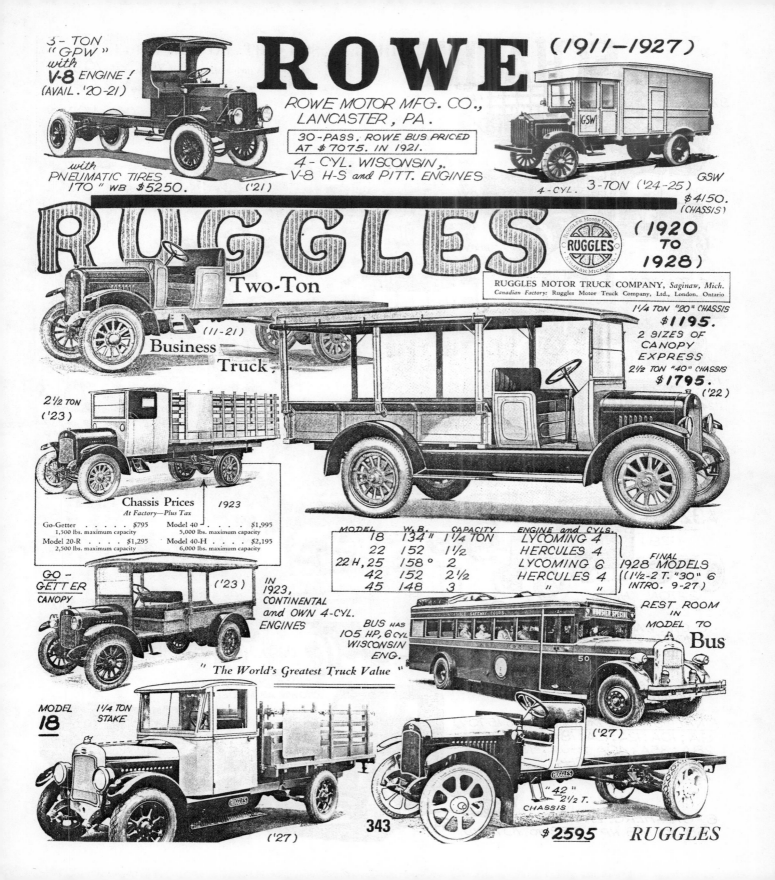

ROWE (1911–1927)

3-TON "GPW" with V-8 ENGINE! (AVAIL. '20-21)

with PNEUMATIC TIRES 170" WB $5250. ('21)

ROWE MOTOR MFG. CO., LANCASTER, PA.

30-PASS. ROWE BUS PRICED AT $7075. IN 1921.
4-CYL. WISCONSIN, V-8 H-S and PITT. ENGINES

4-CYL. 3-TON ('24-25) GSW $4150. (CHASSIS)

RUGGLES (1920 TO 1928)

RUGGLES MOTOR TRUCK COMPANY, Saginaw, Mich.
Canadian Factory: Ruggles Motor Truck Company, Ltd., London, Ontario

Two-Ton (11-21)

Business Truck.

1¼ TON "20" CHASSIS $1195.
2 SIZES OF CANOPY EXPRESS
2½ TON "40" CHASSIS $1795. ('22)

2½ TON ('23)

Chassis Prices 1923
At Factory—Plus Tax

Go-Getter $795	Model 40 . . . . . $1,995
1,500 lbs. maximum capacity	5,000 lbs. maximum capacity
Model 20-R $1,295	Model 40-H $2,195
2,500 lbs. maximum capacity	6,000 lbs. maximum capacity

GO-GETTER CANOPY ('23)

IN 1923, CONTINENTAL and OWN 4-CYL. ENGINES

" The World's Greatest Truck Value "

MODEL	W.B.	CAPACITY	ENGINE and CYLS.
18	134"	1¼ TON	LYCOMING 4
22	152"	1½	HERCULES 4
22 H, 25	158°	2	LYCOMING 6
42	152"	2½	HERCULES 4
45	148"	3	" "

FINAL 1928 MODELS (1½-2 T. "30" 6 INTRO. 9-27)

BUS HAS 105 HP, 6 CYL. WISCONSIN ENG.

REST ROOM IN MODEL 70 Bus

('27)

MODEL 18 1¼ TON STAKE ('27)

"42" 2½ T. CHASSIS $2595 RUGGLES

343

SCHACHT

THE G. A. SCHACHT MOTOR TRUCK CO.

Factory—Cincinnati, Ohio (1904-1938)

New York Branch: Hancock St. and Paynter Ave., Long Island City

3½ TON ('21)

5 TON ('21)

4- CYL. ENGS. BUDA THROUGH '23 WISCONSIN ENGINE ('23 ON)

('22)

(SOME MODELS WITH 10-SPEED TRANSMISSION)

SUPER SAFETY BUS

('25)

6 CYL., 201" W.B.

4-TON "G" ('24)

('25)

1½ TON "H" ('24)

('26)

SHOWING 2 BODY VARIETIES of 1½-TON MODEL H

197, 217 or 237" WB $5900. (BUS CHASSIS)

CHASSIS $2500.

$3275. ('28)

3-TON MODEL L ('26)

('26)

MFR. KNOWN AFTER 1927 AS THE LE BLOND-SCHACHT TRUCK CO.

2-TON "HS" CAB AND CHASSIS

6 CYL. WAUK. ENGS. IN MOST '29 MODELS 2½-TON "ROADMAKER"

2-TON "JW" VAN

('29)

CONT. and HERCULES ENGINES IN 1931.

(1928 - 1929 BUS CHASSIS IS KNOWN AS MODEL "N.")

FINAL '37-'38 MODELS (1 TO 15 TON) 8A; 10A; 12A; 15A; 18A; 20A; 25A; 28A; 35A; 40A; 66A; 75A; TRA ; TRCU ; 115CU ; 120CU ; 125CU ; 128 CU

('37)

6-CYL. HERC. ENGINES 68 TO 148 HP 263 TO 707 CID

STAKE

CAB AND CHASSIS

344

(1913 TO 1932)

Selden Motor Trucks

SELDEN TRUCK CORPORATION, Rochester, N.Y.. U.S.A.

new A SERIES

20

1½ TON	137½" WB	7.0 GR
2½	145	7.75
3½	162	8.75
5	164	10.25

NEW 3½ Ton ("A" Series) →

WORM Drive

5-TON

CONTINENTAL ENGINES (4 CYL.)

1½ - TON

21

IN-BUILT QUALITY Selden MOTOR TRUCKS

3½ - TON

"A" SERIES MODELS CONTINUE (THROUGH '23)

22-23

Bus ("STREET-CAR" TYPE) ('23)

M & W Co-Operative Gas and Oil Co. Indiana. Pa.

BETTER Gasoline

BETTER Oils and Greases

Phones Bell 253 H & G 299 W

For Better Gas

M & W

2½ TON "A" TANKER

345

SELDEN 23

Selden 24
ALL new MODELS

MODELS:

Model	Ton	WB				
30-C	1½ TON	137½" WB				(ALSO,
33	1½	146	70	3½ TON	164" WB	"52"
53	2½	154 OR 172	73	3½	168	BUS)
50	2½	149	90	5	166	

MODEL 53 VAN

25-26

OLD RADIATOR DESIGN CONTINUES ON HEAVY TKS.

('26)

('25)

CONTINENTAL ENGS. CONTINUE

4-TON 73-B 168-193" WB

new 6-CYL. 1¼-TON "PACEMAKER" 20-6 144" WB

new↑ LIGHT 6-CYL. MODELS AVAIL.

ROADMASTER 21-PASS. PAY-ENTER BUS (6 CYL., 190" WB) ("PACEMAKER" and "CENTURY" BUS CHASSES ALSO)

'27 MODELS:

PACEMAKER	1¼ TON
UNIT 34-36	2 *
ROADMASTER	3 *
UNIT 53	3
UNIT 90	3½-4
UNIT 90	5

* 6 CYL.

ROADMASTER CAB and CHASSIS

('27½) (ILCO-RYAN SAFETY LIGHTS)

"47" (3-4 TON)→

('29)

"37-C" PACEMAKER SPECIAL (2-2½ TON)

ROADMASTER DUMP TRUCK

27 ON

MINOR VARIATIONS IN CAB AND HOOD DETAILS

FINAL 4-CYL. MODELS ("25" and "35") IN 1929.

'30 and '31 MODELS: (ALL with 6-CYL CONT. ENGS.)

7	1 TON	124" WB
17, 317	1½	142
UNIT 37	2	151
39-C	2½	164
47-CB	3	151
47-CD	4	151
67-C	5	164
77	5½	170

Culver 3756
Stone 1271

W. J. ELAM & SONS
SAND AND GRAVEL

R-94-16

('28)

346

SELDEN (END)

SERVICE MOTOR TRUCK CO., Wabash, Ind., U.S.A.

(1911—1933)

Service MOTOR TRUCK
With the Red Pyramid on the Radiator

BUDA 4-CYL. ENGINES ON ALL (THROUGH '28, EXCEPT 6-CYL. BUDA IN '28 2½-TON "61," and MIDW. 4-CYL. IN '21-'23 ¾-TON "15."

'19 MODELS = 320, 340, 370, 375, 400 (1-5 TON)

('20)

(9-20 = EARLY '21 MODEL, PYRAMID ON RADIATOR)

'20 MODELS: 220, 31, 36, 51, 76, 101, (1 TO 5 TON)

NOTE UNUSUAL SHAPE OF DOORS.

FROM 1921 TO 1927, RED PYRAMID ON TOP OF RADIATOR TYPIFIED SERVICE TRUCKS.

Look for the Red Pyramid on the Radiator

SERVICE MOTORS, Inc. Wabash, Indiana ('21)

Service

1920s

RADIATOR UPPER PAN

CANOPY EXPRESS ('21)

'23 MODELS :

12	¾ TON
25	1¼
21	1½
32	2
52	3
72	4
77	4
101	6

"51" (2½ TON) ('21) 160" WB

('23)

OHIO POWER COMPANY

33, 42, 61, 81 new MODELS FOR '24 (FALL, '23)

THE E.T. SLIDER CO SAND & GRAVEL

NOTE DISC WHEELS

'27-28 MODELS : 25H (1 T;) 34 (1½ T, '26-7;) 61 (2½ T;) 81 (3½ T;) 103 (5 T;) 61, 81, 103 TT MODELS ALSO

"61" 3-TON ('24) 164½" WB

('24-'26 STYLE)

(RELAY MOTORS CORP. TAKES OVER, LATE '26.)

new '29 MODELS: (20-Z, 25-Z, 5TT-Z, 30-Z, 40-Z, 61-L, 50-Z, 60-Z, 70-Z, 80-Z) have 6-CYL. BUDA ENGINES. 4-CYL. BUDA IN 5-TON "103."

('28) RELAY-AFFILIATE

CHASSIS $3215.

REMOVABLE CYL. HEAD

347

61-L (2½ TON) 174" WB

Service

OWN 4-CYL. ENGINES (TO '22)

('20)

'20 MODELS:

1½ TON	142" WB	7.0 GR
2½	156	7.70
3½	162	8.75
5 (W)	168	8.80
5 (C)	174	7.04
7 TON	174	7.26

STERLING MOTOR TRUCK CO., MILWAUKEE, WIS.

7½-TON CHAIN DR. 4 CYL. (5 x 6¼") 174" WB

('21)

(1907-1958)

Sterling

Since 1907 *

KNOWN AS STERNBERG UNTIL 1913.

*=REGULAR PRODUCTION SINCE 1909.

1920s

4-CYLINDER WAUKESHA ENGINES IN '23

EW-20

('26)

ABOVE: ('24)
5 TON CHAIN-DRIVE TRUCK
4 CYLS., CAST IN PAIRS (5 x 6¼"),
2-WHEEL BRAKES 148" WB
HEAVY CHASSIS = $6000.

'26 MODELS (OWN 4-CYL. ENGS.)

DW-8	1½ TON	EC-29-7½	7½ TON	
DW-10,12,14	2½	EC-35-34	10	
DWS-14	3	DWS-10T	TT	130"WB
DW-18X	4	EW-15T	TT	148
EW-20	4	EW-20T	TT	"
EC-EW-23	5	ECS-24T	TT	"
EWS-25	5	EC-50T	TT	"
ECS 24	5			
EW-EC26-6	6			

DB-8

1½ TON 150" WB 6 CYL.

4 and 6-CYL. ENGS. IN '29; "OWN" WAU. ENGS. (IN '29 1½ TON UP)

('28)

DC-25
6 TON 166' WB

DB 7

('29)
137, 145 OR 150" WB

DB7 (1-1¼ TON) has 6-CYL. CONTINENT. ENG. (3⅜ x 4") 32 x 6 TIRES

DW 18-64

2½ T. 166, 180, OR 148"

DC 26 64

('29)

5½ T.

'29 MODELS: DB7 (1-1¼ TON;) DB8-63 (1½ T;) DB 9 (1½-2 T;) DW12 (2½-3½ T;) DW14-64 (3 T;) DW15 (3½-4½ T;) DW18 (4½-5½ T;) DC21-44 (4 TON, 4 CYL.;) EW 20-44 (5 TON, 4 CYL.;) EW23 (5½-7T;) EW27 (7-8½ T;) D619 (4-5T;) D623 (6-7T;) D626 (7-8½ T;) EC29 (8½-10T;) EC35 (10-12 TON

TYPICAL GAS STATION OF 1929

EC29-66A 6-WHEELER ('29)
218" WB 36 x 6 TIRES

348

1930s

Sterling

('30)

('32)

1933 MODELS: 1½-TON FB-40 to 12-12½ TON
DIESEL FD-195
ALL with WAU. 6-CYL. ENGINES,
EXCEPT FD-195 with CUMMINS "H" 6-CYL. DIESEL.
ALSO, CONTINENTAL "25-A" 6-CYL. ENGINES
IN FB-40, FB-50.
6-WHEELERS
ALSO AVAIL.,
UP TO 16-16½ TON
FDT-250.

('35)
SHELL OIL
TANKERS

('36)

C.O.E.

('36)

MODEL **G** C.O.E.

('37)

DIESEL
HEAVY DUTY

STILL USES CHAIN DRIVE

THIS
TYPE
OF "J"
INTRO.
12-38,
STILL
AVAIL.
1942.
(NOTE THE
ORNATE
GRILLE.)

('39)
J SERIES

349

1940 MODELS: MB, MC, MD, HC, HD, JC, JD SERIES
6=WHEELERS: HBT, HCS, HWS, JWS SERIES
178-251" WB

DIESEL ENGINES AVAIL. IN MOST MODELS.
$2520.-$15,200. 1940 PRICE RANGE

Sterling

6- CYL. WAUKESHA ENGINES, 320 TO 677 CID 86 TO 152 HP ('40)

1940s
ON

4- WHEEL-DRIVE MODELS ALSO AVAIL.

HC-250 (GAS)
HC-250H (DIESEL)
('47)

('46)

('50 - '51.)
('52 - '53 STERLING-WHITE SIMILAR)

('52)

"STERLING WHITE" NAME ON HOOD VENT TRIM

1954 MODELS:
HB-1204 (127" WB)
HA-1304 (160" WB)
HB-1604 (152" WB)
HB-1904 (152" WB)
HB-2254 (CUMMINS DIESEL MODEL has "D" SUFFIX)
6-WHEELERS IN HA, HB, SF, TA SERIES
ENGINES:
WAUKESHA 6, CUMMINS 6 (DIESEL) or BUDA 8 (DIESEL)

('52) MIXER

350

MODEL DD-5160 (4WD)

('20) 3½ TON

Stewart
MOTOR TRUCKS

STEWART MOTOR CORPORATION
BUFFALO, N. Y.
(1912-1939)

20

MODELS=			WB	GR
11	¾ TON	110"		6.0
8(12)	1	130		6.8
9	1½	140		7.6
7	2	156		9.0
10	3½	165		10.0

4 CYLINDERS
CONTINENTAL ENGINES (LE ROI IN ¾ TON)
('20)

2½-TON "7X" INTRO.'21.

EISEMANN IGNITION

21-22

1921 MODELS :

SPEED TRUCK ¾ TON				GR
14 (11)	¾	110" WB	LE ROI ENGINE	6.60
15 (12)	1	130	HALL-SCOTT	6.75
9	1½	140	CONTINENTAL	7.60
7, 7X	2, 2½	156	CONT., BUDA	9.00
10, 10X	3½	165	" "	10.00

MODEL **12** ('21)

35 x 5 TIRES

1-TON SPEED TRUCK 130" WB

2½ - 3 TON

1921 MODELS CONTINUED INTO 1922.

1¼ - 1½ TON STAKE

(1922 MODELS ILLUSTRATED)

Purity ICE CREAM   UTICA ICE CREAM CO

1½ - 2 TON ICE CREAM TRUCK

HEAVY DUCK STORM CURTAINS

TANKER

UNITED CONSUMERS CORPORATION PETROLEUM PRODUCTS

¼ TO 1¼ TON CANOPY EXPRESS

PARIS COAL CO.

3½ - 4 TON COAL DUMP TRUCK

34 x 4½   34 x 4½

128" WB (MAY, 1922)

NAMEPLATE ON COWL

BUMPER NOT USUALLY INCLUDED ON STEWART TRUCK AFTER EARLY 1920s.* * UNTIL 1930s

351

new NAME FOR SERIES : **"Utility Wagon"**

Stewart
MOTOR TRUCKS

1-TON "SPEED TRUCK" STARTS 4-23, with 130" WB 4 CYL., 43-HP ENGINE (3¾" × 5" BORE and STROKE) 34 × 4 TIRES (DISC WHEELS)

MODEL 15 ('23)

'23-'24 MODELS
15 — 1 TON
14X — 1¼
9 — 1½
7X — 2½
10X — 3½

1925 MODELS:
16 (1 TON;) 17 (1½ TON) WITH LYCOMING ENGS.;
7X (2½-3 TON;) 10X (3½-4 T.) WITH BUDA ENGS.

"17" ('25)

MODEL 17 1½ TON STAKE

1-Ton 130" WB ('24)

"Buddy" ¾ Ton Speed Truck 40 HP 6 CYL. CONT'L.

'26 MODELS: 16 — 1 TON (4 cyl.)
16x — 1¼ (6)
17 — 1½ (4)
17x — " (6)
18 — 2 (4)
7x — 2½ (4)
10x — 3½ (4)

23-26

('26) 118" WB

$895 chassis

ALSO LYC. 4, 6 OR BUDA 4 ENGINES ('26)

27-29

MODEL 22 4-TON CAB/CH. 165" WB 6 CYL.

$4200. ('28)

1928 with 4-WHEEL BRAKES

1927 MODELS:

BUDDY	¾ TON	118" WB	6 CYL.	CONTINENTAL ENGINE	
"	1	128	6	"	
1¼ TON	1¼	130	4	LYCOMING	
17, 17X	1½	145	6	"	
18	2	160	4	"	
19	2½	165	6	"	
22	3½	165	6	"	

Ingersoll

1 TON ('28) (¾ TON "BUDDY" LOOKS SIMILAR, BUT has WOOD WHEELS.)

2-TON STAKE

CONTINENTAL BAKING CORP. ('28)

PAINTED RADIATOR SHELLS ON MOST PRE-'29 MODELS

LYCOMING ENGINES IN ALL '29 STEWARTS (4 and 6 CYL.)

4-WHEEL BRAKES

LEXINGTON LUMBER CO. LUMBER 29 LA SALLE AVE.

'28 MODELS:
BUDDY ¾T, 1T;
16, 16x—1¼T;
17, 17x—1½-2T;
18x, 25, 25x—2T;
19—2½-3T; 22—3½-4T

Flint & Kent

1-TON ('29)

("BUDDY w. ROOF-VISOR)

PHOENIX HOSIERY CO.

1929 IS FINAL YEAR FOR DRUM HEADLIGHTS.

3½ TON

Stewart MOTOR TRUCK

"BUDDY" LT. DUTY DISCONTINUED EARLY IN 1930.

ALL 6-CYL. EXC. 4-CYL. "30," "40."

CANOPY 30

31-X

PANEL

PRATT & LAMBERT VARNISH PRODUCTS

STAKE

30

MODEL, TON	WB	CID	POWER
30 1T.	130"	199	50 @ 2600
30X "	"	185	55 @ 2600
40 1½ "	(SAME AS "30")		
34X "	145	224	61 @ 2600
28X 1¾	136	"	"
29X 2 T.	145	278	" "
18X 2½	165	310	85
32X "	"	278	80
33X 3 T.	"	354	90 @ 2750
19X 3½ "	"	"	"

OTHERS ALSO AVAIL.
new MODELS
| 31X 5 T. | | 462 | 100 @ 2000 |
| 27X 6-7 | | | " |

$695. TO $5700

LYCOMING ENGINES, EXCEPT FOR WAUKESHA 462 CID 6 (100 HP) IN *new* "31-X," "27-X" MODELS.

31

the New 8 Cylinder Model with STRAIGHT-8 ENGINE (420 CID, 130 HP LYCOMING) (STARTS 3-31) with 12-SPEED TRANS. 9.00 × 20 TIRES

NEW

38-8 (3½ TON)

6-CYL., 60 HP "40X" JOINS "40" FOR 1931.

"29XS" (85 HP) REPLACES "29X." "35X" IS *new*

CONTINENTAL, LYCOMING, WAUKESHA ENGS.

FB-30
30 ✳ (FINAL 4-CYL.)
30-X

32

19-X, 38-6, OR 38-8

1 Ton

3½ Ton

ALSO,
2-TON "50-X," "29-XS"
3-TON "36-X," "48-8"

15 Models—57 Wheelbases 1 to 7 Ton— $695 to $6190—6 and 8 Cylinder Motors

40-XA

1½ Ton

5 Ton

31-X DUMP

18-X, 32-X, OR *new* 8-CYL. 58-8

2½ Ton

27-XS (7 TON)

Tractor and Trailer

353

33

(NO CONT. ENGINES)

Stewart
MOTOR TRUCKS

LONGER WHEELBASE CHOICES AVAILABLE ON MOST MODELS.

¾-TON =	41 X
1½	42 X
2	43 X, 29 XS
2½	32 X, 58-8
3	18 X, 48-8
3½	19 X, 38-6, 38-8
5	31 X
7	27 XS

JUNE, 1933:
new 1-TON with 6-CYLS., 56 HP, 4-SPEED TRANS., 134" WB.
1½-TON has 62 HP 6, 134" WB.
2-TON has 65 HP 6, and 145" WB.

34

41 XS (1-TON) new in 1934, AS ARE 44 X (1½ TON) and 45 X (2½ TON)

OTHER MODELS CONTINUED FROM 1933, SOME WITH INCREASED TON RATINGS.

1935 MODELS: (65-130 HP)
41H (1 TON;) 46H (1½ T;) 47H (2 T;)
29XS, 48H (2½ T;) 32X, 58-8,
49H (3 T;) 48-8, 18XS (3½ T;)
38-6, 38-8 (3½-5 T;) 31X (5-6 T;)
27XS (7-8 TON)

('35)

VENT DOORS ON HOOD

('35)

("BUDDY" LT. DUTY RETURNS 1935-1937.)

35-36

'36 MODELS

40H (½ TON, 4 CYL.;) 60H (¾ T;)
41H (1 T;) 46H (1½ T;) 47H (2 T;)
48H, 50H (2½ T;) 49H, 32X (3 T;)
58X, 18XS (3½ T;) 38-6, 38-8 (3½-5 T;)
31X (5-6 TON)

new

60H has new CONTINENTAL 170 CID 6 CYL. ENG. (60 HP @ 2800)

1937 MODELS: 40H (½ TON;) 60H (¾ T;)
(INCLUDING new "A" SERIES) 45A (1½-2 T;) 45AS (1½-2½ T;)
47A (2-3 T;) 50A, 50AS (2½-3½ T;)
$595 49A (3-4 T;) 58X, 18XS (3½-4½ T;)
THE NEW 1½ TON 38-8, 38-6 (3½-5 T;) 31X (5-8 TON)

FINAL 8s IN 1937.

"60-A"

('37)

MORE CONTINENTAL ENGINES IN 1938.

1938 MODELS:
40HC, 60H (¾ T;)
61A (1-1½ T;)
45A (1½-2 T;)
45AS (1½-2½ T;)
47A (2-3 T;)
50A, 50AS, 50AD (2½-3½ T;) 49A,
49AD, 51A,

BED EXTENDS FURTHER THAN ILLUS. HERE.

'38 (CONT'D.:)
51AD (3-4 T;) 58A, 58AD, 59A, 59AD
(3½-4½ T;) 38-6 (3½-5 T;) 31X (5-8 TON)

37-39

Stewart
(DISCONTINUED 1941)*

1939 LINE LISTS 4 new C.O.E. MODELS IN 1½ TO 4 TON RANGE with WAUKESHA ENGINES)

new 31-A CONVENTIONAL RATED AT 6-8 TONS.)

354 * "1941-1942" MODELS 38A, 49A, 58A, 59A REPORTED TO EXIST.

STUDEBAKER *Trucks*

STUDEBAKER CORP., SOUTH BEND, IND.

1852–1966

(MOTOR VEHICLES BEGIN 1902. TRUCK PRODUCTION SUSPENDED FROM '17 TO '27; CEASES 1964.

"SEMINOLE" 22-PASS. PARLOR CAR BUS
6 CYL. (3⅞ × 5")
184" WB   34 × 7.50 TIRES

28

4-WHEEL MECHANICAL BRAKES   113" WB   4.6 GR   32 × 6.00 TIRES

¾-TON PANEL DELIVERY 6-CYL.
3⅜" × 4½" BORE and STROKE
ERSKINE PANEL DELIVERY ALSO REPORTED.

29

1929 ERSKINE "52-B" ½-TON 109" WB CONTINENTAL 9-F
6-CYL. ENGINE (2¾" × 4½")   30 × 5 TIRES
"GD-N" 1-TON 140" WB   3⅜" × 4½" 6-CYL. ENG. 30 × 5 TIRES
"76 Sp." 3-TON 184"   3⅞" × 5" 6-CYL. ENG. 34 × 7.50 TIRES
"75 HD" 3½-TON ALSO

BUS ('29)

'29-'30 has FLAT RADIATOR IN STYLE OF STUDE. CAR (ABOVE.)

30

AS OF JULY, 1930,
THE ¾-TON "GN-P" has 115" WB, 6.00×19 TIRES, 221 CID, 6-CYL. (71 HP @ 3200 RPM) 4.7 GR
1-TON "30" has SAME ENGINE, 4.64 GR, 20" TIRES, 130" WB
1-TON "GK-N" has 146" WB, 248.2 CID 6-CYL. ENGINE, (76 HP @ 3000 RPM,) 4.64 GR, 30 × 5 TIRES
1¼-TON "40" has 146" WB, 71-HP ENG., 5.10 GR
2½-TON "77" and "88" have STRAIGHT-8 ENG. (337 CID, 115 HP @ 3200 RPM) with SAME 8-CYL. ENG. IN 3½-TON "99."

EARLY '31 (BLT. '30)

new RADIATOR SHELL ON SOME 1931 TRUCKS.

S-20 1½ TON STAKE

31

S-1	½-TON	114" WB
40	1¼	146
S-20	1½	130
S-50	2	148
88	2½	184
99	3½	"

2-TON "S-50"

70-71 HP 6-CYL. ENGINE (TO 2-TON)

115-HP STRAIGHT-8 CONT'D. ON 2½-3½ TON

355

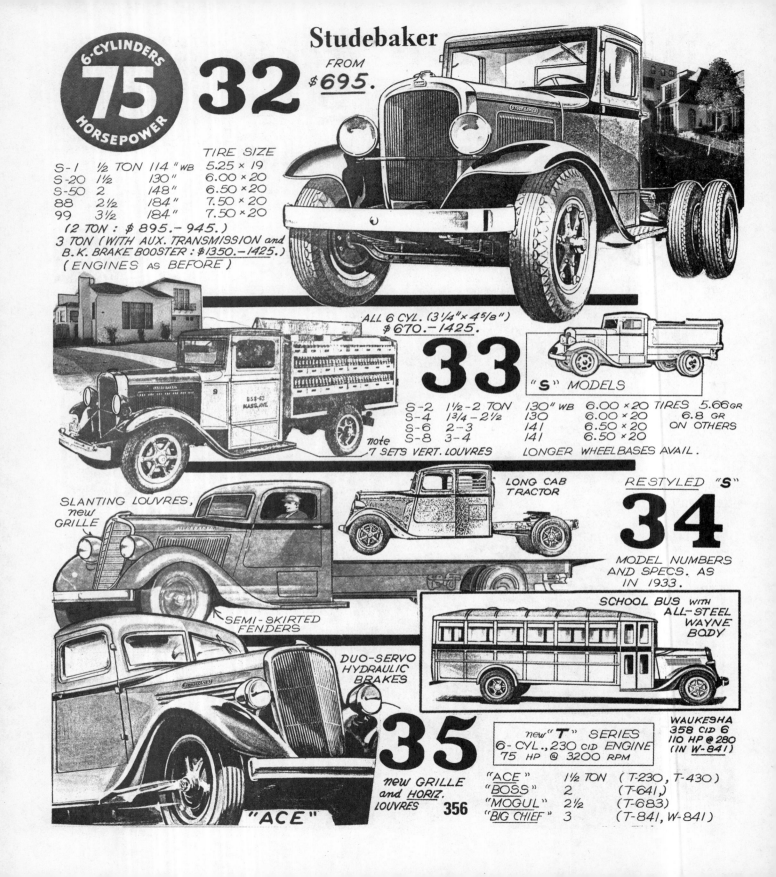

Studebaker

6-CYLINDERS 75 HORSEPOWER

32
FROM $695.

			TIRE SIZE
S-1	½ TON	114" WB	5.25 × 19
S-20	1½	130"	6.00 × 20
S-50	2	148"	6.50 × 20
88	2½	184"	7.50 × 20
99	3½	184"	7.50 × 20

(2 TON : $ 895.– 945.)
3 TON (WITH AUX. TRANSMISSION and B.K. BRAKE BOOSTER : $1350.–1425.)
(ENGINES AS BEFORE)

33
ALL 6 CYL. (3¼" × 4⅝") $670.–1425.

"S" MODELS

S-2	1½-2 TON	130" WB	6.00 × 20 TIRES	5.66 GR	
S-4	1¾-2½	130	6.00 × 20	6.8 GR	ON OTHERS
S-6	2-3	141	6.50 × 20		
S-8	3-4	141	6.50 × 20		

note 7 SETS VERT. LOUVRES
LONGER WHEELBASES AVAIL.

34
RESTYLED "S"

MODEL NUMBERS AND SPECS. AS IN 1933.

SLANTING LOUVRES, new GRILLE

SEMI-SKIRTED FENDERS

LONG CAB TRACTOR

35
DUO-SERVO HYDRAULIC BRAKES

SCHOOL BUS WITH ALL-STEEL WAYNE BODY

new GRILLE and HORIZ. LOUVRES

WAUKESHA 358 CID 6 110 HP @ 280 (IN W-841)

new "T" SERIES
6- CYL., 230 CID ENGINE
75 HP @ 3200 RPM

"ACE"	1½ TON	(T-230, T-430)
"BOSS"	2	(T-641)
"MOGUL"	2½	(T-683)
"BIG CHIEF"	3	(T-841, W-841)

"ACE"

356

Studebaker

4.85 TO 7.8 GEAR RATIOS

73 TO 110 HP

36

ACE, BOSS, MOGUL, and BIG CHIEF MODELS CONTINUE (6-CYL. WAUKESHA ENGINES IN ALL BUT "ACE.")

new C.O.E. "Metro" (OFFERED IN ACE OR BOSS MODELS.)

* "M" AT END OF MODEL NO. MEANS A C.O.E. TYPE.

PAIRS OF HORIZONTAL STRIPS ON 1937 GRILLE

Jacksen STORES INC.

37

"J" SERIES	
J-5	½-TON
J-15 *	1½-2
J-20 *	2-3
J-25 *	2½-3½
J-30 *	3-4

COUPE-EXPRESS STYLED LIKE STUDEBAKER CARS (1937 TO 1939.) NAME REVIVED ON LIGHT 1941 PICKUPS.

new 6 CYL. HERCULES ENGS. REPLACE WAUKESHA (J-20 and up)

INTERIOR

new DIESEL= "J-20-D" TYPES INTRO. JULY, 1937, with 6-CYL., 260 CID HERCULES ENGINES.

68-106 HP HERCULES 6 IN "K 20" and LARGER.

K-15M

('38) C.O.E. CHASSIS $695. UP

('39)

K-20

COUPE-EXPRESS

('38)

K-5 BECOMES L-5 FOR '40 (226 CID 6, 90 HP @ 3400, 4.55-4.82 GR)

MODELS ('38)		
K-5	½ TON	116" WB
K-10	1 "	1130"
K-15	1½-2	
K-20	2-3	
K-25	2½ 4	
K-30	3-5	

(C.O.E. SHORT-WB VARIATIONS ON 1½ TON and UP, WITH M SUFFIX ON MODEL NO.)

38-40

(NO 1940 COUPE-EXPRESS)

357

STUDEBAKER (NO C.O.E.)

COUPE EXPRESS

Full coupe comfort!
Full commercial car serviceability!

('41)

M SERIES STARTS 3-41

M-15 STD. STAKE

M-16 HEAVY-DUTY TANKER

41-45

M SERIES SIMPLIFIED, USING ONLY STUDE. ENG. 3 MODEL TYPES USE SAME BASIC CAB.

('42)

197,661 STUDEBAKER MILITARY VEHICLES BUILT, INCL. AMPHIBIOUS "WEASEL" M-29-C.

HOOD OF MILITARY TRUCK HAS A PRONOUNCED DOWNWARD SLOPE. CAB PROFILE SIMILAR TO "M."

('43)

('47)

HVY. DUTY STAKE

1-TON "M-15-28" STAKE AVAILABLE TO CIVILIANS STARTING AUG., 1945

'46: PAINTED GRILLE, PLAIN BUMPER

('46) 1-TON

46-48

ONLY M-16 HAS 94-HP ENGINE.

POSTWAR "M" SERIES

M5-19053 UP ('47-8 SER. #)

NO HUBCAPS ON STD. and HEAVY DUTY.

1 TON

(9' VAN BODY) ALSO AVAIL. AS 8' PICKUP.

(1949 EXAMPLES ILLUSTR.)

SERIAL #
R-0001 ('49)
R-16001 (1½T) 1950-1951:
R5-42501;
R10-20101;
R15-10801;
1952: 78579;
8355; 3/4T: 31399; 3127

$1262. UP ('49-50)

new 1½-TON with 900-GAL. TANK BODY

CAB DETAIL

2-TON 14' STAKE 171" WB ('49)

TOTALLY RESTYLED

49-53

SERIES 112" OR 122" WB

('49 STARTS JUNE, 1948.)

1953 SER.# 96238; 7424 (3/4 TON: 34250; 5926)

2-TON DUMP TRUCK

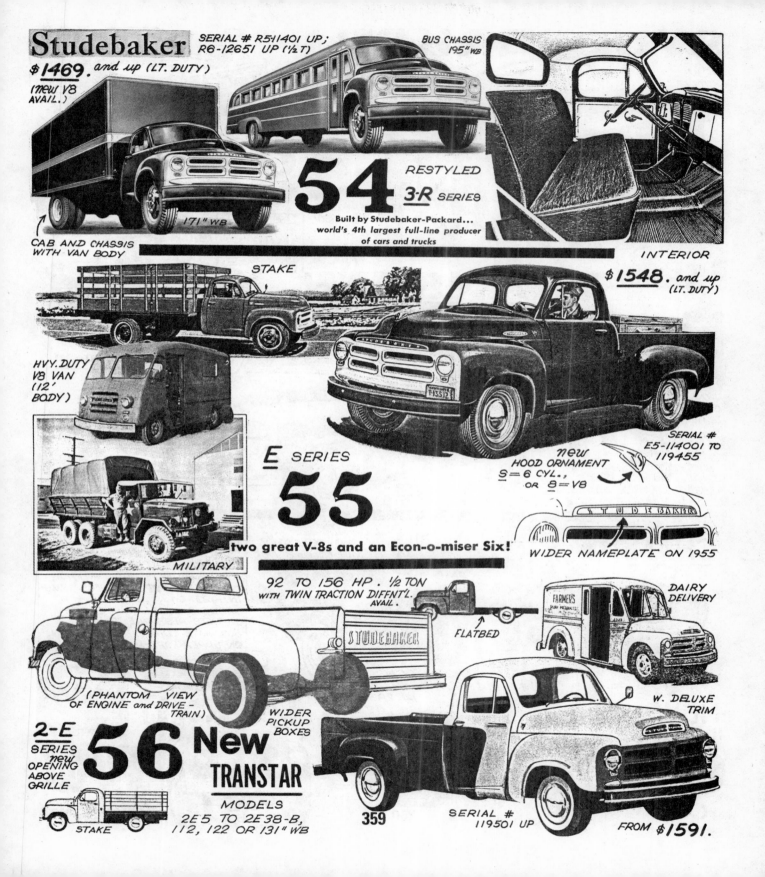

Studebaker

$1469. *and up* (LT. DUTY)

(NEW V8 AVAIL.)

SERIAL # R5-11401 UP; R6-12651 UP (1/2 T)

BUS CHASSIS 195" WB

171" WB

CAB AND CHASSIS WITH VAN BODY

54 RESTYLED 3-R SERIES

Built by Studebaker-Packard... world's 4th largest full-line producer of cars and trucks

INTERIOR

STAKE

$1548. *and up* (LT. DUTY)

HVY. DUTY V8 VAN (12' BODY)

E SERIES 55

two great V-8s and an Econ-o-miser Six!

MILITARY

SERIAL # E5-114001 TO 119455

new HOOD ORNAMENT
6 = 6 CYL., OR 8 = V8

STUDEBAKER

WIDER NAMEPLATE ON 1955

92 TO 156 HP. 1/2 TON with TWIN TRACTION DIFFNT'L. AVAIL.

FLATBED

DAIRY DELIVERY

FARMER'S

STUDEBAKER

(PHANTOM VIEW OF ENGINE and DRIVE-TRAIN)

WIDER PICKUP BOXES

W. DELUXE TRIM

2-E SERIES *new* OPENING ABOVE GRILLE 56 New TRANSTAR MODELS 2E5 TO 2E38-B, 112, 122 OR 131" WB

STAKE

359

SERIAL # 119501 UP

FROM $1591.

STUDEBAKER

PROD. : 10,563

1/2-, 3/4-, 1-Ton Models

57 -58

new GRILLE ('57)

TRANSTAR

('58)

1958 SERIAL #s BELOW:

E5-125401;
E6-16901;
E11-13001; E14-2801;
V8 : E7-9301; E12-3601;
E13-2301 and up

Studebaker-Packard CORPORATION

TRANSTAR DASH ('57)

America's Lowest-Priced Pickup!

new 1958

('58) REAR

STUDEBAKER

Only $1595*

Studebaker Scotsman

TRANSTAR

PROD. : 10,779

AUX. LIGHTS IN GRILLE OF SOME TRANSTAR TYPES IN 1959.
SER. # START WITH
E1-1101;
E3-101;
E11-13501; E14-3101; E16-45301;
V8s : E2-101; E7-11101; E12; E13; E28 SERIES

59

STUDEBAKER NAME ON DOOR

SIMPLE new — S — EMBLEM ABOVE GRILLE ON 1959 SCOTSMAN.

SCOTSMAN REPLACED BY

CHAMP 1/2 ton

FINAL L-HEAD 6s IN 1960. NEW O.H.V. VERSION OF 170 cid 6, 1961.

1961 CHAMP AVAIL. WITH *new* "SPACESIDE" WIDE PICKUP BOX FORMERLY USED BY DODGE.
FINAL NARROW, 9' BOXES IN 1962, ON "7E" CHAMP. FINAL "8E" CHAMP IN 1963-64.
MODELS E-45A and E-45E DIESELS RESEMBLE TRANSTAR BUT HAVE "DIESEL" DESIGNATION ON UPPER BORDER OF GRILLE.

NEW light duty 60 ON

(SOME FINAL '64 CHAMPS WITH "STUDEBAKER" NAME ON LOWER EDGE OF GRILLE)

('60)

PRODUCTION :
12,314 ('60); 7642 ('61);
14,283 ('62);
13,117 ('63);
749 ('64)

TRANSTAR

360

new E-35, E-45 TYPE

('63-64) SHORT CONVT'L. 96" BBC

('33 STYLED LIKE TERRAPLANE CAR.)

TERRAPLANE

MFD. BY HUDSON MOTOR CAR CO., DETROIT

(TRUCKS = 1933 - 1938)
CAB/CHASSIS MODELS AVAIL.

SER. # 373000 UP

34

6-CYL., L-HEAD ENGINE (INCLUDING HUDSON, THROUGH '47.)

212.1 C.I.D.

Pickup $515.

112" W.B. (THROUGH '35)

$595.

88 HP

STEEL ROOF ON CAB

35

3/4-TON SEDAN DELIVERY

$675.

PICKUP $545.

SER. # 51101 UP

36

new BODIES new 2-PIECE V-WINDSHIELD

PICKUP $560.

HUDSON MOTOR CAR COMPANY
SERVICE PARTS

88 HP (100 HP OPTIONAL)

SER. # 61101 UP

new 115" W.B.

FACTORY and PANEL DELIVERY FLEET

new SMALLER REAR WINDOW IN PICKUP

96 HP @ 3900 RPM

$700.

37

SER. # 70101 UP

6.00 x 16 TIRES

new 117"-W.B. MODEL "70" (4.55 G.R.)

new MODEL "78" has 124" W.B., 5.12 G.R. ("BIG BOY")

8,058 SOLD

KNOWN AS "HUDSON - TERRAPLANE"

new SILENT STRAIGHT-THROUGH MUFFLER

SER. # 80-101 OR 88-101 UP

38

96 OR 102 HP

"80" "88" 117-124 " W.B.

new HUDSON "112" SERIES IS LOWER-PRICED MODEL with 112" W.B. SER. # 89-101 UP

Thompson

361

$900. PANEL

SOME 1938 (and all 1939 and LATER) TRUCKS USE THE "HUDSON" NAME.

Traffic Truck

4000 LBS. CAPACITY

Traffic Motor Truck Corporation, St. Louis, U.S.A.
Largest exclusive builders of 4000-lb. capacity trucks in the world.

(1912-1928)

COVERT Transmission and Clutch Ball and Roller Bearings on all Shafts

RUSSEL Internal Gear Drive Rear Axle

FISK Solid Tires 34 x 3½ Front 34 x 5 Rear Pneumatics at extra cost

CARTER Efficiency Carburetor

BOSCH High-Tension Magneto

DETROIT STEEL Products Springs

TIMKEN AND HYATT Bearings

CONTINENTAL Red Seal 3¾ x 5 Motor

STANDARD AND THERMOID Universal Joints

WHEELS Heavy Truck Type Second-growth Selected Hickory

STEERING GEAR Traffic Made Worm and Gear Type

FRONT AXLE Traffic Made Forged I-Beam Timken Bearings in Wheels

PRESSED STEEL DASH Hood and Gasoline Tank Traffic Made

RADIATOR Traffic Made Cast Shell Cellular Core

FRAME Traffic Made 6-in. U-Channel 212 inches long over all

133" WHEEL BASE 122-in. Length of Frame Back of Driver's Seat

(chassis) **$1595** (factory)

MARCH, 1921 PRICE OF 2-TON.

('21)

FACTORY

TOP OF RADIATOR EXTENDS ABOVE HOOD.

TRAVELING GROCERY VAN FOR DOOR-TO-DOOR SALES.

4 CYL.

AFTER 1922, 2 TON MODEL "C" IS JOINED BY 1½ TON "Speedboy", 3-TON "6000", and 4-TON "8000." LATER 2 TONS IN "4000" SERIES.

LATER MODELS USE ZENITH CARB.

(chassis) **$1495** (factory) ('20)

CHASSIS PRICES

$1595

('21)

362

VERSARE

(MFD. 1925-1928 BY VERSARE CORP., ALBANY, N.Y.) (OPERATED 1928 TO 1931 BY CINCINNATI CAR CO.)

A VARIETY OF 4, 6 and 8-WHEELED BUSES and TRUCKS. 8-WHEELERS have ELECTRIC MOTOR AT EACH END, POWERING 4-WHEEL BOGIES. ELECTRICITY GENERATED BY 4-CYL. BUDA ENG. (GAS)

25 -31

WITH ARCH ROOF

WITH CLERESTORY ROOF

THE ALTON TRANSPORTATION COMPANY   No 2

800

MONTREAL TYPE

('25) ALTON TYPE

8-WHEEL BUSES SOLD TO ALBANY, N.Y.; ALTON, ILLINOIS; MONTREAL, QUEBEC. (33 - PASS.)

NEW

"STREETCAR" TYPE BUS (RIGHT) ——→ INTRO. 1927

C SHERBROOKE

THIS TYPE BUS SOLD TO ALBANY, NYC, MONTREAL, BOSTON, CLEVELAND, SALT LAKE CITY, ETC.

truck

HEAVY-DUTY SIDE DUMP TRUCKS ALSO AVAIL.

(VELIE ON NEXT PAGE)

363

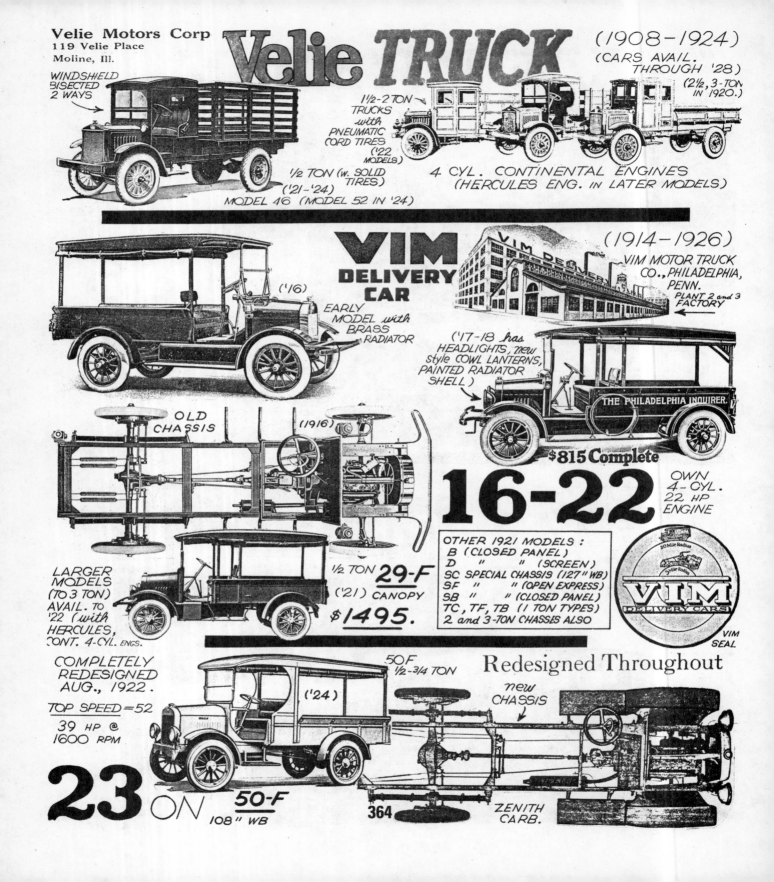

Velie Motors Corp
119 Velie Place
Moline, Ill.

Velie TRUCK

(1908-1924)
(CARS AVAIL. THROUGH '28)
(2½, 3-TON IN 1920.)

WINDSHIELD BISECTED 2 WAYS →

1½-2 TON TRUCKS *with* PNEUMATIC CORD TIRES ('22 MODELS)

½ TON (w. SOLID TIRES)
('21-'24)
MODEL 46 (MODEL 52 IN '24)

4 CYL. CONTINENTAL ENGINES
(HERCULES ENG. IN LATER MODELS)

VIM DELIVERY CAR

(1914-1926)

VIM MOTOR TRUCK CO., PHILADELPHIA, PENN.
PLANT 2 and 3 FACTORY →

('16)
EARLY MODEL *with* BRASS RADIATOR

('17-18 has HEADLIGHTS, *new* style COWL LANTERNS, PAINTED RADIATOR SHELL)

THE PHILADELPHIA INQUIRER.

OLD CHASSIS

(1916)

$815 Complete

16-22

OWN 4-CYL. 22 HP ENGINE

LARGER MODELS (TO 3 TON) AVAIL. TO '22 (with HERCULES, CONT. 4-CYL. ENGS.

½ TON **29-F**
('21) CANOPY
$1495.

OTHER 1921 MODELS:
B (CLOSED PANEL)
D " " (SCREEN)
SC SPECIAL CHASSIS (127" WB)
SF " " (OPEN EXPRESS)
SB " " (CLOSED PANEL)
TC, TF, TB (1 TON TYPES)
2 and 3-TON CHASSES ALSO

VIM
DELIVERY CARS
20 Mile Radius
VIM SEAL

COMPLETELY REDESIGNED AUG., 1922.

TOP SPEED = 52
39 HP @ 1600 RPM

50F ½-¾ TON

Redesigned Throughout

new CHASSIS →

('24)

23 ON 50-F
108" WB

364

ZENITH CARB.

(SINCE 1957)

WABCO
AN AMERICAN-STANDARD COMPANY

LETOURNEAU WESTINGHOUSE, PEORIA, ILLINOIS

69

"35-C" HAULPAK REAR DUMP

(IMPROVED IN 1970, WITH CHOICE OF GM V-12 OR CUMMINS 6-CYL. DIESEL ENG. (GM has 852 CID, 434 HP.)

OVERLAP OF VARIOUS MODEL TYPES

Model 888B and 777B
GRADER (DETR. OR ('72) CUMMINS ENG.)

120-B HAULPAK

GRADER CAB ('72)

WALKER ELECTRIC TRUCKS (1906-1942)

WALKER VEHICLE COMPANY—CHICAGO
BRANCHES AND DEALERS IN PRINCIPAL CITIES
America's Leading Manufacturer of Electric Street Trucks

23

Great Walker Fleets

AMERICAN RAILWAY EXPRESS CO.
Owns 413 Walker Trucks
BUSH TERMINAL COMPANY
Owns 33 Walker Trucks
COMMONWEALTH EDISON COMPANY
Owns 286 Walker Trucks
CUSHMAN'S SONS, INC.
Owns 149 Walker Trucks
MARSHALL FIELD & COMPANY
Owns 276 Walker Trucks
NATIONAL BISCUIT COMPANY
Owns 83 Walker Trucks
NEW YORK PIE BAKING COMPANY
Owns 33 Walker Trucks
STERN BROTHERS
Owns 38 Walker Trucks

UNILLUSTRATED 1928 MODELS :
10 BEVEL (3/4-1 T.)
20 WBD " "
45 WBD (2-2½ T.)
50 WBD (2½-3 T.)
65 WBD (3½-4½ T.)
25 WBD (1-1½ T.)

29

"10 SPECIAL" 3/4-TON STYLED LIKE AN UP-TO-DATE GAS-POWERED PANEL DELIVERY TRUCK (with 2-WHEEL BRAKES)

28

Electric Power—
at half the cost of "gas."

"75" 5 TO 7 TON CHASSIS TOP SPEED=11 MPH $4500.

141", 150", OR 160" WB

128" WB

32 x 6 TIRES

OTHER MODELS TO 7 TON CAPACITY

"DYNAMOTIVE" DELIVERY TRUCKS, STARTING MID-'30s

WALTER

(SINCE 1909)
(CARS, 1904-09)

Walter Motor Truck Co.   Sales Office: 605 Fifth Ave., New York

S
('20-'21)

5 TON CHASSIS

LONG ISLAND CITY; QUEENS, N.Y.

WAUKESHA 4-CYL. (VOORHEESVILLE, N.Y., 1957 ON) ENGINES (SOMETIMES LISTED AS "OWN" ENGINES.)

FRT
('24-25)

$6500.

MODEL S has 168" OR 192" WB

$5600⁰⁰

Walter Patented Automatic Locking Differential and Suspended Drive
EXCLUSIVELY A WALTER ENGINEERING DEVELOPMENT

ELECTRIC MODELS ALSO AVAIL.

"FRT" 15 TO 25 TON TRACTOR TRUCK 100" WB (THIS TYPE INTRO. MAY, 1923.)

MANY MODELS WITH FRONT WHEEL DR.

"FH" TRACTOR TRUCK (11-TON G.V.W. WITH DUMP BED) 136" WB   ('28-29) $7200.

LONG FRONT OVERHANG AHEAD OF AXLE IS TYPICAL OF MOST WALTER TRUCKS.

6 CYLS.

(MFR. AT RIDGEWOOD, L.I., N.Y., 1935-1957)

('36)

('37)

MAUMEE T-1

6-WAK—Butane Engine
6-WAK—Gasoline Engine
6-WAKD—Diesel Engine   ('53)
6-WAKDS—Supercharged Diesel Engine

WALTER
SNOW FIGHTERS
('44)

with SNOW PLOW

WAUKESHA
1197 CU. IN. 6-WAK SERIES
ENGINES

('53)

IN RECENT YEARS, WALTER HAS BUILT SPECIALIZED HVY. DUTY UNITS IN LIMITED PRODUCTION, AND LOW-CAB AIRPORT CRASH TRUCKS IN A STYLE SIMILAR TO THAT OF OSHKOSH.

New Supercharged 6-WAKDS Diesel, with center-mounted turbocharger; 6-cyl., 6¼ x 6½, 1197 cu. in., 352 max. hp.

On the Mesabi Range this 20-tonner hauling iron ore is a Walter Dumper powered by a Waukesha Super-Duty Six 6-WAK Butane Engine

WALTER TRUCKS

WARD LaFRANCE

(ORIG. WARD LaFRANCE TRUCK CORP.)   (EST. 1919)

2B	2½ TON	158"wb	4 CYL.
4A	3½	158	4
5A	5	160	4

(1920-1924 SPECS.; COMPANY RE-ORGANIZED EARLY 1924)

4-CYL. WAUKESHA ENGINES IN 1926, WITH 4 MODELS:

2B	2½ TON	170"	wb
4B	3½	172	
5B	5	164	
7B	7	164	

	2½	170	(1925 SPECS.;
4A	3½	162	4-CYL. ENGINES
A	5	164	CONTINUED)

ADDITIONAL 3-TON 2B-6 (6-CYL.)
AVAIL. IN 1928, AS WELL AS
4-CYL. 4B OR 6-CYL. 4B6
4-CYL. 5B OR 6-CYL. 5B6
4-CYL. 7B OR 6-CYL. 7B6
(TRACTOR-TRUCKS ALSO AVAIL.)

1927 MODELS:	2C	2½ TON	170" wb	4 CYL.
	2B	3	170	4
(WAUKESHA	4B6	3½	172	6 CYLINDERS
ENGINES)	5 to 5½ TON		164	4

1929 MODELS:

	2D	2½ TON	4 CYL.
	2B	3	4
(W.B.s	4B6	3½	6
OPTIONAL)	4B, 4D	3½, 4	4
	2B6, 4D6	3, 4	6
	5B		4
	7B		4
	5B6, 7B6		6

new 1930 MODELS:

25R	3 TON	193-205"wb	6 CYL.	358 cid	WAU. ENG.	77 HP @ 2200	
25B	3	194-206	8	322	OWN	100 @ 2400	
30B	3½	197-209	8	"	"	"	"
30RU	3½	" "	6	381	WAU.	83 @ 2200	
35R	4	OPTIONAL	6	462		97 HP @ 2000 RPM	
4E6	4	"	6	"	"	"	"
45D	4½	"	6	"	"	"	"
50C	5	"	6	"	"	"	"
5B6	5	"	6	548.7		100 @ 1800	
50D, 70C	7	"	6	462		97 @ 2000	
7B6	7	"	6	540		100 @ 1800	

PRIMARILY FIRE TRUCKS, SINCE 1930.

new 1945-1946 CIVILIAN MODELS ILLUSTRATED BELOW

TRACTOR - TRAILER

TRUCK TRACTOR
(AVAIL. IN 2, 4, OR 6-WHEEL DRIVE)
6-CYL. CONTINENTAL ENGINES
127-206 HP MODELS ('46):
D-1, DI-B, DI-C, D2, D3, D5, FD-O, FD-1, FD-2

DUMP TRUCK

GREAT AMERICAN INDUSTRIES, INC.   ELMIRA, NEW YORK (CO. TITLE IN 1945)

WATSON

TRUCKS

WATSON WAGON COMPANY

Largest Manufacturers of Bottom Dump Wagons in the World

41 Center Street   Canastota, N. Y.

(1916 – 1926)

(MFG. WAGONS and TRAILERS SINCE 1889.)

BOSCH, DYNETO, SIMMS and CONNECTICUT IGNITION SYSTEMS USED (VARIOUS)

JOHNSON, STROMBERG, ZENITH and OTHER CARBS.

('17)

WATSON PRODUCTS CORP., 40 West Center St., Canastota, New York

(new CO. NAME AFTER 1918)

RIGHT-HAND DRIVE (THROUGH '19)
5-TON HAS 4-SP. TRANS.,
10.3 GEAR RATIO

$4050.

('19)

16-19

100% WATSON Tractortruck

5-TON HAS 80" WB and
4-CYL. CONTINENTAL ENG.
(11 M.P.H. @ 1100 RPM)

Announcing **new** MODELS START 1920 :

B	3/4-1 TON	128" WB
	1½	
	2½	
N	3½	168" WB

LEFT-HAND DRIVE STANDARDIZED

20 ON ←

new CONVENTIONAL STYLE TRUCKS

CONTINENTAL 4-CYL. ENGINE CONT'D. IN 3½-TON and OTHER HEAVY-DUTY TYPES, INCL. 1923 5-TON 80"-WB TRUCK TRACTOR.

ABOVE : 3/4 1 TON MODEL **B**

4- CYL. WAUKESHA ENGINE IN 1920 MODEL B. STARTING 1922, *new* 1-TON MODEL D USES 4-CYL. BUDA ENGINE.

WATSON
HAULAGE SYSTEMS
MOTOR TRUCKS
ROAD TRACTORS
DUMPING WAGONS
and TRAILERS

Watson Trucks

Wayne Transportation Division
P.O. Box 1447
Richmond, Indiana 47374.

Welles Corporation, Ltd.
2650 Metcalfe Street
Windsor, Ontario N8Y 4R5

Wayne

Wayne Corp
An Indian Head Company

(1931 ON)

JAIL BUS

RIGHT-HAND DRIVE MODEL

1980s

(W. CHEV. CHASSIS)

SPECIAL BUS BODIES ON VARIOUS MAKES OF CHASSIS

FORD CHASSIS

WITH LUGGAGE RACK

CHEV. OR GMC CHASSIS ON CHAPERONE (MINI)

CHAPERONE™

GMC CHASSIS

LIFEGUARD®

BUSETTE ('82)

SINCE 1931, ALSO MFG. OF SCHOOL BUS BODIES

INTERNATIONAL CHASSIS

369

WHEELED COACH

MFD.
BY
WHEELED COACH
ORLANDO,
FLORIDA'

(1984
EXAMPLES
ILLUSTR.)

1500 SERIES
MINIBUS
(WITH SLIDING
DOOR)

1600 / 1800
SERIES
and
INTERIOR

1980s

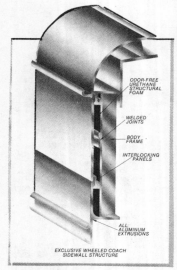

ODOR-FREE
URETHANE
STRUCTURAL
FOAM

WELDED
JOINTS

BODY
FRAME

INTERLOCKING
PANELS

ALL
ALUMINUM
EXTRUSIONS

EXCLUSIVE WHEELED COACH
SIDEWALL STRUCTURE

DETAILS OF
WHEELED COACH
BODY CONSTRUCTION
(SIDEWALLS)

32-PASS.
CITY
TRANSIT BUS
and
INTERIOR
ISUZU CHASSIS
with
DIESEL
ENGINE
AT REAR
130 HP *

196.9" WB

*=150 HP
WITH
TURBO-
CHARGER
(INTRO.
MID-1984)

DOUBLE
SLIDING
SIDE DOORS

370

(SINCE 1900)

← FACTORY

White

THE WHITE COMPANY . Cleveland

4 CYLINDERS

1919 MODELS "GBBF" (¾ TON,) "TBC" (1½ TON,) "TJ" (3 TON,) and "TG" (5 TON) REPLACED BY new NUMERICAL MODELS for 1920.

HEAVY-DUTY ('19).

('21)

19-21

OWN ENGINES

4- SPEED TRANSMISSIONS

1920 MODELS :

15	¾ TON	133½" WB
30	2	157½
40	3	174
45	5	174

"40" and "45" have DRIVESHAFT FOOT BRAKE.

15 EXPRESS   **$2975.**

¾ TON   ('21)

34 × 5 TIRES

40

3½-TON (new '21 CAPACITY RATING)

(DESIGN STILL SIMILAR IN 1925)   ('21)

20

2-TON

(REPLACES "30" FOR '21.)

36 × 4 TIRES   **$3875.**

1921 MODEL "40" has 36 × 5 TIRES (40 × 5 REAR)   MODEL "45" has 36 × 6 TIRES (40 × 6 REAR) "45-D" 5-TON DUMP TRUCK AVAILABLE AT **$5600.**

$4950. CHASSIS PRICE

36 × 6 TIRES

198" WB 4 CYL

STARTING 1922, MODELS "15-45" and "20-45" have LONGER WHEELBASES.

22-24

CLERESTORY-ROOFED CITY BUS ('24)

"50-A" BUS ('24)

1923 GEAR RATIOS

15	5.36
20	9.25
40	11.6
45	11.6

$5100.

"D" SUFFIX AFTER 1924 MODEL NO. INDICATES A SHORTER WHEELBASE.

156" WB

45-D 5 T. POWER DUMP TRK. ('24)

WHITE TRANSPORTATION CO.

371

3/4-TON "15"

133½" WB   34 × 5 TIRES

OWN 4-CYL. ENGINES CONT'D., with "GK"
3¾" × 5⅛" ENG. IN "15" and "20."
"GR" 4¼" × 5¾" ENG. IN
"40" and "45."

45 D

156" WB

5-TON "45-D" POWER DUMP TRUCK

White 25

ABOVE:
50-A
BUS

CHARABANC-STYLE SCENIC BUS

ZENITH CARBS.

$4950. (CHASSIS)

26

50-A BUS
198" WB
4 CYL.

32 × 6 TIRES

1926 "15-45" has 10" LONGER WHEELBASE and LARGER "GR" ENGINE, UNLIKE STD. "15."

52-GRB REFUSE TRUCK

"GRB" new DESIGNATION of 4¼" × 5¾" ENGINE.

There is a complete line of White Trucks to meet every transportation requirement. See these White models at any of the 82 factory branches or at 596 dealers.

TRUCKS
Model 15—1 ton $1,545
Model 20—1½ ton . . . 2,125
Model 50—2 ton 3,125
Model 51—2½ ton . . . 3,750
Model 55—3½ ton . . . 4,850
Model 52—2-7½ ton . . 5,100

BUSSES
Model 53—4 cyl. 16 Pass. $4,250
Model 50B—4 cyl. 25 Pass. 5,350
Model 54—6 cyl. 29 Pass. 7,500

THE WHITE COMPANY
Cleveland

27

MODEL "40" NOW "40-A"

372

CHASSIS: $7500.

MODEL 54 BUS
227" WB 6 CYL.
4 3/8 × 5 3/4 B. + S.

52
174" WB

5 TO 5 1/2 TON

SOLID TIRES

NEW

White
MOTOR TRUCK COMPANY

AVAIL. WITH SIDE DOOR ON VAN BODY

INTER-CITY

51-A
2 1/2 TON
170" WB

30 × 5 TIRES

DRIVER'S COMP'T.

OPEN CAB (TOWN CAR STYLE) WITH SPECIAL HORIZONTAL HOOD LOUVRES

15-B
$1545.
(CHAS.)

PANEL

15-B	1 TON	133 1/2" WB
57	1 1/4	141
20-A	1 1/2	145 1/2
56	2	165
51-A	2 1/2	170
55	3 1/2-5	174

new MODELS ADDED

NOTE FORWARD-SLOPING WINDSHIELD.

28

THESE NEWLY-STYLED URBAN DELIVERY MODELS AVAILABLE SPRING, 1928.

2 and 2 1/2-TON "FAST EXPRESS"

FAST EXPRESS SERVICE

No. 81

LONGER WHEELBASES AVAIL. ON VARIOUS MODELS.

373

(4-CYL. "50-B" and "53" BUS CHASSES ALSO AVAIL.)

new "59"
(SUMMER, '29)

new LOCKHEED HYDRAULIC BRAKES and
new BODY BY BENDER ON "60" and "61."

MCGUNES

51-A

4 CYL.
170" WB
CHASSIS
$3750.

2½-TON

29

new 6-
CYLINDER
L-HEAD
3½" × 4½" ENGINE
IN WHITE SIX "LIGHT DELIVERY" (ABOVE)
(AVAIL. SPRING, 1929.)

"60" = 3-SPEED
"61" = 4-SPEED

ALSO, new 6-CYL.
LIGHT-DUTY CHASSIS AVAIL.

"58" 3-TON MODEL ADDED (with 180" and other WBs.)
ALSO, "52-T" and "51-A" TRUCK-TRAILERS.

"60" CHASSIS
$1850.

"52" HVY. DUTY CHAS.
$5100.

FIGURE "W" CENTER BUMPER GUARD
(ON SOME MODELS)

(NOTE ILLUSTRATIONS
BELOW)

30

new
7½-TON
4-CYL.
(56 HP)
"52" and 6-CYL. (75 HP) "59-A."
ALSO "52-T"
and "51-AT"
TRACTOR-
TRUCKS
ALSO.

1-TON "15-B"
4 CYL., 226.4
31 HP CID
@ 1600 RPM

OTHER
MODELS :
"60" (1-TON)
260 CID 6 (45 HP)   @ 1800 RPM
"57" (1¼-T.) 289 CID 4 (46 HP @ 1700)
"20-A"(1½-T.)226.4 CID 4 (31 HP @ 1600)
"61" (1½-T.) 299 CID 6 (61 HP @ 2000)
"56" (2-T.) 289 CID 4 (46 HP @ 1700)
"51-A" (2½-T.) 326.3 CID 4 (56 @ 1800)
"58" (3-T.) (AS 51-A)
"55" (3½-5-T.)
(AS 51-A)
"52" (5-T.) (AS
51-A)

"63"
STAKE
(new
MEDIUM-H.
DUTY 2½-TN.)
6-CYL. (396 CID)
75 HP @ 2000
RPM

new 2½-
TON
"63"
DUMP
TRUCK

A.B. DORN CO.

29

White

new 3-TON "64" DUMP TRUCK
(518 CID 6) 100 HP @ 2000 RPM
(HEAVY DUTY)

374

('30½)

White

MODEL "54" BUS INTRO. 12-27, has "1-A-1" ENG.

227" WB CHASSIS

INTER-CITY BUS MODEL 54 6-CYL. (4 3/8 x 5 3/4 B.+S.) 519 CID O.H.V.

(1929 PRICES and SPECS. LISTED)

25 TO 29 PASSENGERS
38 x 9.00 TIRES (DUAL REAR)

(VERMONT TRANSIT CO. EXAMPLES ILLUSTR. TOP LEFT and BELOW)

29-30
(CONT'D.)

ROYAL BLUE LINES OF PENNSYLVANIA EXAMPLE AT RIGHT

SUBURBAN and LOCAL TYPE BUSES

note "W" ON FRONT BUMPER

MODEL 54 :
7915 LBS. CHASSIS WEIGHT 18000 LBS. GROSS WT., WITH BODY and NORMAL LOAD of PASSENGERS. METAL-TO-METAL 4-WHEEL FOOT BRAKES, AIR-OPERATED. (HAND BRAKE CONTRACTS ON DRIVESHAFT.)

SOME BODY BUILDERS INCLUDE DECORATIVE RAILING AT REAR, R.R.-STYLE

AS SEEN ON A NEW ENGLAND HIGHWAY, BELOW

CHASSIS PRICES :

4-CYL. "53" $4250.
(16-21 PASS.)

4-CYL. "50-B" 5350.
(25-29 PASS.)

6-CYL. "54" 7500.
(ILLUSTR. TOP, LEFT)

"DRUMHEAD" SIGN SOMETIMES AT REAR

NEW

"60-K" HOUSE-TO-HOUSE DELIVERY (SUMMER, 1931) TRUCK
6 CYL., HYDRAULIC BRAKES
112" WB and up

new 6-CYLINDER HEAVY-DUTY MODELS AVAIL. (with 4-WH. AIR BRAKES or POWER HYDRAULIC BRAKES.)

new HORIZONTAL HOOD LOUVRES (LT. DUTY)

31-32

OVERHEAD-VALVE
6-CYL. "620," "630," "640" SERIES MODELS IN MARCH, 1931.

GROSS WEIGHTS = 8,000 - 40,000 lbs. ('31)

"160-1-2" new for 1931 (1 to 2 TON) with 138" WB. 4 CYL., 45 HP ENGINE, AS FOUND IN new "210," "211," "212" (1½ to 2 TON.)

('31)

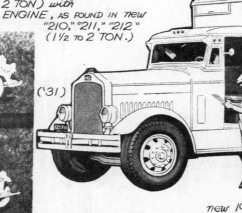

RETAIL DELIVERY

FAST EXPRESS

HEAVY-DUTY DUMP

CITY OR INTER-CITY VAN

HIGHWAY MOTOR FREIGHT. INC.

(note DIFFERENCE BETWEEN CAB OF VAN, ABOVE, FROM THAT OF VAN at LOWER LEFT.)

new 1931 6-WHEELERS with 6 CYL., 96 HP ENGS.:
"64 SW 300" (5 to 7½ TON)
"59 ASW 400" (7½ to 10 TON) ('31)

1932 MODELS: ('31)

Model	Tonnage	Cyl.	HP
602	(1½ to 2 TON)	6 CYL.	54
611	(2 T)	6	61
161, 162	(1-2 T)	4	45
51-A	(2½ T)	4	54
211, 212	(1½-2 T)	4	45
612	(2½ T)	6	61
620	(2½ T)	6	72
58	(3 T)	4	54
640	(3 T)	6	108
621, 630	(3 T)	6	82
631	(3½ T)	6	82
641	(3½ T)	6	108
642	(4 T)	6	108
643	(5 T)	6	108

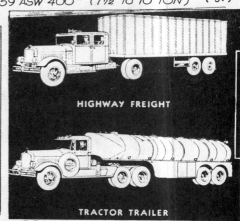

HIGHWAY FREIGHT

TRACTOR TRAILER

6-WHEELERS ALSO

THE FAMOUS WHITE TRUCKS AND BUSES

White

('32-'33)

33

SUMMER, '33 (K)

MODELS :

60-K , 601, 161 (1¼-1½T;)
602 , 162 (1½-2 T;) 611, 211 (2-2½T;)
612 , 212, 620 (2½-3T;) 51-A (2½-4T;)
618, 621 (3-4T;) 630, 640 (3-4½T;)
58 (3-5T;) 631, 641 (3½-6T;) 55 (5T;)
58-SS (7½T;) 642 (4-7½T;) 52 (5-7½T;)
643 (5-9T;) 691 (7-9T;)
   6-WH. : 630SW200 (5-6T;) 642SW320 (7-9T;)
      643SW420 (9-11 TON)

$1700.-$16,000. =TRUCK and BUS PRICE RANGE

new "K" SERIES has CAB PLACED FURTHER FORWARD, with ENGINE PARTIALLY PROTRUDING INTO CAB FIREWALL.

ADDED MODELS FOR 1934 (with MOST PREVIOUS MODELS CONT'D.)

701 (1¼-1½T;) 701-A (1½T;) 702 (1½-2T;) 702-A (2T;)
612-K (2½-3T;) 618-K, 620-K (3-4T;) 630-K, 640-K (3-4½T;) 631-K,
641-K (3½-6T;) 631-X (7½T;)   4.73 to 11.7 GEAR RATIOS

FINAL 4-CYL. CONVENTIONALS ('35)

632-X IS new 10-TON, 215" WB MODEL FOR '35,
WITH 6-CYL., 434 CID ENGINE (105 HP @ 2100 RPM.)
   580 CID, 6-CYL. ENG. IS MOST POWERFUL (130 HP @ 2050 RPM)
of '35 WHITES, USED IN 640,
640-K, 641, 641-K,
642, 643, and
691 MODELS.

new STYLING FOR 1934 →

34-35

WHITE'S FIRST V-12 "10-AB" ENGINE LISTED FOR 1935. EARLY 465 CID VERSION has 128 HP @ 2600 RPM, FOUND IN MODELS 730 and 731.

54-A STREAMLINED BUS ('35) →

731 C.O.E. V-12 ('35)

377

White

MOST 700 *and*
600 SERIES MODELS
CONTINUED, PLUS
7½-TON 586-GS.

IMPROVED 505 CID V-12 "12AB"
ENGINE (143 HP @ 2800 RPM)
IN MODELS 730, 730-X, 731, 731-X.

new
STREAMLINED 1936 MODELS, STYLED BY
ÁLEXIS DE SAKHNOFFSKY
(ALL MODELS
RESTYLED BY
MARCH, 1936.)

IN SOME
'36 MODELS
UNDER 4 TONS,
AN IMPROVED 80 HP
ENGINE (RATED
81 HP @ 3000,
270 CID)

BUS
('37)

*Automatic Air Conditioning is a
new feature of White Cabs that
assures constant ventilation of
clean fresh air. Dunlopillo seats
bring greater driver comfort.*

**36-38
NEW**
TOTAL RESTYLING

*Beautifully designed aero-type
instrument panel adds to the
de luxe appearance of the cab.*

new C.O.E.
MODELS ('37)

1937 C.O.E.s : 730, 731, 731-H,
805, 809, 810, 812, 818

new 900 SERIES
6-WHEELERS ('37)
INCLUDE 904,
918, 920, 922,
942, 991.

('37)

*The new White has been com-
pletely modernized with smart
streamline styling.*

STREAMLINED TANKER

FINAL V-12 TRUCKS
IN 1938.

68 TO
143 HP
IN 1938,
6-WHEELERS TO
16½ TONS.

378

IMPROVED FLOATING RIDE CABS and "SUPER POWER" 6-CYL. ENGINES (6-CYL. ONLY, IN 1939 CONVENTIONALS.)

FROM 76 HP @ 3000 RPM

1940 MODELS 510, 700, 800 SERIES and up 95" WB UP

LONGER WHEELBASES IN 1941; 4.45 TO 9.5 GEAR RATIOS

MID—
39-40s

White

('41)

new WA SERIES STARTS 1941.

CONV. 134" and 136" WB

White Horse

← 99" WB, 4 CYL. AIR-COOLED REAR ENG.

NEW FOR 1939. (SOME '40-41 WHITE HORSES W/O VERT. FRONT CHROME.)

1½ - 10 TON 1941 MODELS:

WA-14	250 CID	90 HP @ 2800	B/M
WA-18	270	100 @ 2600	
WA-20	318	110 @ 2600	
WA-22	362	125 @ 2600	
WA-26	and WA-34 ALSO		
720	529 CID	133 @ 2400	
722	97" and 100 WB C.O.E.s:		

(MODEL #s 100 DIGITS HIGHER THAN CORRESPONDING CONVENTIONALS LISTED ABOVE. WA-114 has SAME ENG. AS WA-14, and SO FORTH. 820 and 822 LIKE 720 and 6-WHEELERS: 722 SPECS.) WA-2064, WA-2264, WA-3464, 920, 922 MODELS.

'41-'42 WHITE HORSE (note CHANGES)

('42) CITY BUS

White 46

C.O.E.

LINEMAN'S UTILITY TRUCK

"WHITE HORSE" DELIVERY STILL MFD. (LIMITED PROD.) TO EARLY 1950s.

47-48

WHITE CONVENTIONAL TRUCK STYLING CHANGES VERY LITTLE DURING MID-1940s.

TRACTOR-TRAILER COMBINATION

ENGINE (COOLING DETAILS SHOWN)

49

"SUPER POWER" FRONT DETAILS

"WC" SUPER POWER SERIES

380

49-50

('49)

new
743-CID
CUMMINS NHB 600
DIESEL ENGINED TRUCKS INTRO.
SUMMER, 1949. 200 HP @ 2100 RPM,
134" TO 245" WHEELBASE RANGE.

White
SUPER POWER
3000

POWER LIFT CAB
RAISES IN LESS
THAN 30 SECONDS,
TO PROVIDE EASY
ENGINE ACCESS.

new
TILT-
CAB

(INTRO.
SPRING, 1949)

VAN
BODY
VARIATION
ILLUS.
AT
TOP
RIGHT

new C.O.E.s IN
3000 SERIES

WHITE DIESEL POWER

HIGHWAY POST OFFICE COACH

TRANSIT BUS

White

('50)

EXPRESS MAIN 44

DIESEL ENGINES have 743 CID, 175-200 HP @ 1800 RPM

C.O.E.s 3014, 3015, 3016, 3018, 3020, 3022, 3026

('51):

WHITE 3000

50 -53

White SUPER POWER

184 HP

ALL 6-CYLS.
136", 134" WB and up

MORE POWER with WHITE MUSTANG ENGINE

1951 MODELS:	(TRUCKS)			
WC-16	298 CID	110 HP	@	3100 RPM
WC-18	318	114	@	3000
WC-20	340	120	@	"
WC-22	362	125	@	"
WC-26	386	135	@	"
WC-28	481	170	@	"
WC-32	504	184	@	"

TRUCK- TRACTORS have "T" SUFFIX ON MODEL NO.; DIESELS have "D" SUFFIX.

('53)

CONV. WC-24PLT TRACTOR 10.00 x 20 TIRES

COMPACT DIESELS ('54)

$12,300.

WHITE

WHITE - FREIGHTLINER (BUILT IN AFFILIATION WITH WHITE MOTOR CO., FROM 1951 TO 1975,) SHOWN IN SEPARATE FREIGHTLINER SECTION.

WITH 6 CYL., 200 HP CUMMINS DIESEL ENG. TILTED 20° TO RIGHT, ALLOWING 2 CYLS. TO BE SET BACK INTO CAB.

MASON-DIXON 2835

MASON-DIXON 2849

MASON-DIXON 2839

2592

2581

2592

('56)

new (AVAIL. IN CANADA)

2000-B SCHOOLBUS CHASSIS ('56½)

SCHOOL BUS

WITH 6-CYL., 298 CID "WHITE MUSTANG" ENG. (110 HP @ 3100 RPM)

DIESELS (ABOVE)

FLEET OF 225 WHITE 9000's NOW IN SERVICE

54-59

2064 TANDEM →

PROD.: 23,384 ('58) 25,335 ('59)

C.O.E.

new White "5000" Cab made of **FIBER GLASS**

New EMBLEM

white

"2064" TANDEM TRUCK

('59)
383

GASOLINE POWERED

('60)

White

('61)

DURING EARLY 1960s, SOME OLDER CONVENTIONAL TYPES CONTINUED.

SEE FOLLOWING PAGE FOR C.O.E. TYPES OF 1960s.

('67)

('69)

193

60-70

with MIXER BODY

WESTERN STAR MFD. IN WHITE'S KELOWNA, B.C. FACTORY (WHICH OPENED 5-67)

('69-70)

('69)

PRODUCTION, 1960 TO 1970:

18,389   ('60)
19,474   ('61)
26,450   ('62)
28,161   ('63)
21,342   ('64)
27,316   ('65)
32,422   ('66)
24,664   ('67)
29,982   ('68)
31,520   ('69)
22,288   ('70)

9000 SERIES TRUCK TRACTOR

(C.O.E.s ON NEXT PAGE)

384

THIS TYPE AVAIL. DURING MOST OF 1960s, WITH ONLY MINOR CHANGES.

White

CAB PIECES MOULDED OF "ROYALEX" ON THIS MODEL.

THE TREND

('67)

C.O.E.s

60-70
(CONT'D.)

available with either White Super Mustang gasoline engines or Cummins and Detroit Diesel diesels and a compatible range of transmissions.

('69)

PDQ DELIVERY

AVAIL. 1960-1966

TILT CAB RAISED, SHOWING ENGINE DETAILS

COMPACT SERIES

855 CID 270 HP

('70)

6000 →
XPEDITOR

new FOR 1970 → (EARLY TYPE W. NO SMALL EXTRA LTS. AS SEEN ON LATER MODEL AT LEFT.)

ABC COMPANY

385

MIXER

VARIOUS 4000 OR 9000 SERIES CONVENTIONALS AS OF 10-71.

White

WHITE TRUCKS

CONSTRUCKTOR

Model	BBC
C4364-G	108"
C4664D-G	118"

WHITE CONSTRUCKTOR

Stokely·Van Camp
Stokely's Finest

4000 SERIES CONV.

M77 · M77

OBSOLETE OR DAMAGED MODELS CAN BE REBODIED WITH

CONSTRUCKTOR

GLIDER KIT

71 ON

"ALLEY CAT"

NATIONAL DISPOSAL SERVICE

REFUSE TRUCK (new) (STARTS SPRING, '71)

1500, 1600 OR 7000 SERIES C.O.E. TYPES AS OF 10-71.

C.O.E.

REAR (WEST. STAR)

W

WHITE

WHITE WESTERN STAR

SOME HAVE 2 HEADLIGHTS INSTEAD OF 4.

WHITE

CAB (WEST. STAR)

4900 WD, 4864 WD OR 4964 WD SERIES

72½ ON
New

White

ROAD COMMANDER

(REPLACES 7400 SERIES C.O.E.s)

TORSION BAR TILT CAB

SINGLE ACCESS DOOR puts the wiper motors and radiator cap right at your fingertips. Also gives you fewer things to go wrong.

"ROAD COMMANDER 2" LIGHTWT. STARTS MID-1977.

73
ON

ROAD BOSS 2 and WESTERN STAR CONVENTIONALS AVAIL. 1978, 195-475 HP DIESEL ENGINES.

Western Star
(WINDSHIELD HEIGHT INCREASED 2")

(ROAD XPEDITOR 2 and ROAD COMMANDER 2 C.O.E.s ALSO AVAIL. 1978, 195-450 HP DIESEL ENGINES.)

ROAD BOSS
(NEW)

"ROAD BOSS 2" FROM 1977 ON

(C.O.E.s ON NEXT PAGE)

('73)

387

WHITE

ROAD XPEDITOR
new low cab forward

74
ON
diesel power
CHOICE OF
13 DIFF.
engines.
210 TO 335 HP

Inside the Cab
Two inches more headroom
2-Tone padded vinyl interior with
wood tone dash
RCCC instrument panel — all controls
standardized
118% bigger speedometer and
tachometer — easier to read
Quick disconnect dash access panel

ROAD XPEDITOR

(DOOR EMBLEM)

1974 C.O.E.
ROAD
COMMANDER
has
new BUMPER and
GRILLE LIKE THAT of
ROAD BOSS CONVENT'L.

C.O.E.
84
ON

NEW
HIGH CABOVER

388

WHITE

83 *WESTERN STAR*

Conventional:

New 84 ON

HAS TANDEM REAR AXLES

Cab features maximum efficiency with wraparound instrumentation (including electric tach and speedometer) and removable instrument panels for easy servicing.

DASH (ABOVE) ('84)

AERODYNAMIC SHROUD

4 RECTANGULAR HEADLIGHTS

new DIAGONAL RADIATOR BAND SHOWS VOLVO AFFILIATION

WHITE

Integral Sleeper:

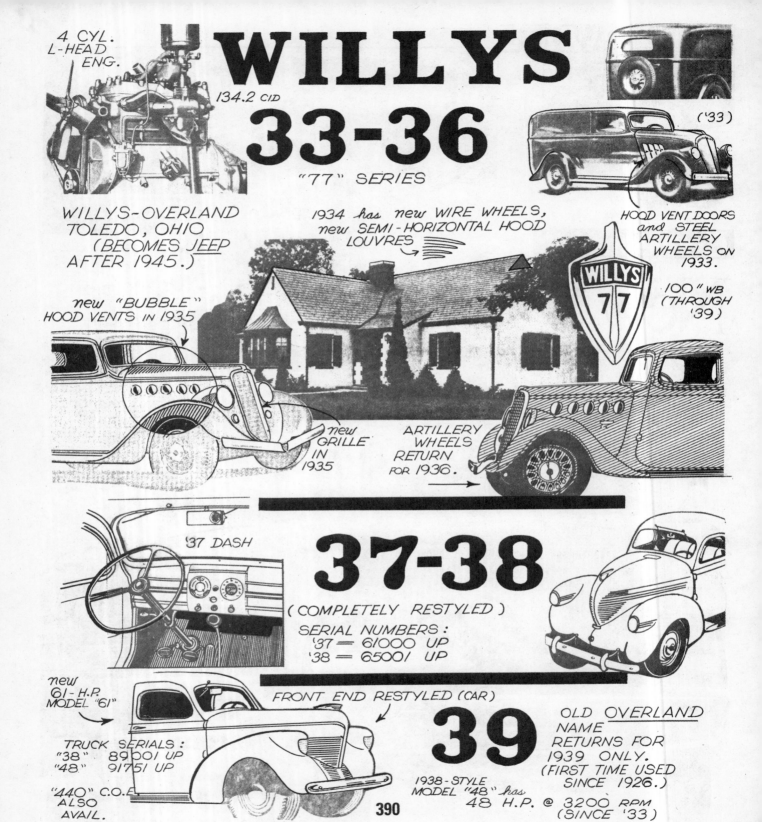

WILLYS
33-36
"77" SERIES

4 CYL. L-HEAD ENG.

134.2 CID

('33)

WILLYS-OVERLAND TOLEDO, OHIO (BECOMES JEEP AFTER 1945.)

1934 *has* new WIRE WHEELS, new SEMI-HORIZONTAL HOOD LOUVRES

HOOD VENT DOORS and STEEL ARTILLERY WHEELS ON 1933.

WILLYS 77

new "BUBBLE" HOOD VENTS IN 1935

100" WB (THROUGH '39)

new GRILLE IN 1935

ARTILLERY WHEELS RETURN FOR 1936.

37-38

'37 DASH

(COMPLETELY RESTYLED)
SERIAL NUMBERS:
'37 = 61000 UP
'38 = 65001 UP

new 61-H.P. MODEL "61"

FRONT END RESTYLED (CAR)

39

OLD OVERLAND NAME RETURNS FOR 1939 ONLY. (FIRST TIME USED SINCE 1926.)

TRUCK SERIALS:
"38" 89001 UP
"48" 91751 UP

"440" C.O.E. ALSO AVAIL.

1938-STYLE MODEL "48" has 48 H.P. @ 3200 RPM (SINCE '33)

WILLYS 40

"OVERLAND" NAME CEASES.

"WILLYS" NAME ON SIDE OF HOOD (SEE ARROW) ← FANCY ORNAMENT

SPLIT GRILLE IN 1940

100" WB, EXC. ON EARLY "441" MODELS LISTED IN 1940.

SC-440
4 CYL.
58 HP
@
3600 RPM
4.7 TO
5.11 G.R.

SCOF-440-P
48 HP @ 3200 RPM
5.11 GEAR RATIO
(OTHERS AVAIL.)

('41)

VAN

THE WALK-IN WILLYS VAN (AT LEFT) IS EXTREMELY SCARCE, AND SELDOM SEEN!

C.O.E. VERSION OF **441** SERIES 104" WB

1941 WILLYS

41-42

441 104" WB **442 →**
new GRILLE, HOOD (LIKE '41)

UNSOLD 1941 AND 1942 MODELS (CIVILIAN TRUCKS AND CARS) RELEASED ON A LIMITED BASIS DURING THE WARTIME YEARS.

"442" SERIES (LISTED AS AVAILABLE AS LATE AS 1947.)

FOR POST-WAR MODEL SEE "JEEP" SECTION.

391

"WILSON— THAT'S HAUL!"

Wilson

New One-Ton

J. C. Wilson Company, Detroit, Michigan

TRUCKS 1915–1925

(BLT. DRAYAGE WAGONS SINCE 1880s)

NO 1-TON MODEL FROM '20 THROUGH '23

$3300. EA 2½ TON

('20)

('21)

4-CYL. CONT'L. ENGINES

TYPICAL RADIATOR

POSTAL TELEGRAPH-CABLE COMPANY

UNITED STATES US CARTRIDGE CO.
METALLIC AMMUNITION   THE BLACK SHIELD
U.S.C.Co.

("F" WHEELBASE INCR. TO 140")

new C 1-TON

MODELS		('20)	
F	1½ TON	136"WB*	6. GR
EA	2½	152	7.75
G	3½	160	8.75
H	5	160	10.25
C	1 TON	142"WB ('24-5)	

1½-2½-3½-5 Ton, All Worm Drive

('24-'25)

Winther Motor Truck Company (1917–1927)

Manufacturers of Motor Trucks and Motor Cars

Kenosha, Wisconsin

FRONT DETAIL ('18)

WORMLESS ('19)

("WINTHER-MARWIN" 4-W-D TRUCKS ALSO)

FINAL 1927 WINTHER TRUCKS RE-NAMED "WINTHER-KENOSHA."

4 CYLINDERS WISCONSIN ENGINES; H.-S. ENG. INTRO. IN new ¾-1 TON "751" (STARTS '21)

1½ TO 7-TON MODELS ALSO.

(CARS ALSO)

('21)

$1795.= "The Winther Delivery Special"

WOLF WAGON

(1956-1960s)
MFD. BY WOLF ENGINRG., DALLAS, TEXAS (AFTER 1960, MFD. BY ST. LOUIS CAR CO., ST. LOUIS, MO.

TRAILER-LIKE TRUCKS COULD BE JOINED TOGETHER LIKE A TRAIN!

POWELL TRUCK LINES, INC.

('58)

392

MISC. A

('25) 2½ TO 3 TON MODEL W AMERICAN LA FRANCE

ARGOSY COMPACT PASSENGER BUS
('77)

O. Armleder Co
Cincinnati, Ohio,
ARMLEDER
('20)

ARROW TERMINAL TRACTOR

ATLAS
('70-'71)
('20-'21)

AVAILABLE
(GRAHAM-DOANE SIMILAR)

('46)

EARLY BACKUS TRUCK
('26)

AVERY
6- CYL.
('20)

BACKUS

B BACKUS MOTOR TRUCK CO., E. RUTHERFORD, N.J.
(1925 - 1937)
AFTER 1927, BUS PRODUCTION PREVAILED.

CHARTERED

('37)

('38) BANTAM PANEL MODEL 60 393

MISC. B

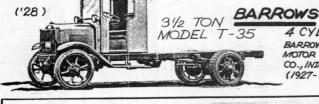

('28) **BARROWS**

3½ TON MODEL T-35 4 CYL.

BARROWS MOTOR TRUCK CO., INDIANAPOLIS (1927-1928)

BECK

('56) A CLOSE IMITATION OF GMC'S "SCENICRUISER."

BECK ALSO BLT. OTHER BUSES, 1934-1957.

BESSEMER 4-TON ('22)

6 × 6, Tractor, Wrecking, Type C-2 (Biederman)

BIEDERMAN

6-WHEELER (1940s)

BLAZER BY CHEVROLET

('81)

(C. '34)

"BOTTLE" TRUCK, ON 6-CYL. DODGE CHASSIS. TYPICAL OF VARIOUS SPECIAL-BODIED ODDITIES BUILT FOR ADVERTISING PURPOSES.

BRONCO BY FORD

('78)

(c. 39)

Brown

MISC. C

COLEMAN LITTLETON, COLO.

4 DRIVE   4 STEER
7   7   (EARLY 1960s)

COLEMAN

CLYDESDALE

CONESTOGA
('19-'20)

COMET
4-CYL.
1½-TON
('20)

('25)

COMMERCE MODEL "25"
2½ TON

CRANE CARRIER ('81)
REFUSE TRUCK

CROSLEY
PANEL DELIVERY
4-CYL.
('51)

('51)

COOK BROS.   "BE WISE"

C.T.
ELECTRIC
MODEL H-1
½ TON 108" WB
(1908-1928, PHILADELPHIA, PA.)

CUSHMAN
"TRUCKSTER"
1960s

Crown   ('71)

SCHOOL BUS

('28)

school coach   395

MISC. D

DELCAR

('20)

MODEL BW

DEARBORN TRUCKS

DeMartini

('25)

DJB ('82)

2½ TON "K-5" ('26)

('21)

Capacity Two-Ton

DORRIS

DUTY

('47)

"DRAGON WAGON"
8-WHEEL DRIVE
(BY LOCKHEED)

LOCKHEED

DRAGON WAGON

('72)

MISC. E-F

('72)

EUCLID DIVISION
GENERAL MOTORS CORPORATION
Cleveland 17, Ohio

(EST. 1931)

GM MORE POWER FOR YOU

('57)

EAGLE (EAGLE EMBLEM ON FRONT)
BUS (SINCE 1956)
ORIGINALLY BUILT IN BELGIUM. AMERICAN FACTORY OPENED AT BROWNSVILLE, TEXAS IN 1975. MOST BUILT FOR CONTINENTAL TRAILWAYS. ALSO NAMED "GOLDEN EAGLE" and "SILVER EAGLE" SINCE '50s.

Euclid Equipment
FOR MOVING EARTH, ROCK, COAL AND ORE

FORMERLY
The EUCLID ROAD MACHINERY Co.
CLEVELAND 17, OHIO

(SINCE 1977, EUCLID A SUBSIDIARY OF DAIMLER-BENZ.)

FABCO
FABCO, DIV. of KELSEY-HAYES CO., OAKLAND, CALIF. (SINCE '54)
(GAS OR DIESEL)

('72)

UV new FOR 1972

FARGO
"CLIPPER" 6 CYL. ('29) 3/4 TON
(1/2-TON "PACKET" MODEL ALSO IN '29)
MF'D. BY CHRYSLER CORP., DETROIT, SINCE 1928.

from **$795** F.O.B. Marion, Ind.

('51)

FARMOROAD
BY CROSLEY

FISHER MODEL 16 1-TON (ABOVE)

FLXETTE
BUS

('81)

('59)

FOX

('26)

1½ TON
Fisher Fast Freight
A SPEEDY 1½ TON TRUCK

397

('36)

GAR WOOD

MISC. G

('75)

('25)

Gotfredson Truck

GILLIG

GILLIG BROS.

SCHOOL BUS GILLIG BROS., HAYWARD, CALIF. (SINCE 1932) IN SAN FRANCISCO TO '38.

('20)

GRAMM PIONEER BERNSTEIN

GRAHAM - DOANE

('47)

GRAY

('25)

1-TON CHAS. 4 CYL.

(1924 SIMILAR)

('29)

('34)

GRASS-PREMIER

GUILDER

"JB" 4-TON ICE CREAM TRUCK

J.M.HORTON ICE CREAM CO.

HORTON'S ICE CREAM

NEW YORK

MISC. H-J

Model 140
Two-Ton Truck

HENDRICKSON ('39)

HUFFMAN ('20)

('30)

(2 VIEWS)

INDIANA

(ABOVE, LEFT)

Jackson

FOUR WHEEL DRIVE TRUCKS

JACKSON MOTORS CORP.,
JACKSON, MICH.

EISEMANN IGN. and ELECTR.
SYSTEM. WITH SELF-STARTER.

"No Hill Too Steep—
No Sand Too Deep"

JACKSON MODEL "C-1920"
WITH 4-CYL.
CONTINENTAL ENGINE
(4½" × 5½")
150" WB
4 SP. TRANS.
9.18 GEAR RATIO
(LISTED 9.17, '21)
36 × 7 SOLID
TIRES
12 M.P.H. (@
1027 RPM)
1921 SAME, BUT IS
"4WD" MODEL.

3½
TON
"C-1920'

('20)

('33)

J. C. JARRETT MOTOR
AND FINANCE CO.,
COLORADO SPRINGS,
COLO. (1921-1934)

6-CYL. WAUKESHA ENG.

Nelson Motor Truck Company
SAGINAW, MICH.

JUMBO MOTOR TRUCKS

4 CYL.
BUDA
ENG.

('20)

JARRETT

399

MISC. K - L

KAISER
60' ARTICULATED BUS

> BLT. BY PERMANENTE METALS CORP.
> DIV. OF KAISER INDUSTRIES,
> PERMANENTE, CALIF. (1 BUS ONLY)
> WITH 6-CYL. CUMMINS DIESEL ENGINE.
> USED ON SAN FRANCISCO TO LOS
> ANGELES ROUTE OF SANTA FE
> TRAILWAYS UNTIL 1951.

('46)

Swing-away cab for pallet cargo

('71) **KARRY-ALL**

('20)

KELLAND
KELLAND MOTOR CAR CO.
NEWARK, N. J.

('66) **KW-DART**

LECTRA D-100
ELECTRIC truck →

('26)

('81)

LEHIGH
MOTOR TRUCKS

2 Ton
4 Cylinder Model
$1695
F. o. b. Allentown, Pa.

LINN

T-3
8 TON

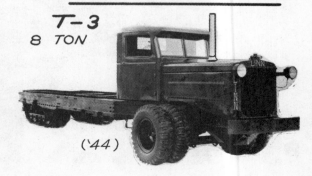

LE MOON
1200-D
DIESEL

('38)

('44)

400

MISC. M - N

('25)

MASON
"ROAD KING
MODEL 215

MASON   4 CYL.
MOTOR TRK. CO., $1776.25
FLINT, MICH.   (CHASSIS)

(A DIV. OF DURANT)

(ABOVE)
MacDONALD (C. '48) LOW-LOADER

MacDONALD TRUCK and MFG. CO.
SAN FRANCISCO, CALIF. (1920-1952)
(A DIV. OF PETERBILT AFTER W.W. 2)

MASTER TRUCK

ENGINEERED FIBREGLASS CO.,
FOUNTAIN VALLEY, CALIF.
(INTRO. 1972) DETROIT
DIESEL, OTHER DIESELS AVAIL.

160" WB

('72)

"MICRO-COACH"
(BY GILLIG)

('71)

('21)

MAXWELL

(1905—1925)
ORIGINALLY
MAXWELL-BRISCOE MOTOR
CO., TARRYTOWN, N.Y.,
CARS and TRUCKS TO 1912.
(CARS ONLY, 1913-1916.)
1917-1925, MFD. IN DETROIT
BY MAXWELL MOTOR CO.

('25)

GILLIG BROS., HAYWARD CALIF. (INTRO. 1971)
ON FORD P-500 DLVRY. CHASSIS (330 CID FORD V8, 190 HP)

NATIONAL TRANSMARK 30' BUS

4 CYL.

Northway

('85)

('85)

NATIONAL
COACH CORPORATION

('20)

401

MISC. O-R

Onan
"WESTCOASTER" (MAILSTER)

('74)

OTIS ELECTRO BUS

$450 CHASSIS PRICE F.O.B. Toledo

('61)

U.S. MAIL

OVERLAND

('22) 4-CYL.

RAINIER TRUCK

RHODE ISLAND LACE WORKS

('20)

REHBERGER 3-TON ('25)

REHBERGER

DETAILS OF CAST ALUMINUM RADIATOR, DASH PANEL →

Reliance Truck
EVERY INCH WORTHY THE NAME

('20)

REYNOLDS

('20)

('25) 6 CYL. 230 CID

ROCKET

LIST PRICE only $1390

RUGBY EXPRESS & FAST MAIL

6 CYL. 128" WB

('28)

RUGBY   1-TON EXPRESS

MISC. S

SANFORD ('28) S-2-T 2 TON
171" WB
6 CYL. SERIES N "CUB"
160" WB ('29)

SIGNAL MOTOR TRUCK CO DETROIT
CANADIAN AEROPLANES LIMITED
SIGNAL ('19-20)

SKILLCRAFT BUS
SKILLCRAFT INDUSTRIES, VENICE, FLA.
('81)

2½-TON MODEL "2½-K" ('25)

STANDARD

Star DELIVERY WAGON w PANEL TOP and VESTIBULE FRONT 109" WB ('24)

STAR SIX

STAR DURANT MOTORS

ONE TON CHASSIS $975 f. o. b. Lansing
Box and cab not included 40 HP ('27)

COMPOUND FLEETRUCK

The greatest single step forward in a quarter century of Motor Transportation. A new type of transmission with the *economy shift*—a 4th forward gear that increases motor efficiency, gasoline mileage, speed and power range. Easy to operate—a forward push on gear lever instantly changes from 3rd to 4th, reducing fuel cost 20%.

The Stoughton Wagon Co. Stoughton Wis.
('20)

STOUGHTON

('36)
STUTZ PAK-AGE-CAR
STUTZ PAK-AGE-CAR

MISC. T-U

Toppins Truck Unit with Fordson Power Plant

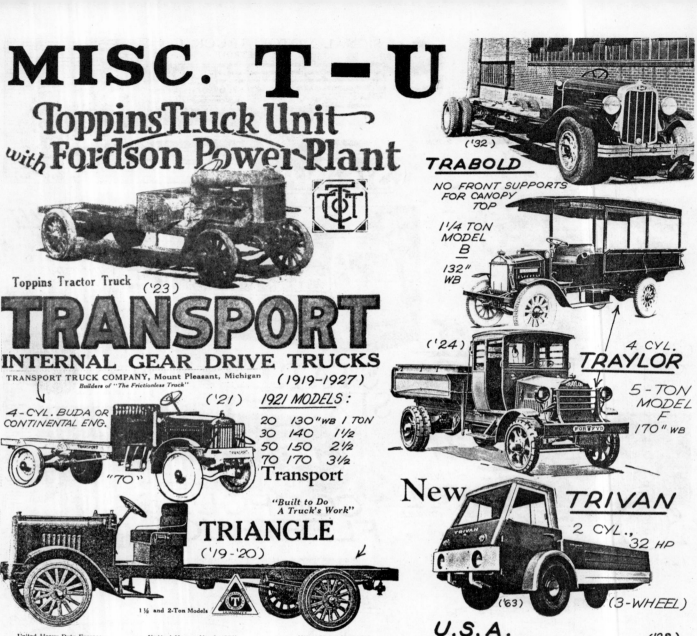

Toppins Tractor Truck

('32) **TRABOLD**

NO FRONT SUPPORTS FOR CANOPY TOP

1 1/4 TON MODEL B 132" WB

TRANSPORT

INTERNAL GEAR DRIVE TRUCKS

TRANSPORT TRUCK COMPANY, Mount Pleasant, Michigan
Builders of "The Frictionless Truck"

('23)
(1919-1927)

4-CYL. BUDA OR CONTINENTAL ENG.

('21)

1921 MODELS:

20	130" WB	1 TON	
30	140	1 1/2	
50	150	2 1/2	
70	170	3 1/2	

Transport

"70"

"Built to Do A Truck's Work"

4 CYL. **TRAYLOR**

('24)

5-TON MODEL F 170" WB

TRIANGLE

('19-'20)

1 1/2 and 2-Ton Models

New **TRIVAN**

2 CYL., 32 HP

('63)

(3-WHEEL)

U.S.A.

('28)

United Heavy Duty Express
For full ton-and-half load chassis $1445

United Heavy Haul "35"
For all service up to 3500 lb. chassis $1595

United Heavy Haul "50"
Capacity, 5000 lb. chassis $1795

UNITED

UNITED MOTORS PRODUCTS CO., Grand Rapids, Mich.

$895
Chassis

MISC. W-Z

('26)

Ward Electric

('29) MODEL K CHASSIS

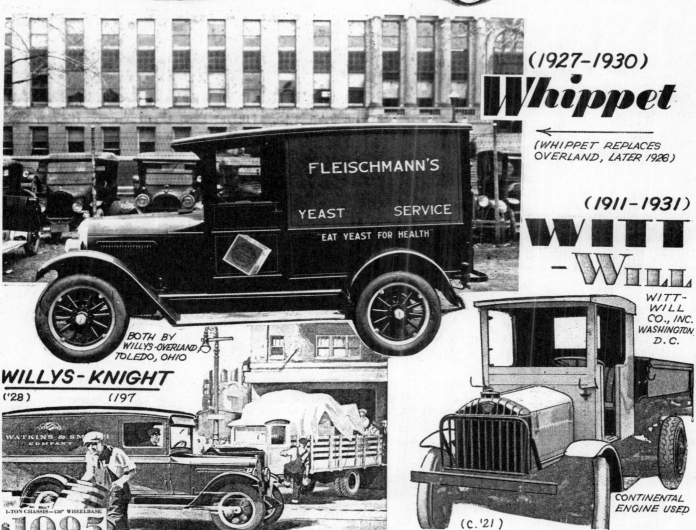

(1927-1930)
Whippet

(WHIPPET REPLACES OVERLAND, LATER 1926)

(1911-1931)
WITT-WILL

WITT-WILL CO., INC. WASHINGTON D.C.

FLEISCHMANN'S

YEAST SERVICE

"EAT YEAST FOR HEALTH"

BOTH BY WILLYS-OVERLAND, TOLEDO, OHIO

WILLYS-KNIGHT

('28)   (197

WATKINS & SMITH COMPANY

1-TON CHASSIS—130" WHEELBASE

$1095

CONTINENTAL ENGINE USED

(C.'21)

YELLOW-KNIGHT
1-TON MODEL **T-2** CHASSIS

4 CYL. 124" WB

('26)

ZELIGSON
6-WHEELER DIESEL
TULSA, OKLA.

('79 ON)

American-Built Trucks & Buses Mfd. Between 1920 and 1985

(* = illustrated in miscellaneous sections starting on page 393)

A AND B—American and British Mfg. Co., Bridgeport, CT; Providence, RI (1914–1923)

AA—All-American (1918–1927)

ACASON—Acason Motor Truck Co., Detroit, MI (1915–1925)

ACE—American Motor Truck Co., Newark, OH (1918–1928)

A.C.F.—American Car and Foundry Motors Co., Detroit, MI; Philadelphia, PA; Berkeley, CA (1926–1953)

A.C.F./BRILL—See A. C. F.

ACME—Acme Motor Truck Co., Cadillac, MI (1915–1932)

ACME—Acme Wagon Co., Emingville, PA (1916–1921)

ACME—Acme Harvesting Machine Co., South Bartonville, Peoria, IL (1920)

ACORN—Acorn Motor Truck Co., Chicago, IL (1924–1931)

AEROCOACH—General American Transportation Corp., East Chicago, IL (1940–1952)

AHRENS-FOX—Ahrens-Fox Fire Engine Co., Cincinnati, OH (1911–1953); C. D. Beck Co., Sidney, OH (1953–1956)

AIR-O-FLEX—Air-O-Flex Auto Corp., Detroit, MI (1918–1920)

AJAX—(1920–1921)

AKRON MULTI-TRUCK—Thomart Motor Co., Kent, OH (1920–1922)

ALENA STEAM—(1921)

ALL-AMERICAN—See AA

ALL-POWER—All-Power Truck Co., Detroit, MI (1918–1923)

ALLIED TRUCK—(1920)

AMERICAN—American Motor Truck and Tractor Co., Portland, CT (1920–1924)

AMERICAN AUSTIN (BANTAM)*—American Austin Car Co., Inc., Butler, PA (1930–1934); American Bantam Car Co., Butler, PA (1935–1941) Cars, light delivery trucks, early military Jeeps

AMERICAN BANTAM—See American Austin (Bantam)

AMERICAN BUS AND TRUCK—(1926)

AMERICAN CARRIER EQUIPMENT—American Carrier Equipment, Fresno, CA (1971 on) Bus also known as Shuttlecraft

AMERICAN COMMERCIAL—(1918–1923)

AMERICAN LA FRANCE—Various company titles; originally American La France Fire Engine Co., Elmira, NY, now a division of A.T.O., Inc. (1910 on)

AMERICAN MOTOR BUS—See Chicago Motor Bus

AMERICAN STEAM TRUCK—American Steam Truck Co., Elgin, IL (1918–1922)

AM GENERAL—AM General Corp., Wayne, MI; Mishawaka, IN (1974 on) Trucks, buses, military vehicles

AMTORG—(1930–1935)

ANSUL—(early 1970s)

APEX—Hamilton Motors Co., Grand Haven, MI (1918–1921)

APPERSON—Apperson Bros. Automobile Co., Kokomo, IN (1905–1920) Cars also

APPLETON—Appleton Motor Truck Co., Appleton, WI (1922–1934)

ARANDSEE—(1920)

ARCO—Arco Iron Works, Inc., Topeka, KS (1959)

ARGOSY—Argosy Mfg. Co., Versailles, OH (1976 on)*

ARKLA—Arkansas-Louisiana Gas Co., Little Rock, AR (1965)

ARMLEDER—Originally O. Armleder Co., Cincinnati, OH; after 1928, Le Blond-Schacht Truck Co., Cincinnati, OH (1909–1936)*

ARROW—Arrow Mfg. Co., Denver, CO (since 1960s)*

ASTOR—M. P. Möller Motor Car Co., Hagerstown, MD (1925) Principally taxis

ATCO—American Truck and Trailer Corp., Kankakee, IL (1919–1923)

ATLANTIC/ATLANTIC ELECTRIC—Atlantic Vehicle Co., Newark, NJ (1912–1921)

ATLAS—Martin Carriage Works; Martin Truck and Body Co.; Martin-Parry Corp.; Atlas Motor Truck Co.; Atlas Div., Industrial Motors Corp., York, PA (1916–1923)*

AUBURN—Auburn Automobile Co., Auburn, IN (1900–1937) Basically cars, but professional vehicles in 1936

AULTMAN-TAYLOR—The Aultman-Taylor Co., Mansfield, OH (1906–1923)

AUSTIN—See American Austin

AUSTIN UTILITY COACH—Austin System, El Segundo, CA (1933–1934)

AUTOCAR—The Autocar Co., Ardmore, PA (1897–   )

AUTOHOE—The Autohoe Co., West De Pere, WI (1950)

AUTOHORSE—One-Wheel Truck Co., St. Louis, MO. One-wheel tractor for attachment to horse-drawn vehicles (1917–1926)

AUTOMATIC—Automatic Machine Co., Bridgeport, CT (1920) Industrial trucks and tractors

AUTOMATIC—Automatic Electric Transmission Co.; Automatic Transportation Co., Buffalo, NY. Electric car and van (1922)

AUTOMOTIVE SYNDICATE BUS—Automotive Syndicate, Indianapolis, IN Steam bus, one only (1928)

AUTORAILER—(1946)

AUTO TRACTOR—Auto Tractor Corp., Chicago, IL (1930)

AVAILABLE—Available Truck Co., Chicago, IL. In 1957 a division of Crane Carrier Corp. (CCC), Tulsa, OK (1910–1957)*

AVERY—The Avery Co., Peoria, IL (1910–1923; also tractors until 1950)*

BACKUS—Backus Motor Truck Co., East Rutherford, NJ (1925–1927)*

BACKUS BUS—Backus Motor Truck Co. (1927–1937)*

BAKER—Baker Steam Motor Car & Mfg. Co., Pueblo, Denver, CO; Steam Appliance Corp. of America; Baker Motors, Inc., Cleveland, OH (1920–1928)

BANKS—Banks Motor Corp., Louisville, KY. Funeral vehicles (1923)

BANTAM—See American Austin*

BARKER—Barker Motors Co., North Los Angeles, CA (1911–1920)

BARROWS—Barrows Motor Truck Co., Indianapolis, IN (1927–1928)*

BARTLETT—(1921–1922)

BATTRONIC—Battronic Truck Corp., Philadelphia, PA (1962 on)

BAUER—(1925–1927)

BEAN—John Bean Div., FMC Corp., Lansing, MI; Tipton, IN (1973 on)

BEAVER—Beaver State Motor Co., Portland, Gresham, OR (1914–1920)

BEAVER BUS—Beaver Transit Equipment Co.; Beaver Metropolitan Coaches; National Coach & Mfg. Co. (1934–1956)

BECK—Beck-Hawkeye Motor Truck Works (after 1918) Cedar Rapids, IA (1911–1922)

BECK—(1947)

BECK BUS—C. D. Beck and Co., Sidney, OH (1934–1957)*

BECK-HAWKEYE—See Beck

BEGGS—Beggs Motor Car Co., Kansas City, MO (1918–1928) Cars also

BEL—(1923)

BELL—Iowa Motor Truck Co., Ottumwa, IA (1919–1923)

BELMONT—Belmont Motors Corp., Lewiston, PA (1919–1926)

BESSEMER—Bessemer Motor Truck Co., Grove City, PA (1911–1923); Besser-American Corp., Plainfield, NJ (1923–1926)*

BETHLEHEM—Bethlehem Motors Corp. (1917–1927)

BETZ—Betz Motor Truck Co., Hammond, IN (1919–1929)

BIEDERMAN—Biederman Motors Co., Cincinnati, OH (1915–1956)*

BIG FOUR—(1920–1923)

BILL—Bill Motor (See Curtis-Bill)

BINGHAMTON—(1922)

BIRCH—Birch Motor Cars, Inc., Chicago, IL (1916–1923)

BLAW KNOX—(c. 1968)

BLUE BIRD—Blue Bird Body Co., Fort Valley, GA (1932 on) Bus, truck and motor home

BOBBI-KAR—Geo. D. Keller, Huntsville, AL (1946–1947; name changed to Keller)

BOLLSTROM—Bollstrom Motors, Inc., Detroit, MI (1916–1921) 4-W-D vehicles reportedly available

BOWMAN—(1921)

BOYERTOWN—(early 1970s)

BRADFIELD—(1929–1930)

BRADFORD—Bradford Motor Car Co., Haverhill, MA (1919–1920)

BRADLEY—Bradley Motor Car Co., Cicero, IL (1920–1921) Principally ambulances and hearses

BRIDGEPORT—Bridgeport Motor Truck Co., Morrisey Motor Car Co., Bridgeport, CT (1920–1929)

BRILL—See A.C.F.

BRINTON—Originally Chester County Motor Co., Coatesville, PA (1913–1916); Brinton Motor Truck Co., Philadelphia, PA (1916–1926)

BRISCOE—Briscoe Motor Corp., Jackson, MI (1914–1922) Cars also

BROCKWAY—Brockway Motor Trucks, Cortland, NY (1912–1977)

BROMFIELD—Bromfield Mfg. Co., Boston, MA (1930)

BROWN—St. Cloud Truck Co.; Brown Truck Co., Duluth, MN (1922–1924)

BROWN—Brown Industries, Spokane, WA (1936–1938)

BROWN—Brown Truck and Equipment Co., Charlotte, NC. Originally built in fleets for Horton Motor Lines, postwar models available for sale to public (1939–1953)

BUCK—The Buck Motor Truck Co., Bellevue, OH (1925–1927)

BUDA—Industrial trucks, 1920; also built engines for other makes of trucks since then

BUFFALO—Buffalo Truck and Tractor Co., Clarence, NY; Buffalo, NY (1920–1926)

BUFFALO FIRE TRUCK—Buffalo Fire Appliance Corp., Buffalo, NY (1927–1948)

BUFFALO-SPRINGFIELD—Buffalo-Springfield Roller Co., Springfield, OH (1907–1921)

BUICK—Now a division of GM (trucks 1910–1918; 1922–1923)

BULL DOG—Bull Dog Motor Truck Co., Galena, IL (1924–1925)

BUS AND CAR—See Silver Eagle, Eagle

BUSSING—(1929–1930)

BYRON—E. W. Byron Co., New Haven, CT (1933)

CADILLAC—Now a division of GM (est. 1902) Chassis available for custom-built trucks and professional cars

CAPITAL—(1912–1922)

CAPITOL—Capitol Motors Corp., Fall River, MA (1919–1923)

CARAVAN—(1920)

CARPENTER SCHOOL BUS—Carpenter Body Works, Inc., Mitchell, IN. Also custom-built bus bodies on other makes of chassis (1923 on)

CASCO—Casco Motor Truck Co.; Sanford Automotive Corp., Sanford, ME (1921–1930)

CASE—J. I. Case Threshing Machine Co., Racine, WI. Farm equipment since 1880; trucks, tractors and automobiles

CATERPILLAR—Holt Mfg. Co.; Caterpillar Co., Peoria, IL. Tractors since 1924; trucks since 1962; also manufactures diesel engines for other brands of trucks

C.C.C./CRANE CARRIER—Crane Carrier Corp. Division of C.C.I. Corp., Tulsa, OK (1953 on)*

CEDAR—(1921)

CHALMERS/CHALMERS-DETROIT—Chalmers Motor Co., Detroit, MI (1907–1923; replaced by CHRYSLER in 1924) Mainly cars

CHAMPION—Direct Drive Motor Car Co., Pottstown, PA; Champion Motors Corp., Harrison Bldg., Philadelphia, PA (1918–1925) Unusual trucks, in that power was applied directly to rear wheel rim

CHAMPION BUS—Also mobile homes and motor homes. See Champion

CHAMPION-ROTARY—(1922–1923)

CHASE—Chase Motor Truck Co., Syracuse, NY (1907–1920) Early models also known as Motor Wagon

CHECKER/CHECKER CAB/successor to COMMONWEALTH—Checker Cab Mfg. Co., Kalamazoo, MI (1922–1982) Known principally for taxis, airport buses, stages, and cars

CHEVROLET—(1918–

CHICAGO—Chicago Motor Truck, Inc., Chicago, IL (1919–1923); Robert M. Cutting Co., Chicago, IL (1923–1932)

CHICAGO MOTOR BUS—Chicago Motor Bus Co., Chicago, IL (1916–1923)

CHICAGO MOTOR WAGON—Chicago Motor Wagon Co., Chicago, IL (1910–1912; also 1930?)

CHRYSLER—Chrysler Corp., Detroit, MI. (since 1924; a corporation since 1925) Also mfg. Dodge, Fargo, Plymouth, etc. Production mostly automobiles, except for Dodge trucks

CHUTING STAR—Forward, Inc., Huron, SD (1976 on)

CLARK—Clark Equip. Co., Benton Harbor, MI (1960 on)

CLARKSPEED—Clarkspeed Truck Co., Pontiac, MI (1928–1931)

CLARK TRUCKTRACTOR—(1921)

CLERMONT-STEAMER—(1923)

CLEVELAND—(1960–1961)

CLEVELAND ELECTRIC—(1955–1960)

CLIMBER—Climber Motors Corp., Little Rock, AR (1920–1923) Also cars

CLINE—Cline Truck Mfg. Co., Kansas City, MO, until 1972; Cline Truck Div., Isco Mfg. Co., Kansas City, MO 1972 on (also ISCO)

CLINTON—Clinton Motors Corp., New York, NY (1920–1923); Reading, PA (1923–1934) Bus chassis also

CLYDESDALE—Clydesdale Motor Truck Co., Clyde, OH (1917–1938)*

C.M.C.—(1920)

COACHETTE BUS—The Coachette Co., Dallas, TX (1954–1968)

COAST—Coast Apparatus Inc., Martinez, CA (1958–1974)

COLEMAN—Coleman Four Wheel Drive Co., Denver, CO; Coleman Motors Corp., American Coleman Co., Littleton, CO (1925 on)

COLES—(1955)

COLLIER—The Collier Co., Cleveland, OH; Collier Motor Truck Co., Bellevue, OH (1917–1922)

COLUMBIA—Columbia Motor Truck & Trailer Co., Pontiac, MI (1916–1926)

COLUMBIA NITE COACH—(c. 1927–1940) Double-deck sleeper bus similar in concept to Pickwick Nite Coach. See Greyhound

COMET—Comet Automobile Co., Decatur, IL (1916–1925) Trucks, tractors and cars

COMMERCE—Commerce Motor Car Co., Detroit, MI (1907–1922); Commerce Motor Truck Co., Ypsilanti, MI (1923–1926); Relay Motors Corp., Lima, OH (1926–1933)*

COMMERCIAL—Commercial Truck Co. of America, Philadelphia, PA (1909–1929)

COMPOUND FLEETRUCK—See Star*

CONCORD—Abbott-Downing Truck and Body Co., Concord, NH (1916–1933)

CONDOR—Condor Motors, Inc., Chicago, IL (1929–1943)

CONESTOGA—Conestoga Motor Truck Co., Lancaster, PA (1917–1920)*

CONSOLIDATED—(1934)

COOK—Cook Motor Corp., Kankakee, IL (1920–1923)

COOK BROS./COOK—Cook Bros. Equipment Co., Los Angeles, CA (1950–1964)*

COOPER—Fred E. Cooper, Inc., Tulsa, OK (c. 1955 on) Oil rig trucks

CORBITT—See CORBITT

COUPLE GEAR—Couple Gear Freight Wheel Co.; Couple Gear Electric Truck Co., Grand Rapids, MI (1904–1923) Gasoline and electric trucks and fire engines

COURIER BUS—See M.C.I.

CRAWFORD—(1904–1924)

CRESCENT—Industrial trucks (1920)

CROFTON/CROFTON BUG—Crofton Marine Engine Co., San Diego, CA; also Brawny Bug (1959–1961)

CROSLEY—The Crosley Corp., Cincinnati, OH (1939–1952) Also cars, and Farm-O-Road*

CROW/CROW–ELKHART—Crow-Elkhart Motor Co., Elkhart, IN (1912–1925) Also cars

CROWN—Crown Coach Corp., Los Angeles, CA (1933 on) Buses and fire trucks*

CRUSADER BUS—See M.C.I.

C.T./C.T. ELECTRIC—Commercial Truck Co., Philadelphia, PA (1908–1928)*

CUB—Cub Industries, Inc., White Pigeon, MI (1950–1951)

CUNNINGHAM—James Cunningham, Sons & Co., Rochester, NY (1909–1936) Principally ambulances and hearses; also cars

CURRAN—New York, NY (1928)

CURTIS-BILL—Bill Motors Co., Oakland, CA (1933) Truck & bus

CURTIS-NATIONAL—National Bus Lines, Los Angeles, CA (1934) Two buses

CUSHMAN—Cushman Motors; now OMC-Lincoln Div., Outboard Marine Corp., Lincoln, NE (1936 on)*

CYCLONE—Cyclone Motors Corp., Greenville, SC (1921–1923)

CYCLONE STARTER—(1920)

DAIRY EXPRESS—Eastern Dairies, Inc.; General Ice Cream Corp., Springfield, MA (1926–1930)

DART—Dart Motor Truck Co.; KW-Dart Truck Co., various other names; Anderson, IN; Waterloo, IA; Kansas City, MO (1903 on)

DAY-ELDER—National Motors Mfg. Co.; Day-Elder Truck Co.; Day-Elder Motor Truck Co.; Irvington, NJ; National Motors Mfg. Co., Newark, NJ (1916–1937)

DEARBORN—Dearborn Motor Truck Co., Chicago, IL (1919–1926)*

DEFIANCE—Defiance-Century Motor Truck Co., Defiance, OH (1917–1931)

DE KALB—De Kalb Wagon Co., De Kalb, IL (1914–1921)

DELCAR—American Motors, Inc., Troy, NY. Not related to present American Motors Corp. (1946–1949)*

DELIVR-ALL—Marmon-Herrington Co., Inc. (1945–1952) Front-drive delivery

DELLING—Supersteam Service Co., Trenton, NJ (1930)

DELMORE—Delmore Motor Corp., New York, NY (1923) Light three-wheel truck

DE MARTINI—De Martini Motor Truck Co., Inc., San Francisco, CA (1919–1934)*

DENEGRE—(1923)

DENBY—Denby Motor Truck Corp. (1915–1931)

DEPENDABLE—Dependable Truck & Tractor Corp., Galesburg, East St. Louis, IL (1914, 1925)

DE SOTO—Chrysler Corp., Detroit, MI (cars, 1929 to 1961 models; De Soto name applied to some export models of Dodge trucks, from 1937 on. Some De Soto trucks assembled in Turkey in recent years.)

DETROIT—Anderson Electric Car Co.; Detroit Electric Car Co., Detroit, MI (1907–1938) Cars also

DIAMOND REO—A Division of White Motor Company, Lansing, MI (1967–1975; 1977 on)

DIAMOND T—Diamond T Motor Car Co., Chicago, IL (est. 1905)

DIEHL—Diehl Motor Truck Works, Philadelphia, PA (1918–1927)

DIFFERENTIAL—The Differential Steel Car Co., Findlay, OH (1931–1936); Differential Co.; Difco Co., Findlay, OH (1960 on)

DISPATCH—(1921)

DIVCO/DIVCO-TWIN—Divco Corp., originally Detroit Industrial Vehicle Co., Detroit, MI (1926 on)

DIXON—Dixon Motor Truck Co., Altoona, PA (1921–1933)

DMX BUS—Dittmar Mfg. Co., Harvey, IL (1936–1940)

DOANE—Doane Motor Truck Co., San Francisco, CA (1916–1946); Graham-Doane Truck Co., Oakland, CA (1946–1948)

DOBLE—Doble Steam Motors, Emeryville, CA (1918–1930) Mainly cars

DODGE/DODGE BROS—(est. 1917)

D'OLT/D-OLT—D'Olt Motor Truck Co., Woodhaven, NY (1920–1925)

DORRIS—Dorris Motor Car Co., St. Louis, MO. Cars also (1906–1927)*

DORT—Dort Motor Car Co., Flint, MI (1915–1924) Cars joined by trucks in 1921

DOUBLE DRIVE—Double Drive Motor Truck Co., Chicago, IL (1919–1922); Double Drive Truck Co., Benton Harbor, MI (1922–1930); also mfr. of front-drive trucks

DOUGLAS—Douglas Motors Corp., Omaha, NE (1917–1935)

DOVER—Manufactured by Hudson Motor Car Co. (1929–1930)

DRAKE—Drake Motor and Tire Mfg. Co., Knoxville, TN (1921–1923)

DRAYMASTER—(1931–1933)

DRIER—(1929)

DUER—Duer Motor Truck Co., Chicago, IL (1926–1928)

DUMORE—American Motor Vehicle Co., Lafayette, IN (1920)

DUPLEX—Duplex Truck Co. (1908–1961)

DURANT—Durant Motor Co.; Durant Motors; Detroit, Lansing, MI (1928–1932; cars also, 1922–1932.) See also Star* and Rugby*

DUTY—Duty Motor Co., Greenville, IL (1913; 1920–1923)*

DYNAMIC—(1920)

EAGLE—Eagle Motor Truck Co., St. Louis, MO (1920–1932)

EAGLE BUS—See Silver Eagle, and Eagle*

EARL—Earl Motors, Inc., Jackson, MI (1921–1924) Cars also, replaces Briscoe

EASTERN DAIRIES—(1925)

ECKLAND—Eckland Bros. Co., Minneapolis, MN (1931) Trucks and buses

ECONOMY—Economy Motor Corp., Tiffin, OH (1918–1920)

EDISON—The Edison Co., Detroit, MI (1910–1928)

EDWIL—(1934–1940)

EHRLICH—(1920)

EIGHT WHEEL TRUCK—(1923)

EIMCO—The Eimco Corp., Salt Lake City, UT (1957 on)

EISENHAUER—Eisenhauer Mfg. Co., Truck Division, Van West, OH

ELBURTO—(1920) Multi-wheel truck (1945–1948)

ELCAR—Elcar Motor Co., Elkhart, IN (1920–1930) Cars also

EL DORADO—Motor Transit Co., Los Angeles, CA (1925–1930)

EL DORADO/FALCON/EMC BUSES—See El Dorado

ELECTRIC—(1923)

ELECTROBUS—Electrobus, Inc., Van Nuys, CA (1974); Electrobus Div., Otis Elevator Co., Stockton, CA (1974–1975) See also Westcoaster

ELECTROCAR—The Electrocar Corp., New York, NY (1922)

ELECTROMOBILE—Industrial electric trucks (1920)

ELECTRUK—Electruk Corp., New York, NY (1916–1925) British truck of same name mfg. 1937–1961)

ELGIN—Elgin Motor Car Corp., Elgin, Argo, IL (1916–1924) Cars also

ELKHART—(1928–1931) See also Huffman

ELLSWORTH—Mills-Ellsworth Co., Keokuk, IA (1916–1920)

ELMIRA—Elmira Commercial Motor Car Co., Elmira, Oswego, NY (1916–1921)

ELWELL-PARKER—Electric industrial trucks (1920)

ELYSEE—M. P. Möller Co., Hagerstown, MD (1926–c.1932)

EMERY—(1950–1952)

ERIE—Erie Motor Truck Co., Erie, PA (1914–1923)

ERSKINE—The Studebaker Corp., South Bend, IN (1927–1930) Mainly cars; trucks available 1928–1929

ESCO—Esco Motor Co., Pittsburgh, PA. Only 50 Esco trucks produced (1930–1946; no production 1938 to 1944) Similar design to Sterling

ESSEX—Hudson Motor Car Co., Detroit, MI. Cars and trucks. Similar to Hudson's other subsidiary, Dover truck.*

EUCLID—Original Euclid Crane Hoist Co. Cleveland, OH. Other ownerships and company titles; currently (since 1977) Euclid Div. of Daimler-Benz AG, Cleveland, OH (1934 on)*

EUGOL—Eugol Motor Truck Co., Kenosha, WI (1921–1923)

EVO—Lodal, Inc., Kingsford, MI (1968 on)

FABCO—F.A.B. Mfg. Co.; Fabco Div., Kelsey-Hayes Co., Oakland, CA (1938–1939; production resumes since later 1950s)*

FACTO—Facto Motor Trucks, Inc., Springfield, MA (1920–1926)

FAGEOL—Fageol Motors, Oakland, CA (1916–1954) affiliated with Twin Coach Corp., Kent, OH (est. 1927)

FAIRBANKS-MORSE—Fairbanks-Morse and Co., Chicago, IL (1908–1921) Tractors also

FAIRFIELD—Automotive Development Corp., Stamford, CT (1927)

FALCON BUS—See El Dorado

FAMOUS—Famous Truck Co., Inc., St. Joseph, MI (1917–1923)

FARGO—Fargo Motor Car Co., Chicago, IL (1913–1923)

FARGO—Chrysler Corp., Fargo and Dodge Truck Divisions (1928 on)

FARM-O-ROAD—See Crosley; also Farm-O-Road*

FEDERAL—Federal Motor Truck Co., Detroit, MI (1910–1959)

FIELD—(1920)

FIFTH AVE. COACH—Fifth Avenue Coach Co., New York, NY (1914–1930) Also New York Transportation Co., New York, NY; principally buses

FIREBAUGH—(1947)

FISHER/FISHER-STANDARD—Standard Motor Truck Co., Detroit, MI (1912–1934) See Fisher* and Fisher Fast Freight

FITZJOHN—Fitzjohn Body Co., Muskegon, MI (1938–1939); Fitzjohn Coach Co., Muskegon, MI (1939–1958); principally buses

FIVE BORO CAB—M. P. Möller Motor Co., Hagerstown, MD (1930–1931)

FLECKWICK—Fleckwick Motor Coach Works, Inglewood, CA (1933) Principally buses

FLEXI-TRUC—See IBEX

FLINT—Durant Motors, Inc., Long Island City, NY (1924–1927) Cars also

FLXIBLE—See Flxible and Flxette bus, 1963 on*

FMC—Motor Coach Div., FMC Corp., Santa Clara, CA (mid-1970s) buses and motor homes

FOAMITE-CHILDS—(1924) Foamite-Childs Corp., Utica, NY

FORD—Ford Motor Co., Detroit, MI (est. 1903)

FORSCHLER—Originally Philip Forschler Wagon Co., New Orleans, LA (1914–1918); Forschler Motor Truck Mfg. Co., New Orleans, LA (1919–1923)

FOX—Fox Body Co., Janesville, WI (1959)*

FREEMAN—Freeman Motor Co., Detroit, MI; Freeman Quadrive Corp., Detroit, MI (1921–1934; may not have been in production each of these years)

FREEMAN—Chicago, IL (1928–1931) May be same as Freeman Motor Co.

FREIGHTLINER/WHITE FREIGHTLINER—Freightliner Corp., Portland, OR (est. 1939)

FREMONT—(1919–1925)

FRISBEE—Frisbee Truck Co., Webberville, MI (1921–1923)

FRONT DRIVE—Front Drive Motor Car Co., Kansas City, MO (1921–1929)

FRONT DRIVE—Double Drive Motor Truck Co., Benton Harbor, MI (1925–1928)

FULTON—Fulton Motor Truck Co., New York, NY (1916–1925)

FWD—FWD Corp., Clintonville, WI (est. 1912)

GABRIEL—Gabriel Motor Truck Co.; Gabriel Auto Co., Cleveland, OH (1913–1920)

GARDNER—Gardner Motor Co., Inc., St. Louis, MO. Professional cars; company also built automobiles, (1919–1931)

GARFORD—Garford Motor Truck Co., Lima, OH (1909–1933)

GAR WOOD—Gar Wood Industries, Detroit, MI (buses, 1936–1938)* Military vehicles, 1957 to early 1960s

GARY—Gary Motor Truck Co., Gary, IN (1916–1927; bus chassis, 1923)

GEARLESS—Gearless Steam Auto Mfg. Co., Denver, CO (1921) Cars also

GEM—Gem Auto Truck Co., Watervliet, NY (1921–1922) Also another Gem mfd. 1917–1919 in Grand Rapids, MI

GENERAL CAB—Yellow Truck & Coach Mfg. Co., Pontiac, MI (GM) (1930–1938) Replaces Yellow cab. Also known as General Motors cab

GENERAL-DETROIT—General Fire Truck Corp., Detroit, MI (1937–1955) Western subsidiary: General Pacific Corp., Los Angeles, CA 1948–1955

GENERAL-MONARCH—General Fire Truck Corp., St. Louis, MO (1932–1935)

GENERAL-PACIFIC—General Pacific Corp., Los Angeles, CA (1948–1955)

GERSIX—Gerlinger Motor Car Co., Portland, OR (1915–1917); Tacoma, WA (1917); Gersix Mfg. Co., Seattle, WA (1917–1922) Predecessor to Kenworth

GIANT—Giant Truck Corp., Chicago Heights, Chicago, IL (1915–1923) Reportedly known as Chicago Pneumatic Tool Co. (1918)

GILLIG BUS—Gillig Bros., San Francisco, CA (1932–1938); Gillig Bros., Hayward, CA (1938 on) Also built German Neoplan buses under license, starting 1977

GLOBE—Globe Furniture Co., Northville, MI (1916); Globe Motor Truck Co., Northville, MI (1917–1919)

GLOBE—Globe Motors Co., Cleveland, OH (1916–1921) Relation to the Globe Furniture Co. uncertain

GMC—General Motors, Pontiac, MI (est. 1911)

GO-GETTER—A model of Ruggles

GOLDEN EAGLE—A variation of Silver Eagle

GOLDEN GATE—(1927)

GOLDEN STATE—(1928–1935)

GOLDEN WEST—(1919–1920)

GOLIATH—(1920)

GOODWIN/GOODWIN-GUILDER—Goodwin Car and Mfg. Co., New York, NY (1922–1925) Developed into Guilder truck

GOODYEAR—Goodyear Tire and Rubber Co., Akron, OH (1920–1926) Limited number of trucks and buses

GORHAM-SEAGRAVE—Seagrave Co., Columbus, OH (1912–1920)

GOTFREDSON—Gotfredson Truck Co., Ltd., Detroit, MI (1923–1929) Originated 1920 in Canada, by Gotfredson & Joyce Corp., Walkerville, Ontario. Canadian production until 1932. Detroit production cont'd. 1929–1948 by Robert Gotfredson Truck Co., Detroit, MI.* Buses also

GOULD—(1954–1955)

GOVE—Gove Motor Car Co. (1922–1923)

GP—(1929–1935)

GRADALL—Warner and Swasey Co., Lansing, MI; Winona, MN (1955 on)

GRAHAM BROS.—(1917–1929)

GRAHAM-DOANE—See Doane*

GRAMM—Gramm Motors, Inc.; Gramm Motor Truck Corp.; Gramm Truck and Trailer Corp., Delphos, OH. Also Chicago, IL after 1932 (1926–1942)

GRAMM-BERNSTEIN—Gramm-Bernstein Motor Truck Co., and other titles, Lima, Delphos, OH (1912–1933)*

GRAMM-KINCAID—Gramm & Kincaid Motors, Inc., Lima, OH (1925); Delphos, OH (1925–1928)

GRAMM-PIONEER—Gramm-Bernstein Motor Truck Co., Lima, OH (1918–1925)

GRANT—Grant Motor Car Corp., Findlay, Cleveland, OH (1913–1923) Cars also; trucks added 1918

GRASS-PREMIER—Grass-Premier Truck Co., Sauk City,. WI (1923–1937)*

GRAVELY—(c. 1972)

GRAY—Gray Motor Corp., Detroit, MI (1922–1926)* Cars also

GREAT EAGLE—(1920)

GREAT LAKES—(1949–1956)

GREENVILLE—(1926)

GREYHOUND—(truck, 1975 on)

GRUMMAN/GRUMMAN OLSON—Grumman Allied Industries, Inc., Garden City, NY; also branches in several cities (since 1963) buses and vans. See also Flxible*

GUILDER—Guilder Engineering Co., Poughkeepsie, NY (1922–1936)*

GV ELECTRIC—General Vehicle Co., New York, NY (1906–1920)

G.W.W.—Wilson Truck Mfg. Co., Henderson, IA (1919–1925)

HAHN—Original W. G. Hahn & Bro., Hamburg, PA (1907–1913). Other titles during interim; moved to Allentown, PA, (1927). Selden-Hahn Motor Truck Corp. (1930–1931); Hahan Motors, Inc., Hamburg, PA (since 1931). Trucks and fire trucks

HAHN-SELDEN—(1931–1933; see Hahn)

HAL-FUR—Hal-Fur Motor Truck Co., Cleveland, Canton, OH (1919–1932)

HALL—Lewis-Hall Iron Works, Detroit, MI (1915–1923)

HAMILTON—(1917–1921)

HAMPDEN—(1923)

HANLEY—Hanley Engineering Service, Prospect, OH (1940–1941) Fire trucks, some with V-16 engines. Engines of that type built by Hanley, but based on Marmon V-16 design

HANOVER—(1922–1926)

HARRISBURG—(1920)

HARVEY—Harvey Motor Truck Works, Harvey, IL (1911–1933)

HATFIELD—Cortland Car & Carriage Co., Sidney, NY (1916–1924) Cars and trucks. Trucks also by related companies, (1907–1908; 1910–1914)

HATHAWAY-PURINTON—Hathaway-Purinton, Peabody, MA (1924–1925)

HAULPAK—Le Tourneau-Westinghouse, Peoria, IL (1957–1968)

HAWKEYE—Hawkeye Truck Co., Sioux City, IA (1916–1933)

HAYES-ANDERSON—(1928–1934)

H.C.S.—H.C.S. Motor Co., Indianapolis, IN (1920–1927) Mainly cars

HENDERSON—Henderson Bros. Co., N. Cambridge, MA (1915–1927)

HENDRICKSON—Hendrickson Motor Truck Co., Chicago, Lyons, IL; Hendrickson Mfg. Co., Lyons, IL (1913 on)

HENNEY—John W. Henney Co.; Henney Motor Car Co., Freeport, IL (1915–1932) Professional cars, some automobiles. Professional cars on Packard chassis in later years (including a few automobiles) until 1954.

HERCULES—(1961)

HERTNER ELECTRIC—(1934–1936)

HERTZ—Yellow Cab Mfg. Co., Chicago, IL (1925–1928) Rental vehicles

HEWITT-LUDLOW—Hewitt-Ludlow Auto Co., San Francisco, CA (1912–1921)

HICKS-PERRETT—(1922)

HIGHWAY—A model of United

HIGHWAY—Highway Products, Inc., Kent, OH (1960–1975) including buses. Twin Coach bus name revived by this company, 1968–1975. See Fageol

HIGHWAY-KNIGHT—Highway Motors Co., Chicago, IL (1919–1922) Used R and V Knight sleeve-valve engine

HIGRADE—Higrade Motors Co., Grand Rapids, MI (1917–1918); Harbor Springs, MI (1918–1921) Leftovers may have been available to 1923

HOADLEY—(1914–1922)

HOLMAN—(1922)

HOLMES—Holmes Motor Mfg., Littleton, CO (1921–1923)

HOLMES—Ernest Holmes Co., Chattanooga, TN (wrecking trucks and conversions since 1930s.)

HOLT—(1912–1925)

HOOVER—Hoover Wagon Co., York, PA (1917–1920)

HOOVER ELECTRIC—Hoover Wagon Co., York, PA (1911 only)

HOWE—Howe Fire Apparatus Co., Anderson, IN (1932 on)

H.R.L.—H.R.L. Motor Co., Seattle, WA (1921)

HUDSON—Hudson Motor Car Co., Detroit, MI (1938–1947 trucks)

HUFFMAN—Huffman Bros. Motor Co.; Valley Motor Truck Co.; Elkhart Motor Truck Co., Elkhart, IN (1916–1929)*

HUG—The Hug Co., Highland, IL (1922–1942)

HUNT—Electric industrial trucks (1920)

HUPMOBILE—Hupp Motor Car Co., Detroit, MI (trucks, intermittently, 1912–1925. Cars, 1908–1940)

HURLBURT—Hurlburt Motor Truck Co., New York, NY (1912–1915); Hurlburt Motor Truck Co., New York, NY (1915–1919); Harrisburg Mfg. and Boiler Co., Harrisburg, PA (1919–1927)

HURON—Huron Truck Co., Bad Axe, MI (1912–1923)

HURRYTON—Menominee Motor Truck Co., Clintonville, WI (1923–1928)

IBEX—(est. 1946)

IDECO—(1980s?) Oil derrick trucks

I.H.C.—International Harvester Co., Chicago, IL (est. 1907)

INDEPENDENT—Independent Motor Co., Youngstown, OH (1915–1923)

INDEPENDENT—Independent Motor Truck Co., Davenport, IA (1917–1934) Company may have been inactive in later years

INDIAN—Indian Motorcycle Co., Springfield, MA. Three-wheel light delivery in 1930

INDIANA—Harwood-Barley Mfg. Co., Marion, IN (1911–1919); Indiana Truck Corp., Marion, IN (1920–1932); Indiana Motors Corp., Marion, IN (1932–1933); Indiana Motors Corp., Cleveland, OH (1933–1939) Affiliated with Brockway and White during 1930s* Buses also

INDIANA TRUCK CORPORATION—Acquired by Brockway Motor Trucks in 1928

INDUSTRIAL—(1921–1922)

INLAND—Inland Motor Co., Evansville, IN (1919–1921)

INTERNATIONAL/INTERNATIONAL HARVESTER—See International

ISCO—Isco Mfg. Co., Inc., Kansas City, MO (1972 on)

ITALIA—Italia Motor Truck Co., San Francisco, CA (1921–1925)

J. & H.—Lorain Motor Truck Co., Lorain, OH (1920–1921)

J. & J.—Lorain Motor Truck Co., Lorain, OH (1920–1921)

JACKSON—Jackson Motor Co., Jackson, MI (1907–1923) Cars also*

JARRETT—J. C. Jarrett Motor and Finance Co., Colorado Springs, CO (1921–1934)*

JEEP—Willys-Overland, Inc., Toledo, OH (later models found in Pickup and Van Spotter's Guide)

JONES—Jones Motor Car Co., Wichita, KS (1918–1920) Cars also

JUMBO—Nelson Motor Truck Co., Saginaw, MI (1918–1924) Jumbo name appears on some lists as late as 1932; could be the Jumbo mfd. in the Netherlands using Ford components

KAISER BUS—Permanente Metals Corp., Oakland, CA and plant at Permanente, CA. Single experimental articulated bus, in use a few years. (See misc. section) Kaiser-Frazer also built cars, 1946–1955. Car Mfg. moved to Argentina after 1955, continued there to 1962. Kaiser Jeeps also mfd. in USA.

KALAMAZOO—Kalamazoo Motor Vehicle Co., Kalamazoo, MI (1913–1919); Kalamazoo Motors Corp., Kalamazoo, MI (1920–1924)

KALAMAZOO CRUISER BUS—See Pony Cruiser

KANKAKEE—Kankakee Automobile Co., Kankakee, IL (1918–1925)

KARAVAN—Caravan Motors Co.,; Caravan Motor Corp., Portland, OR (1920–1922)

KARDELL—(1918–1920)

KARIVAN—Tri-Car Inc., Wheatland, PA (1955) Three-wheel van also used chassis of Tri-Car automobile.

KARRYALL—Built by Koehring (mid-1960s)

KARRY LODE—Electric industrial trucks (1920)

KASTORY—(1924)

KAWS QUALITY—Kaws Truck and Bus Mfg. Co., Indianapolis, IN (1921–1925)

KEARNS/KEARNS-DUGHIE—Various company titles include Kearns Motor Buggy Co., Kearns Motor Truck Co., Kearns Motor Car Co., Beavertown, PA (1909–1920), and Kearns-Dughie Corp., Danville, PA (1920–1928). After move to Danville also built fire trucks, some under name of Childs Thoroughbred

KECK-GONNERMAN/K. G.—Keck-Gonnerman Co., Mt. Vernon, IN (1898–1926) Trucks probably not mfd. during the entire period

KELDON—House Cold Tire Setter Co., St. Louis, MO (1919–1920)

KELLAND—Kelland Motor Car Co., Newark, NJ (1922–1925) Electric

KELLER—Geo. D. Keller, Huntsville, AL (1947–1950) Formerly Bobbi-Kar; production mainly automobiles

KELLY-SPRINGFIELD—Kelly-Springfield Motor Trucks, Springfield, OH (1912–1928) Formerly known as Kelly

KENOSHA-WINTHER—Kenosha Fire Engine and Truck Co., Kenosha, WI (1918–1928)

KENWORTH—Kenworth Truck Co., Seattle, WA (since 1923)

KEYSTONE—Keystone Motor Truck Corp., Oaks, PA (1914–1924)

KIDDER—(1920)

KIMBALL—Kimball Motor Truck Co., Los Angeles, CA (1917–1926)

KING-ZEITLER—King-Zeitler Co., Chicago, IL (1919–1930)

KISSEL—Kissel Motor Car Co., Hartford, WI (1908–1931)

KLEIBER—Kleiber Motor Co., San Francisco, CA (1914–1937) Cars also

KLEMM—E. R. Klemm, Chicago, IL (c. 1915–1920)

KLONDIKE—F. W. Kohlmeyer, Logansville, WI (1918–1920)

KNIGHTSTOWN—Knightstown Funeral Car Co., Knightstown, IN (1933)

KNOX—Knox Motors Co., other titles included Martin Tractor Co., Martin Rocking 5th Wheel Co., most recent location Longmeadow, MA. Formerly Springfield, Chicopee Falls, MA (1900–1926)

KNUCKEY—Knuckey Truck Co., San Francisco, CA (1943–mid-1950s)

KOEHLER—H. Koehler Co., H. J. Koehler Motor Corp. (originally H. J. Koehler Sporting Goods Co.) Newark and Bloomfield, NJ (1910–1928)

KOEHRING—Koehring Co., Milwaukee, WI (also Dumptor) One type for railroad tracks

KREBS—Krebs Commercial Car Co., Clyde, OH (1912–1916); Krebs Motor Truck Co., Bellevue, OH (1922–1926)

KUHN—(1918–1920)

KURBMASTER/KURBMASTER JUNIOR—J.B.E. Olson Corp., Garden City, NY. Later Grumman Olson (1968 on)

K.W.—See Kenworth

KW-DART—See Dart and KW-Dart*

K-Z—(1921–1923)

LA FRANCE—American La France Fire Engine Co., Elmira, NY (1910–1920) Trucks usually do not have American prefix, fire trucks do

LA FRANCE-REPUBLIC—La France-Republic Corp., Alma, MI (1929–1932); La France-Republic Division of Sterling Motors Corp., Alma, MI (1932–1943)

LAMMERT AND MANN—(1922)

LAMSON—Lamson Truck and Trailer Co., Chicago, IL (1911–1920) 1–5 ton models

LANDSHAFT—William Landshaft and Son, Chicago, IL (1911–1920)

LANE—Lane Motor Truck Co., Kalamazoo, MI (1916–1920)

LANG—(1912–1931)

LANGE—H. Lange Wagon Works, Pittsburgh, PA (1911–1912); Lange Motor Truck Co., Pittsburgh, PA (1912–1932)

LANSDEN/LANSDEN ELECTRIC—The Lansden Co. Inc., New York, NY (1904–1928)

LANSING ELECTRIC—Lansing Co., Lansing, MI (1917–1920) Also Lansing

LAPEER—Lapeer Tractor Truck Co., Lapeer, MI (1916–1920)

LARRABEE/LARRABEE-DEYO—Larrabee-Deyo Motor Truck Co., Binghamton, NY (1915–1933)

LA SALLE—Cadillac Division of GM (1927–1940) Mostly cars; only a few commercial applications on chassis

LAUREL—Laurel Motor Corp., Anderson, IN (1916–1921)

LEACH—Leach Motor Car Co., Los Angeles, CA (1920–1923; mainly cars)

LEASE—(1923)

LE BLOND-SCHACHT—See Schacht

LECTRA HAUL—Unit Rig and Equipment Co., Tulsa, OK (since 1963)

LEHIGH—The Lehigh Co., Allentown, PA (1925–1927)*

LE MOON/NELSON-LE MOON—Nelson and Le Moon, Chicago, IL (1910–1927); Nelson-Le Moon Truck Co., Chicago, IL (1927–1939)*

LETOURNEAU—Letourneau-Westinghouse Co., Peoria, IL (1950 on) See also Wabco

LEWIS-HALL—Lewis-Hall Iron Works, Detroit, MI (1920–1930)

LIBERTY—Gramm-Bernstein Co., Lima, OH; Liberty Motor Vehicle Co., Cleveland, OH (1917–1930) Liberty title also applied to standardized truck for use in World War I, mfd. by various American truck builders to standardized design.

LINCOLN—Lincoln Motor Co., Division of Ford Motor Co., Detroit, MI. Originally an independent company 1920–1922 (1921–1930) Principally cars built during this period, though a few factory adaptations for commercial use, and many private adaptations of used models, such as wrecking car conversions

LINK-BELT—Link-Belt Speeder Corp., Cedar Rapids, IA (1949 on) Crane trucks

LINN—Linn Mfg. Corp., Morris, NY (1916–1950) Acquired by Republic in 1927. Half-track trucks

LION—Lion Motor Truck Corp., New York, NY (1920–1921)

LITE WAY—(1953–1955)

LITTLE GIANT—Chicago Pneumatic Tool Co., Chicago, IL and Franklin, PA (1910–1925) Also built trucks with C.P.T. and Chicago nameplates. Company in business in recent years, but no longer mfg. trucks.

L.M.C.—Louisiana Motor Co., Shreveport, LA (1919–1923)

LOADSTAR—A model of International

LOCOMOBILE—Locomobile Co. of America, Bridgeport, CT (1902–1929) Principally automobiles, but trucks available 1912–1916 and later by special order or by custom application on Locomobile chassis

LOMBARD—Lombard Auto Tractor-Truck Corp., Waterville, ME; New York, NY (1901–1923)

LONE STAR—Lone Star Motor Truck and Tractor Co. (or Assn.), San Antonio, TX (1920–1923)

LONGEST—Longest Bros. Co., Louisville, KY (1910–1916, but listed as available in 1925)

LORRAINE—Pilot Motor Car Co., Lorraine Car Co., Richmond, IN. Light trucks and professional cars (1919–1924)

LO TRUK—(1940)

LOW-BED MOTOR TRUCK—(1929)

LOYAL—Loyal Motor Truck Company, Lancaster, OH (1918–1920)

LUEDINGHAUS—Luedinghaus-Espenschied Wagon Co., St. Louis, MO (1919–1933)

LUVERNE—Luverne Motor Truck Co., Luverne Automobile Co., Luverne, MN (1916–1921) Cars, trucks, fire trucks (1912–1923) Fire trucks on other brands of chassis after 1923

LUXOR—Luxor Cab Mfg. Co., Framingham, MA. M. P. Möller Motor Co., Hagerstown, MD. Also built Astor cab, Dagmar auto, others (Luxor available 1924–1927)

LYNCOACH—Lyncoach and Truck Mfg. Co., Oneonta, NY (1938–c. 1970) Also operation in Troy, AL (1960–c. 1970) Also Lyn Airvan and Lyn Arrow

LYONS—Lyons Iron Works, Manchester, NH (1919–1921)

MACCAR—Maccar Truck Co., Scranton, PA (1912–1935)

MacDONALD—MacDonald Truck and Tractor Co.; Union Construction Co.; MacDonald Truck and Mfg. Co., San Francisco, CA; MacDonald Truck and Mfg. Co., Division of Peterbilt Motors Co., Oakland, CA (1920–1952) Peterbilt affiliate after World War II

MACK—Mack Trucks, Inc. (since 1909)

MADSEN—Jay Madsen Equip. Co., Inc., Bath, NY (1948–1973) Bus, fire, refuse

MAGIRUS-VOMAG—Magirus-Vomag Machine Co., Wehawken, NJ (1924–1926) German Magirus and Vomag components, sold in USA

MAIBOHM—Maibohm Motors Co., Racine, WI; Sandusky, OH (1916–1922) Cars also

MAJESTIC/MAJESTIC CAB—(1925–1927) Larrabee-Deyo Co., Binghamton, NY

MANLY—Manly Motor Corp. (1917); O'Connell Manly Motor Corp. (1918); O'Connell Motor Truck Corp. (1919–1920) Waukegan, IL

MARMON/MARMON-HERRINGTON—(est. 1902)

MARSHALL—(1919–1921)

MARTIN—Martin Motor Truck Corp., Garden City, NY (1929–1932)

MARTIN-PARRY—(1920–1921)

MASON/MASON ROAD KING—Mason Motor Truck Co., Flint, MI (a Durant product, 1922–1925)*

MASTER—Master Motor Car Co., Cleveland, OH (1907–1920)

MASTER—Master Trucks, Inc.; Master Motor Corp.; Master Motor Truck Co., Chicago, IL (1917–1929) Trucks and bus chassis

MASTER TRUCK—Engineered Fiberglass Co., Fountain Valley, CA. Master Truck, Division of Hallamore, Inc., Fountain Valley, CA (1972 on)*

MAXI—Six Wheels, Inc., Los Angeles, CA (1940–1942) Large off-highway

MAXIM—Maxim Motor Co., Middleboro, MA (1914 on) Principally fire trucks

MAXWELL—Maxwell Motor Co., Detroit, MI (1913–1925) Cars & taxis also; absorbed by Chrysler. Maxwell-Briscoe trucks in earlier years

MAYBRATH—(1949)

McBRIGHT—McBright Inc., Lehighton, PA (1953–1955) Rear-mounted White engine, two-, three- or four-axle models

McCARRON—W. E. McCarron Corp., Chicago, IL (1927–1929)

McCORMICK-DEERING—McCormick-Deering, Rock Island, IL (c. 1928) Road tractor

MCI BUS—Motor Coach Industries, Pembina, ND

MECHANICS—(1926–1928)

MEECH-STODDARD—(1922–1927)

MENGES—Menges Motor Co., Greenville, MS (1921)

MENOMINEE—D. F. Poyer Co., Menominee, MI; Menominee Motor Truck Co., Clintonville, WI (1911–1928); Utility Supply Co., a subsidiary of FWD, Clintonville, WI (1928–1937)

METEOR—Meteor Motor Car Co., Piqua, OH (1913–1932; 1941) Mostly professional cars, but some automobiles, one bus known

METRO/METROPOLITAN—Metropolitan Coach and Cab Co., New York, NY (1926–1927)

METZ—Metz Co., Waltham, MA (1909–1921) Cars also. Truck production centered mainly between 1916–1917

MGT—(1947–1950)

MICHIGAN—Michigan Hearse and Carriage Co., Grand Rapids, MI (1915–1921)

MICRO-COACH—Gillig Bros., Hayward, CA (intro. 1971)*

MID WEST—Mid West Steam Motor Co., Laramie, WY (1925)

MILBURN—Milburn Wagon Co., Toledo, OH (1914–1925) Electric trucks and cars; few trucks if any after 1915

MILFORD—(1946)

MILLER—A. J. Miller Co., Bellefontaine, OH (1917–1924) Mainly professional cars, built bodies on other chasses up to late 1950s

MILLER METEOR—Fort Pitt Commerce Corp., Washington, D.C. (1949)

MILLER-QUINCY—E. M. Miller Co., Quincy, IL (1921–1924) Professional cars

MILWAUKEE—(1951)

MINIBUS—Passenger Truck Equipment Co., Huntington Park, CA (1963–1967); Minibus, Inc., Pico Rivera, CA (1967 on)

MINNEAPOLIS—(1920) May be connected with earlier 1912–1913 models of Minneapolis Motor Cycle Company, Minneapolis, MN

MINNEAPOLIS STEEL—(1910–1928)

MITCHELET—(1923)

MITCHELL—Mitchell Motor Corp.; Mitchell-Lewis Motor Co., Racine, WI (1903–1922) Most trucks (1905–1908)

MOBIL—(c. 1969)

MOHICAN—Mohican Motor Corp., New York, NY (1921; possibly 1920 also) Trucks for export

MOLINE—Moline Plow Co., Moline, IL (1920–1923)

MÖLLER—M. P. Möller Motor Car Co., Hagerstown, MD (1927–1931) Taxis. Also mfr. of Astor, Aristocrat, Luxor, Blue Light, 20th Century,

Paramount, Super Paramount, Five Boro Cab, etc. Town Taxi (1933) used Möller body on Diamond T chassis, and Möller built taxi bodies for Ford V-8s from 1932–1936.

MONARCH—(1926–1927)

MOORE—Moore Motor Vehicle Co., Minneapolis, MN; Danville, IL (1916–1921)

MORELAND—Moreland Motor Truck Co., Burbank, CA (1911–1941)

MORT—Meteor Motor Car Co., Piqua, OH (1923–1926) Professional cars

MORTON—Morton Truck and Tractor Co., Harrisburg, PA (1917–1920) Affiliated with Harrisburg Mfg. and Boiler Company and used their factory, which also produced Hurlburt truck (1919–1927)

MOSES AND MORRIS—(1920)

MOTOX—(1921)

M.P.C.—Milwaukee Parts Corp., Milwaukee, WI (1925–1928)

MURTY/MURTY BROS.—Portland, OR (est. 1949)

MUSKEGON—Muskegon Engine Co.; Muskegon Truck Co., Muskegon, MI (1917–1920)

MUTUAL—Mutual Truck Co., Sullivan, IN (1919–1926) After 1921, possibly sales of unsold trucks in stock

NAPCO POWER PAK—(1955–1956) These trucks used Chevrolet engines

NAPOLEON—Napoleon Auto Mfg. Co., Napoleon, OH; Traverse City Motor Co., Traverse City, MI; Napoleon Motors Co. and Napoleon Motor Cars and Trucks, Traverse City, MI (1919–1923) British version known as Seabrook-Napoleon

NATIONAL—(1926)

NATIONAL—National Bus and Mfg. Corp., San Antonio, TX (1948)

NATIONAL/NATIONAL COACH—National Coach Corp., Gardena, CA; Carson, CA; and E. Brunswick, NJ (since 1979?)*

NATIONAL–KISSEL—Kissel Motor Car Co., Hartford, WI (1927–1930) Also Kissel; professional cars and automobiles

NELSON-LE MOON—See LeMoon

NEOPLAN BUS—Basically German, but some American production undertaken by Gillig Bros., Hayward, CA, starting 1977, using Ford engines.

NEPPER—Richard C. Nepper Co., Cincinnati, OH (1961 on) Fire trucks

NETCO—New England Truck Co., Fitchburg, MA (1914–1938)

NEVIN—(1927)

NEWCOMER—(1926–1930)

NEW STUTZ—See Stutz

NEW YORK—Tegetmeier and Riepe Co., New York, NY (1913–1926) Actual production may have ended around 1921

NEW YORK AUTO-TRUCK—(1920–1921)

NILES—Niles Car and Mfg. Co., Niles, OH; Niles Motor Truck Co.; South Main Motor Co., Pittsburgh, PA (1916–1926)

NILSON—(1921)

NOBLE—Noble Motor Truck Co., Kendallville, IN (1917–1932)

NOLAN—(1924)

NORTHWAY—Northway Motors Corp., Natick, MA (1918–1925)*

NORTHWESTERN—Star Carriage Co., Seattle, WA (1913–1930) "Built in Seattle for Seattle's Hills," actual production may have ceased in 1923.

NORWALD—(1911–1922)

NORWALK—Norwalk Motor Car Co., Martinsburg, WV (1911–1922) Most trucks probably during 1918–1919

NUCAR—Nucar Forwarding Corp., Trenton, NJ (1930)

NYE—Hood Manufacturing Co., Seattle, WA (1920–1921) Large logging trucks

OAKLAND—Pontiac, MI (1907–1931) A Division of GM from 1909; mostly cars

O. B./O. B. ELECTRIC—O. B. Electric Vehicles, Inc., New York, NY; O. B. Electric Truck Inc., New York, NY (1921–1933) Also O. B. Truck (1923–1933)

O'CONNELL—See Super Truck

OGDEN—Ogden Motor and Supply Co., Chicago, IL; Ogden Truck Co., Chicago, IL (1919–c. 1929) Production may have ended by 1926

OGREN—Ogren Motor Car Co., Milwaukee, WI (1921–1923) Cars also

O. K.—Oklahoma Auto Manufacturing Co., Muskogee, OK (1917–1921); Nolan Truck Co., Okay, OK (1921–1929)

OLD HICKORY—Kentucky Wagon Mfg. Co., Inc., Louisville, KY (1915–1923)

OLD RELIABLE—Henry Lee Power Co., Chicago, IL (1910–1912); Old Reliable Motor Truck Co., Chicago, IL (1912–1927)

OLDSMOBILE—A Division of General Motors Corp.

OLSEN—Swedish Crucibile Steel Co., Detroit, MI (1921) Ford parts used

OLYMPIC—Olympic Motor Truck Co., Tacoma, WA (1921–1928) Production may have ended considerably before 1928

OMAHA—(1921)

OMORT—Greenville Mfg. Co.; Omort Truck Div., American Aggregates Corp., Greenville, OH (1923–1934) Name stood for "One Man Operated Road Truck." Mainly dump and road construction trucks

ONAN WESTCOASTER—Onan Div. Studebaker-Packard Corp., Minneapolis, MN (1950s and 1960s)*

ONEIDA—Oneida Motor Truck Co., Green Bay, WI (1917–1931)

OREN—Oren-Roanoke Corp., Roanoke, Vinton, VA (1949–1974) Fire trucks; acquired by Howe in 1974

ORLEANS—New Orleans Motor Truck Mfg. Co., New Orleans, LA (1920–1921)

OSGOOD-BRADLEY—(1930–1932)

OSHKOSH—Oshkosh Motor Truck Mfg. Co., Oshkosh, WI (est. 1917)

OTTAWA—(1960 on)

OVERLAND—See Willys and miscellaneous section

OVERTIME—(1915–1924)

PACIFIC—Pacific Car and Foundry Co., Renton, WA (1942–1945)

PACKARD—Packard Motor Car Co., Detroit, MI

PACKET—(1919–1922)

PACKET—A model of Fargo

PAIGE—Paige-Detroit Motor Car Co., Detroit, MI

PAK-AGE-CAR—Pak-Age-Kar Corp., Union Stock Yards, Chicago, IL (1926–1932); Stutz Motor Car Co. of America, Inc., Indianapolis, IN (1932–1938); Pak-Age-Car Corp., Subsidiary of Auburn Central Co., Connersville, IN (1938–1941); Diamond T Motor Car Co., Chicago, IL (sales and service, 1939–1941) Originally called Pac-Car. See Stutz in miscellaneous section

PAN—Pan Motor Co., St. Cloud, MN (trucks 1920; cars 1918–1922)

PAN-AMERICAN—Pan-American Motors Corp., Decatur, IL (1919–1922)

PANTHER—(1920)

PAR-KAR—Par-Kar Coach Co., St. Louis, MI (1922–1923)

PARKER—Parker Motor Truck Co., Parker Truck Co., Inc., Milwaukee, WI (1918–1933) Originally Stegeman truck

PATERSON—(1908–1924) Mainly cars

PATRIOT—Hebb Motors Co., Lincoln, NE (1917–1926)

PAYSTAR—A model of International

PEERLESS—Peerless Motor Car Co., Cleveland, OH (1905–1932) Cars also. Truck production primarily between 1911–1918; some custom applications, also, on chassis.

PEET—Peet Motor Corp., Hollis, New York, NY (1923–1926)

PENDELL LOW BED—Mechanics Mfg. Co., Los Angeles, CA (1925–1928)

PENN—Penn Motors Corp., Philadelphia, PA (1921–1927)

PENNFORD—(1924)

PENTON—Penton Motor Co., Cleveland, OH (1928)

PERFECTION—Perfection Truck Co., Minneapolis, MN (1923–1926)

PETER PIRSCH—Peter Pirsch and Sons, Kenosha, WI (1926 on) Mainly fire trucks

PETERBILT—Peterbuilt Motors Co., Newark, CA (since 1939)

PETERS—(1924)

PETROLEUM—(1923)

PETTIBONE—reportedly still available, origin unknown

PHILADELPHIA—Philadelphia Motor Car Co., Philadelphia, PA (1924–1925) Includes bus chassis

PICKWICK/PICKWICK NITE COACH—Pickwick Stages Systems, Los Angeles, CA; Pickwick Motor Coach Works, Los Angeles and Inglewood, CA; (1927–1933) Origins of company as early as 1912. See Greyhound

PICKWICK SLEEPER—Columbia Coach Works, 1936.

P.I.E./P.I.E.–FRUEHAUF—Built for Pacific Intermountain Express (1956)

PIEDMONT—Piedmont Motors, Lynchburg, VA (1917–1923) Cars also

PIERCE—(1955)

PIERCE-ARROW—Pierce-Arrow Motor Car Co., Buffalo, NY

PILOT—(1922)

PIONEER/PIONEER ALL-STEEL—Pioneer Truck Co., Chicago, IL; Valparaiso, IN (1920–1925)

PIONEER STAGE—California Body Building Co., San Francisco, CA (1923–1927); California Body Building Co., Oakland, CA (1927–1929); Pioneer Motor Coach Mfg. Co., Oakland, CA (1929–1930) Buses and stages. Body mfg. operations as early as 1914

PITMAN—½-cab models (1957)

PITTSBURGH—Pittsburgh Model Engineering Co., Pittsburgh, PA (1920–1925)

PITTSBURGHER/PITTSBURGER—Pittsburgher Truck Mfg. Co., Pittsburgh, PA (1919–1925)

PIZZA EXPRESS—Continental Body Corp., Chicago, IL (1983 on)

PLAINS—(1923)

PLYMOUTH—Division of Chrysler Corp.

POLE—Commercial Truck Co., Philadelphia, PA (1913–1920)

PONTIAC—Division of General Motors

PONY—Minnesota Machinery and Foundry Co., Minneapolis, MN (1920–1923) Very light, cycle-car-type delivery van

PONY CRUISER—People's Rapid Transit Co., Kalamazoo, MI (1938–1940); Kalamazoo Coaches, Inc., Kalamazoo, MI (1940–1951)

PORT ALBANY—(1929)

POWELL—Powell Mfg. Co., Compton, CA (1954–1956)

POWER—Power Truck and Tractor Co., Detroit, MI (1920–1925)

POWER TRUCK—Power Truck Co., St. Louis, MO (1925) Move to St. Louis may have been earlier than 1925

PREMIER—Premier Motor Mfg. Co., Indianapolis, IN (1903–1925) Most of production devoted to automobiles

PREMOCAR—Preston Motors Corp., Birmingham, AL (1920–1923)

PRESTON—(1920–1923)

PREVOST BUS—Prevost Car Co., Canada (since 1947)

PROSPECT—Prospect Fire Engine Co., Prospect, OH (1924–1934)

PROSPECT–BIEDERMAN—(1924–1930) Fire truck

P.R.T.—Philadelphia Rapid Transit Co., Philadelphia, PA (1927) Includes public service vehicle

PULLMAN BUS—Pullman-Standard, Chicago, IL. Factory at Worcester, MA (1932–1952) Electric city transit trolley buses

QMC—Goodyear Tire and Rubber Co., Akron, OH. For US Army (1926–1927)

RAINIER—Rainier Motor Corp., Flushing, NY (1916–1924); Rainier Trucks Inc., Flushing, NY (1924–1927)* Possibly connected with Rainier Motor Car Co. of Saginaw, MI dating as far back as 1905

RANGER—Southern Motor Mfg. Assn., Houston, TX (1920–1923)

RAPID TRANSIT—a model of Republic

RAUCH AND LANG, RAULANG: BAKER R AND L—Rauch and Lang Electric Car Mfg. Co., Chicopee Falls, MA (1922–1935) Previously in Cleveland, OH as early as 1905, building electric cars. R and L (1923–1924)

R. AND B.—(1929–1941)

READING—Middleby Auto Co., Reading, PA (1920–1925)

RED BALL—Red Ball Transit Co., Indianapolis, IN. Red Ball Motor Truck Corp., Frankfurt, IN (1923–1927)

REDFORD—(1924)

REHBERGER—Arthur Rehberger and Son, Inc., Newark, NJ (1923–1938)* Buses also

REILAND AND BREE—Reiland and Bree Mfg. Co., Northbrook, IL (1923–1931)

RELAY—Relay Motors Corp., Lima, OH (1927–1934)

RELIANCE—Racine Motor Truck Co., Reliance Motor Truck Co., Appleton Motor Truck Co., Appleton, WI (1917–1927) Production may have actually ended between 1923 and 1927*

REO—REO Motor Car Co., Lansing, MI (1904–1967)

REPUBLIC—Republic Motor Truck Co., Alma, MI (1913–1929)

REX—Royal Rex Motors Co., Chicago, IL (1921–1923)

REX—Rexnord Engrg. Co., Milwaukee, WI (c. 1976 on)

REX VIAPLANE—Rex Finance Corp., Chicago, IL (1932) One bus only

REX-WATSON—(1925)

REYA—The Reya Co., Napoleon, OH (1917–1920)

REYNOLDS—Reynolds Motor Truck Co., Mt. Clemens, MI (1920–1927)* Trucks and buses

RIDDLE—Riddle Mfg. Co., Ravenna, OH (1916–1926) Professional cars

RIKER—Locomobile Co. of America, Bridgeport, CT (1916–1922) Operated by Hare's Motors after 1920. Original Riker trucks were electric, 1898–1903, and not mfd. by Locomobile, which had once built trucks bearing the Locomobile name.

RIMPULL—Rimpull Corp., Olathe, KS (1975 on)

RITE-WAY—American Rite-Way Corp., Dallas, TX; Riteway of Indiana, Ft. Wayne, IN; Arlan Mfg. Co., Arlington, TX (since early 1960s)

ROAD KING—A model of Mason

ROADMASTER—A model of Selden

ROAMER—(1923) Cars also (1916–1930)

ROBINSON—Thomas F. Robinson, Minneapolis, MN (1909–1910); Robinson-Loomis Truck Co., Minneapolis, MN (1910–1912); Robinson Motor Truck Co., Minneapolis, MN (1912–1920) First one-ton forward-control model known as Gopher

ROBINSON—Robinson Fire Apparatus Mfg. Co., St. Louis, MO (1911–1920)

ROBINSON—Golden West Motors Co., Sacramento, CA (1915–1920)

ROCKET—Northway Motors Corp., Natick, MA (1925–1926)*

ROCK FALLS—Rock Falls Mfg. Co., Sterling, IL (1912–1925) Professional cars

ROCKNE—The Studebaker Corp., South Bend, IN (1932–1933) Cars also

ROGERS: ROGERS UNA-DRIVE—Rogers Una-Drive Motor Truck Corp., Sunnyvale, CA (1919–1922) Four-wheel drive, power transmitted to central transfer box with driveshafts leading to front and rear axles

ROMER—Romer Motors Corp., Taunton, MA (1921)

ROSS CARRIER—The Ross Carrier Co., New York, NY (1933)

ROUSTABOUT—See Trivan

ROWE—Rowe Motor Mfg. Co., Lancaster, PA (1911–1927)

ROYAL—Royal Coach Co., Rahway, NJ (1923–1927) Buses

ROYAL REX—See Rex

RUGBY—Durant Motors, Inc., Lansing, MI (1927–1932)* Earlier Rugby trucks were Stars made for export to British Commonwealth

RUGGLES—Ruggles Motor Truck Co.

RUMELY—Advance-Rumely Thresher Co., La Porte, IN. Also Rumely Products Co. (1885–1928; truck production 1919–1928) Also tractors

RYDER—Ryder System, Miami, FL (1973 on) First known as Paymaster. Aerodynamic line-haul tractors built for Ryder by the Hendrickson Mfg. Co.

S AND S—Sayers and Scovill Co., Cincinnati, OH (1907–1935) Professional cars. Automobiles also built, S and S and Sayers Six

SAFETY—(1926–1928)

SAFEWAY BUS—The Six Wheel Co., Philadelphia, PA (1924–1928)

SAF-T-CAB—1926 model of Checker. Also 1933–1936, built by Checker for Auburn

SAINT CLOUD/ST. CLOUD—St. Cloud Truck Co., St. Cloud, MN (1920–1923) Some reports give 1921 production cutoff date

ST. LOUIS—St. Louis Car Co., St. Louis, MO (1921–1922; 1930–1951) Buses, mostly electric trolley coaches from 1930s on

SAMSON—Samson Tractor Co., Janesville, WI; a GM subsidiary (1920–1923) Trucks and tractors

SANDOW—Moses and Morris Motors Corp.; Sandow Motor Truck Co., Chicago Hts., IL (1912–1929)

SANFORD—Sanford-Herbert Co., Syracuse, NY (1911–1913); Sanford Motor Truck Co., Syracuse, NY (1913–1937); Sanford Fire Apparatus Corp., East Syracuse, NY (1969 on) Earliest trucks named Sanbert Trucks, bus chassis, and fire engines (fire engines exclusively after 1969)

SAURER—Swiss origin, but American manufacture also, by Saurer Motor Co., Plainfield, NJ (1911–1918) Saurer trucks imported to the USA as early as 1908

SAXON—Saxon Motor Co., Detroit, MI (1914–1916) Cars also, until 1922

SAYERS: SAYERS AND SCOVILL—See S and S

SCHACHT—The G. A. Schacht Motor Truck Co., Cincinnati, OH (1904–1938)

SCHOONMAKER—(1921)

SCHWARTZ—Schwartz Motor Truck Corp., Reading, PA (1920–1923; followed by Clinton)

SEAGRAVE—The Seagrave Co., Columbus, OH (1907–1919); a Corporation in 1919–1963; Seagrave Fire Apparatus Div., FWD Corp., Clintonville, WI (1963 on) Fire trucks

SECURITY TWIN-DRIVE—(1923)

SELDEN—Selden Truck Corp., Rochester, NY (1913–1932)

SENECA—Seneca Motor Car Co., Fostoria, OH (1917–1925) Cars also

SERVICE—Service Motor Truck Co., Wabash, IN (1911–1933)

SHAW—Walden W. Shaw Livery Co.; Walden W. Shaw Corp.; Yellow Cab Mfg. Co., Chicago, IL (1912–1921) Trucks and cabs; cars also

SHELBY—Shelby Truck and Tractor Corp., Shelby, OH (1912–1923)

SHUTTLECRAFT BUS—See American Carrier Equipment

SIGNAL—Signal Motor Truck Co., Detroit, MI (1913–1924)*

SILVER EAGLE: GOLDEN EAGLE: EAGLE—Originally Belgian (1961–1974) American models introduced 1975 on, by Eagle International, Brownsville, TX. Majority of Eagles sold to National Trailways Bus System. Some Belgian models still in production

SIOUX HAWKEYE—(1931) See Hawkeye

SIX-WHEEL TRUCK AND BUS—The Six-Wheel Co., Philadelphia, PA (1922–1928) Buses also known as Safeway; trucks also mfd.

SKOOTMOBILE (tri-van)—Skootmobile, Inc., Chicago, IL (1939) ¼-ton light delivery scooter vehicle

SLEEPER COACH—Sleeper Coaches, Inc., Detroit, MI (1937) Only one bus built, with rear-engined Reo chassis.

SMITH FLYER—A. O. Smith Co., Milwaukee, WI (1917–1920) Buckboard-type 5-wheel light delivery. Standard-type trucks built by same manufacturer 1912–1915, known as Smith-Milwaukee

SOUTHERN—Southern Automobile Co., Atlanta, GA; Memphis, TN (1920–1923)

SOUTHERN—Southern Truck and Car Corp., Greensboro, NC (1919–1921)

SOUTHERN—Southern Coach Mfg. Co., Evergreen, AL (1945–1961) Buses. Company formed 1941 to rebuild other buses. Also known as Southern Coach buses

SOUTH MAIN MOTOR—(1922)

SPA—(1930)

SPACKE—Spacke Machine and Tool Co., Indianapolis, IN (1919–1920)

SPANGLER—D. H. Spangler Eng. and Sales Co., Hamburg, PA (1946–1949)

SPARTAN—Spartan Coach and Mfg. Co., Inc., Sturgis, MI (1946–1949) Buses

SPARTAN—Spartan Motors, Inc., Charlotte, MI (1975 on)

SPEED—(1921–1922)

SPEEDBOY—A model of Traffic

SPEED WAGON—A model of REO

SPEEDWAY—A model of Traffic

SPENCER—Research Engineering Co., Dayton, OH (1922)

SPRINGFIELD—(1922)

STANDARD/FISHER-STANDARD—Standard Motor Truck Co., Detroit, MI (1912–1934) See also Fisher

STANDARD/STANDARD-WARREN—Warren Motor Truck Co., Warren, OH (1917–1923)

STANLEY: STANLEY STEAMER—Stanley Motor Carriage Co., Newton, MA (1901–1924); Stanley Vehicle Corp. of America (1924–1929); cars also, 1897–1927. Stanley Mountain Wagon open hotel bus (1909–1916) and trucks

STAR—Durant Motors, Inc., Elizabeth, NJ and Lansing, MI; offices at Star Motors, Inc., New York, NY (1922–1932) Rugby trucks also. Star automobiles 1922–1928.

STATES—States Motor Car Co., Kalamazoo, MI (1916–1920)

STEAMOBILE—Winslow Boiler and Engineering Co., Chicago, IL (1919–1922)

STEAMOTOR—Steamotor Truck Co.; Amalgamated Machinery Corp. (1917–1920)

STEAM-O-TRUCK—Steam Automotive Works, Denver, CO (1918–1921)

STEARNS/STEARNS-KNIGHT—F. B. Stearns Co., Cleveland, OH (1911–1930) Cars also (1899–1930)

STEIN-KOENIG/STEINKONIG—World Motors Co. See World (1926–1927)

STEINMETZ—Steinmetz Electric Motor Car Co., Baltimore, MD (1920–1927) Electric truck chassis and cars

STEP-N-DRIVE—Buffalo Commercial Co., Buffalo, NY (1928–1929) Door-to-door light delivery truck, drivable from runningboard

STEPHENSON—(1930)

STERLING—Sterling Motor Truck Co., Milwaukee, WI (1907–1958)

STERLING—Sterling Custom Built Trucks, Inc., Kansas City, KS (1973 on)

STERLING-WHITE—Another name for 1952–1953 Sterling trucks built by White

STEWART—Stewart Motor Corp., Buffalo, NY (1912–1939)

STOUGHTON—Stoughton Wagon Co., Stoughton, WI (1919–1928)*

STRICK—Strick Corp., Fairless Hills, PA (1978 on) Cab-under type, also known as Strick Cab Under

STUART—(1920)

STUDEBAKER—Studebaker Corp., South Bend, IN (1852–1966)

STUEBINN—(1926)

STUTZ: NEW STUTZ—Stutz Fire Engine Co., Indianapolis, IN (1919–1930); New Stutz Fire Engine Co., Hartford City, IN (1931–1940) Separate operation from the Stutz Motor Car Co. of America, Indianapolis, IN (1912–1934) which built Pak-Age-Car for a time.

SUCCESS—(1920)

SULLIVAN—Sullivan Motor Car Co.; Sullivan Motor Truck Co., Rochester, NY (1910–1926) Production may have halted in 1923

SUMNER TOPP-STEWART—(c. 1921)

SUPER; SUPER-TRUCK—O'Connell Motor Truck Co., Waukegan, Chicago, IL (1919–1936) Includes a line of unusual two-way reversible-control trucks with driver's seat that swung around steering column

SUPERIOR—Superior Motor Truck Co., Atlanta, GA (1915–1922)

SUPERIOR—Superior Coach Corp., Lima, OH (1938–1948) Buses (built bus bodies as early as 1923)

SUTPHEN—Sutphen Fire Equipment Co., Amlin, OH (1967 on) Previously built fire equipment on other chassis

SWAMPBUGGY FABCO—(1946)

TAIT—Tait Bros., Inc., Springfield, MA (1914–1926) Later known as Dairy Express.

TEC/TEC-TRUCK—Terminal Engineering Co., New York, NY (1920–1922) Electric

TECHNO—Techno Truck Co., Cleveland, OH (1962) Only one completed, converted from B-170 short conventional International truck which carried container that could be raised and lowered hydraulically

TECO—(1948)

TEREX—Terex Div., General Motors Corp., Hudson, OH (1972 on) Giant earth-moving off-road dump trucks to 550 tons capacity

TERRAPLANE—Hudson Motor Car Co., Detroit, MI

TEXAN—Texas Motor Car Assn., Ft. Worth, TX (1918–1923) Cars also

TEXAS—(1921)

THOMART—(1923)

THORNE—Thorne Motor Car Corp.; Thorne Gas Electric Corp., Chicago, IL (1929 to late 1930s) Door-to-door delivery vans

THREE POINT—Three Point Truck Corp., New York Air Brake Co., Watertown and New York, NY (1917–1926)

THRIFT-T—(1947)

TIFFIN—Tiffin Wagon Works; Tiffin Wagon Co., Tiffin, OH (1913–1925)

TITAN—American Machinery Co., Newark, DE (1916–1920)

TITAN—Titan Truck (and Tractor) Co., Titan Truck Service Co., Milwaukee, WI (1917–1932)

TMC—Transportation Mfg. Corp., Roswell, NM (1975 on) A subsidiary of Greyhound, which, like MCI, builds buses for that line. Buses the same as MCI except for name.

TOPPINS—Toppins Tractor Truck Co., Milwaukee, WI (1923)*

TOPP-STEWART—(1919–1928)

TORBENSENS—(1923)

TORO—(1923)

TOWER—Tower Motor Truck Co., Greenville, MI (1915–1925)

TOWN TAXI—Town Taxi Co., Hagerstown, MD (1933–1935) Body by M. P. Möller Co.

TRABOLD—Trabold Truck Mfg. Co., Johnstown, PA (1911–1922); Trabold Motors, Inc., Johnstown, PA (1922–1924); Trabold Motors Co.,

Ferndale, PA (1924–1929); The Trabold Co., Johnstown, PA (1929–1932)* Also built truck bodies until 1960

TRAC-TRUCKS—(1934)

TRAFFIC—Traffic Motor Truck Corp., St. Louis, MO (1912–1928)

TRANSCOACH—Transcoach Div., Sportscoach Corp., Chatsworth, CA (1974 on) Buses

TRANSICOACH—Built at Richmond, IN, offered by both Crown and Wayne (1948–1950) Buses

TRANSIT—Transit Motor Car Co., Louisville, KY (1912–1913); Transit Motor Truck Co., Louisville, KY (1913–1920)

TRANSIT—Transit Buses, Inc., Dearborn, MI (1948–1949) Buses. Originally formed in 1941 to sell Ford Transit Buses. January, 1950: company sold to Checker. Cab Service Parts Corp., Detroit, MI (1947–1955)

TRANSPORT—Transport Truck Co., Mt. Pleasant, MI (1919–1927)* Production may have ceased 1925–26

TRANSPORTATION—(1935)

TRANSTAR—A model of International

TRAVELALL—A model of International

TRAVELER—Taxicab Mfg. Co., New York, NY (1925)

TRAYLOR—Traylor Engineering and Mfg. Co., Cornwell Hts., Allentown, PA (1920–1931)*

TRIANGLE—Triangle Motor Truck Co., St. Johns, MI (1917–1925)*

TRIUMPH—Triumph Truck and Tractor Co., Kansas City, MO (1919–1923)

TRI-CAR—(1955)

TRIVAN/TRI-VAN—The Roustabout Co., Frackville, PA (1962–1964)* Successor to Roustabout truck; three-wheeler

TRI-WHEEL—(1950) Light delivery

TROJAN—Toledo Carriage Woodwork Co., Toledo, OH (1914–1915); Commercial Truck Co., Cleveland, OH (1916–1920)

TROJAN—Trojan Truck Mfg. Co., Los Angeles, CA (1937–1940) Large dump trucks for strip mining

TRUCK-BUILDER—(1919–1920)

TRUCKETTE—Motorette Corp., Buffalo, NY (1947–1948)

TRUCKSTELL—Truckstell, Inc., Cleveland, OH (1937–early 1940s?) Built own trucks; also parts and equipment for other brands

TUCKER—The Tucker Co., Grass Valley, CA; Medford, OR (1947 to ?)

TURBO-TITAN—A model of Chevrolet

TWENTIETH CENTURY CAB—M. P. Möller Motor Co., Hagerstown, MD (1925)

TWIN CITY—Twin City Four Wheel Drive Co., Inc., St. Paul, MN; Four Wheel Drive Mfg. Co., Minneapolis, MN (1917–1926) Manufacturing plants operating simultaneously in Minneapolis and St. Paul

TWIN CITY BUS—Minneapolis Steel and Machinery Co., Minneapolis, MN (1918–1929) Also Twin City trucks

TWIN COACH—See Fageol

TWIN PARTS—(1921)

TWISTER DRAGON WAGON/DRAGON WAGON—Lockheed Missiles and Space Co., Inc., Sunnyvale, CA (starts 1972)*

ULTIMATE—Vreeland Motor Co., Inc., Hillside, NJ (1919–1925)

UNION—Union Motor (Truck) Co., Bay City, MI (1915–1926)

UNION CONSTRUCTION—(1923)

UNITED—United Motor Truck Co. (1915–1916); United Motors Co. (1916–1922); United Motors Products Co. (1922–1926)* All of Grand Rapids, MI; and Acme Motor Truck Co., Cadillac, MI (1927–1930)

UNITED—United Four-Wheel Drive Co., Chicago, IL (1917–1920)

UNITED STATES/U.S.—United States Motor Truck Co., Cincinnati, OH (1909–1930)

UNIVERSAL—Universal Motor Truck Co., Detroit, MI (1910–1916); Universal Service Co., Detroit, MI (1916–1920)

UPPERCU—Aeromarine Plane and Motor Corp., Keport, NJ (1924–1927) Buses, etc.

URSUS—(1920–1921)

U.P.S.—United Parcel Service, New York, NY (1937–1938) Possibly later; delivery trucks custom-built for United Parcel Service

U.S.—See United States

U.S.A.—See Liberty

U.S.A.—(1928)*

UTILITY WAGON—A model of Stewart

VALLEY—Valley Motor Truck Co., Elkhart, IN (1927–1929) Also known as Valley Dispatch. See also Huffman

VANETTE—(1946)

V-CON—Marion Power Shovel Co. Inc., Vehicle Constructors Div., Dallas, TX (1971 on) Giant diesel-electric end-dump trucks to 270 tons capacity

VELIE—Velie Motors Corp., Moline, IL (1908–1924)

VERSARE—Versare Corp., Albany, NY

VIALL—Viall Motor Car Co., Chicago, IL (1913–1926)

VICTOR—Victor Motor Truck and Trailer Co., Chicago, IL (1918–1920)

VICTOR—Victor Motors, Inc., St. Louis, MO (1922–c. 1928) Another Victor truck manufacturered in Buffalo, NY (1910–1914)

VIM—Vim Motor Truck Co., Philadelphia, PA (1914–1926)

VIRGINIA—(1932–1934)

VOMAG—Robert Remer, Inc., Weehawken, NJ (1922–1926) This name better known in Germany

VULCAN—(1922)

WABCO—Letourneau Westinghouse, Peoria, IL (since 1957)

WACHUSETT—Wachusett Motors, Inc., Fitchburg, MA (1922–1930)

WALKER ELECTRIC—Walker Electric Co., Chicago, IL (1906–1942)

WALKER-JOHNSON—Walker-Johnson Truck Co., East Woburn, MA (1919–1920); Boston, MA (1920–1925)

WALTER—Walter Motor Truck Co., New York, NY

WALTHAM—Waltham Motors Corp., Chicago, IL (1921)

WARD ELECTRIC—Ward Motor Vehicle Co., New York, NY (1910–1914); Ward Motor Vehicle Co., Mt. Vernon, NY (1915–1934)*

WARD LA FRANCE—Ward La France Truck Corp., Elmira, NY (est. 1919)

WARE—Ware Motor Vehicle Co., St. Paul, MN; Ware Twin Engine Truck Co., Minneapolis, MN; Successor: Twin City 4-wheel-drive Co. (1912–1921)

WARFORD—(1940–1941)

WARNER-SWASEY—(1955–1977)

WATEROUS—Waterous Engine Works, St. Paul, MN (1906–1923) Fire engines

WATSON—Watson Products Corp., Canastota, NY (1916–1926)

WAYNE BUS—Wayne Corp.

WERNER—(1935)

WESTCOASTER—West Coast Machinery Co., Stockton, CA (1927–1970); Westcoaster Co., subsidiary of Otis Elevator Co., Stockton, CA (1970–1975) Light three- and four-wheel delivery and mail-carrying vehicles. See Onan Westcoaster*

WESTERN—Western Motor Truck Co., Cleveland, OH; Western Truck Mfg. Co., Chicago, IL (1907–1928) May not have been in production for that entire time span

WESTERN STAR—See White

WESTRAK—(1950)

WHARTON—Wharton Motors Co., Inc., Dallas, TX (1921–1922)

WHIPPET—Willys-Overland, Toledo, OH (1927–1930) Also cars. Whippet cars for 1927 first introduced as Overland Whippet in Summer of 1926.

WHITCOMB—Whitcomb Wheel Co., Kenosha, WI (1927–1935) Trucks and buses. Production may have ceased in early '30s, with sell off of remaining stock 'til 1935.

WHITE—The White Co., Cleveland, OH (since 1900)

WHITE FREIGHTLINER—See Freightliner

WHITE HICKORY—White Hickory Wagon Mfg. Co.; White Hickory Motor Corp., Atlanta, GA (1916–1922)

WHITE HORSE—See White

WHITE STAR—White Star Motor and Engineering Co., Brooklyn, NY (1912–1921)

WICHITA—Wichita Motor Co.; Wichita Falls Motor Co., Wichita Falls, TX (1911–1932)

WILCOX; WILCOX TRUX—H. E. Wilcox Motor Car Co.; H. E. Wilcox Motor Truck Co.; H. E. Wilcox Motor Co.; Wilcox Trux, Inc.; all of Minneapolis, MN (1907–1928) Production ended 1927 when factory sold to Will. Buses also

WILL—C. H. Will Motors Corp., Minneapolis, MN (1927–1931) A subsidiary of Greyhound. Bus manufacturing for Greyhound Lines. Western division begun in Oakland, CA in 1929 where Pioneer-Will and Western Will buses also produced. Final delivery of Will buses to Greyhound was in January, 1931. See Greyhound

WILLYS—Including Overland (1903–1963). From 1908 on, Willys-Overland Co., Toledo, OH, until 1963 when name Kaiser-Willys appeared, nearly a decade after the Kaiser and Willys merger. Principal output automobiles, but Overland and Willys trucks, as well as various Jeep vehicles after 1941. Jeep line expanded to civilian station wagons, pickups, etc., in 1946. See Jeep*, Willys*, and Overland*

WILLYS-KNIGHT—Subsidiary of Willys-Overland, Toledo, OH (1914–1933) Principally cars until 1929*

WILSON—J. C. Wilson Co., Detroit, MI

WINNEBAGO BUS—Winnebago Industries, Inc., Forest City, IA. Primarily a manufacturer of motor homes, Winnebago introduced a small (159 inch wheelbase) bus in 1973.

WINTER AND HIRSCH—(1923)

WINTHER—Winther Motor Truck Co., Kenosha, WI (1917–1927)

WINTHER-KENOSHA—Kenosha Fire Engine and Truck Co., Kenosha, WI (1927)

WINTHER-MARWIN—(1918–1921) A 4-W-D model of Winther

WISCONSIN—Wisconsin Motor Truck Works, Baraboo, WI (1912–1915); Myers Machine Co., Sheboygan, WI (1915–1918); Wisconsin Truck Co., Loganville, WI (1919–1926) Trucks and also bus chassis

WISCONSIN—Wisconsin Farm Tractor Co., Sauk City, WI (1921–1923) Principally tractors

WITTENBERG—Wittenberg Motor Co., Midway, WA (1966 on) Military-type trucks built on reconditioned chassis of GMC, Dodge, Reo, etc. Originally dealt in used military vehicles, which developed into Wittenberg rebuilts.

WITT-WILL—Witt-Will Co., Inc., Washington, D.C. (1911–1931)*

W. J.—(1921)

W.M.C.—Stands for Will Motors Corp., another name for Will buses

WOLF WAGON—Wolf Engineering, Dallas, TX (1956–1960s)

WOLVERINE—American Commercial Car Co., Detroit, MI (1918–1922)

WOLVERINE-DETROIT—Pratt, Carter, Sigsbee and Co., Detroit, MI (1911–1922) Relation, if any, to other Wolverine uncertain

WOODS: WOODS BROS.—(successor to Patriot) Patriot Mfg. Co., Havelock, NE (1927–1929); Patriot Mfg. Co. div. of Arrow Aircraft and Motors Corp., Lincoln, NE (1929–1931) Woods trucks listed as available as late as 1933.

WOODWARD—(c. 1921)

WORLD—World Motors Co., Cincinnati, OH (1927–1932) Successor to Stein-Koenig; Worlds (1927–1930) may be same

WRIGHT—(c. 1921)

YALE—Yale Motor Truck Co., New Haven, CT (1920–1922)

YELLOW CAB—Yellow Cab Mfg. Co., Chicago, IL (1915–1925); Yellow Truck and Coach Mfg. Co., Chicago, IL (1925–1928); Yellow Truck and Coach Mfg. Co., Pontiac, MI (1928–1929) Taxis and trucks. Yellowcab truck introduced in 1924

YELLOW COACH/GMC COACH—(since 1923) Buses—Yellow Coach Mfg. Co., Chicago, IL (1923–1925); also Yellow Motor Coach Co.; Yellow Truck and Coach Mfg. Co., Chicago, IL (1925–1928); Yellow Truck and Coach Mfg. Co., Pontiac, MI (1928–1942); GMC Truck and Coach Div., General Motors Corp., Pontiac, MI (1943 on) Also see GMC Greyhound

YELLOW KNIGHT—Knight-engined (sleeve-valve) Cabs and trucks, as part of Yellow Cab line (1926–1927)*

YOUNG—Young Motor Truck Co., Geneva, OH (1920–1923)

YOUNG—Young Fire Equipment Corp., Lancaster, NY (1970 on) Fire trucks, beginning with two-axle Bison and three-axle, low-cab Crusader.

ZELIGSON—Zeligson Co., Tulsa, OK (1946 on)